The Software Engineer's Guidebook

Navigating senior, tech lead, and staff engineer positions at tech companies and startups

Gergely Orosz

 The Pragmatic Engineer

The Software Engineer's Guidebook

by Gergely Orosz

Published by Pragmatic Engineer BV, Amsterdam, Netherlands.

Edited by Dominic Gover.

ISBN: 9789083381824

First Edition: November 2023, version 1.01

engguidebook.com

Keep up-to-date with the tech industry

This book has taken four years to write, and within its pages, I try to capture observations and advice that will stand the test of time. This means that changeable parts of the tech industry – like the job market, levels of funding for startups, and emerging technologies – are not within the scope of this book. This is despite the fact I write about these timely matters every week, as the author of The Pragmatic Engineer Newsletter.

The Pragmatic Engineer Newsletter is one of the most-read online technology publications and the #1 technology newsletter on Substack. It's a weekly newsletter offering an inside look at Big Tech and startups, with its finger on the pulse of the tech market. The newsletter is highly relevant for software engineers, engineering managers, and anyone working in tech.

Bloomberg describes my newsletter like this[1]:

> "In his newsletters, [Gergely Orosz] speaks with inside knowledge and authenticity about the industry. The Pragmatic Engineer covers a lot of ground, from sweepy pieces about the state of Big Tech and layoffs in the industry, to how employees should prepare for performance reviews."

Subscribe here:

pragmaticurl.com/newsletter

I hope you enjoy this book, and find it useful for keeping up-to-date with the tech industry, together with the newsletter.

– Gergely

---

[1]https://pragmaticurl.com/bloomberg

Contents

PREFACE

I've been a software engineer for about 10 years, and a manager for five more. During my first few years as a developer, I received little to no professional guidance. But I didn't mind, as I assumed hard work would eventually lead to progress.

However, this changed a few years into my career when I was passed over for a promotion to a senior engineer role which I thought I was ready for. Not only that but when I asked my manager how I could get to that next level, they didn't have any specific feedback. It was then that I decided that if I ever did become a manager, I'd always offer team members useful advice on how to grow.

It was when I was working at the riding-hailing app Uber that I became an engineering manager. By then I was a seasoned engineer, but I still remembered my earlier promise to myself. So, I did my best to support people on my team to improve professionally, get the promotions they deserved, and give clear, actionable feedback when I thought colleagues weren't ready for the next level, just yet.

As my team grew and I took on skip-level reports, I had less and less time to mentor team-mates in-depth. I also started to see patterns in the feedback I gave, so began to publish blog posts of the advice I found myself giving repeatedly; about writing well, and doing good code reviews. These posts were warmly received, and a lot more people than I expected read and shared them with colleagues. This is when I began writing this book.

By year two of the writing process, I had a draft that could be ready to publish. However, at that time I launched The Pragmatic Engineer Newsletter. The focus of this newsletter is keeping the pulse of today's tech market, plus regular deepdives into how well-known, international companies operate, software engineering trends, and occasional interviews with interesting tech people. Writing the newsletter made me realize just how many "gaps" were in the book draft. The past two years have been spent rewriting and honing its contents, one chapter at a time.

After four years of writing, I can say with conviction that "The Software Engineer's Guidebook" and The Pragmatic Engineer Newsletter are complementary resources. This is despite the fact there is very little overlap in their contents.

Writing this book helped me kick off the newsletter because it was obvious there are plenty of timely software engineering topics to write about, which would make little sense to cover in a book with a longer lifespan than a weekly newsletter. The newsletter has helped me improve the book; I've learned lots about interesting trends and new tools that feel like they are here to stay for a decade or longer, such as AI coding tools, cloud development environments, and developer portals. These technologies are referenced in this book in much less detail than you will find in the newsletter.

I hope you discover useful ideas in this book, which serve you well for years to come.

INTRODUCTION

This is the book I wish I could have read early in my career as a software developer; especially when I joined a larger tech company for a healthy pay rise, and found a very different engineering culture with surprisingly little guidance for navigating my new environment.

This book follows the structure of a "typical" career path for a software engineer, from starting out as a fresh-faced software developer, through being a role model senior/lead, all the way to the staff/principle/distinguished level. It summarizes what I've learned as a developer and how I've approached coaching engineers at different stages of their careers.

We cover "soft" skills which become increasingly important as your seniority increases, and the "hard" parts of the job, like software engineering concepts and approaches which help you grow professionally.

The names of levels and their expectations can – and do! – vary across companies. The higher "tier" a business is, the more tends to be expected of engineers, compared to lower tier places. For example, the "senior engineer" level has notoriously high expectations at Google (L5 level) and Meta (E5 level,) compared to lower-tier companies. If you work at a higher-tier business, it may be useful to read the chapters about higher levels, and not only the level you're currently interested in.

Naming and levels vary, but the principles of what makes a great engineer who is impactful at the individual, team, and organizational levels, are remarkably constant. No matter where you are in your career, I hope this book provides a fresh perspective and new ideas on how to grow as an engineer.

How to read this book

It is composed of six standalone parts, each made up of several chapters:

- Part I: Developer Career Fundamentals
- Part II: The Competent Software Developer
- Part III: The Well-Rounded Senior Engineer
- Part IV: The Pragmatic Tech Lead
- Part V: Role Model Staff and Principal Engineers
- Part VI: Conclusion

Part I and Part VI apply to all engineering levels, from entry-level software developer, to principal-and-above engineer. Part II, Part III, Part IV, and Part V cover increasingly senior engineering levels and group together topics in chapters, such as "Software Engineering," "Collaboration," "Getting Things Done," etc.

This is a reference book you can return to as you grow in your career. I suggest focusing on topics you struggle with, or the career level you are aiming for. Keep in mind that expectations can vary greatly between companies.

In this book, I've aligned the topics and leveling definitions to expectations at Big Tech and scaleups. However, there are topics that are also useful at lower career levels which we dive deeper into, later in the book. For example, in Part V: "Reliable Software Systems," we cover logging, monitoring, and oncall in-depth, but it's useful – and often necessary! – to know about practices below the staff engineer level. I suggest using the table of contents by topic, as well as by level when deciding which chapters to prioritize.

And now, let's jump in...

Part I

Developer Career Fundamentals

For the first few years of my developer career, I didn't care too much about career-related stuff. I assumed that if I worked hard and delivered good work, the rewards would follow. At developer agencies, promotions were rare and career development was much more limited, but I didn't feel like I missed out on anything while my title and level stayed the same at the first few places I worked.

It was when I moved to larger companies like JP Morgan and Microsoft that I noticed it's not always those who work hardest or deliver the highest quality work, who are awarded the biggest bonuses and win prized promotions. When I became an engineering manager at Uber, I had a team of engineers who required regular performance feedback and support in their professional growth, such as getting promoted to the next level.

This chapter summarizes observations of how different companies function, and career advice I gave to engineers on my team.

Something I wish I'd had a better understanding of much sooner is the different types of company you can work at as a developer – from well-known Big Tech giants, through startups, all the way to more traditional businesses, consultancies, and academia. Crucially, it can get increasingly hard to transition between different categories of workplace – which may be an unwelcome surprise a decade into working in one segment.

The other thing I missed out on was how to own your career. It was only when I became a manager that I realized what a difference it makes when a developer takes ownership of their career path – which also greatly helps their manager to advocate for them.

Most engineers I met assumed their manager would take care of most things career-related, and that glowing performance reviews and promotions would materialize as if from thin air. Perhaps this may conceivably happen at some small companies and startups, but at larger tech companies additional work is needed for career recognition. In most cases, it's not much additional work; it's just that many engineers don't know which additional activities to do.

The observations, concepts, and approaches in this chapter are applicable to all seniority levels, from entry-level engineer, all the way to staff-and-above.

1

CAREER PATHS

When it comes to careers, everyone's path is different. Some career elements are easy to be specific about, like where you work, your job title, and total compensation. However, many other important things are harder to measure, such as what working with colleagues is like, opportunities for professional growth, and work/life balance.

Career paths are diverse, and there's no simple way to define what a "good" career path looks like, as this varies from person to person. The best you can do is figure out which career path is interesting and achievable for you.

The routes people take into software engineering also vary; there are more common ways, like graduating from university with a computer science-related degree, and there are also self-taught engineers and career switchers. I worked with a colleague who'd been a chemical engineer for twenty years before teaching themself to code and becoming a developer.

In this chapter, we cover career-related topics:

1. Types of tech companies
2. Typical software engineering career paths
3. Compensation, and company "tiers"
4. Cost centers, profit centers
5. Alternative ways to think about career progress

1. Types of Companies

There's no way to categorize companies definitively, but they do share some common characteristics from the software engineer's point of view. Common types of company are:

Big Tech

Large, publicly traded tech businesses like Apple, Google, Microsoft, and Amazon. These typically employ tens of thousands of software engineers, and their market caps are in the billions of dollars.

Big Tech engineering jobs are usually the most sought-after, due to their top-of-the-market compensation, career growth opportunities beyond staff engineer level, and the chance to do work that impacts hundreds of millions of customers. There could also be the opportunity to work with best-in-class coworkers from across the industry.

Medium to large tech companies

Tech-first companies with software engineering at the core of their business. These companies are smaller than Big Tech and may employ hundreds or thousands of software engineers. Examples include Atlassian, Dropbox, Shopify, Snap, and Uber.

These companies tend to offer similar compensation to Big Tech, and career paths beyond staff engineer level. The user bases are usually somewhat smaller, but engineers' work can still impact tens of millions of customers.

Scaleups

Venture-funded, later-stage companies with product-market fits, which are investing in growth. These businesses may be making a loss on purpose, in order to invest in growing market share. Examples include Airtable, Klarna, and Notion.

These places usually move fast under high pressure to grow the business in order to justify a valuation, capitalize on future funding rounds, or prepare to go public.

A subset of scaleups is "unicorns:" businesses with a private valuation of $1B or more. In the 2010s, there were relatively few unicorns, and being one signaled a company might be the next big thing. Today, unicorns are much more common, so being one is less of a differentiator.

Startups

Venture-funded companies which have raised smaller rounds of funding, and are aiming for a product-market fit. This involves building a product that attracts customer demand.

Startups are inherently risky; they often lack meaningful revenue and are dependent on raising new rounds of funding to operate – for which a product-market fit is needed.

An example of a successful startup that graduated to a scaleup was Airbnb in 2011. Founded in 2008, the company won seed investment from Y Combinator. By 2010, Airbnb's product had gained traction, and it raised $7.2M Series A. In 2011, the company raised a $112M Series B, as investors saw its potential.

An example of a startup that didn't make it past the startup stage is Secret, an anonymous sharing app. Founded in 2013, Secret allowed users to share their secrets, incognito. The company enjoyed good traction and raised $35M in funding over two years. However, in 2015, it shut down and part of its funds were returned to investors.

Startups tend to offer the most freedom to software engineers, but also the least stability. These companies can also be demanding in work-life balance terms, as their existence depends on achieving a product-market fit before the money runs out. Meanwhile, founders greatly influence the environment of a startup. Some put a "work hard, play hard" culture in place, while others focus on a sustainable working culture. Startups offer the most variety of work, labor force, and growth opportunities.

Startups which offer employees equity are high-risk/high-reward places. If the business thrives and eventually exits via a public offering or acquisition, early employees with significant quantities of stock do very well financially. This happened at Airbnb when the company went public with a market cap of $86B in 2020, and at design collaboration tool Figma, which Adobe acquired for $20B in 2022.

Traditional, non-tech companies with tech divisions

These places have a core business with little to do with technology, which is just another division. Some are more than 50 years old and were founded before the software development era. Others are in sectors where technology is not a main source of value.

Examples of such companies include IKEA (home furnishing,) JPMorgan Chase & Co (financial services,) Pfizer (pharmaceutical,) Toyota (automotive,) and Walmart (retail.)

Many such companies have embarked on digitalization and aim to make software development more strategic to their businesses. However, the reality is that tech is more of a cost center than a profit center at these places, and these places tend to offer lower compensation than Big Tech and many scaleups.

On the other hand, traditional companies tend to offer more job stability and a better work-life balance than most tech-first companies. The downside for software engineers is usually fewer career options than in Big Tech and at scaleups, and career paths above staff engineer are also rare.

Traditional but technology-heavy companies

An interesting subset of more traditional companies are those where technology is central to their offering in the form of hardware, software services, or both. These companies were often standout successes in their early days, and are now mature, reliable, and profitable businesses. However, with their age and slowdown in growth comes a more rigid organizational structure that is different from younger technology companies.

Examples of such companies include Broadcom, Cisco, Intel, Nokia, Ericsson, Mercedes-Benz and Saab. Hardware-heavy businesses, as well as automotive ones, can frequently be in this category.

These companies are commonly seen as less desirable to work at than Big Tech or scaleups. Compensation-wise, they are almost always below Big Tech and usually don't adopt new ways of working as quickly as younger companies do.

At the same time, these companies do offer complex engineering challenges that can be very satisfying to work on as an engineer, and the impact of your work can be at a scale that's more typical of Big Tech. They are also usually very stable places, and tend to offer a more predictable work-life balance than Big Tech or scaleups. Also, the tenure of software engineers at such companies can also be surprisingly lengthy, which contributes to predictability and stability that's much rarer at younger companies.

Small, non-venture funded companies

Bootstrapped companies, family businesses, and lifestyle businesses (which exist for the benefit of the founder's lifestyle,) are all examples of smaller companies without venture funding. This means two things:

1. No investor pressure to grow at all costs
2. Profitability is required, or the business will fail

These characteristics mean such small companies are rarely high-growth and are conservative in hiring and their business approach. However, they can be friendly, stable places to work, thanks to a comfortable pace of work, profitability, and because many people choose to stay longer at stable companies than at more hectic places.

Public sector

There is constant demand for governments to invest in software development, and they do.

The upside of public sector jobs is stability, and that compensation is usually clearly communicated and follows a formula. Many positions also have healthy perks in terms of time off and benefits.

Downsides may include a slow, bureaucratic approach, and the need to support legacy systems which are hard to change. In some countries, it can also be harder to move from a government job to the private sector.

An example of a government organization with a good reputation is the UK's Digital Service division, which builds and maintains many state websites. It is exemplary in how it works; for example, by publishing much of its work on GitHub (at https://github.com/alphagov.) Another public sector organization with a good engineering culture is the British Broadcasting Corporation (BBC.)

Nonprofits

These exist to serve a public or social cause. Examples include Code.org, Khan Academy, and the Wikimedia Foundation.

Non-profits typically offer less compensation than venture-funded companies, but in return they have a different mission than generating returns for investors and profits for owners. Working environments vary; some are excellent places for technologists to work, but tech is usually more of a cost center.

Consultancies, outsourcing companies and developer agencies

So far, we've covered companies that build products and services, for which they employ software engineers. However, there is considerable demand for "renting" software engineering expertise via an agency or outsourcing provider.

Outsourcing companies provide as many software engineers as a customer needs, and the customer decides where to allocate the engineering talent within its business. Meanwhile, a consultancy makes contracts with customers to build complex projects end-to-end, by providing software engineers who do this work. The consultancy is typically responsible for building and shipping the whole project.

Examples of consultancies and outsourcing companies include Accenture, Capgemini, EPAM, Infosys, Thoughtworks, and Wipro.

Developer agencies are usually small to midsize companies that take on smaller consulting projects, like building websites, apps, and similar projects for clients. They can also handle service maintenance for customers. Consultant engineers often bill customers at a daily or hourly rate, while being full-time employees of the developer agency.

The upside for software engineers of consultancies, outsourcing companies, and developer agencies, is that they're usually the easiest places to get hired, especially if you're less experienced. This is because these companies often have high demand for talent, and offer less compensation than their customers in the other categories.

Other upsides are that training for less experienced engineers is often available, there's opportunities to work on a variety of projects, and to get a peek into many different workplaces as a contractor.

There are downsides to working at consultancies. The most common:

- Career development-wise, these companies usually don't offer paths to above staff engineer-level, which is one step above senior engineer.

- The scope of work is limited to what the customer sets. Consultancies are generally hired for projects that a customer considers to be outside its core competency.
- Not much focus on good software engineering practices. Clients pay for short-term results, not for a developer to work on long-term things like reducing tech debt.
- It might be hard to switch to product-focused companies later. Companies that build products like Big Tech, startups, and scaleups tend to have very different cultures where maintainability is important, as is taking the initiative. Working at a consultancy for too long can make the switch to these places harder.

Academia and research labs

These institutions usually are part of, or work closely with, universities, and work on long-term research projects. Some focus on applied research, while others do basic research.

An upside of working in research labs is applying your skills to less explored fields, and the stability of being in an environment with fewer to no commercial pressures.

Which type of company best fits your career goals?

As we see, there are many types of companies and organizations to consider as a software engineer. So which one fits you best?

There's unlikely to be opportunities simultaneously at all ten types of place listed above. So narrow the list down to realistic options, based on your circumstances. It's helpful to talk with friends, family, and people in your network who are engineers, if possible. Get their opinion on whether they like their workplace, and what their job is really like.

Don't forget, there can be huge differences between companies in the same category, and teams differ significantly in the same workplace. Someone working in a traditional business's tech division on a fantastic team likely has a better time than someone in a struggling team at a Big Tech giant.

2. Typical Software Engineering Career Paths

Career paths for software engineers are pretty simple within a *company*. The two most common are the single-track and the dual-track career paths.

Single-track career path

The single-track career path of an individual contributor (IC) and a manager typically looks like this:

Level	Individual contributor	Manager
1	Software Engineer	
2	Senior Engineer	
3	Staff/Principal Engineer	Manager
4		Director
5		VP of Engineering
6		CTO

A typical single-track career path. Compensation rises by level, as do expectations

At smaller and non-tech first companies, there's a de facto career ceiling for software engineers at level 3 – the staff/principal level –, beyond which growth is only possible by switching to the manager track.

One downside of switching paths is that plenty of engineers come to believe management isn't for them, and so they quit to work elsewhere, meaning an employer loses some of their best engineers who become managers, or who exit the business entirely because they dislike managing.

Dual-track career path

Companies where engineering grows to above 30-50 people, or which are more forward-thinking, often have a dual-path career ladder, to avoid engineers having to choose between being stuck at a level with similar compensation to a line manager or becoming managers themselves. This is what the dual-path approach typically looks like:

Level	Individual contributor ladder	Manager ladder
1	Software engineer	
2	Senior engineer	
3	Staff engineer	Manager
4	Senior staff engineer	Director
5	Principal engineer	Senior director
6	Distinguished engineer	VP of engineering
7	Fellow	Senior VP of engineering
8		CTO

A typical dual-path career ladder: Once again, compensation rises by level, as do expectations

At companies with dual-path career progression, there are a few different approaches:

1. Individual contributor. Progress from software engineer, through senior, and to increasingly challenging IC levels.
2. Engineering manager. Change to an engineering manager from senior or staff engineer, then progress along the management track. With some luck, get to director-and-above positions.
3. Switch between the IC and manager tracks. Go back to being an engineer after a manager role, and perhaps repeat in future. This approach is more common than you might expect at such companies

All career paths are unique

In reality, many people switch jobs pretty frequently in tech. The majority of software engineers I've known do switch jobs every few years, which changes their career trajectory. This creates varied career paths, which you can see in the LinkedIn profiles of experienced former software engineers. Here's a few examples.

The 20-year career path of Tanya Reilly[1], author of the excellent book, "The Staff Engineer's Path," is pretty linear and has stayed on the software engineer path:

- systems administrator (Fujitsu, Eircom)

---

[1]https://www.linkedin.com/in/tanyareilly

- → software engineer (Google)
- → senior software engineer (Google)
- → staff systems engineer (Google)
- → principal software engineer (Squarespace)
- → senior principal software engineer (Squarespace)

The 20-year career path of Nicky Wrightson[2] – a head of engineering a the time of publishing –, stayed on the software engineering path for a long time, before moving into leadership:

- software developer (consultancy)
- → specialist consultant and developer (telecom companies)
- → developer (BNP Paribas, JP Morgan, Morgan Stanley)
- → six-month sabbatical
- → principal engineer (Financial Times, River Island, Skyscanner)
- → fractional CTO (venture builder firm Blenheim Chalcot)
- → Head of Engineering (topi)

The career path of Mark Tsimelzon[3] – director of engineering at WhatsApp at the time of publishing – has varied over three decades, from starting as a software engineer, to alternating between being a founder and building stuff, and leadership positions:

- software engineer
- → engineering manager
- → founder (startup later acquired by Akamai)
- → product manager (Akamai)
- → founder (at a startup later acquired by Sybase)
- → director of engineering (Yahoo)
- → entrepreneur in residence (venture capital firm)
- → VP of engineering (startup acquired by Yahoo)
- → senior director of engineering (Yahoo)
- → VP of engineering (Syapse)
- → chief engineering officer (Babylon Health)
- → director of engineering (Meta)

Common career paths

The software engineering industry is dynamic and ever-changing, so it should be little surprise that software engineers have lots of opportunities to shape their careers by taking opportunities that come along. I've observed at least a dozen "common" career paths:

---

[2]https://www.linkedin.com/in/nickywrightson
[3]https://www.linkedin.com/in/marktsimelzon

1. **The lifelong software engineer**. An engineer who stays a software engineer, becoming increasingly senior (e.g. senior engineer, staff, principal engineer,) and moving between companies. They often move stacks and broaden their skillset with each new position.
2. **The software engineer turned specialist**. A developer who comes to specialize in a domain, like native mobile or backend, and stays for an extended time.
3. **Generalist/specialist pendulum**. An engineer who specializes in a technology, and then spends time in a more generalist position. Rinse and repeat.
4. **Software engineer specializing in a niche field**. For example, a software engineer who transitions to a site reliability engineer, or a data engineer, where they do some coding, but the work mostly doesn't resemble software engineering.
5. **Software engineer turned contractor/freelancer**. Having reached senior engineer status, this person becomes a contractor or freelancer, often earning more and worrying less about internal politics and career development.
6. **Software engineer turned tech lead**. A developer who starts by leading a team, though not necessarily doing management tasks. Even when they switch jobs, they eventually return to the tech lead position.
7. **Software engineer turned engineering manager**. A developer who becomes an engineering manager, and then progresses on that career path.
8. **Software engineer turned founder/business owner**. Following a career as a software engineer, this person starts or co-founds a business.
9. **Software engineer turned non-software engineer**. A person who moves into another tech field like developer relations (DevRel,) product management, technical program management (TPM,) tech recruitment, or other. Their experience as a software engineer is relevant, and they get to explore fields they've developed an interest in.
10. **Software engineer/manager pendulum**. A software engineer who becomes an engineering manager, and then returns to being an engineer, often repeating this switch a few times. CTO Charity Majors writes about this increasingly common path in The Engineer/Manager Pendulum[4].
11. **Combination of some of the above**. For example, a software engineer turned engineering manager, turned product manager, turned founder, or any other combination.
12. **A non-linear career path**. For example, a software engineer who becomes an engineering manager, then takes a long career break to have a family, or pursue a different career. They return to the field as a director of engineering. Non-linear career paths develop in ways unique to each person.

In this book, we explore a more typical career path within a company, from entry-level engineer to staff+ engineer. However, while such a career path is typical for an IC progressing

---

[4]https://charity.wtf/2017/05/11/the-engineer-manager-pendulum

within a company, it's not necessarily common for software engineers. By detailing the sheer variety of career paths from starting as a software engineer, I hope to show there's not one "good" career path. Opportunities and preferences vary by person, and you should feel empowered to venture into less conventional areas.

3. Compensation and "Tiers" of Companies

It is tricky to quantify every aspect of a job, its professional challenges, flexibility, and work/life balance.

One thing that is easier to quantify is total compensation – with the caveat that equity packages in private companies can be tricky to quantify. As a hiring manager, I've observed what seemed like a trimodal distribution of compensation packages, and also confirmed this distribution by analyzing thousands of self-reported data points submitted to TechPays.com – a site I built prior to the publication of this book. Here's the distribution:

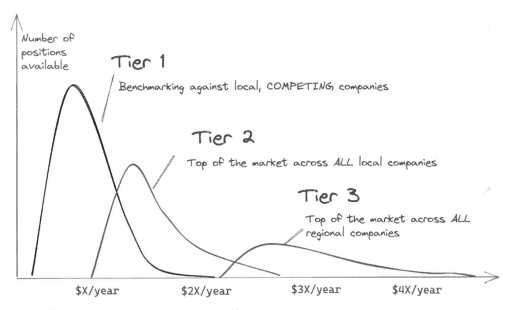

The trimodal nature of software engineering salaries: Why a comparable position can (and does) pay very differently. Tier 1: local companies; Tier 2: top of the local market; Tier 3: top of the regional market

The same role and title can vary in compensation by a factor of 2-4 times at different types of companies, the data reveals. A senior engineer at Google is likely to make at least double – and potentially even quadruple – the total compensation of a senior engineer at a non-tech company, or a small family-run business. Total compensation means the combination of three values:

- Base salary
- Cash bonus
- Equity: at publicly traded companies, this is liquid, and at privately owned startups and scaleups it is illiquid.

Let's talk about the three tiers of the tech market as they relate to compensation.

Tier 1: local market

Companies that benchmark against the local market. Companies in this group are typically:

- Local startups
- Small, non-venture funded companies
- Traditional non-tech companies with tech divisions
- Public sector
- Nonprofits
- Consultancies, outsourcing companies, and developer agencies
- Academia and research labs

Tier 2: top of the local market

Companies that aim to pay at the top of the local market to attract and retain standout local talent. Typical companies in this group:

- Some medium-sized tech companies, especially ones that optimize compensation for the local market
- Some scaleups
- Some startups, usually those with healthy funding and a regional focus
- Some traditional companies with tech divisions, especially those doubling down on tech investment

Tier 3: top of the regional/international market

Companies that aim to pay the best across the region, and compete with peer tier 3 companies, not local rivals. Typical companies in this group:

- Big Tech
- Most medium-sized tech companies
- Well-funded scaleups which compete for talent with Big Tech and midsize tech companies
- Startups with strong funding that hire from the above groups

Compensation at tier 3 companies tends to have three components:

- Base salary
- Equity, issued annually
- Cash bonus, issued annually

When publicly traded companies issue stock, it can be sold upon vesting as part of the total compensation package. This is how staff-level software engineers at Big Tech and similarly large companies earn more in stock compensation annually than their base salary.

Many startups and scaleups also issue equity for software engineers. However, at private companies, this equity is not liquid and so any stock increase is "paper gains" only, until the company has an exit like a public offering or is acquired. These exits are how early employees with significant stock holdings make small fortunes, as happened to early Uber employees. Of course, privately traded companies are riskier because many never achieve an exit. This happened to early Foursquare employees in 2023 when their stock grants simply expired[5] and "vanished," 14 years after the company was founded.

Contractors and freelancers

So far, we've covered fulltime total compensation. However, we need to look into compensation for contractors and freelancers, who often do similar work to permanent fulltime employees but are paid differently.

They bill the company an agreed rate, usually hourly or daily. From the Human Resources point of view, they're not employees and have a business-to-business contract to provide software engineering services to a client. The terminology varies by country; the US and UK use contractors, while in many European countries they're called freelancers. This book uses "contractor."

As a contractor, a major contrast to being fulltime is that compensation can be significantly higher. The rates senior-and-above software engineers can charge as contractors, almost always place them above Tier 2 compensation packages. Meanwhile, some high-end contractors can earn the equivalent of Tier 3 compensation packages.

In some countries – especially in Europe – fulltime employment income is heavily taxed, while income from contracting may be less so.

From an employer's point of view, the biggest difference between contractors and fulltime workers is flexibility: they can recruit contractors quickly and terminate their contracts equally rapidly. Also, there's no need to worry about career progression, training, or sever-

---

[5]https://www.theinformation.com/articles/the-private-tech-company-that-let-employee-stock-grants-evaporate

ance terms. Vacation is also usually outside the scope of such agreements; when a contractor takes a day off, they don't bill for that day.

Performance management and the career ladder are also different for contractors. There are no performance reviews or opportunities for promotion. As a result, there's no need for many of the activities full-time employees do for good performance management outcomes. Plenty of people choose contracting because they don't want more career progression based on internal company levels, and welcome the opportunity to focus more on their work, and less on performance management processes and office politics.

A downside for contractors is that their job is often less secure than an equivalent permanent role. Fulltime employees' jobs are protected by rules and regulations in most countries. But for contractors, the redundancy process is very simple by design; usually, the employer simply does not extend a fixed-term contract or else serves notice according to a contractual timeframe. Contractors are very easy to hire and fire, so tend to be the first team members who are let go when times get tough.

However, contractors tend to be comfortable with lower job stability in return for higher compensation. Many are senior-or-above engineers who are content to not climb the corporate career ladder.

Tradeoffs between tiers

How do company tiers, based on compensation philosophies, compare? It's tricky to be objective as each company is different, and each working environment has upsides and downsides. Below are some observations about tiers 1, 2, and 3 for full-time employees. Contractors are not covered in detail, as there are no assigned levels or promotions to aim for. However, great contractors tend to embody many traits we cover in the "Senior" and "Staff" sections of this book.

Area	Tier 1 (local)	Tier 2 (top of local)	Tier 3 (top of regional)
How hard to get a job	Easiest	More challenging	Very challenging
Performance expectations	Usually reasonable	Often demanding	Almost always demanding
Career paths as an individual contributor	Usually up to senior or staff	Sometimes beyond staff	Almost always beyond staff
Work/life balance	Can be a focus	Usually less of a focus	Usually less of a focus

Comparing the three tiers of companies

The highest-paying companies predictably tend to attract the most candidates for jobs, which means they can – and usually do – place the highest demands upon software engineers.

4. Cost Centers, Profit Centers

Many companies apply the concept of "profit centers" and "cost centers" to their business. Which one of these you work in can have implications for your career.

A profit center is a team or organization that directly generates revenue for the business. A classic example is the Ads organization at Google, which is directly responsible for generating the majority of Google's income. There are many teams that help with this effort; the Search team brings visitors to the site and therefore also contributes heavily, for example. But without the Ads team building tools for advertisers to spend their ad budgets, Google would make much, much less money.

A cost center refers to teams or organizations which do not directly generate revenue, but are still needed for the company to operate smoothly. A good example is an engineering team working on compliance, ensuring the company is GDPR-compliant in Europe. Their activities are required, but generate no revenue, and so are cost centers from a business point of view.

What are the implications of working at cost centers or profit centers at larger companies? Here are a few:

- **Promotions**: these are almost always easier in profit centers. It's easier to sell a promotion case by displaying the impact on revenue generation. An exception is at Big Tech, where for staff-and-above positions, solving organization-wide engineering challenges is an expectation on top of organization-wide business impact. Such requirements incentivize experienced engineers to work on platform teams in order to progress their careers.
- **Performance reviews and bonuses**: there's usually no difference in working at either type of organization between entry-level and up to senior engineering level. At higher levels, those in profit centers frequently get better "scores" and bonuses. This is because most businesses naturally tilt toward money-makers when all else is equal in engineers' contributions.
- **Internal transfers**: it's understandable if workers want to be in a profit center. However, this is frequently not the case; many engineers are drawn to complex and interesting work, and that mostly happens on "Big Bet" projects which are not (yet) profit centers. Conversely, profit centers are often among the more "boring" teams in an organization, so fewer people want to join. Imagine getting into Meta and choosing a team to work on; would you rather work on Ads infrastructure and increase ad revenue by 0.005%, or a new team building an exciting, innovative way to connect with

friends?

- **Attrition**: cost centers almost always have higher turnover as more employees leave the company, or transfer to profit centers because career advancement in these teams can be easier.
- **Job security**: cost centers are a prime target for job cuts when a company needs to make cost savings.

So, how do you know if your team or organization is a profit or cost center? Here are some ways to find out:

- Does your team or organization report its revenue generated in every period? If so, you're likely in a profit center.
- How does your company make money, and which organizations bring in revenue? Does Sales get all the credit, or is it the front office if you work at a bank? Is Tech credited for generating revenue? Which teams within Tech get credit?
- Look at the org chart. How high up is technology represented in the organization? To where does engineering and product report? How many VPs are there in engineering, compared to marketing, finance, operations and other groups?
- Which teams do the CEO call "strategic" during all hands meetings, and credit for increasing revenue? Is your team or organization among them?
- Is your company publicly traded? If so, read quarterly reports for a sense of the corporate focus, which will likely be areas where profit centers are.

Software engineering can be a cost or profit center:

- In Big Tech, at midsize tech companies, and at startups and scaleups where tech is core to business activities, tech and software engineering are frequently seen as profit centers.
- At traditional companies and public sector employers, it's common to treat tech as a cost center that's a "means to an end."
- At consultancies and developer agencies, development is what the company provides as a service, meaning this activity is usually a profit center.

Working both in cost centers and profit centers gives you perspective. It's easy to feel superior to cost centers when you work in a profit center. However, effective companies need both types of teams and organizations, so it's a useful skill to know how to thrive in each.

5. Alternative ways to think about career progress

Believe it or not, there is much more that matters in your job and career, than titles and compensation. Your rank, a company's reputation, and pay are the easiest things to talk about because they're concrete, and compensation numbers offer an easy way to compare positions. Here are some other factors that contribute to how satisfying your job is:

- People whom you work with and team dynamics
- Your manager and your relationship with them
- Your position within the team and the company
- Company culture
- The mission of the company, and what it contributes to society
- Professional growth opportunities
- Your mental and physical health in this environment
- Flexibility. Can you work remote, or from home? If so, how often, and on what notice?
- Oncall. How demanding and stressful is it?
- Life beyond work: how easy is it to "leave work at work?"
- Personal motivations

Visualizing this:

How many people think about their career

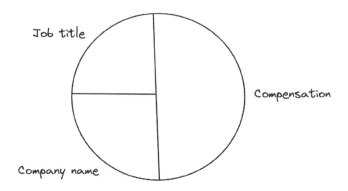

An alternative way to think about your career

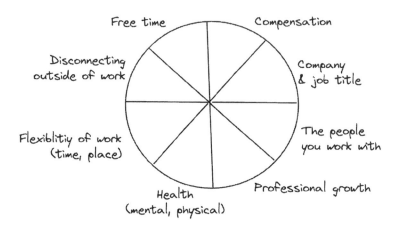

An alternative way to think about where you are in your career

Weigh the areas in the charts above against the compensation packages of the positions you apply for. It's not uncommon for long-serving professionals to take a pay cut in order to get an "upgrade" in one or more of these areas. Find the balance which works for you in your job, and in the next one. You will have a much more satisfying career than people who optimize only for easy-to-measure parts of jobs.

2

OWNING YOUR CAREER

The single best career advice for any software engineer is:

Own it!

Why? Because nobody cares about your career as much as you do. This is a lesson I've learned, which really hit home when I became a manager and tried to help people grow professionally, reach their goals, and achieve their ambitions.

In this chapter, we explore the topic of owning your career:

- You're in charge of your career
- Being seen as someone who "gets things done"
- Keep a work log
- Ask for feedback
- Make your manager an ally
- Pace yourself

1. You're In Charge Of Your Career

I've had several managers during my career; some cared about my aspirations and others didn't. Some promoted me after only a few months, while others provided little to no feedback on how to grow, even after we'd worked together for more than a year.

When I first became a manager, I vowed to be a great manager and to care about the careers of all my direct reports. I sat down with them, discussed their career goals, and tried hard to make them a reality. However, I noticed some things:

- Many software engineers had never had a career conversation with a manager before, and I was the first to ask about their goals; not only their goals in our workplace, but where they wanted to get to when they inevitably left the company.
- Some people were easier to help than others. I had better conversations with those who knew what they wanted, than colleagues who'd not figured this out – or didn't want to think about it.
- I wanted to help everyone, but as a manager my time was limited. I could spend a little time with everyone but had many other matters to focus on.

Eventually, I had to admit that even though I wanted to help every report's career, I was not the best person to do this. The best person was the individual themself; as proved when people performed better by taking the initiative, setting goals, tracking them, and continuously improving. This didn't happen to people who put in little to no effort or waited for me to set goals and nudge them to work towards them.

All those colleagues had a manager who genuinely cared about their professional development. But many people have managers without the bandwidth or motivation to grow their careers.

Take ownership of your career path if you want to be successful. Don't hang around waiting for a manager to step in. Even if you get lucky with a great manager, they have a dozen other people to think about and will be able to dedicate only a fraction of the attention to your career that you can.

There are plenty of ways to own your career, such as telling your manager and peers what you care about, sharing work that you do which they might not notice otherwise, and creating opportunities for people to give you feedback.

2. Be Seen As Someone Who "Gets Things Done"

When I talk with engineers who want to better their careers, they often ask how they can make better cases for promotion, or improve at office politics. Both these have their place, but if you're not seen as someone who "gets stuff done," then nothing else will matter.

Get stuff done!

Finish the work you're assigned, and deliver it with high-enough quality and at a decent pace. Over-deliver when you can, shipping more and better than expected. For most engineers, "shipping" means shipping code in production which works, and launching features, services, and components.

Get plenty of impactful things done

There's a big difference between getting meaningless stuff done, such as shipping small refactoring tasks which make no real difference to customers and fellow developers, and getting impactful things done which make a difference to the business and your team. Be the person who gets lots of impactful things done. Where to start with this? It's just a matter of understanding your team's priorities and the business's. So find out!

Make sure people know you get stuff done

A common mistake software engineers make is to assume everyone around them – their team, manager, product manager, and colleagues on other teams – will know when they ship a feature or complete a complex project. This isn't the case.

You need to tell your manager and team when you get things done. If what you do is impactful, measure the business impact and share it. Share when the work is unusually complex or involves heroic effort, otherwise many people won't know the challenges you faced and overcame!

Finish the work you commit to, focus on important tasks, and let others know when you get things done. Then your work won't go unnoticed.

3. Keep A Work Log

What did you work on this week and last week? What about ten months ago? If you're like most software engineers, it's easy to recall recent work. But further back in the past, the details can be fuzzy, which isn't a problem – until it is.

For example, it can be an issue at the end of the year when you summarize your contribution, which influences the performance review or promotion prospects. Or when your manager is preparing performance reviews and asks you to summarize what you've been doing all year. If you have no notes, you'll miss important work due to overlooking it, or waste time tracking down the details of previous projects.

Instead, record key work each week, including important code changes, code reviews, design documents, discussions and planning, helping out others, postmortems, and anything else which takes time and has an impact. Former Stripe software engineer Julia Evans calls this a "brag document[1]."

This document has so many benefits, not just for performance reviews but also for yourself by capturing just how much you do. Here's an example of this approach:

---

[1] https://jvns.ca/blog/brag-documents

Current

- Project Zeno
  - Called meeting on the project being at risk / cutting scope

Week of 6 Dec

- Project Zeno
  - Code: T43322, T43321
  - First time sending out Thanos update email
- Helping out the Chat team
  - Lots of chat support with Val and Nick
  - 7pm call with SF the last minute
- Design proposal: retire proxies. Will circulate it next week.
- Emergency version bump: T23232
- Sue: paired 4x this week.
- 1:1 with PM: proposed adding tech debt removal to the backlog. Added J32129!

Week of 30 Nov

- Project Zeno
  - Finished the design doc
  - Code: T23444 (refactoring the controllers), T34324, T42321
  - Code reviews: many! A notable one: T43242 (agreeing on approach to refactor)
- Postmortem for Zeus outage
- First mentoring session with Sue!
- 2x interviews and 1 hire!
- Cleaned up the Tech Debt project

An example of a work log document. See the template here[2]

Some of the most productive engineers I've worked with keep a "work log" in some form. It helps in several ways:

- **Priorities**. The more productive an engineer is perceived as being, the more that people approach them with requests. Engineers who list the work they do – or need to do – have an easier time knowing their top priorities than colleagues with no such document.
- **Feeling good about stopping work at the end of the day**. At larger tech companies, it's not uncommon to start the morning wanting to get a pull request in, but this still isn't done by evening time because other tasks came up. Recording what you do puts the day into perspective.

---

[2]https://pragmaticurl.com/work-log

- **Saying "no."** When there's too much on your to-do list and something new comes in, you need to either reject it or remove something from your log to make room for the new task. Engineers who know everything on their list can easily turn down new work, or negotiate which tasks to stop.
- **Performance reviews, promotions, and quantifying impact**. When performance reviews come around, writing a self-review is one of the best ways to ensure fair feedback. This takes less time with a work log, and the same applies to software engineering promotions.

Is keeping a work log weird?

When I first started to write this document, it felt almost silly. And when I suggested it to people as a manager, many were reluctant.

Some engineers felt it would be just stating the obvious, and why record work that's done and dusted? Others believed it would be a form of bragging, which felt wrong. And for some other engineers, it just didn't feel like a priority, and that updating a log would be a distraction from "real" work.

For me, starting a work log was a bit similar to giving meditation a go, and I'd heard people say meditation works when you do it regularly. What finally pushed me to meditate was a friend telling me: "I know it sounds stupid to listen to a recording for ten minutes a day, and I thought the same. But just do it for two weeks, and you'll see what I mean." I did, and a fortnight later I understood what my friend meant.

The same is true for writing a work log/brag doc. It may sound silly, and it does take time, but just do it for two months; every week, write down the work you do. Show this doc to your manager in a one-on-one every few weeks. At the end of two months, you'll understand why it's useful. I've yet to hear someone regret doing it, *after* resolving to stick with it!

4. Ask And Give Feedback

One of the best ways to grow as a professional is via feedback from colleagues. What do they think you're doing well, and where can you improve?

Ask for feedback

As a software engineer, there are plenty of easy ways to get feedback, and you might already be utilizing some:

- Code reviews. A great way to get another pair of eyes on your code changes, spot issues, spread knowledge, and receive feedback on your work.

- Ideas and suggestions. Share proposals or ideas for projects with teammates and ask for thoughts and feedback.
- Design documents. If your team or company utilizes these documents, you can get feedback on project implementation proposals.
- Peer performance reviews. Your company may run a more formal performance review process. If so, people may be asked to share feedback about their peers; what they do well, and how they could improve. This is valuable feedback you might not otherwise get.

You can also be proactive in seeking feedback from colleagues such as teammates, your manager, your product manager, or others with whom you work. My suggestion is to avoid asking for personal feedback. Instead, ask for feedback about something specific you did, or worked on. For example:

- "Could you help give feedback on my coding approach, based on my last few pull requests? Are there areas you think I could change in my approach, or where I'm not following unwritten coding guidance?"
- "How do you think this architecture planning meeting went, which I facilitated? What did you like about it, and do you have suggestions on how it could've been more productive?"
- "The outage last night which I commandeered: how do you think I did? This was the first outage I took charge of; what could I change next time to mitigate things more effectively?"

Feedback is a gift because it's always much easier to simply not give it, especially if it would be unflattering. So, if someone shares constructive feedback with you, remember it would've been easier for them to say nothing. Keep this in mind if your instinct is to react defensively.

It's a fact most people don't give feedback when it's not sought. So, you'll have to seek feedback by asking questions about specific situations. In my experience, asking for feedback is especially helpful when doing something for the first time, or when still figuring things out in a new group or environment.

Reflecting on work is another great way to grow and learn, and feedback helps you do precisely this.

Give feedback to others

Giving feedback contributes to colleagues' growth, but how do you do this when it's always easier and more convenient to stay quiet? Here are approaches I've consistently seen work well:

- **Call out good work!** When you see someone do solid work, tell them! Say what you liked about it, which can be as simple as adding a positive comment to a code review, saying the refactor you've reviewed is a neat approach. Or tell the person directly that the latest feature they pushed out is polished.

- **Be specific**. Tell people what you liked. "Good job" or "well done" are not really helpful feedback, so be clear about what you liked and why.
- **Only give positive feedback when you mean it**. Don't tell people you like something or that they did a good job, if you didn't mean it. Fake compliments don't help anyone.

Giving critical feedback is harder. As an engineer, you don't want to come across as attacking someone, which is how negative feedback can appear. There are a few ways to minimize the risk of a misunderstanding:

- **Focus your observation on a situation and its impact**. For example, say you want to give feedback after a colleague pushed a bug to production, which could have been avoided with more thorough testing. Describe the situation, that you observed a bug in production and the impact it had. Then, ask the colleague for their opinion of this situation, and for ways to reduce the likelihood of it happening again.
- **Avoid saying "you should do this."** Unless you're the person's manager, avoid making it sound like you're giving them instructions. Instead, help them come up with solutions. You can suggest what you would have done differently in the situation.
- **Give negative/constructive feedback in-person**. It's easier for someone to misunderstand your intent if you provide feedback over email or chat. Talk with them in person or via video, so you can see their reaction.
- **Make it clear from the start you're on their side**. Most people have the "fight or flight" response to negative feedback. Ease this by making it very clear you want this person to become an even better professional, and that it would be easier for you to stay silent and not say anything, but your goal is to help them get better. Ask them to hear you out first, and keep in mind you are sharing feedback because you believe it will benefit them.
- **Make it clear it's just your observation, which they can ignore if they wish**. I like to give constructive feedback to a peer by stating the power dynamics: tell them you are not their manager, just a peer, and that your observation doesn't mean they need to change anything. In the end, this is just your feedback, which they're free to ignore if they think it's invalid.
- **End the discussion positively**. The goal of giving any feedback is to help the other person and the team. Don't forget it's unlikely to help the team if you and the person who receives your feedback are on worse terms after the conversation. So, try to end the discussion in a mutually satisfying way. This could mean by closing with honest, positive feedback, or just thanking them for being so open in listening to you.

"Decode" poorly delivered feedback

Giving feedback constructively is an art that takes practice. This means most engineers are not very good at it. Heck, even some managers should practice more! It's almost certain you will receive poorly delivered feedback, even when the person's intentions are clear. Here's how to get something useful out of it:

- **Insist on specific examples of what the feedback applies to**. Most low-quality feedback is such because it's vague. For example, your manager might say, "I think your code quality could use some improvement." In response, ask questions like, "could you give me a specific example, could we look at specific pull requests?"
- **Clarify the impact**. Often, it will be unclear why the feedback is important. For example, a teammate might say, "I don't think you should have made that refactor." To this, ask what impact it had on them and others in the team.
- **Ask for suggestions**. Much badly delivered feedback makes no suggestions about what behavior to change or do instead. If a teammate says you didn't deploy to production carefully enough and caused a bug as a result, ask: "How could I deploy more carefully, how would you go about this, and which steps would you take?"
- **If you disagree: explain why this is the case**. While it's helpful to consider all feedback, you do not need to agree with it. If you disagree, explain why this is. The person delivering the feedback might be missing context, and your explanation could help provide them with that missing piece of information.

Feedback is a gift, both when given and received. Poorly delivered feedback is also a gift, but some work is needed to turn it into something useful you can act on!

5. Make Your Manager An Ally

Your manager is the colleague who has the single biggest impact on your career within a company. It's your most significant workplace relationship. A manager who believes in you, advocates for you, and supports you in your career goals, makes a huge difference; especially compared to one who's unaware of much of your work, doesn't know your professional goals, and provides no feedback.

You cannot control all aspects of your relationship with your manager, but there are plenty of ways to improve and optimize it, and hopefully create an allyship where you mutually support each other.

How do you make it great?

Have regular 1:1 time with your manager

Use this to catch them up with work you've been doing, and to share your work log of wins and challenges. Discuss your professional goals and ask about their challenges, and how you could help them and the team.

Tell them, don't assume they know

Many software engineers assume their manager must know the work they do, but this isn't the case. Your manager has lots on their plate, and won't review every pull request you do, and especially won't know that you spent half a day helping a colleague debug an issue.

So tell them! This is why regular 1:1s matter.

Understand your manager's goals

A little empathy goes a long way, so get a sense of what's important for them in the context of the team. The easiest way is to ask about the biggest upcoming challenges of the next month and half-year; there might be opportunities to help.

For example, if your manager shares that the biggest thing on their mind is that the team recently had several high-priority outages, then you could greatly help by taking the initiative to improve reliability.

Deliver what you agree on, and give updates when you cannot

There will be plenty of times when you agree to do something by a certain date, like putting a plan together for a migration and distributing it to the team. Make a point to do this by the agreed date and let your manager know when it's done, or notify them upfront if it will be late.

Managers get a sense of who's reliable on their team; who doesn't need chasing up on commitments, and who does. Aim to be in the "reliable" group. For this, it can be better to not make commitments you're unsure you can deliver.

Establish mutual trust with your manager

Many things are easier when you and your manager trust each other. However, trust is not given; it's earned over time.

When you start with a new manager, aim to be open, honest, and transparent with them. Hopefully, this will be mutual. If so, you should get comfortable with telling them the unvarnished truth, without fear of being judged.

Get your work recognized

As an engineering manager, my goal was always to recognize the work people on my team did. After all, this was a win for us both; it brought the engineer well-earned recognition and made my team look good. It also indirectly helped my career as a manager because when everyone on my team did well, my chance of a good performance review or promotion significantly improved.

Some team members made it easier for me to know about their work, recognize it, and give honest feedback on how to improve. This is how they did it:

- Came prepared to our 1:1 meeting, and ensured I knew what they'd done, the challenges they'd solved, and where they needed help or feedback.
- Completed agreed work related to their career. For example, if we agreed that they'd come back in two weeks with goals they'd like to achieve, they prioritized this work.
- Were clear about their professional goals by stating what they wanted to achieve.
- Were interested in team challenges and those I faced as a manager, and considered solutions that also benefited their career goals.
- Asked for specific feedback on their work. For example, asking me to share one positive and an improvement area in how they ran a project, or how they could improve a design document, or seeking feedback on a lengthy code review, including whether I thought their approach was helpful or overbearing.
- Kept a log of their work in some form, which they shared with me. This was invaluable when I prepared for performance reviews and promotion discussions.
- Asked for help when they were stuck on something and understood how I or my network could help them get unstuck.

In short, these colleagues made it simple for me to help them, as their manager!

6. Pace Yourself

Athletes pace themselves to optimize for peak performance, and for the longevity of their careers. What about software engineers, for whom the average career lasts much longer than an athlete's – up to 40 years. But burnout is a high risk for software developers, like career-threatening injury is for athletes. Are there lessons we can take from sports, for having a good career and keeping pace with the pack, without burning out?

I've found the "stretching, executing, and coasting" model useful for pacing yourself as a software professional. Factors like the environment, the project, motivation, externals, and more, determine pace.

Stretching

Stretching yourself is the most fun, at least initially. This is when you're learning new things fast and applying them as you go. It involves fresh challenges which require you to step up. As a manager, I actively looked for opportunities to stretch people, get them out of their comfort zones, and accelerate their learning.

Starting at a new company and getting up to speed is always a stretch. Joining a project that uses a different language/technology than you're used to, is a good challenge. Taking the lead on a type of project you've not led before, is too. So is working on a project with a tight deadline that forces quick, pragmatic decisions.

While stretching helps you grow faster, being in stretch mode for too long can backfire if it slows you down over time, or even causes burnout. If doing stretch work comes with overtime, then you'll become physically and mentally exhausted. If being stretched means falling behind in parts of your work, then this can cause anxiety. Without a way to relax and get back to normal, mental and physical exhaustion and stress can cause burnout. Even if it doesn't trigger burnout, over time your motivation and output may drop.

The coaches of athletes notice when they're over-stretching themselves, by observing movement, times, and other outputs. As a software engineer, look to people in your life who can tell if you're pushing too hard, like colleagues, friends, family, or others who give honest feedback.

Executing

This is the "normal" way of working and involves using your skills and experience to get things done well. You pull your weight – and sometimes go beyond "the call of duty" – in ways which don't overstretch you. You keep learning new things at a normal, not accelerated, pace.

An excellent way to execute is coding in a language/framework you're an expert in, on a project with reasonable timelines. You get your work done and help others without the need for overtime. In general, familiar work with few surprises is when executing is pretty straightforward.

After a period of stretching, it's common to sidestep the risk of burnout by scaling back to heads-down execution. I've seen people who are stretched make a list of additional things they're doing, which add up to too much. So they find colleagues to take over work, or start saying "no" to some tasks. They ask for support and let their manager know they intend to stop or hand over a piece of work in order to keep executing well, and not burn out.

Coasting

This means doing less and lower quality work than you're capable of. Coasting might be a temporary, short-term breather after a tough project, catching up on other things, or taking a mental break. Coasting can be a result of personal circumstances that distract you from work, or a symptom of low motivation. People who coast are rarely proactive and often need nudging on day-to-day tasks.

Coasting for more than a few days is counterproductive for everyone. It's not good for the "coaster," their project, or team. Teammates notice when someone has "checked out" and will assume they can't be relied on much. Others on a project will have to step up and pull more than their own weight to deliver it on time. And the person coasting will enjoy little to no professional growth, while their current skillset grows rusty.

If you find yourself coasting for longer than a little while, and the reason is low motivation, ask yourself what needs to change, and then be proactive in making changes. Why are you unmotivated? Are you in the right environment, the right team, or the right company? Do you have the right skills to get the work done, and if not, can you invest in improving your capabilities? Can you set yourself more challenging goals and take on more ambitious work? If nothing changes, your motivation may keep dropping until your manager has to have a hard conversation about your place on the team, or the company. Get ahead of this by catching yourself when coasting for too long, and look for ways to stretch yourself again.

Mix up stretching, executing, and the occasional period of coasting to optimize for long-term professional growth and avoid burnout, a bit like professional athletes change their pace of work for long-term performance and to avoid injuries.

3

PERFORMANCE REVIEWS

For many professionals at large companies and some startups, performance reviews are a significant and sometimes stressful exercise. They determine bonuses and eligibility for promotion. They're also that rare time when you're rated according to a quantitative system.

The good news is there is almost always plenty you can do to achieve better performance review results! However, there's little you can do at the last minute, which means advance preparation is important. In this chapter, we cover:

1. Start early: gather context and set goals
2. The power of habit
3. Before the performance review
4. The performance review

1. Start Early: Gather Context And Set Goals

Every company is different. What's important in your workplace, and what is rewarded? How is impact measured? Answers to these questions and others differ wildly at a seed-stage startup versus at a Big Tech giant.

A crucial starting point is figuring out the context in which you need to succeed. Determine which goals are helpful for you, your team, and the company.

Identify and understand the most important factors

What things do your team and employer care about most? People who typically achieve outstanding performance reviews and promotions help the business achieve success or hit very ambitious goals. How can this be you? It begins by understanding what's valued, which means identifying what matters first:

- **Ask your manager**. An obvious place to start. Ask what the team's goals are, and how they tie into company goals. Ask about your manager's personal goals, and what's important to them. The more you can help with this, the more valuable you'll be to your manager and the team.
- **Ask tenured people on your team**. Talk with experienced teammates and ask what they see as important team and company goals.

- **Listen to the company's leaders and executives**. Better-run companies are clear about their goals at the corporate and organizational levels. Finding out the most important priorities is usually as simple as attending all-hands meetings, re-watching recordings of meetings and presentations, or reading emails from the leadership that explain priorities. In Big Tech, you might have to listen to several all-hands at your organization's level, the product org, the parent organization, the tech organization, etc.
- **Ask people with influence**. Seek 1:1s with colleagues who play key roles in the business and are also accessible. They could be your product manager, your skip-level manager, a business stakeholder, or others.
- **Understand how the performance review system works**. There are a few common systems for performance reviews. However, there's lots of variety in how these work, while better companies refine their systems to fit evolving needs as they grow.

What performance review system is in place?

These are the most common performance review systems:

- **Unstructured/ad hoc**. Managers do performance reviews but with no real structure or cadence. Every now and then, your manager might give some feedback, typically when pay rises are announced. This is a common setup at smaller companies, where performance reviews matter less. The upside is you don't need to worry much, and it doesn't consume much time. The downside is that your rating pretty much rests on your manager's personal opinion of you.
- **Manager-only input and feedback**. This is more structured. For example, there might be a lightweight expectations document for your role. The review itself consists of your manager giving feedback. With this system, it's important your manager knows about your work. You're also likely to achieve better reviews by having a good relationship with them.
- **A peer feedback-based performance review process**. There's a regular process for team members to give feedback on some peers, which the manager reviews. They deliver feedback about you with a rating. In this system, your relationship with your peers is influential in getting a decent review – or not.
- **A formal, heavyweight process**. Much of Big Tech and several later-stage startups run a more heavyweight process to counter common biases. In a typical setup, you write feedback for your peers, produce a self-review, and your manager compiles a written review based on the inputs. An upside of this process is that you typically get specific feedback. A downside is the amount of time and effort it takes.

Gather these important details about your performance review:

- **Who makes the final decision?** It will almost certainly be your manager, but it's worth clarifying this.

- **Who has major input in your performance review?** Based on how the system works, it may be peers and stakeholders who have meaningful input, or only your manager.
- **When does the review happen?** What are the key dates? For organizations with structured processes, there's typically a deadline by which peer reviews and self-reviews are due, a timeframe within which calibrations happen, and a time when outcomes are communicated.
- **Advice to ensure a fair performance review**. Talk with tenured peers within your team, and outside. They're likely to have tips about what can help or hinder a fair review.

Discuss your goals with your manager

Set goals based on all you learn about the wider context. Some should support team and company goals – and perhaps your manager's, too. And of course, they should help you.

Share your goals with your manager and ask for feedback. If you have a mentor in the organization, share them with this person, too; what do they think, which goals do they like best, what's missing, and what suggestions do they have?

Agree goals with your manager

One of the best ways to get your manager on-side is for them to endorse your goals. Therefore, iterate your goals to the point where your manager can support them and make sure your goals are recorded.

If you achieve every goal, it may be a good opportunity to ask your manager how they rate your performance. However, be aware that a responsible manager cannot say, "if you do X, you'll get an above-average performance review." It just doesn't work like this because performance reviews are compiled by comparing your results and outputs with teammates', usually on a calibration. Your manager cannot predict how colleagues will do, nor how the calibration will go.

A fair question to ask your manager is whether your goals would help you meet expectations, or to stretch yourself and exceed expectations at your level. You won't get any guarantees, but there may be some pointers.

2. The Power Of Habit

Performance reviews typically happen once or twice a year, but your daily work is important all year round. There are easy ways to ensure a fair performance review, which take little time and effort, such as:

Record your wins

Most performance reviews suffer from recency bias. When review time arrives, you and your manager most easily recall the most recent successes and results. Conversely, some great work from months ago could be overlooked.

To counter this, record your wins as they happen, for example, weekly or bi-weekly. Capture projects you complete, and take screenshots of praise for your work in emails or chats, and other evidence that speaks to your performance.

Keep a work log

This is an easy way to keep track of the good work you do – not only the wins. I've observed most people who follow this method use a living document, in which they record notable work, add links to relevant pages, and record the impact of their work. We covered the benefits of a work log – and shared an example – in Part I: Owning your career.

Share progress with your manager

Hold regular 1:1 catch-ups with your manager every few weeks, to share work you've been doing, discuss wins and challenges, and show you're managing things effectively.

As a manager, I was regularly surprised by how much work my colleagues did that I didn't know about. This was especially true for more experienced engineers who took plenty of initiative. If they hadn't shared the details, I would have been unaware; not because I didn't care, but because I simply didn't know about it.

For this reason, I suggest erring on the side of oversharing what you do and don't assume your manager has knowledge of it. A good approach is to share a work log every now and then, and take your manager through everything on your plate.

Get things done

Most advice is worth nothing if you're seen as someone who does "busywork" – work that takes effort but provides no real value – or plays politics, but doesn't get meaningful stuff done. It's important to ship great work because it builds your reputation as someone who really does "get things done," and will help you be recognized for this in a performance review.

What great work is depends on your environment. If possible, ensure your work has the right balance of quality and speed. At startups, great might lean towards shipping things quickly, while at larger companies, it might mean well-tested and clean code, or code changes which are straightforward to review, or maintainable solutions.

Get familiar with what great means in your engineering organization, and gather regular feedback from peers and managers for a sense of how your work measures up. When you build a reputation as someone who does great work, others will trust you.

Help others

You won't get far if you only look out for yourself, focus on your own work, and never lift a finger unless it benefits your performance review or promotion case. Most people are observant enough to spot colleagues who are overly self-interested, and may start to dislike you for this, and even claim – justifiably – that you're a poor team player.

Depending on your situation, it's good to balance work which helps you, with that which helps your team and company.

So, lend a helping hand when there's an opportunity; it could be trivial things like doing code reviews, offering to pair up to write code, giving feedback on projects and planning documents, helping with research, offering to do work in an area you're expert in, unblocking other people or teams, and much more.

Capture work you do to help others

A downside of spending too much time helping others is that they get the credit for a job well done, but your manager – and even your peers – might not see your input. Be aware that when you spend a good chunk of time helping others, you might be mistakenly seen as unfocused in your own work, while your contributions elsewhere could go unrecognized.

Principal software engineer Tanya Reilly calls the task of regularly helping your team to succeed, "glue work." She wrote a thoughtful article about its pros and cons, "Being Glue[1]."

My advice is to ensure the meaningful work you do is noticed, at least by your manager. This is when having a work log is helpful. Also, if you notice you're spending most of your time helping, but very little time on "getting things done," then you might need to re-evaluate how you spend your time, or your manager's expectations of your current role and level.

Ask for specific feedback, every now and then

A classic way performance reviews go wrong is when a manager gives negative feedback on something that happened months ago. As engineers listen to this bad news, they're likely to be fuming and wondering, "why didn't you tell me this earlier?"

I believe managers owe it to their reports to share feedback as soon as possible. However,

---

[1] https://noidea.dog/glue

you can't control how your manager behaves. Also, a performance review may not be the best setting to call them out for not notifying you earlier. What you can control are your actions.

Seek feedback from your manager and peers well ahead of a performance review. Do this as early as possible to avoid unpleasant surprises at the review. Good feedback is timely, specific, and actionable. In order to gather good feedback, ask for it in advance, focus on specifics, and identify which actions to take based on it.

Here are some situations for getting useful feedback:

- **Facilitating a meeting**. Set up a meeting for your team, and after it's done, ask a more tenured engineer how they thought the meeting went, and one thing that could have been better.
- **Resolving an outage**. You were in charge of resolving an outage in a system, and think you did a great job. But did you? How about asking your manager and an engineer how it went, and what could've been better?
- **Presenting in front of a larger group**. After presenting on behalf of your team at an all-hands, it's normal to wonder whether it went great or terribly. Why not ask one or two attendees how you did, and what could have been clearer? You could even record your presentation and review your performance for areas of improvement.
- **Proposing a new initiative**. You proposed a new project to the product manager and engineering manager, which was greenlit. Great! But why not ask some people involved in the process how you could have made your case even better?
- **Leading a project**. While leading a project, invite feedback about what team members like and what's confusing. After the project's completed, invite people to share feedback on how you did as project lead and how you could improve, as well as running a retrospective.
- **Criticizing someone else's code**. A peer puts up a code review with lots of issues. You provide feedback pointing this out. But are you overly harsh, or too soft? Ask an experienced peer what they think of your review's tone, content, and style.

You can – and should! – seek feedback when doing something for the first time. This could be a new activity, or working with a new group of people.

Take feedback seriously, but remember that it's opinion and not a directive. Just because people give you feedback, doesn't mean you need to act on it. Listen to what they have to say, then figure out if it's valid. If so, what do you want to change?

Figuring out which feedback to act on and which is redundant is a whole other topic. However, it all starts with feedback, otherwise there is no food for thought.

3. Before The Performance Review

When the performance review date draws near, it often makes sense to spend time on a few activities to ensure a fair review. The more formal the review process, the more time it's wise to spend on preparation in advance.

How much can you rely on your manager as your champion?

No matter what the performance feedback structure, your manager plays a key role in the feedback process. So try to get a sense of these things:

- What is your standing with your manager, how do they view you, do they think you're meeting expectations, falling short, or exceeding them? The easiest way to find out is to ask.
- What is your standing within your team and among your peers? Performance reviews can sometimes be comparison exercises. Even if not, your manager will know whom they consider "top performers," who are "solid performers," and the few who are "bottom of the pack." Be honest with yourself; which group do you think you're in? Don't expect any decent manager to give a direct answer.
- What is the level of trust with your manager, how much do you trust them, and they you, how many review cycles have you completed together, were there surprises in the past?
- What is your manager's standing in the organization? How much tenure do they have, and how influential are they within their peer group? The more influential and the longer tenured your manager, the more they can push successfully for their desired outcomes during calibration.

If you have a new manager, one who doesn't have much influence or tenure, or one with whom trust is low, then expect it to negatively affect your performance review and prepare for this outcome. You might need to overcompensate and make it hard for your manager to give unfavorable feedback.

Find out the important deadlines

What's the deadline for completing documents, when is the calibration meeting that decides ratings, when's your manager likely to finalize their preparation? Hint: it will be close to the date of the meeting.

Knowing key dates is critical because it's pointless to give your manager extra context after decisions have been made. Fill in any knowledge gaps about your contributions before this. Offer your manager a summary of your work which they can use before the performance calibration.

Gather feedback from peers

If there's already a formal process for peers to share feedback, ensure you select colleagues with sufficient context of your work, and who are willing to give feedback. Say you'd be grateful if they took time for this.

If there's no such process, then you'll have much less feedback, which isn't good for your professional growth or for your manager to get a clear sense of you in a team context.

I suggest privately seeking feedback from peers; ask what you're doing well, and also areas for growth. I strongly suggest writing down what you're told. Depending on the level of trust with your manager, you could show them this feedback.

Create a self review

You can make your manager's job easier by handing them a self-review ahead of time. They will have to write up a summary of your work, with feedback on your performance, and might also have to include calibration to justify ratings, as well as compare individuals for the final performance scores. For this reason, provide lots of ammunition for your performance review.

Write up a document, listing:

- The "what." Results you've delivered over time, to help your manager avoid recency biases by including older work. This is where a work log is really useful.
- The "how." Qualitative examples such as helping others, mentoring, pushing for excellence, making pragmatic decisions, etc.
- Original goals and outcomes. Reflect on the goals you set and those you achieved.
- Examples of competencies. If your organization has competencies listed for your role, show how you fulfill them.
- Feedback from peers. If there's no formal peer feedback process, list some feedback you've collected.
- Praise and positive feedback. Collect written or verbal positive feedback you've received because it's easy to overlook these interactions. Collecting it will help you and your manager to factor in work where you went above and beyond.

Two questions to consider are whether to rate yourself in this summary document, and whether you see yourself as meeting, exceeding, or being below expectations. This depends on your own approach and your relationship with your manager; it's their job to assign a rating, and some people may see it as pushy to rate yourself.

On the other hand, assigning an honest self-review rating is a good thing, in my view. It shows what you truly think of your performance. Plus, your manager will give the rating they want, regardless. Perhaps your own rating will reveal a disconnect between you both. I suggest you write your own assessment of your performance unless there's a good reason not to.

4. The Review

Once you've submitted documents for your performance review and the process is underway, there's nothing left to do but wait. This can be an anxious time, especially if you're focused on getting an above-average performance review, or a bonus. Here are some things that might be worth doing during this period.

Remember performance reviews are snapshots of a point in time

The feedback is just one data point. Of course, it feels really important, but in reality it holds little long-term relevance for your career.

I've seen people get poor performance reviews and change jobs as a result, who go on to thrive. I've also observed people who keep getting amazing reviews but feel trapped in their job, and worry about leaving for a new place where they'd have to start from scratch.

Know the dynamics of the performance review

As a rule of thumb, about 20% of people tend to get above-average reviews, 60-70% get average ones, and about 10-15% score below average.

Look around your team and your organization. The chances are, you'll see many motivated people who all want to achieve a great review. But some will be disappointed in this.

A reliable way to avoid disappointment is to set realistic expectations. Personally, if around 80% of people were expected to get average or better reviews, I tended to ground myself to expect an average review, as long as I knew that I wasn't beneath expectations, and to treat anything better as a welcome bonus.

Avoid being too dependent on the outcome

I've observed some people plan how to spend their bonus before it's been awarded, especially at companies where performance reviews map directly to compensation. But you can't fully predict performance reviews, nor the size of any bonus. So, I advise against making plans based on an outcome you don't control.

Biases are very real

Your colleagues and manager have many unconscious biases, as do you. This matters because your manager's biases may well play into a performance review. Some common biases which come up during performance reviews are:

- Recency bias: more attention paid to recent work
- Strictness bias: excessively demanding when evaluating some team members
- Leniency bias: more leniency than usual for some individuals
- Horns bias: negative feedback from your manager in one area overshadows the whole review
- Halo bias: a single positive event uplifts the whole review. Common when someone is seen to have "saved" a major project
- Similarity bias: your manager gives better reviews to people like them
- Central tendency bias: your manager rates everyone on the team similarly because it feels fairer than to differentiate
- Contrasting bias: your manager keeps comparing you to teammates, not to your role's expectations

Know that not all managers are equally capable of giving feedback:

- Few managers are truly great at it. Typically, those who are have the experience to give wise feedback, are practiced at doing so and spend considerable time preparing fair feedback.
- Lots of managers are bad at giving feedback. A surprising number of managers have never seen what effective feedback looks like. Many don't educate themselves on this, or seek feedback before giving their own. Others just don't prioritize it.
- Most managers are in the middle. They might not have seen what giving effective feedback looks like, but they try to improve. Over time, some of these people become great at giving feedback.

Once you've been through a performance review cycle, you'll have a sense of which group your manager is in. Don't forget the outcome also depends on how clearly your manager can articulate their feedback, not only your work.

Be open to negative feedback and don't dismiss it

Nobody likes hearing their performance was less impressive than they thought. However, getting negative feedback can be a good thing, as long as it's specific and actionable.

I suggest pushing back on vague feedback which neglects specifics. Your manager should give feedback that's specific enough for you to reflect on. However, once you know the specifics, reflect on the message and think about whether you can – or want – to take action.

Remember, you and your manager are on the same side

Your manager's interest is to build and operate a high-performance team. The better everyone performs, the better the team works, and the greater the rewards for everyone.

In a healthy setup, your manager gives difficult feedback because they want you to grow, and they trust you to take it in the spirit it's given. Keep in mind everyone is in the same boat, rowing in the same direction.

Play the long game

Your career will likely be measured in decades, not by performance review cycles. Whether you get a "meets" or "exceeds" in one cycle is unlikely to have an outsized impact across this timeframe. Instead, the projects you work on, the people you develop strong relationships with, the skills you acquire, and the challenges you tackle, all have more influence.

Don't forget the big picture

Individual performance reviews hold little significance in the context of a decades-long career. Of course, they matter, but adopting a long-term perspective may help you avoid fixating on performance reviews more than they merit.

4

PROMOTIONS

Career levels tend to be pretty well defined at tech organizations bigger than a few dozen software engineers. Meanwhile, levels are less important at early-stage companies, but over time it becomes useful to differentiate expectations for an entry-level engineer, a senior engineer, principal level, etc.

Once levels are established at a company, it's only natural to ask what it takes to get promoted to the next rung on the ladder. In this chapter, we cover:

1. How promotions are decided
2. Promotion processes
3. "Terminal level"
4. Promotions in Big Tech
5. Advice for getting promoted
6. A long-term career view

1. How Promotions Are Decided

When should someone be promoted? The reasons are similar at most companies:

- **Performing at the next level**: many businesses promote people who are performing at next-level expectations. Needless to say, this means performing above expectations at the current level.
- **Impact at the next level**: lots of places promote people who contribute large enough impact.
- **Business case for a promotion**: there are companies that only approve promotions when a budget increase is available. This is sometimes the case for staff-and-above roles. So even if you're performing above expectations, there won't be a promotion unless there's a business need for a staff engineer and a budget for one.
- **Opportunity and space for a promotion**: if an organization has budgeted for a staff engineer and a senior engineer is operating at that level, there's an opportunity for promotion. Having a space into which to be promoted is increasingly a requirement at more senior levels.
- **Raise the bar at the next level**: this is rare, but some organizations justify promotions by asking, "how does this person raise the bar at the next level?"

In practice, several more things are required for a promotion to happen:

- **Perception**. How others perceive your impact can be more important than the actual business impact you make. This is especially true when companies grow, and it gets harder to map someone's direct impact on the business.
- **Support of others**: promotions only happen with decision-makers' support. Who these decision makers are is different at a five-person startup, than at a mega-corp of thousands.
- **Internal politics**. Politics refers to the influence and standing within an organization of a candidate for promotion. The more decision-makers are in a promotion process, the more complex the organization, and the more senior the position, the more complicated that promotion politics is.
- **Promotion process mechanics**. Different promotion processes reward different types of visibility.

2. Types Of Promotion Processes

Different companies run different promotion processes. Below are three of the most common approaches, and what each tends to reward.

An informal promotion process

This is common at startups and small companies. The process is usually ad hoc, where the CTO and some senior managers hold a meeting and discuss who's ready for promotion, and decide on a promotion on the spot.

This type of non-structured decision-making is typical for companies of up to about 50 engineers, or sometimes more. In such companies, being visible to managers who make promotion decisions makes promotion much easier. For example, if you worked on a project in which you talked with the CTO frequently, you'll have an upper hand over people who never interacted with anyone 'in the room.'

The upside of such a process is simplicity and a low admin overhead. However, it can become a biased process which overlooks people who do good work but have low visibility.

A lightweight promotion process

As a company grows, getting all managers together can become difficult, and the biases of the process are more visible. So, the leadership often aims to put a process in place that's more scalable and fairer. This usually begins by writing down basic expectations for each engineering level and inviting managers to submit short documentation on why an engineer on their team is ready for promotion.

In these settings, it's usually still a manager-only group that decides promotions. However, there are some rules, and the expectations of what it takes to be promoted to the next level are clearer.

Lightweight promotion processes are common for most mid-sized companies and even some larger ones. At large tech businesses, it's more common to have a lightweight promotion process until the senior engineer level, and a more heavyweight one above it.

This environment favors people with managers who are tenured, well-connected in the organization, and politically influential. This doesn't mean people without such managers won't be promoted. However, new managers are often less able to show the same level of conviction for their reports as some more experienced managers.

A heavyweight promotion process

As companies grow, they often aim to standardize promotion criteria and remove bias from the process. This leads to heavyweight promotion processes where getting promoted requires the following documents:

- A self-review from the promotion candidate
- A manager review by the manager of the candidate
- Peer reviews by people the candidate worked with, saying whether or not they support the promotion. Peers include engineers, other managers, product folks, and tech people. The more senior the peer, the more weight their opinion likely has.

This process favors professionals who work on high-impact projects that are easy to quantify, those with lots of written artifacts, and managers and individual contributors who express themselves effectively in writing.

Outcomes in this setup depend the least on managers, but the promotion process is very exhausting and takes the longest time. It's also a setup in which it's necessary to start preparing well in advance by producing and organizing artifacts which aid a case.

Hybrid models

Hybrid approaches to promotions are increasingly common at large tech companies. For example, at Amazon and Uber, promotions up to the senior engineer level are usually decided by a manager-only committee at the org level. Promotions at staff-and-above levels are typically done with an org or company-wide committee approach. This is also the case for engineering managers, where the process becomes committee-like at the senior engineering manager-and-above level.

3. "Terminal Level"

The concept of "terminal level" – sometimes called "career level" – is common at several tech companies. It's the level software engineers are expected to win promotion to over time, with no expectation of promotion beyond it.

For example, in around 2015 the terminal level was L5 at Google, E5 at Meta, and L5A at Uber – all senior engineer levels. Engineers who didn't progress fast enough to these levels would sometimes be exited from the company, or put on performance improvement plans (PIP.) It was a kind of "get promoted or get fired" system.

In recent years, all three companies have changed their approaches. Google changed its terminal level to L4, a level below senior software engineer. Both Meta and Uber have relaxed their approaches by not pressuring engineers to grow beyond E4 / L4.

The point of defining terminal levels, or career levels, is twofold:

- Making clear it's mandatory for engineers to strive to get to this level. Terminal levels usually come with the expectation that engineers are fully autonomous.
- Clarifying that there's no guarantee engineers will get promoted beyond this level. This is because the higher levels are increasingly difficult to reach. Often, levels above the terminal level need budget allocation, and not all teams have the budget to make a case for a higher-than-terminal-level position.

Companies with terminal levels often have an "up or out" culture that pushes engineers to continuously improve until they hit the terminal level. This approach creates pressure, but it's usually coupled with a well-understood promotion system, in a workplace where you can rely on managers and experienced engineers to help you level up.

Even companies without terminal levels will expect engineers to hit certain career levels. Terminal levels are almost always at senior engineer levels – the notable exception being Google, where the terminal level is L4 (Software Engineer III), which is a level below the senior engineer level. Expectations at the terminal level include:

- Be fully autonomous
- Unblock yourself
- Help your team succeed, and support and mentor junior teammates

It's reasonable for any company to expect engineers to eventually get to this level, with enough time and support. In this book, we cover expectations in depth in Part III: "Senior Engineer."

Figure out if your company uses the terminal level or career level concepts. If so, getting promoted to these levels should be a main focus.

4. Promotions At Big Tech

Compensation, promotions, performance, and how they connect, differ at Big Tech from most companies. At many "traditional" companies, getting promoted is the obvious – and often the only – way to earn more. End-of-year bonuses are often tied heavily to company performance, sometimes fully independent of your own performance.

Compensation and promotions

Big Tech also takes a different view of promotions and compensation with regard to base salary, bonuses, and equity compensation:

- **Pay for performance is a common approach**. Your cash bonus and equity refreshers are tied to performance, relative to peers. The highest-performing people often get outsized bonuses, 5-10x times that of an "average" bonus.
- **Rules for promotion eligibility**. Most companies require at least a 12-month tenure in a role in order to be eligible for promotion, and some also mandate that only top performers – those calibrated in the upper half of ratings – be nominated for promotion. While most companies publish promotion criteria, some organizations can apply stricter criteria, for example, on tenure expectations.
- **A promotion moves compensation to the bottom of the next band**. Pay bands are for base salary and total compensation targets. When someone's promoted, they receive a minimum salary increase (usually 8-10%) and move to somewhere near the base of the next level's compensation band. Equity refreshers are allocated in this approach; promotion winners typically get some additional equity refresh, although this can be delayed by a cycle and is often less than hoped for.
- **A top-performing employee at a lower level can make more than an average performer at the next level**. It might be surprising, but those recognized as top performers – usually 3-5% of a peer engineering population – can take home more total compensation than average performers at the next level up. This is due to top performers being rewarded with outsized cash bonuses and equity grants.
- **Promotions are not the only way to reward impact**. High-impact people can be rewarded with major bonuses, retention grants, and more. From the senior engineering level, promotions are less pressing for many engineers, because the financial incentive is lower compared to performing well at their current level.

Expectations for promotion

Expectations of impact and competency are common ways Big Tech companies frame performance and promotion conversations, and they document expectations for all engineering and engineering management levels. To be promoted, candidates must demonstrate performance at the next level in two dimensions:

- **"What"** – impact of the work. Engineers are expected to demonstrate business impact at the next level. For example, for a staff engineer this expectation might be to deliver a long-term effort that solves a meaningful problem at the organization level. The impact is typically easier to quantify for customer-facing product work than for some Platform work. Product work is often tied to company key performance indicators (KPIs) like incremental revenue or cost savings. Platform work is often tied to KPIs one level below, like decreasing systems' latency, increasing reliability, or increasing developer productivity.
- **"How"** – measuring against competencies. Each company defines its dimensions of expectations at each level, called competencies. For example, at Uber these competencies were software engineering, design & architecture, execution and results, collaboration, creating efficiency and citizenship. Performing at the next level in these areas almost always means working well with stakeholders and other colleagues. In practice, some competencies carry more weight than others, and these differences are unique to each company, the promotion process, and sometimes even to a group within the company.

One of the biggest challenges of senior-and-above promotions at Big Tech is the continuously widening impact radius and complexity of problems. For example, to get promoted to the senior engineering level, it's typically expected to showcase team-level impact. Staff engineers need to show organization or company-wide impact.

Senior engineering managers and directors face similarly raised expectations. While a company grows rapidly, there are plenty of opportunities for this. A hyper-growth company has no shortage of organization-wide issues for engineers and managers to solve. If they succeed, promotions typically follow.

However, the more mature a company becomes, the fewer of these opportunities there are, and the more complex and time-consuming they are to solve. Opportunities may be so hard to find that failure isn't an option because it would blow a rare opportunity.

Having fewer "promotion-worthy" opportunities also incentivizes success criteria like turning a failing project into something that can be perceived as successful. And why would people not do this? They put in the effort, did the work, and admitting failure would result in poorer performance reviews and promotion outcomes. *I'm playing devil's advocate here.*

Promotion-driven development

An unfortunate consequence of the impact-driven nature of promotions and performance reviews at Big Tech is what can be called "promotion-driven development." With each level, your work is expected to impact larger groups and drive more impactful business outcomes.

How can you impact a large group of engineers, and drive a major business outcome? An obvious answer is to solve an engineering problem the organization has. However, to get promoted, the "what" (impact) is not enough. You also need to perform at the next level of the "how" (competencies.) In practice, this means building something non-trivial that involves coordinating large groups and is a difficult engineering challenge.

This is exactly why engineers working towards staff promotions often create their own, in-house solution instead of using an existing third-party framework for an organization-wide issue. To justify this, they find edge cases where existing solutions are inadequate and execute a complex, impactful, promotion-worthy solution.

Building custom tooling is sometimes justified by unique needs, but there's little to no incentive for an engineer to choose an off-the-shelf vendor solution that solves the problem. This approach would be labeled "trivial" and not meet the complexity expectations of software engineering and architecture/design at senior-and-above levels.

Promotion-driven development is one reason why all of Big Tech has built custom solutions for everything from developer and observability tools, to rebuilding products that didn't take off. I'm not exaggerating: Google built 20 different chat products in 16 years, often in parallel[1]. It's a certainty each of these chat projects got dozens of engineers and managers promoted to the next level, and then a different group made a case to start a complex project from scratch with an even larger impact, rather than fix the existing product.

5. Advice For Getting Promoted

You hope to be promoted in the next cycle, so what can you do ahead of time to improve your chances? Here are some things:

- **Be realistic**. How was your last performance review? Did you exceed expectations? If not, there's little chance of promotion. Work towards exceeding expectations in the next review cycle.
- **Understand how promotions work**. Who nominates, who decides, what are the criteria, and which processes does your company follow?
- **Understand how promotions really work**. In reality, who gets promoted doesn't always map to an officially documented process. Talk with people who have been through the process, and also with any mentors. Common differences that are undocumented can include completing a "promotion project" that's shipped to produc-

---

[1]https://arstechnica.com/gadgets/2021/08/a-decade-and-a-half-of-instability-the-history-of-google-messaging-apps

tion, peer feedback being much less important, feedback from staff-level engineers or directors being much more important, and the influence of managers being bigger than official guidance suggests.

- **Self-evaluate**. Assuming there's a clear set of expectations, like a career ladder with competencies, evaluate where you are in relation to your current level and the next. A self-review template might be helpful.
- **Get feedback from peers**. Ask for feedback about how you're doing, especially from more senior colleagues. Come promotion time, you'll likely need peers to support your case. Get ahead by consulting people who'll give peer feedback. Questions could include: "which areas could you see me improve in, am I operating at the next level, what gaps do you see, any advice on how to grow from here?"
- **Find a mentor at the next level**. Reach out to someone who's at least one level higher on the career ladder, ideally who was promoted to that level at your company. Set up a 1:1 and ask if they can share their experience of growing to the next level, and give advice and feedback. Obviously, this doesn't guarantee a promotion, but you get another ally and one more person to give actionable feedback.

Organizing your work

"Produce, organize, publish" is a good framework for thinking about the buckets of work you do, as described[2] by product leader, Shreyas Doshi. It's not enough to do good work, you need to work with others and publish your work so that people are aware of it. Here's a good way to think about this model:

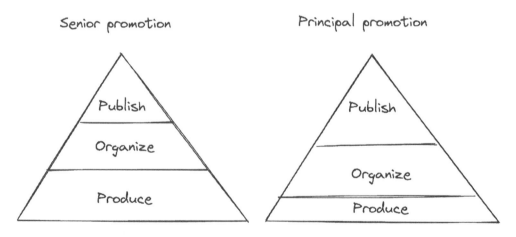

The produce, organize, publish framework. The more senior you are, the more you'll be expected to organize and publish at the next level

---

[2]https://twitter.com/shreyas/status/1332889515556364288

Produce work day by day, creating artifacts like code, design docs, postmortems, code reviews, and more.

Organize things that help to get things done. This might mean organizing meetings, setting up initiatives, and introducing better ways of working within groups, such as workflow improvements or bug bashes.

Publish your work and promote it via 1:1s, presenting at organization or company-wide meetings, knowledge-sharing sessions, other internal or external events, etc.

In most organizations, as you become more senior, your focus shifts to organizing and publishing, instead of producing. This is no accident. Both staff engineers and directors spend more time organizing and publishing than producing, compared to lower levels.

Keep track of your achievements. The most practical way to do this is to write down what you do, every week. Summarize key achievements each month and quarter. If you start this now, write down your key achievements of the past year. It's good to have examples that show you continuously deliver highly impactful work.

The importance of your manager

Talk with your manager and raise the topic of promotion. Ask where they think you are, and what it would take them to support your bid. Show them your self-review. Your manager usually has the final say on which projects you work on, and if you don't work on projects that prove you're ready for the next level, you won't have a strong promotion case.

Get your manager on your side. If they're not supportive, promotion will be hard, if not impossible. So start on this well ahead of decision time. How can you reassure them you're ready, what will make them support your case?

For staff-and-above promotions: get your skip level manager on your side. Promotions above the senior engineering level typically have significant input from the manager chain. Even your manager being on-side might be insufficient; your skip-level manager also needs to advocate for you. Have 1:1s with these people and ensure they know about and support the work you're doing and understand its impact. If possible, try to hold a recurring 1:1 every few months.

When a promotion would mean a change of manager, getting full support from your skip-level is even more important. For example, some companies have a rule that an engineering manager can't manage staff engineers. Should you be promoted to staff, you would stop reporting to your current manager. This is potentially delicate, as some managers might not see it as in their interest. The more challenging a promotion is, the more important strong relationships and clear expectation-setting are with your management chain.

Make an actionable plan. Set goals with your manager to reach that next level, or get closer to promotion. Do this in writing and deliver on them. Keep your manager in the loop about your progress and get feedback. It's great to do this in a document.

What if your manager changes? Your manager could leave your team or company at any time, so consider if your promotion is over-reliant on their advocacy. If so, change this by ensuring your work is visible to more people via 1:1s. The publishing activity in the "Produce, organize, publish" framework is key here.

Be realistic

Don't get obsessed by promotion because it risks alienating your manager and peers if you're seen as the person "working only for promotion." Have a plan, work towards it, and avoid the perception that personal advancement is the only thing you care about. This doesn't just apply to perception; avoid it being your one and only goal. Find other goals within your control which give you satisfaction.

Be realistic about promotion rates. The higher the level you're aiming for, the fewer promotion bids typically succeed. At most of Big Tech, about 30-40% of promotion cases to senior levels are rejected. This rate is typically lower at the levels below, and even higher at levels above.

Prepare to not be promoted. Nothing is guaranteed, but can you set goals that make you a better professional, regardless of the outcome? Successfully shipping a complex and impactful project, becoming more visible inside or outside the company, and mastering a new technology are all worthy achievements that make you more valuable, more employable, and more promotable in future.

Help others so they help you. What goes around, comes around. Helping others is a good thing to do in itself, and also builds up goodwill. Here are things you can do to help others:

- Mentor someone a level below you. Can you help them grow to where you are now?
- Mentor people outside your company. You'll not only help, but also learn a lot.
- Support others whom you know are working towards a promotion. Can you give them constructive, helpful feedback, and other assistance?
- Volunteer for things that help the team which colleagues ignore. At the very least, this will help the team, and managers are more likely to support promotion candidates who help the whole team succeed, not only themselves.
- Share that you're working towards a promotion with some teammates. If they know it's important to you, they may be more likely to help.

6. A Long-Term Career View

Career paths are not always straightforward, and plenty of successful people endure twists and turns in their careers along the way. It's helpful to zoom out and look at your career in a bigger context, not just a period of months or a year. Below are suggestions to build a successful career, long term.

Don't let promotions and titles define your self-worth

It's tempting to compare yourself with people at the next level. For example, a senior engineer might look at a staff engineer and feel frustrated that they do many things better than their staff-level colleague but are not at staff level, too.

Resist this envy! Getting promoted isn't based on skill alone; it's about demonstrating sufficient impact and having the chance to do this when such opportunities are not evenly spread. People at the next level could have had more chances to demonstrate next-level impact, or be better at selling their achievements during interviews.

Starting at the staff level, titles tend to be less meaningful and are harder to compare. So what's the point? Focus on your career and your path, and you'll be better off.

Avoid "elbowing" people out of the way

If you need to choose between hitting a professional goal and damaging professional relationships for it, ask if it's really worth it. Maybe there's a different way. People remember who shoved them aside, and the tech industry can feel surprisingly small, so a reputation for caring only about your advancement may return to bite you later.

Many career investments only pay off much later

Take these two subjects:

- Person A optimizes for immediate career progression. They go from software engineer to senior software engineer, and then push for – and get – a staff engineer promotion. They then stay at this level. When they look for opportunities elsewhere, they do interviews but can't secure an offer above senior engineer. But they don't want to take a "title cut," and so stay put.
- Person B optimizes for their curiosity, and is less concerned about titles. They're a software engineer and get an internal promotion to senior engineer. They then switch stacks to work on something new and take a step down to a software engineer role at another company in a different environment. They repeat this learning curve a few times. Later, their breadth and depth of expertise stand out, and they get staff-and-above offers at interesting companies.

Person A might have "faster" career growth at first, but Person B invests in the long-term by picking up new stacks and sampling a variety of experiences by working at a few companies.

Professional choices such as moving sideways, or onto a new stack, may have no instant career payoffs, but can be good longer-term investments. And even if these investments don't pay off in the form of a promotion, perhaps it was simply worthwhile and interesting to work in an exciting new area?

Happiness shouldn't be defined by titles and career levels

There's much more to being satisfied at work than our titles and responsibilities. Keep in mind what's good about your current position, what's not so good, and figure out what you *really* care about.

5

THRIVING IN DIFFERENT ENVIRONMENTS

Each company is different in culture, values, pace of work, and more. This means there's no single way to be successful in all environments. However, there are enough similarities among types of companies like Big Tech or high-growth startups for some common approaches to work. In this chapter, we cover:

1. Product teams and product-minded engineers
2. Platform teams
3. "Peacetime" versus "wartime"
4. Types of companies

1. Product Teams and Product-Minded Engineers

Product teams are engineering teams that build a product for external customers. They are noticeably different from platform teams which serve internal customers, and service teams which don't work on their own products but provide a service for customers or contribute to a product.

On product teams, engineers who tend to make the most impact are what I call product-minded engineers. They are developers with an interest in the product itself; they want to understand why decisions are made, how people use the product, and love being involved in product decisions. They would likely make a good product manager if they ever gave up the joy of engineering. I've worked with many great product-minded engineers and consider myself this type of developer. At companies building world-class products, product-minded engineers elevate teams to new levels of impact.

Places where product-minded engineers can make this impact include teams working on user-facing features, or collaborations with product managers. They often become key contributors; the go-to team member for product managers, who frequently advance to be team leads.

Product-minded engineers

Here are a few traits product-minded engineers share:

- **Proactive with product ideas and opinions**. Do not settle for simply implementing a specification they receive. Instead, they consider alternatives and approach the product manager with them. They often challenge existing specifications by suggesting other approaches that may work better.

- **Interest in the business, user behavior, and relevant data**. Take time to understand how the business works, how the product fits in, and what its goals are. They're empathetic with how users feel about and use the product. They dive straight into business and user data by accessing it directly if possible, or via the product manager and data scientists.

- **Curiosity and a keen interest in "why?"** Questions like, "why build this feature, but not another one?" are asked by them, and they seek the answer by consulting the product manager and colleagues with this and other product-related questions. They always have questions but manage not to annoy others because they've built up strong relationships.

- **Strong communicators with great relationships with non-engineers**. They like talking with colleagues from outside engineering, and learning what people do and why. They are accomplished communicators, with an interest in discovering how other disciplines work. You may see them grabbing coffee, lunch, or having hallway chats with non-engineers.

- **Offering product/engineering tradeoffs upfront**. With a strong understanding of a product's "why" and the engineering side of things, product-minded engineers can – and do! – make suggestions few others can.

- **Pragmatic handling of edge cases**. Quickly map out edge cases and think of ways to reduce their workloads, often with solutions that require no engineering work. They're focused on the "minimum lovable product concept" and evaluate an edge case's impact and the effort of handling it. They offer good middle-ground suggestions by mapping what can go wrong and suggesting which edge cases need addressing, even before shipping an early version.

- **Quick product validation cycles**. Before a feature they're working on is production-ready, product-minded engineers find creative ways to get early feedback. This could be via hallway testing with colleagues, showing a work-in-progress feature to the product manager, organizing a team bug-bash on the beta build, and more. They always ask: "how can we validate that people will use this feature the way we think they will?"

- **End-to-end product feature ownership**. Most experienced engineers own their work end-to-end, from getting the specification, through implementing it, to rolling it out and validating that it works correctly. Product-minded engineers often go a step further and consider their work "done" only after getting user behavior and business metrics. Post-rollout, they actively engage with product managers, data scientists, and customer support, to learn how the feature is being used in the real world. It can take weeks to get reliable data to draw conclusions.

- **Strong product instincts through repeated cycles of learning**. After each project, their product understanding deepens and they refine their product instincts. Next time, they'll offer even more relevant input. Over time, they become a go-to person for product managers, with their advice sought well before projects kick-off. They build a strong reputation outside the team, which opens more doors to career growth.

Becoming a product-minded engineer

If you work on a user-facing product, here are a few tips for growing your "product muscle:"

- **Understand how and why your company is successful**. What's the business model, how is money made, which areas are most profitable and expanding fastest, and why? Where does your team fit in?
- **Build a strong relationship with your product manager**. Most product managers will jump at the chance to mentor product-minded engineers, as they help managers to scale themselves. They ask the product manager product-related questions, take time to build the relationship, and are clear that they want to be involved in product matters.
- **Engage in user research, customer support, and related activities**. Get involved in activities to learn how the product works. Pair with designers, UX folks, data scientists, operations colleagues, and others who interact with users.
- **Bring feasible product suggestions to the table**. Take the initiative when you have a good understanding of the business, the product, and its stakeholders. You could bring small suggestions to a project you're working on, or suggest a larger effort by outlining the engineering and product work and making it easy to prioritize in the team's backlog.
- **Offer product/engineering tradeoffs for projects**. Suggest product tradeoffs that reduce engineering effort, in addition to engineering tradeoffs for the product feature being built. Are open to feedback.
- **Seek regular feedback from the product manager**. Being a product-minded engineer means having good product skills on top of your engineering skillset. The best person to give feedback on this is your product manager, so reach out for feedback on whether your product suggestions are viable, and for their thoughts on growth areas for you.

2. Platform Teams

Platform teams are the building blocks that product teams use to ship business-facing functionality. Products are built on top of platforms which enable product teams to move faster. Platform teams are key in scaling up high-growth engineering organizations. They share these characteristics:

- **Focused on a technical mission**. Concentrate on technical goals like scaling a key area, achieving performance or availability targets, or building architecture that's easy to extend and maintain, which serves multiple teams and areas.
- **Customers are usually internal**. Most customers of a platform team are engineers on other product teams or, in rare cases, colleagues on the business side who also use the platform.
- **Used by multiple teams**. Each platform typically has multiple customers, products, or other services utilizing its offering.

Here are a few examples of a platform team:

- The infrastructure team at a scaleup. This team provides compute and storage resources for other teams on in-house platforms, or support teams to use and manage cloud environments.
- A payments platform team at a large tech company. This team offers internal software development kits (SDK) for teams to integrate into their products to enable payments. They interface with payment providers, so other internal teams don't need to.
- The CI/CD team at most companies. This team owns and manages continuous integration and continuous deployment. They often help drive practices like automated testing approaches, linting, and other approaches to increase the quality of software, and give feedback.

Platform teams tend to be formed when multiple product teams start building solutions for a problem like storage, infrastructure, or for a business capability like payments. In many cases, a dedicated team owns the problem areas, and providing one solution via a platform team avoids duplication while making everyone else's lives easier.

Platform teams tend to attract some of the most experienced engineers because they often have an engineering mission to build scalable solutions that developers enjoy using. The customers of platform teams are software engineers on other teams, meaning platform teams also attract engineers who want to work with software engineers, not less technical customers.

Upsides of working in a platform team

- **Engineering complexity**. Platform teams are home to some of the most complex engineering challenges, especially infrastructure platform teams providing storage or compute.
- **Wide impact**. The work of a platform team is not limited to one product; it powers multiple products and has a wide, indirect impact.
- **More engineering freedom**. Many platform teams don't have product managers, and it seems like engineers run things. This gives freedom to work on tasks like removing technical debt or introducing novel engineering ideas.
- **Less day-to-day pressure**. Being more removed from customers, these teams tend

to face less pressure to ship new features or products. This allows for more long-term building and avoids having to use hard-to-maintain hacks.

- **Seniority**. Platform teams tend to attract senior-and-above engineers because they benefit from this type of seniority. Engineers who enjoy working with more experienced folks usually enjoy working on these teams.

Downsides of working in a platform team

- **The business impact is harder to define**. A product team can easily claim its latest feature boosted revenue, or that another feature attracted more users. But platform teams cannot so easily cite metrics the business cares about.
- **Frequently seen as a cost center**. If it's a struggle to demonstrate impact which the business values, platform teams will more likely be seen as cost centers. This means it will be harder to make a case for headcount and to grow. Relatedly, if a company decides to downsize, these teams may be more affected than profit centers.
- **More distant from customers**. Many platform teams are so far removed from customers that engineers often forget their ultimate task is to make customers' lives easier. When teams lose touch with customers, it can lead to misplaced incentives and frustration with product teams.

Thriving in a platform team

Here's what I've observed productive platform engineers do:

- **Build empathy for customers**. Most platform teams assume their customers are only software engineers in product teams. But this isn't true, the other customers are end users whom the product teams serve. Never forget this and build empathy with them.
- **Talk to engineers using your platforms**. Make it easy for engineers who build on top of your platform to communicate with you. Introduce yourself, and invite them to ping you any time with questions. Have easy-to-access email lists and chat rooms where an engineer can ask a question about your platform, and make a point to get back to them, or jump on a call with them. If you don't build these relationships, you risk becoming an "ivory tower platform engineer" who works on things nobody wants.
- **Work side by side with platform customers**. Most platform engineers build platforms as part of a team. However, standout platform engineers sometimes move to the "other side" and work with a product team on integrating or implementing their platform. Aim to do this when possible, as it gives you a much better appreciation of how teams use your platform. It's also a lot of fun!
- **Do a rotation working on a product team**. Similarly, rotate and spend a few weeks working on a product team if possible; especially if you've not done so for a long time. Product teams use everything you build, so have a connection with them.
- **Aim for *some* urgency and focus**. A benefit of working on a platform team is that

there's much less urgency to ship things, and there are usually fewer interruptions. This is great because it allows you to do focused, uninterrupted work. On the other hand, the lack of any kind of pressure can make your focus slip from getting important tasks done. Ensure to be clear about what the most important thing you need to do is, and try to make progress and keep focus.

Working on both a product and a platform team makes you more well-rounded. A product team and platform team are not superior to each other. An engineer develops a personal preference for one or the other by working on both.

To become a well-rounded engineer, consider working on a new type of team. After working on a product and on a platform team, you'll understand both better and more deeply appreciate the challenges each faces. And you'll likely know which one you prefer to work in!

3. "Peacetime" vs "Wartime"

When I joined Uber in 2016 the company was doing well, at least that's how it seemed from the outside after raising $5.6B on a $66B valuation a few months earlier. On the inside, I found things were fast-paced, hectic, and many projects felt like "life or death" matters.

Large parts of Uber operated in "wartime" mode for lengthy periods. This wasn't a vague feeling, we had terms for it; teams often called for a "war room" meeting to get important projects done, and at the San Francisco HQ, one large meeting room was actually named the "War Room." Critical initiatives were given "code red" or "code yellow" labels. Conflicts between teams were common because all were focused on moving fast and launching their features.

Uber's transition to "peacetime" was obvious when it came. In late 2017, Dara Khosrowshahi became CEO and the frantic pace rapidly cooled. Initially, he announced company-wide priorities at the start of 2018, and we ran a more detailed planning cycle. There was a new sense of stability in the air which was absent before.

So, what are "wartime" and "peacetime" at companies, and how was this term popularized? It was in the early 2010s when Ben Horowitz – cofounder of VC firm Andreessen Horowitz – published the article "Peacetime CEO/Wartime CEO." He wrote:

> "Recently, Eric Schmidt stepped down as CEO of Google, and founder Larry Page took over. Much of the news coverage focused on Page's ability to be the "face of Google" as Page is far more shy and introverted than the gregarious and articulate Schmidt. While an interesting issue, this analysis misses the main point. Eric Schmidt was much more than Google's front man; as Google's

peacetime chief executive he led the greatest technology business expansion of the last ten years. Larry Page, in contrast, seems to have determined that Google is moving into war and he clearly intends to be a wartime CEO. This will be a profound change for Google and the entire high-tech industry."

Here's how Horowitz defined peacetime and wartime:

> "Peacetime in business means those times when a company has a large advantage vs. the competition in its core market, and its market is growing. In times of peace, the company can focus on expanding the market and reinforcing the company's strengths.

> In wartime, a company is fending off an imminent existential threat. Such a threat can come from a wide range of sources, including competition, dramatic macro-economic change, market change, supply chain change, and so forth. The great wartime CEO Andy Grove marvelously describes the forces that can take a company from peacetime to wartime in his book, "Only The Paranoid Survive."

The terms "wartime" and "peacetime" became popular in tech and stuck. Basically, companies operate in "wartime" when their existence is at risk, and are in "peacetime" when things are calm and steady.

Here's how the two phases differ:

Area	Wartime	Peacetime
Business environment	Existential pressure	Little to no pressure
Focus on competition	Obsessed with rivals outcompeting or threatening the business	No need to be obsessed with competition
#1 priority for dev teams	Shipping quickly	Shipping thoroughly validated features
Deadlines	Meeting deadlines is a must	Meeting deadlines is a bonus
Meetings	Reduce meetings in favor of getting things done. "Done is better than perfect"	Normal to have lots of meetings to make sure everyone is aligned. "Alignment is more important than speed"
Conflict	Okay if it helps get things done	Not okay and isn't how things get done
Process	Break the process if it helps get stuff done	Follow the process, it exists for a reason
"Nice to have"	No focus on "nice to have" work	Lots of focus on "nice to have" work
Workplace frustration	Expressing emotions like stress and frustration is okay. Rarely repercussions for doing so.	Not okay if it involves behaving unprofessionally. Potential repercussions.
Work-life balance (WLB)	Work-life-what?	A considerable focus, and common to have WLB-friendly policies.

Common differences between wartime and peacetime modes

Leadership is different in wartime vs peacetime. Here's how:

Area	Wartime leadership	Peacetime leadership
Decision-making	Decisive	Seeks consensus
Prioritization	Ruthlessly prioritizes getting critical things done	Supports promising work streams
Conflicts	Tackles head-on	Avoids
Imposing pressure on employees	Common to "light a fire under people's asses"	Avoids pressurizing employees
Unpopular decisions	Frequent: leaders do what it takes to meet priorities	Rare: little to no need to make people unhappy, especially employees
Visibility of leadership	Visible and involved in the fine details	Less visible and not involved in most details
Style	Raw, sometimes to the point of seeming unprofessional	Measured and professional

Typical leadership behaviors in wartime vs in peacetime

Thriving in wartime

If your company is operating in wartime mode, how can you thrive? Here are approaches that can work in this context:

- Getting things done: do it quickly with *good enough* – as opposed to perfect – quality. Speed is usually much more important than quality. Follow the "done is better than perfect" doctrine.
- Handling conflicts: be unafraid of disputes if they help you move faster, but don't take them personally because they're usually not personal, but are caused by the wartime context.
- Allies: don't worry too much about making allies and just focus on getting the work done. If it's necessary to work with another team to get things done, do so. But there's no need to build alliances right now, as there's no time since everyone is heads-down.
- Internal politics: If you have good standing with your manager and skip level, then all's good.
- Priorities: Work only on things the business needs, right now.
- Job stability: Work like your job depends on it – because it might.
- Pace yourself: Constantly sprinting can end badly, so pace yourself.
- Burnout: This is a big risk to avoid.

Thriving in peacetime

For companies with less stressful environments, other approaches tend to work better:

- Getting things done: Get things done with high quality. Slow and stable beats fast and wobbly in this context.
- Handling conflicts: Avoid disputes, even if they'd help you move faster. Figure out why your conflicts occur because they're unwelcome in peacetime.
- Allies: Make allies across the teams you work with, as they will help you get things done and may aid your career.
- Internal politics: Important for career advancement, especially in senior positions. Manage upwards, sideways, and down as well.
- Priorities: Work on longer-term initiatives that benefit the business.
- Job stability: Job security exists, with time and space to do things well.
- Pacing yourself: A slow and steady pace can become too slow, so switch up gears sometimes.
- Stagnating: Avoid becoming bored at work in peacetime, which is a risk.

Alternating between modes

Most companies shift between wartime and peacetime modes. For a successful venture-funded startup that eventually IPOs, the pattern is generally this:

- Founding: wartime. Founders work long hours to build a prototype and hope it clicks with early customers.
- Fundraising: wartime. The team works around the clock to show investors there's something worth putting money into.
- After fundraising: brief peacetime. With funding secured, the team has breathing space to think long-term: grow the team, build the core idea, and do a few experiments on the side. The earlier the startup stage, the shorter this period is.
- Between fundraising rounds: the same rhythm as above. If funding starts running out or competitors appear, then it's back to wartime more.
- A year before an IPO: wartime. In the final push to get business metrics where they should be, the company prioritizes areas investors care about.
- After the IPO: it depends. With a successful IPO and the share price rising, it's hard for the culture to not switch to peacetime. However, if the IPO doesn't go well and the business struggles, wartime tactics are likely to be used.
- As a public company: more of a pull to operate in peacetime mode at businesses that do well on the market over time. Of course, this depends on leadership.

Companies alternate between wartime and peacetime because they have to, not because they want to. Some leaders would likely prefer to always operate in a high output mode like wartime. But this has several drawbacks:

- Much higher attrition
- Talented people leave due to burnout, who might stay if the stress was lower
- Hard to execute a long-term strategy because priorities are all short-term

- Hard to motivate people to stay in wartime mode if the business is thriving

The result of a successful wartime focus is that the company gets ahead in the market and creates enough time and space to recoup. This cycle then repeats.

The sooner you figure out how to be effective in both modes, the better off you'll be. Whatever company you're at, you'll notice the shift when it happens. Figure out where your team and organization are right now, employ strategies to do well in that context, and assume things will change sooner or later, and that you'll need to readapt.

4. Types of Companies

How do tech companies operate, in general? There's no universal rule because each business is different, but there are patterns of behavior at Big Tech, larger tech companies, high-growth scaleups, and early-stage startups.

Big Tech and larger tech companies

Here's a couple of modes of operation which are common in the biggest tech businesses:

- Product vs platform: these companies tend to invest most in platform teams. At larger companies, up to a quarter of engineers may work on platform teams.
- Peacetime vs wartime: these businesses tend to operate in peacetime, as a consequence of enjoying the success which fuelled growth. However, they sometimes switch gears to wartime. Signs this is happening tend to be pretty easy to spot: layoffs, stricter performance reviews, leadership changes, very clear communication from the top about the need to focus, and more.

Advice for thriving at large tech companies:

Keep track of your individual impact. Performance reviews and promotions are usually more heavyweight at these companies. To get fair performance reviews and a promotion, it's useful to keep track of personal achievements, and the impact your work has at the team and company levels.

Build allies and a network. The benefit of large companies is working with a lot of people! Personal relationships are rarely unimportant in achieving success at work. Help others and gain allies who may later help you get work done better and faster, and could perhaps even assist your professional growth. People tend to come and go at big companies, so those whom you know could help you – or you help them – years later in different workplaces.

Mid or late-stage scaleups

Scaleups are venture-funded startups that have passed the early stages and are focused on expanding their market. They are businesses in the Series B, C, D, or later stages of funding, but are not yet publicly traded.

- Product vs platform: these companies overwhelmingly have product teams. Platform teams are usually in their very early stages – if they exist at all.
- Peacetime vs wartime: it's normal for these companies to operate in wartime mode. Talk to people at the company and pay attention to how leadership acts, and you should be able to figure this out quickly.

Advice for thriving in high-growth organizations:

Tenure is a differentiator. For companies that grow rapidly, it's common for 50% or more employees to have joined in the past year. At these places, tenured engineers tend to be in demand, as they have a better understanding of how internal systems have evolved than new joiners do.

If you've been at a company like this for a few years, there are typically lots of internal transfer options, as most teams welcome knowledge and experience. You'll also likely find it easier to do well in performance reviews.

Hiring and onboarding is a focus. These companies tend to spend a lot of time hiring, but many put less effort into onboarding. If you're a more experienced engineer, you can make a large, positive impact just by improving the onboarding experience for new engineers.

Are you in a cost center or a profit center? High-growth companies don't always care about revenue, and value other growth metrics like the number of active users. Figure out what the company's main focus is, then get a sense of whether the leadership sees your team as a cost center or a profit center.

High growth phases end. At some point, high-growth companies stop growing or drop to a lower pace of growth, or realize they've over-expanded and make layoffs. During cuts, cost centers are more likely to be affected, along with perceived low performers. This is another reason for working in a profit center.

Early-stage startups

- Product vs platform: startups rarely if ever have platform teams. Product teams do the majority of work.
- Peacetime vs wartime: at most startups it's wartime. Much depends on the company's leadership; some founders create less stressful and more balanced working environments. Others don't.

Advice for thriving at early-stage startups:

Figure out how you can help the company achieve product-market-fit. Until a startup gets its product-market fit – meaning there's customer demand for its offering – the business is at risk of going under due to running out of money.

Your most important job is to help the company succeed by reaching a product-market fit. Talk with the founders, your team, and with customers to figure out how you can help, beyond doing your assigned projects and tasks. Startups are the best places to take the initiative and make a company-wide impact, so do this!

Know that startups are risky. Among all types of companies, startups are the most likely to let people go, and the most likely to run out of money and go bankrupt.

Take advantage of the autonomy you have. A major upside of working at a startup – which often compensates for some of the risks – is a high level of autonomy for employees. At most startups, doing stuff without getting permission first and then seeking forgiveness later, is an accepted way of working. Hopefully, you have autonomy; if so, take advantage of it!

Tell the founders about your work. You work at a small company, so it's fair to assume the founders know about your work, right? In my experience, this isn't always the case. When you do work that's impactful, challenging, or both, tell your team and the founders about it.

Good work can easily be overlooked amid the hectic pace of startups.

Don't forget the most important thing about working at a startup: get things done! Everything comes second to this. Ensure you get the *right* things done – i.e., work that creates value for the startup – and execute quickly!

Approaches to thrive at any type of company

There are a few strategies to help you succeed professionally, regardless of which type of company you work at:

Do standout work. "Standout" work means different things at different companies; some places value quality above speed, while at other places, it's vice-versa. Figure out what your company values, and aim to over-deliver on expectations of software engineers.

Help others around you. The software industry is small, which is something many engineers don't realize for years until they unexpectedly bump into former colleagues in different workplaces. Why not forge strong relationships with your peers and help them where possible – even if it's personally inconvenient? People will hold you in good stead, which can open doors later in your career.

Don't burn bridges. Try to resolve conflicts that arise, treat others with respect, and learn to disagree agreeably, and professionally. Why? For the same reason as above: tech is a small industry.

6

SWITCHING JOBS

It's rare for a software engineer to work at the same company for their entire career. Even Satya Nadella, who became CEO of Microsoft in 2014 after joining the tech giant as a software engineer 22 years earlier in 1992, had an engineering job at Sun Microsystems before joining Microsoft.

So, what are sensible approaches for switching jobs, and knowing when to pull the trigger and take an opportunity elsewhere? We cover:

1. Exploring new opportunities
2. Waiting for a promotion vs switching jobs
3. Preparing for tech interviews
4. Down-leveling
5. Up-leveling
6. Onboarding to a new company

1. Exploring New Opportunities

There are plenty of reasons to explore job opportunities, and they fall into a few categories.

Actively looking for a job

The most obvious case is when you want or need a new job. This could be for several reasons, such as:

- You're a new graduate seeking that first opening in your career.
- You lost a job and need to replace it.
- Your personal circumstances change and you need a job that fits. Cases may include moving to a new location, needing more flexible work arrangements, and more.
- You're unhappy at work, which could mean there are problems with your manager, your team, or the environment. Moving internally isn't an option.
- You realize you are paid well below market rate, and want to correct this by changing jobs and earning the market rate.

When actively looking, it's good to lean into the process, which means searching job openings, and at the very least, responding to inbound messages. You should probably set your

LinkedIn profile to display the "open to new opportunities" ribbon, and be clear with re-cruiters and hiring managers that you're seeking new opportunities, and have a decent idea of what these would be.

Passively open to opportunities

Other times, you're okay with your current job, but keep an open mind for anything interesting that may come along. You're not actively searching job openings, but read inbound messages from recruiters, and follow up with some. If an inbound opportunity piques your curiosity, you'll talk with the recruiter and engage in the recruitment process.

In this situation, you don't feel much pressure to get the job you could interview for. You also have pretty high expectations: usually a step up in compensation and opportunity. You can afford to be picky, as you're okay in your current job.

However, the longer you passively engage in interview processes, you might admit to yourself that you're ready to leave your current job for something that's more than okay.

When you're happy in a job

There are reasons why it's good to engage in the job search and interview process when you're satisfied with your current job:

- To establish your market value. "Am I being paid my worth?" is a question many people ask. An approach that's hard to beat for answering this is to contact recruiters for a sense of the salary range on offer. You don't even need to go through the whole interview process; just ask a recruiter or hiring manager what range to expect. If this is well above what you currently earn, you may decide to pursue the job vacancy.
- To get a sense of how employable you are. It's easy to get rusty with tech interviews. Interviewing while employed can be a way to keep your interview skills sharp.
- To level up via a new job. You could interview in the hope of getting a better offer than you currently earn; which would mean you don't have to wait for a pay rise via promotion at your current workplace.

There is no single "best" approach for exploring new opportunities. The thing about opportunities is that you don't really control how and when they arise. What you do control is whether to engage with them and how seriously to take them.

I have personal experience of passing on opportunities while being happily employed that I wish I'd considered more closely. In 2011, I ignored a reachout from a small startup that had just raised $8M in seed funding. I didn't think too much about this startup, from which someone with the title "QA testing" wanted to talk with me about building their Windows Phone App. Years later, I realized this person was Jan Koum, CEO of a messaging company called WhatsApp. You may have heard of it; Facebook bought it for a historic $19.3B in

2014, when WhatsApp had about 50 engineers. I was happily employed at the time, but had I been able to predict the future, I would've interviewed for the role.

Of course, I had interviews that ended up being wasted time because the opportunity or offer was underwhelming. I regret opportunities that I pursued and turned down much less than I regret failing to engage with potentially interesting ones.

2. Waiting on a Promotion vs Switching Jobs

You feel you have what it takes to perform at the next level. In this case, it's tempting to get out there on the job market, and not wait months for a grueling promotion process in your current workplace. Why not do external interviews? Maybe you'll get an offer with the title you want and more money as well. This is an obvious option, especially when the job market is hot like it was in 2021-2022. However, before applying for positions, there's some nuance to consider.

Promotions are typically backward-looking

To get promoted, you are expected to perform at the next level for 6-12 months, and a promotion confirms you did. What it also means is that you might be able to switch companies to reach that higher level and earn more. In fact, if you can move to a company in a higher tier – according to the trimodal compensation model we cover in the "Career Paths" chapter – your compensation might increase significantly.

The backward-looking nature of promotions also means you could progress faster in your early career if you can get external offers at the next level, and don't have to wait around to be promoted in your current workplace.

The more senior you are, the riskier a new job is

Changing jobs is different at the staff and principal engineering levels than at more junior levels because doing well in these senior roles requires good political standing. This means understanding how a new organization works and its unwritten rules, building trust with new key stakeholders, and knowing how to influence decisions that impact larger groups.

Building a network of colleagues, you trust and who trust you, and figuring out how the organization works, takes significant time. When you switch to a new position, you have to start from scratch. If you don't get up to speed quickly enough, you can find yourself in a stressful situation of trying but struggling to meet heightened expectations.

Tenure becomes increasingly important as you get more senior. While it's common for early-stage career professionals to change jobs often, not staying anywhere for at least 2-3 years can become a red flag in above-senior engineering recruitment.

Staff and principal engineers need time to build connections, and to execute longer-term, impactful projects. Driving this impact is done by understanding the context, making sense of the business, and prioritizing work correctly. Learning how to do this usually takes at least a year at most places.

Tenure also brings the perspective which leaders need. By staying on the same team and at the same company for years, your old decisions come back to bite you and others. You appreciate how something which nobody considered at the time, can grow into a big problem, or how doing a bit more work early, can avoid a large amount of work later.

Before quitting, consider what you'd leave on the table. This is especially true if you have not been long at a company. Building platforms that see large adoption takes years. Launching a product then iterating through each growth stage, also takes years. One reason why engineers and managers who work at high-growth startups for several years become increasingly sought after is that they see several growth phases play out in one place, and can harness that valuable experience elsewhere.

While researching this book, I talked with several Uber alumni who are now staff engineers, CTOs, and VPs of engineering at venture-funded startups. All spent a solid amount of time at the ride-sharing company, and all told me the same thing: their years at Uber and going through its various growth phases, have given them an edge today. They're making strategic decisions with confidence because they know what will happen in 6, 12, or 24 months' time. How? They spent long enough at Uber to see decisions play out along those time frames.

Don't get me wrong, tenure is not what you want to optimize for. However, if you've worked in the industry for 8+ years but didn't spend more than 2-3 years in any one place, then it could be a good idea to target staying in your next position for this long, in order to gain the perspective which only comes with tenure.

The more senior you are, the harder it is to get promoted

Lack of internal opportunities to grow to the next level becomes more common with seniority. For example, you could come up against budget constraints, like when there's no money for a second staff engineer, but this is your next level. Not having space to grow is especially common for managers, who typically need to take on larger teams and deliver more impactful outcomes to get promoted.

If you hit this wall, it can be sensible to look for external opportunities, especially if you're learning less, or are determined to keep progressing in your career.

When you get an offer, don't just assess it based on compensation. Instead, consider other important dimensions, such as career progression, colleagues you'd work with, challenges, company mission, flexibility, etc.

Finally, don't forget that missing out during a promotion cycle might feel like a big deal, but you probably won't remember it a decade later. Play the long game and think about your strategy across that timeframe.

3. Preparing for Tech Interviews

How do you prepare for software engineer interviews? Luckily, there's no shortage of preparation materials to help, in the form of online resources. This section is a short overview of what to expect in a typical interview process for senior-level engineers.

Mid-sized and larger tech companies tend to use similar interview processes, which are sometimes referred to as "Google-like," given their resemblance to how the Big Tech giant conducts interviews.

Type of interview	Done by
Initial screening	
Resume screen	Recruiter, inbound sourcer, or hiring manager
Initial call	
Technical screening	
Technical phone screen (TPS)	Software engineer, or hiring manager
Take home coding exercise	Software engineer
Onsite interview	
Coding interview	Software engineer
Systems design interview (also known as the architecture interview)	Software engineer
Hiring manager interview, also known as behavioral interview	Hiring manager
Bar raiser interview	Dedicated bar raiser interviewer, or hiring manager

Typical interviews for senior-level software engineers

Let's look into the different types of interview:

Initial screening

The goal here is to decide whether it's worth progressing a candidate to the technical screening, based on the following parameters:

- Has the basic qualifications for the role. For example, if it's a staff-level role for which a candidate is expected to have 5+ years of industry experience, including in the backend domain, then candidates lacking this do not proceed.
- Has the required soft skills. This is confirmed in an initial conversation with the recruiter or hiring manager.
- Is motivated for the interview process. A candidate can look great on paper, but are they motivated for the interview process? There are candidates who apply for roles out of curiosity, and some aren't motivated to engage with the process. In this case, proceeding would be a waste of time.

The initial screening is done by the tech recruiter responsible for filling the position, the hiring manager, or an inbound sourcer.

"Inbound sourcer" is a specialized recruitment role usually found at larger companies, where every vacancy gets hundreds or even thousands of applications. Each one needs to be reviewed by a human, so these companies have a dedicated role for reviewing only inbound applications.

The inbound sourcer role is usually the least coveted recruitment position because it's rarely exciting. But these people are very efficient at reviewing resumes and deciding whether a candidate is viable. When I was a hiring manager at Uber, I worked with several inbound sourcers who combed through many resumes per day.

The initial screening is done in two phases: the resume screen, and the initial call with the hiring manager.

The resume screen: a resume is reviewed, and a decision is made on whether the applicant has the basic qualifications for the role. For this reason alone, there's a lot to be said for writing an effective software engineer resume. I wrote the book, "The Tech Resume Inside Out," about precisely this task.

Here are a few suggestions for writing an efficient resume:

- Remember, the goal is to convince the person doing the screening that it's worth doing an initial call with you. The goal is not to describe your career in minute detail.
- Tell the story you want the recruiter or hiring manager to hear for the position you're applying to. Highlight relevant experience.
- Tailor your resume. Don't send the same resume with every application. Instead, consider having a "master" version and tweaking it each time.

- Use an easy-to-scan template. The more easily a recruiter or hiring manager can scan a resume, the better. Avoid flashy formats and two-column layouts. See The Pragmatic Engineer's Resume Template[1] for a free template which checks these requirements.
- Stand out in results, impact, and numbers. Aim to present your achievements as specifically as possible. Define the impact of your work, ideally with numbers.
- A positive referral usually helps more than a fantastic resume. Seek out referrals from your network.

For more advice, see my book The Tech Resume Inside-Out[2].

The initial call with a recruiter or hiring manager: for candidates whose resumes pass, the next step is a phone call. The goal of this call is to gather more information about the applicant; their situation, and what they are looking for, and to give them more context about the position. Sometimes, this turns into a sales call to tell candidates why a vacancy is a compelling opportunity.

When the call is with a recruiter, they usually gather some "soft" signals, like how clearly the candidate communicates, and how interested they are in the position.

When this call is with the hiring manager, they usually go a step further by gathering more signals and doing a "stricter" screening. I know hiring managers who deep dive into projects the candidate has done and delve into behavioral topics. Their goal is to progress people whom they'd be comfortable hiring, assuming they do well in the technical interviews.

Technical screening

Once a candidate passes the initial screen, the employer is pretty certain they're interested, and – on paper – has the desired qualifications. The next step is the technical screening, to validate that a candidate has the technical expertise which their resume claims.

The goal is to ensure a candidate:

- Is technical enough for the role's requirements. Are they up to date with core technological concepts, and are they hands-on enough with technologies?
- Is hands-on enough with coding. It's hard to tell just how hands-on a candidate is with coding without verifying it. The technical screening almost always involves coding tasks which provide signals about this.
- Is worth inviting to a final interview. For everyone involved, interviews are a time investment. It's only worth proceeding to the final round with candidates who perform well in this screening.

---

[1] https://blog.pragmaticengineer.com/the-pragmatic-engineers-resume-template
[2] https://thetechresume.com

The technical screen is almost always done by software engineers – and more rarely – by engineering managers. There are several popular ways to conduct this round:

- **A synchronous coding challenge**. The candidate does a live session or a video call, where they solve a problem by writing code on the spot while conversing with the interviewer, who's a software engineer.
- **A take-home coding challenge**. This is an asynchronous coding exercise, which candidates complete in their own time. The coding exercise can be time-boxed – for example, 90 minutes to complete it. Some exercises are less strict, come with guidance about how much time is usually spent on the exercise, and let the applicant decide how long to take.
- **Another format to probe technical skills**. Some companies prefer a synchronous interview where interviewers discuss technology concepts, but don't do coding. Some companies give candidates technology quizzes to complete, and some do a debugging session with candidates. There are no formal rules, and many companies innovate here.

How to prepare for the technical screening:

- **Gather information on what to expect**. The easiest way is to ask your recruiter contact what the format is, and any advice they can offer on preparation. Once you've passed the initial screening, the recruiter will be on your side and interested in you doing well. Some employers send preparation materials for the technical screening, so candidates aren't caught off guard.
- **Understand how the challenge is evaluated**. What's more important: functionality, code quality, or testing? Does the choice of language matter? Get answers to these questions before you start the challenge. Again, the recruiter is your best source of information.
- **For synchronous exercises, question the interviewer**. In technical interviews done on the spot, it's expected that candidates ask clarifying questions of interviewers, especially for senior-and-above roles. Sharing your thought process and occasionally seeking feedback can be a positive.
- **For asynchronous tasks, set expectations for completion**. Some asynchronous coding tasks involve significant time commitment, which you have to plan for. Communicate your circumstances to the recruiter and confirm whether they can accommodate your timeline.
- **Find out if detailed feedback is provided before you invest time**. Some take-home exercises demand tens of hours of work. There are few things more demotivating than putting in the time but getting no feedback later, except a rejection message. So before you start, ask the recruiter if there is written feedback in the case of a rejection. Of course, this doesn't guarantee you will always get feedback, but it will make it more likely.

Onsite interviews

The final round of the interview process is often an onsite interview. The name refers to the common practice of holding the final set of interviews at the employer's offices. These are typically split into the following categories:

Coding interview: validating a candidate's coding and debugging. It could be an algorithmic interview, or solving a real world coding challenge.

There are plenty of resources on how to prepare for these interviews. A few books I recommend:

- "Cracking the Coding Interview" by Gayle Laakmann McDowell
- "De-Coding the technical interview process" by Emma Bostian

System design interview: also known as the "architecture interview." This gathers signals about how well an engineer can design a system from scratch, based on business requirements, and how they can respond to scaling challenges.

Books on how to prepare for this interview:

1. "System Design Interview – An Insider's Guide" by Alex Xu
2. "System Design Interview – Volume 2" by Alex Xu

Domain deepdive: an interview for revealing how capable candidates are in key technologies for the role. For example, for a backend engineer, this could be a deep dive into distributed systems and the Go programming language. For an iOS engineer, it could be on Swift and more advanced mobile application development topics. As a note, interviewers tend to go into domain concepts during the coding interview and the system design interview.

The hiring manager interview: also referred to the behavioral interview. An engineering manager almost always conducts this interview. The goal is to determine if a candidate is a good fit for the team. This interview tends to go deep into:

- Motivation
- Handling conflict
- Approaching difficult situations
- Does the candidate demonstrate or "live" the company's values?

The hiring manager interview tends to vary by company, and often differs between hiring managers within the same company. For advice on navigating the hiring manager interview and interview process, I made a video called Confessions of a Big Tech Hiring manager[3].

---

[3] https://pragmaticurl.com/confessions

The bar raiser interview is special to Amazon and a few other larger tech companies like Uber. A long-tenured engineer or manager determines whether a candidate can "raise the bar." These interviews tend to be a mix of technical, design, behavioral, and culture interviews.

Other interview types: smaller companies often have a session where candidates meet their potential future teammates and take questions from them. At some places, engineers meet their potential product manager (PM) or other business stakeholders, who also interview them. All these interviews are hard to prepare for upfront. Arriving well rested, in a calm frame of mind, and treating it as an exercise in learning something new are among the most effective approaches I know.

Staff-and-above interview loops

For staff-and-above roles, the interview process tends to be more bespoke. It's common for the hiring manager to build a custom interview process. At some companies, staff+ engineers typically go through the coding and systems design interviews which other engineers also need to clear, and for the coding interview to be a bit more forgiving. Some companies even drop the entry-level coding interview from the process.

Staff+ interviews tend to have several additional rounds, such as:

- A domain deep dive interview. When hiring for areas like payments, mobile, or distributed systems, there's almost always an interview to validate the depth of a candidate's expertise.
- A product manager interview, where they evaluate how well a candidate might work with product folks.
- A director-level interview, conducted as a bar raiser or a hiring manager interview.
- A second systems design interview, conducted by a staff-or-above engineer.

4. Down-Leveling

In tech, switching jobs often comes with a financial or title upside, but not always with both. Switching for higher compensation can result in a "lower" title, like going from senior software engineer to SWE 2, or from VP engineering to senior engineering manager. This is what happened to me when I went from principal engineer at Skyscanner to senior engineer at Uber, while my compensation increased.

This is what I call the seniority roller coaster.

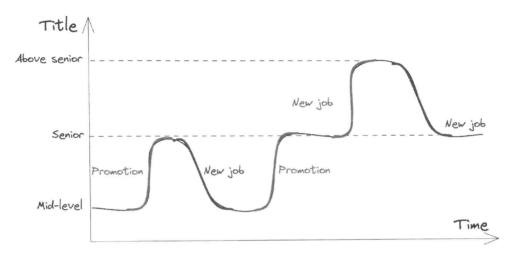

The seniority roller coaster

There can be several reasons for dropping in title while gaining in compensation, such as:

- Moving up a "tier." A common reason is that moving to a higher-tier company brings raised expectations, but also more compensation. You may see your title slashed but your compensation increases.
- Titles across companies have different expectations and compensation. For example, a senior title in Big Tech typically demands more of an engineer than it does at a small developer agency, a non-tech-first company, or a new startup.
- Interview performance. How a candidate performs at interview almost always feeds into leveling decisions, and is the most common reason for down-leveling. Candidates whom interviewers are unsure about, often get offered a position a level below the one they interviewed for.
- Changing companies and technology stacks might lead to a lower-level offer. Non-tech-first companies and developer agencies that judge candidates by years of experience in a given technology, might offer a lower title to someone who "only" has a year of experience with Java, even though they've been a software engineer for ten years. Down-leveling for this reason is common for roles in which interviews focus on a specific technology.

Down-leveling is especially common when joining a Big Tech company for the first time because expectations are typically high, onboarding takes longer than at smaller places, and companies often aim to hire people who "raise the bar" at a given level.

Dealing with down-leveling

If you get an offer at a level "below" your current title but with better pay, how do you proceed?

Know that down-leveling is common when moving up a tier. Employers can be tiered by their expectations of engineers at each level. At the top are the likes of Google, Meta, and other Big Tech giants, where engineers impact millions of users with each change they make. Engineers are expected to know – and follow – more processes and best practices than at companies whose leadership is less technical, or engineering impact is magnitudes smaller.

It should be no surprise that a senior engineer at an agency building niche apps with thousands of users, has different and easier-to-meet expectations than a senior engineer building an app with hundreds of millions of users.

Do your research on what the "lower" title means. Ask for the definition of the level and the next one as well, so you can evaluate whether you're missing skills or the experience needed. If so, it might be an opportunity to gain them. All companies with strong engineering cultures will have well-defined competencies and clear expectations for different levels.

Tell the hiring manager if you disagree with the leveling. Voice your opinion, show examples of your experience, and ask if the hiring committee could consider you for the next level. There's nothing to lose and everything to gain, as long as you do it in a respectful way.

When I was a hiring manager, several candidates challenged leveling decisions. In each case, it made me look closer at interview signals and expectations for the level. Sometimes, we offered the next level.

Consider rejecting an offer if you disagree with its leveling. Titles carry significance for your career and signal your status within an organization. If after getting more information, you disagree with the assessment, then consider rejecting the offer.

Interviews always have a subjective component which can produce false negatives. These will result in offers not being extended to excellent candidates or offers made at a lower level than candidates merit.

5. Up-Leveling

While down-leveling is more common, the opposite can also happen. You may get a higher-level offer than you expected or believe you're ready for.

When I worked at Microsoft, I was an L62 software engineer one level below L63 senior software engineer. Yet, I received an offer from Skyscanner at the principal level, which was a level above the senior engineer level. What happened?

In my case, my level at Microsoft likely did not reflect where I was in my career, and I could have been down-leveled. At the same time, my experience was relevant for Skyscanner; I interviewed well and enjoyed a good connection with the hiring manager. I also had little intention to leave Microsoft except for a really good offer. And so Skyscanner gave me an uplevel offer, which sealed the deal.

To get an up-level offer, several things need to be present:

- Perform well at the interview. Convince the hiring panel you're an outstanding candidate.
- Possess leverage to get a higher level. You have leverage if there's another offer at a higher level, or you're willing to walk away from an offer that's not a step up in levels.
- Have some people inside the company "fight" for you, internally. Making a successful case for an up-level is usually down to one or more people on the interview panel – or who referred you – convincing the hiring manager or hiring committee.

A word of caution, after you secure a higher level, be aware that expectations will be raised from day one. Be sure to clarify these and work hard to live up to them as you progress in your elevated role.

6. Onboarding to a New Job

You've accepted a new job, congratulations! Take time to celebrate this achievement. But don't relax; onboard successfully to your new company so that you hit the ground running.

Perceptions of you are shaped during your first few months in a new workplace, and often last years. This means that if you onboard at a good pace and your contributions exceed baseline expectations, you can easily be seen as a great hire. In contrast, if your onboarding is seen as slow or somehow difficult, you might be perceived as being less efficient; an assumption which may take longer to undo than your onboarding took.

As a new joiner you can – and should! – take ownership of your onboarding, and not just hope to be welcomed with a fabulous onboarding process. Doing so means you'll onboard faster and look like someone who hits the ground running. This perception should make life in your workplace easier, long into the future.

Here are ways to own your onboarding from before day one.

At all companies and levels

Helpful approaches:

- If there's a long notice period after signing a new contract, consider catching up with your future manager before you start. Ask for suggestions on how to prepare to hit the ground running.
- Read the book "The First 90 Days" by Michael D Watkins. It shares some of the best advice on how to create a great image when starting at a new place.
- Keep a work log/brag document from the start. This will help you reflect as you onboard, and serve as a great resource for manager 1:1s, performance reviews, and promotions.
- Keep a weekly journal. Write down three things you learned, and three things you don't understand during the first few months.
- Clarify your goals with your manager for the first month, the next 3 months, and the first 6 months.

Onboarding to a smaller company

Some helpful activities at startups and small organizations:

- Clarify the work you'll do before you join.
- Connect with the most senior person, early on. They'll often have long tenure.
- Don't assume how things work; ask. This is especially important when arriving from a larger company. You could come across as ignorant if you suggest things that make little sense in your new environment.
- Aim to ship something in week one. There's no excuse not to at a small company.

Onboarding to a larger company

Large organizations are more complex, so tame this complexity from day one:

- Get an "onboarding buddy," even if not assigned one. They are ideally someone on the team whom you can go to with questions, and who's ready to be interrupted in order to help you get up to speed.
- Keep a "cheat sheet" document in which you record everything that's new. This could be acronyms and their meanings, build commands, bookmarks to key resources, and much more. Doing this will speed up your learning, and could be extra material for the onboarding documentation.
- Familiarize yourself with the company's tech stack. Brush up on new languages or frameworks you'll be working with.
- Accept that many things don't make sense at first, especially if you arrive from a smaller company. Don't worry, this is normal!

Onboarding to a senior-or-above role

As a more experienced engineer, add structure to your onboarding:

- Connect with a senior-or-above peer. Understand how they organize and measure their work.
- Prioritize being productive on the team's codebase, and becoming hands-on with it.
- Clarify 3, 6, and 12-month expectations with your manager.
- Understand current and future projects and the team's priorities. What is the team working on, and why does it matter, how does all this fit into the company's strategy and priorities?
- Find and browse outage documents like postmortems which are relevant to your team and area, in order to understand problem areas, and not be caught off guard when familiar issues reoccur.
- Start a list of engineering teams worth knowing. When you hear a new team mentioned, add its name to this list. Then, introduce yourself to a member of that team and learn what they do, and how your teams are connected. Making this type of contact is very easy as a new recruit, as you have an excuse to introduce yourself because you're new! You can learn a lot about other teams this way, and make contacts who can be useful in future.

Onboarding to a staff-or-above role

Staff+ roles vary across companies. Aim to figure out what's expected of you, and then build your network so you can solve challenging problems and deliver the impactful results expected at this level:

- Meet your team early and make a friendly impression.
- Also meet peer staff+ engineers early. You'll rely heavily on them to understand how things work, especially at larger companies. Try to make a few new buddies.
- Staff+ roles differ by company, so figure out what's expected and what's not in your role.
- Clarify 3, 6, and 12-month expectations with your manager, and also ideally with your skip. What are the team's top priorities and the biggest problems to address?
- Spend time with product folks to understand their current concerns and plans.

Takeaways

The tech industry is fast-moving and most developers tend to change jobs every few years. At the same time, most of us working in tech can expect our careers to last decades. In the article A forty-year career[4], CTO and author Will Larson reflects on a typical career outside of tech:

> "My father retired a few years ago, having worked as a professor at the University of North Carolina Asheville for the significant majority of his adult life. Since then I've spent more time than expected reflecting on his retirement and his preceding career. In particular, reflecting on the idea that my career is something I can deliberately develop over a forty-year horizon. Not four IPOs, not fourteen two-year stints, but forty years.
>
> It's strange to realize that I lost sight of the forty-year career model, because for a long time it was the only model I knew. (...) If you have the good fortune to start on the long-term career conveyor belt, do your best to avoid tripping, and ride it to success, home ownership, and eventually retirement."

Keeping in mind that developer careers normally run for a similar length of time, it's helpful to map out opportunities you could consider embracing, in the form of different types of companies, and how to navigate performance reviews, promotions, or switching jobs. This chapter presents a variety of approaches for all of the above.

But if you take just one thing from this chapter, make it this:

No one cares about your career as much as you do. Not your managers, and not your coworkers. So figure out how much you care about career progression and put the appropriate amount of work into it.

For additional reading on this section, check out the online, bonus chapter for Part I:

Working at a Startup vs in Big Tech

pragmaticurl.com/bonus-1

---

[4]https://lethain.com/forty-year-career

Part II

The Competent Software Developer

Software development is a craft that takes years to master. Every engineering leader understands this, as do leaders of tech companies. Better companies put reasonable expectations in place for entry-level software developers and for the levels below senior developer, and senior engineer.

Titles for software developers typically vary. The most common forms are:

- Software Engineer (SWE,) SWE 2 (most of Big Tech and many startups/scaleups)
- Developer, Software developer (SDE,) SDE 2 (traditional companies, some startups and some scaleups)
- Member of Technical Staff (MTS.) Some companies founded between the 1970s and 1990s took this title from the iconic Bell Labs, which gave it to senior employees. Businesses using it today include Oracle and OpenAI. OpenAI applies the title "MTS" to all staff, similarly to how other companies use "software developer" or "software engineer."

Almost all companies expect software developers to progress to the senior level. In this section, we cover common expectations for competent developers at most tech companies.

There are plenty of things that most tech companies expect of entry-level and mid-level developers. Below is a set of common expectations. *Keep in mind, every company is unique, and no two have identical expectations.*

Area	Typical expectation
Scope	Tasks or smaller projects
Guidance	Works with some guidance
Getting things done	Seeks help when stuck
Taking the initiative	Not always expected and is a bonus
Software development	Follows team practices
Software architecture	Follows team practices, seeks feedback on designs
Engineering best practices	Follows those in place
Collaboration	Other developers on the team
Mentoring	Seeks mentorship
Learning	Hungry to learn
Typical years of industry experience	0-5

Common expectations for entry-level software developers

7

GETTING THINGS DONE

As an engineering manager, I always knew which engineers on my team "got things done," and did so reliably. These colleagues were good at breaking down work, realistic in their estimates, autonomous in unblocking themselves, and delivered quality work. When an important project came up, I ensured at least one of these engineers was on the project team.

Building a reputation for getting things done is helpful in several ways.

You will be given more impactful and challenging projects, which will accelerate your learning. You will almost always get more autonomy, as your manager views you as reliable and not in need of "hand-holding." And your career will likely progress faster with a strong track record of making an impact and achieving results, which is good for performance reviews and promotions.

However, getting engineering tasks and projects done is far from trivial. In this chapter, we cover several approaches to growing as a reliable developer:

1. Focus on the most important piece of work
2. Unblock yourself
3. Break down the work
4. Estimate the duration of work
5. Seek out mentors
6. Keep your "goodwill balance" topped up
7. Take the initiative

1. Focus on the Most Important Piece of Work

Whether you work at a startup or a large company, lots of things are on your plate. Tasks to complete, projects to work on, code reviews to address, emails to answer, meetings to attend… the list goes on. It's easy to get overwhelmed and feel like you're not making progress – even while working extra hours.

For this reason, it's good to simplify your work life. Ask what is the most important work; the single most important task on your list? No, really; if you could only do one thing this week, what would it be? Answer this question.

Your answer is your #1 priority. When you identify it, make sure you definitely, absolutely deliver that piece of work within the agreed timeframe.

Make a habit of always completing your #1 priority

Make sure the most important project on your plate always gets done, even if it means turning down other tasks, skipping meetings, and pushing back on other matters. If you consistently deliver the most important work as expected by your manager and team, you'll be seen as a reliable developer who gets things done.

On the other hand, if you get everything done except for the most important task, you may be perceived as unreliable. After all, you somehow found time for less important stuff, but not the most important task.

Learn to say "no"

Saying "no" is sometimes necessary. At many companies, software developers are pulled in several different directions, sometimes at once. If you're lucky, your manager protects the team, organizes requests from the business, and ensures developers are not directly pinged with requests to get something else done.

Even so, over time tasks stack up, like requests to debug customer issues, fixes for bugs the product manager just found, cover for an interviewer who's off sick, and so on. Usually, balancing everything is manageable, until there's so much on your plate that you have no time to work on the most important stuff.

For this reason, eventually you have to decline incoming requests. The more experienced you are, the easier this is. The sooner you learn to say "no," the more helpful this skill will be – and it truly is a skill.

The easiest way to turn down a request is to reply, "yes, I'd like to help, BUT…" For example, if a product person asks you to look at a bug at once, but you have more urgent work, you could reply:

"Yes, I'd like to help, BUT I'm working on implementing the Zeno feature, which is my #1 priority. I can either look at this when I've finished my pull request, or I will have to push back on my commitment to get the Zeno feature done on time because I can't do both."

Similarly, if another team invites you to a planning meeting which you don't have time to attend, your response could be something like:

"Yes, I'd like to go, BUT I am swamped with work I need to finish. Would you mind sending over the meeting notes afterward so I can catch up? I'd be grateful. Thanks a lot!"

You don't need to turn down everything, but when push comes to shove, and you're at risk of not completing your #1 priority task, then do say, "no." Better yet, reply: "yes, I'd love to help, BUT ⋯"

Unblock Yourself

Building software is complex and often has unforeseen obstacles, like errors with messages that make no sense, about which a Google search offers no support, or an integration or API that doesn't work as it should. There are thousands of things you stumble upon that must be solved before progressing further.

The larger the company, the more blockers are not technology problems. For example, you could be blocked by not knowing which team owns a piece of functionality you need to change, or not having access to a configuration to be changed. Perhaps you're blocked on waiting for a code review from another team, or pretty much anything that involves input from colleagues.

Software engineers perceived as reliable are able to solve blockers faster than colleagues. How do they do it? And how can you get better at unblocking yourself when there are so many ways to get blocked?

Know when you're blocked

The first step in unblocking yourself is the awareness that you're blocked. Have you ever thought, "I'm so close to getting this done – almost there!" and yet, six hours later, you're still stuck on the same problem? You haven't perceived that you're blocked.

Productive engineers catch themselves treading water and admit they're stuck. This can be harder than it sounds to do. You might be working and making progress with a new approach, researching a tool, system, or framework, but making zero real progress toward building the feature or finding the root cause of a bug.

A rule of thumb for catching yourself being blocked is that if you go more than 30 minutes without meaningful progress – or an hour at most – then admit you're blocked.

Try different unblocking approaches

When blocked, what can you do? The most obvious approach is to seek help from someone on what to try. But what if you don't have anyone to turn to? Here are a few approaches for when blocked on a coding-related problem:

- Do rubber-ducking. Explain your problem and the approaches already tried to a "rubber duck:" an object or yourself. Verbalizing a problem sometimes triggers a train of thought which leads to a solution.

- Draw it on paper. Sketch out the problem on a sheet of paper. Visualizing it might prompt ideas for what else to try.
- Read documentation and references for the technology on which you're blocked. Could you be using a language feature, framework, or library, in a way it wasn't designed for? Could you be neglecting features which are readily available to solve the problem? Check documentation and code samples for clues.
- Use an AI tool. Input your problem and the fixes you already tried, to see approaches the AI tool suggests.
- Search online for similar problems. Describe your problem in various ways, as others might have used different terms for the same issue.
- Post a question on a programming Q&A site. If your company has an internal Q&A site, use it. Also, check sites like Stack Overflow, or relevant forums. Explaining the problem you have can also give you additional ideas on how to solve it!
- **Take a break**. Go for a walk or switch to an unrelated task. When you come back to the problem, you might see it from a new perspective, or notice something you missed earlier.
- **Start from scratch, or undo all changes**. If you are stuck on broken code to which you made many changes, go back to the last point at which the code worked and restart by making small changes, one at a time. This might mean undoing a lot of work, but in return you'll pay closer attention to the process and may discover the cause of the breakage.

Get support to unblock yourself

Some blockers are due to a lack of knowledge from not having seen a problem before, while other blocks stem from a lack of access to the right people. Whatever the case, it's sensible to contact other developers who could help; they could share knowledge you don't have, or connect you with colleagues who can help.

The easiest way to start to get unblocked is to tell your team: "hey, I'm stuck on this problem. Can anyone lend a hand, perhaps pair with me on it?"

Sometimes, you'll be blocked by waiting on somebody. A special kind of blocker is knowing what you need to do, but not being able to do it for this reason. For example, you might want to push your code to production, but first, someone must sign it off with a code review. Or you need one of your dependencies to make a change to their API, but the team which owns the API endpoint hasn't responded to your email or the ticket. So, you're stuck waiting and doing nothing. It's frustrating.

The bigger your workplace is, the more common it is to be blocked by waiting on someone else. If you work with teams in different timezones, waiting on responses to chat messages and emails, code reviews, and design document feedback, all go in this bucket.

Learn how to escalate without ruffling feathers

The art of escalation is important in environments where blocking happens. Colleagues will ignore your messages, not necessarily because they don't want to help, but because they might assume your message is a lower priority than their other tasks.

What is escalation in this context? It means asking your manager or somebody higher in the chain of command, to communicate your message using the authority of their position. It can also involve reaching out to someone with authority elsewhere, for example, the manager of the person being unresponsive to your requests.

Escalation can speed things up, but it also has the potential to harm relationships if used carelessly. Imagine your manager telling you: "I'm hearing you've been ignoring Jim on the Marketing Engineering team. Now he's messaged the director saying you're blocking the new campaign."

You may have no idea how this happened, as you've been coding all day. So, you check and sure enough, four hours ago Jim sent a chat message that you missed. Let's step back and consider Jim's reaction to your silence. Which words describe Jim's behavior in contacting the director: was it necessary, or an overreaction? It will certainly feel like an overreaction for most people, even if from Jim's perspective, he did note he would escalate – but didn't check that this message was actually read.

Aim to not harm personal relationships when you escalate. Good relationships are more important long-term, than getting a task done a bit quicker. An engineer who likes working with you is more likely to help in future if they don't see you as aggressive, or as someone who makes them look bad to their manager.

When considering whether to escalate beyond your team, discuss it with your manager and teammates, first. What's the norm in your workplace? Do people go straight to their manager, who sets their priorities? Or are engineers more autonomous, prefer to handle things themselves, and know when to get their manager involved?

My approach to escalating is this:

1. **Explain**. First, I explain why help is needed, giving context so they understand the importance. For example: "Joe, I really need you to take a look at this code review as soon as possible, as this is blocking the last piece of work on the Zeno project. This project's deadline is next week, and if the code isn't merged by tomorrow, we will miss the deadline."
2. **Ask**. If nothing happens, ask why. "Joe, can you please give me an update on where you are with the code review? I appreciate you have lots of things on your plate. Can you tell me when you think you'll get around to it? Again, this is blocking the Zeno project, and it's a big deal at my end."

3. **Warn**. If still nothing happens, I raise the prospect of escalation: "Joe, I still haven't heard back. We need to move on the Zeno project. If you won't be able to do the code review by the end of the day, I'll be pinging your manager to request merging the code with no reviews from your team."

4. **Escalate**. And if still nothing happens, I'd escalate by involving my manager, the other person's manager, or both.

You might work at a company where it's common to go to managers to clarify priorities, and engineers don't mind at all. At other places, this might be seen as aggressive, and as making colleagues look bad.

Aim to make an escalation a win-win outcome. When you have to resort to escalation, try to be nice about it, so the other person doesn't feel like you threw them "under the bus."

And when the other person does what you requested, be sure to thank them and let people involved know that they helped. It can be as simple as a "thank you" in a direct message, an email, or a message to the manager describing how Joe went the extra mile to give you a hand. Aim to strike a balance between unblocking yourself, while maintaining strong relationships with colleagues beyond your team.

"Help! I'm blocked!" – a cheatsheet

Below are common situations that indicate you are blocked, and some approaches for handling them.

Planning

- Not enough clarity on what to do ("missing information" blocker.) Make clear what information is missing and escalate to colleagues who can help.
- Not knowing who to consult for information about a certain area ("missing information" blocker.) Ask for help from your lead or manager in identifying these people, then make a list of points of contact. Consider sharing it with your team.

Building

- New language or framework ("missing information" blocker, again.) You'll have to learn it, which is a fantastic opportunity to grow your skillset. If it's a language or framework, ask for recommended learning resources. If it's an internal framework, find the documentation, source code, and the colleagues who created it. Start small by learning just enough to solve your problem, before diving deeper in.
- Error messages that make no sense and googling doesn't help ("missing information" blocker.) Consider pairing with a teammate after trying to solve it yourself. If the error message is related to an internal component, reach out to the team who built it. If you get stuck for some time, ask your team for help and fresh ideas.

- Puzzled about how something works ("missing information" blocker,) such as a tool, a framework, or some coding construct. Try decomposing it by drawing it, looking at the source code, and doing some research. If you don't make progress, ask for help from a more experienced colleague and explain what you've done so far. If there's nobody experienced enough on your team, try further afield: ping people you know or ask your manager who to contact.

- Build problems ("missing information" or "waiting on others" blockers,) like a build failing, strange errors, or unusual slowness. If you're feeling brave, read up on the build tooling and see if you can figure it out. A safer bet is to contact the person or team who set up the build and ask for pointers on debugging the issue. If there's a dedicated person or team for the build, they might need to do the work, so ask and then escalate, if needed. Or offer to do the actual work of investigation and making a fix, and only ask for pairing. Not only will you expand your skillset into tooling, but the person helping you may appreciate you being proactive.

- Missing dependency on another team/service that arises midway through a task ("waiting on others" blocker.) This could be an API not working as needed, or components or systems not being ready. There's not much you can do, beyond letting the other party know they're a blocker, escalate, and pause this workstream – or try to do a workaround. It's a good idea to involve your manager, or at least inform them.

- Access problems ("waiting on others" or "missing information" blocker.) No access to systems or data for making changes as part of your work. This is common at larger companies, where you might need permissions to access logs, configs, or to do deployments on certain systems. Your manager is your best contact, as access rights almost always go through them. Explain the problem and why you need access. You can also ping more tenured colleagues, who probably went through the same problem before, and should be able to tell you who grants access. If you don't hear back, escalate to your manager.

- Misleading documentation ("missing information" blocker.) When building something, a framework or system doesn't behave as documented. Oh, great! You wasted a bunch of time on it. Contact the team owning the documentation and offer to fix it. If you can modify the documentation and make the changes, while letting the documentation owner know, then do so. If you need help to progress, the documentation owner is a good source of guidance.

- Outages, or systems being down, which prevent you from working or validating that what you built is working ("waiting on others" blocker.) Flag the outage and escalate it; there's a chance you're the first person to notice it. Once you get acknowledgment, there's not much to do but wait and work on other things.

Testing

- Tests fail non-deterministically ("missing information blocker.) These are tricky and require debugging to understand what's happening and why. Try pairing with a team member or ask in the chat if anyone's had similar issues.

- Missing data to test, such as data to reproduce a test case, or production-like data ("missing information" blocker.) Figure out how to get this data; it could be as easy as finding the right logs, or as complex as requesting access to production data, which may mean waiting on others, or escalating.
- Tests are too slow ("waiting on the machine" blocker). This can be a drain in the long run and usually isn't a pressing blocker. Still, it's a good opportunity to step up and look for ways to make tests faster, and do some performance analysis of where slowdowns occur.

Reviewing

- Waiting on code review ("waiting on others" blocker): we discuss this scenario above. Ping reviewers to ask for reviews directly, and escalate if you don't hear back in a reasonable time. Seek support from team members and your manager on how to handle these situations.
- Merge conflicts: these are time-consuming, and there's no avoiding them. After resolving a conflict, it's sensible to retest your work and also the previous change to ensure nothing's broken. Keep pull requests small to make merge conflicts less problematic, and to iterate faster.

Deploying

- Permissions/access problems ("waiting on others" blocker): find colleagues who can give access, and escalate if needed. At bigger workplaces, there's almost always a dedicated team or process for approvals.
- Deployment is too slow ("waiting on the machine" blocker). Similarly to slow tests, this shouldn't be swept under the rug. If there's a team that owns deployment tooling, contact them and see if they can prioritize speeding things up. If you can tweak the deployment setup, consider getting your hands dirty to shorten the wait time for deploys to complete. If the deployment cannot be sped up, can health checks be put in place, so there's no need to manually verify that things work correctly after a deployment?

Operating systems and maintenance

- Bugs which can't be reproduced ("waiting on others" blocker.) For customer bug reports you struggle to reproduce, more information must be sought. This might mean adding extra logging to the code and asking the customer to try again, or requesting information from them. Either way, you'll very likely be waiting on a response, with no way to escalate.
- Not enough logs to debug system issues ("missing information" blocker.) You might be unable to debug customer problems, or monitor and alert issues. The issue is the system doesn't have enough debugging information for your needs, so add more logs,

monitoring, or alerts, and deploy these, then try again to debug the production issue. Depending on how complex the issue is, pairing with a teammate could be sensible.

- Outages ("missing information" or "waiting on others" blocker.) Systems your team owns go down, either due to an outage, or because of an issue at your end. Alert your manager and team, and if possible, jump in to mitigate the outage. After the issue's resolved, there will likely be an investigation into the root cause, and a postmortem.

2. Break Down the Work

As a developer, you get more complex pieces of work as you progress. To get these done, it's important to know how to break the work down, estimate timelines, and deliver on them.

Think about stories, tasks, and subtasks

It's easy to go down a rabbit hole when breaking down tasks. You could start with a project, take the biggest part of it, and then descend all the way down to defining how a small component works at the coding level.

Avoid falling down this rabbit hole by being a bit more strategic. For example, take a project to add two-factor authentication to an app:

1. Begin at the higher level. What are the main pieces of work to do? If these are sizable, they might map into several parts. You can call these parts "epics," "stories," or "chunks." Epics could include adding a two-factor authentication method, using two-factor authentication to log in, and handling edge cases and errors around two-factor authentication.
2. Once you have your chunks or stories, break them down again into tasks which are pretty straightforward. For example, a task in the "epic" of adding a two-factor authentication method would be to create the screen for adding two-factor authentication code. Another would be to add links to this page from every part of the app, where useful.
3. If needed, divide complex tasks into subtasks. For example, the task of adding links to the two-factor authentication page could comprise three subtasks:
   a. Add the link to the user profile page
   b. Add the link to the final step of the onboarding flow
   c. Add the link to the FAQ document.

The easier it is to understand what needs to be done, the easier it is to estimate how long it will take. Break down the work into small parts, and then challenge yourself to make them even smaller! For example, divide the task of adding a two-factor authentication page into:

- Scaffolding

- Add business logic
- Tweak UI

Or split the work into:

- A barebones implementation that only works for the most important user flow for the product (the "golden path")
- Make edge cases into separate tasks

A good time to stop breaking things down is when the tasks are clear enough to you.

Prioritize work which gets you closer to shipping something

When the work is broken down into smaller tasks, how do you set an order of priority?

A good approach is to focus on an order of work that gets you closer to working functionality. The sooner you have something you can test end-to-end, the sooner you can get feedback on whether you're on the right path. Once you have a basic case in working order, decide the next priority, and which tasks you need to solve to achieve it.

Don't be afraid to add, remove and change tasks

Some developers tend to work on what the task defines, even if they realize midway through that new work is needed, or that some tasks no longer make sense.

Don't be this person! Remember, the goal is to build software that solves customers' problems, not to close tasks.

Tasks are just a tool for organizing work; don't forget this. Use this tool but be ruthless in changing and adding tasks as needed, or removing redundant ones. If you come across new work or run into blockers and new constraints, then your original plan probably needs revising. In this case, overhaul the tasks!

Don't forget that tasks or other ways of organizing work must boost productivity. Don't invest more time in dealing with tasks than on writing code.

3. Estimate the Duration of Your Work

"How long will this take?" is a question many software developers dread. However, it will be asked, despite that. Businesses need to plan, and like it or not, you will be asked to estimate the lengths of time for your tasks. The only way to get better at this is to do it.

There are some developers who say it's impossible to accurately estimate, and they advocate no-estimate approaches. However, reliable engineers I know are solid estimators: they give accurate estimates and are clear about "unknowns" and delays.

Estimation is a learnable skill. However, its challenges differ by the type of work at hand.

Estimating work similar to what you did previously

This is the easiest type of estimate to make. Let's say you need to add a new feature which closely resembles some work you did before. This could be adding yet another page to a website, or yet another endpoint to the API. You can realistically estimate the time for the new task, based on how long it took last time.

Estimating work you've not done before

This is where things get more interesting because you don't have the benefit of experience to use as a baseline. However, there are plenty of ways to come up with an accurate time estimate, based on the type of work. Here are seven common categories of work, and how to estimate them precisely.

#1: Similar work to that of a colleague. There will often be teammates who have coded something similar to what you're tackling for the first time. You're not starting from scratch!

A developer who's coded something similar can estimate how long it should take. The only difference is that you'll definitely take more time to complete the work, as you need to learn some of the context. If you consult them and break down their approach, you can come up with a realistic estimate. Make your estimate a bit longer as you're doing it for the first time.

#2: Refactoring. You change the structure of code but add no new functionality. If you've done refactoring before, you can use that experience for a baseline time estimate, even if the type of refactoring at hand is new. Alternatively, ask teammates if they've done similar refactoring work and whether they can share how easy or complex it was.

You could also simply timebox the work. Timeboxing means assigning a period of time to a task and only working on it for that long, and no longer.

#3: Greenfield work using a technology you know well. In this scenario, technology is not a big risk and you're unlikely to get stuck on some bug in the language or framework. The biggest risk is that business requirements are unclear. But if the task is clear, a good enough estimate can be made.

#4: Integrating with a system you don't know well, using a well-known technology. Things become a lot harder to estimate when you have to build on top of, or integrate into a system you're unfamiliar with. This could be integrating with an endpoint owned by another team or third party.

The biggest risk is opening a can of worms marked "unknowns" about how the system works. It may behave differently than is documented, there might be edge cases you did not think of, or documentation may be absent which makes integration time-consuming.

In such a case, consider prototyping first, and making an estimate only when you've built a simple proof-of-concept that tests the other system or API. If prototyping is not possible, you can always give an "ideal estimate," which assumes no issues with the system. Also provide a "worst-case" estimate which assumes the system will behave strangely and that workarounds will be needed. A worst-case time estimate is high by definition.

If there's pressure to give an estimate, provide a worst-case one. Some eyebrows will be raised, but it will help you make the case for a timebox in which to prototype, so you can give a more accurate estimate.

My suggestion is always to build a prototype because it enables you to provide an accurate estimate.

#5: Building something simple with a mature technology you don't know well. Let's say you're building a project with a stable technology of which you have little experience. Here, learning the new technology – the language or framework – is the biggest effort.

The best way to get a realistic estimate is to ask an engineer who has used the technology. They can give pointers on where to start and help you estimate how long it should take to get up to speed. Treat their estimate with a pinch of salt, as they may underestimate the difficulty of picking up this technology.

If possible, pair with a developer who knows this technology well because it will shorten the time taken to implement your work, and speed up your learning process.

If you cannot pair with a developer, you could always use a timeboxed estimate to get up to speed with the technology. Make this timebox big enough to go through some tutorials, do coding, and find out if your first few iterations of code need more debugging than usual.

#6: Building something simple with a new technology you don't know well. New frameworks or languages carry more risk than mature technologies. There are fewer learning materials and fewer people who can answer questions. Also, a new language or framework is likely to have bugs.

It's hard to estimate how long working with a new technology will take, unless you do some prototyping. So, do this. Build a proof-of-concept with the new tech, and don't make an estimate until you're confident using it.

#7: Building something complex and integrating with a system you don't know well, using an unfamiliar new technology. In this case, there are simply too many unknowns to make a sensible estimate. Things you don't know:

- The system you're integrating with
- The technology
- Unknowns

In order to estimate accurately, you need to reduce the quantity of unknowns. This can be done in two ways:

1. Prototype. You can make an estimate with learnings from the prototype.
2. Break up the work more! Separate it into smaller parts, each of which contains only one unknown. For example:
   - A small task that uses the new technology
   - Build a feature on top of the new technology
   - Integrate with the new system
   - Wrap up by implementing the other parts

Breaking up this work may feel overly granular. However, with this approach, you can efficiently divide and conquer the unknowns. Your estimates might still be imperfect, but each estimate will be impacted by a single unknown, not many of them.

4. Seek Mentors

Mentors are experienced engineers whom you can turn to in confidence with questions and doubts. Some companies have formal mentorship programs, but at most places you need to find mentors by yourself – and it won't be a "formal" relationship.

When it comes to mentoring, think not just in terms of one individual mentor, but a group of people you can learn from. It's great if you can identify a dedicated mentor with whom to discuss pressing issues regularly. However, you can learn just as much from ad hoc mentorship, including experts online.

Aim to find mentors within the workplace whom you can rely on. At the same time, experiment with tools which offer advice for when you're stuck on coding work. These include Q&A websites like StackOverflow, and also AI coding tools like ChatGPT and Bard, which can help unblock you on certain tasks. Just remember, the output of AI tools may not be fully trustworthy – so always verify it!

We cover more on mentorship in Part III: Collaboration and Teamwork.

The tech tribe of mentors

Nielet D'mello[1] is a software security engineer at Datadog. In her article, The tech tribe of mentors[2], she shares the observation that a "tribe" of mentors can help you more efficiently than one person can, alone. She writes:

"Although our mentors can be multi-faceted and experienced in many areas, one individual cannot specialize in everything. Plus, everyone's experiences are different and diverse. Tapping into this is a great way to learn and grow in our careers. That's why I believe in the idea of a tech tribe of mentors.

1. **The dedicated mentor**
   I like the idea of having a dedicated mentor with whom I have a great rapport and feel comfortable sharing my lows and highs. The interactions on a regular cadence set defined goals to work on and are great motivators for constant improvement.
   To find a dedicated mentor, it is best to reach out to someone you have interacted with before, or someone whose work you admire and who falls in line with your goals.

2. **The ad hoc mentor**
   Sometimes, it makes sense to schedule 1:1s with people with whom you may not work closely, but whose work intersects with your path.
   For example, I would schedule a 1:1 with an architect to understand how better to approach designing a new service, by sharing some of my ideas and getting feedback. Another example would be meeting with a senior leader to learn about their career journey and get insights on improving in the areas I wish to. These are no-commitment, ad hoc 1:1s, that might lead to follow-up 1:1s if more ideas can be discussed.

3. **The internet mentor**
   As weird as it may sound, I do have internet mentors. What I mean by that is individuals/ leaders who share their career journey and learnings on their blogs, books, podcasts, etc.
   Over time, I have identified individuals whose writing style and ideas resonate with me, and the advice/ideas presented are viable to try out. Not every advice/idea will make sense to you in your context."

5. Keep Your "Goodwill Balance" Topped Up

There will be times when you feel stuck treading water and getting nowhere. There could be several reasons for this: a tricky bug, a framework/technology you've not used before, or a tool you struggle to figure out. Either way, you come to realize you need help.

---

[1] https://dmellonielet.com
[2] https://dmellonielet.com/2020/10/20/tech-tribe-of-mentors.html

Before you reach out to colleagues, keep in mind the potential implications for goodwill between yourself and others.

Everyone has a goodwill balance

When you help others, your goodwill balance increases. When you ask for favors, it can go down. And when you interrupt people for no good reason, it definitely reduces.

The more junior or new on a team you are, the higher your goodwill balance is. People are willing to help; in fact, they expect to. But this balance will quickly drain if you don't take time to solve things yourself, ask too many trivial questions, or frequently interrupt others.

Avoid using up your goodwill balance too quickly. Go through the most common debugging and information-gathering steps before seeking help. If a solution can be sought, do so online, or in the internal company knowledge base. When there are issues with a framework or technology, read the relevant documentation thoroughly, first.

With code your team owns, look through the source code history and recent commits. If you are debugging a bug, step through the code, record variable values, note assumptions, and do a structured analysis of where something is going wrong. If none of this works, identify the person who might be able to help you and ask them.

Go prepared when asking a colleague for help. Explain the problem clearly, summarize what you've tried so far, and what your next step would be if they cannot help. If they're busy, respect their time as they probably have other priorities. In this case, ask them for a quick pointer.

Regularly top up your goodwill balance

How do you build up your goodwill balance? By doing the opposite of activities that decrease it:

- Make yourself available to others. Sit with them and help solve their problems
- Share your expertise to make others' work easier
- When someone helps you, and it solves your problem, thank them – perhaps even publicly in a team setting

There's a fine line between getting stuck too often without seeking help and asking for help too much. Of course, this all applies after you onboard to your team. During onboarding, you have a large goodwill balance. But once you've onboarded, don't take it for granted; increase this very important balance by helping others.

Avoid working alone, when possible

As an engineering manager, I rarely saw it end well when less experienced developers or new joiners were left to their own devices for weeks or months. Usually, their work took a lot longer to do, and people told me they felt less productive and lonelier. In response, we decided during retrospectives to assign them a "project buddy." But what can you do as a developer if your lead doesn't do this?

Take steps to fix the issue of working solo. For example, ask an engineer on your team to be your buddy for a project, by doing a quick check-in with you each day, reviewing your planning, and doing code reviews.

If an engineer politely declines, talk with your manager or lead, and try to convince them of the productivity benefits for the team. Sure, the more experienced developer will need to spend a little bit of time with you. However, in return you will get things done quicker, and also grow faster. Soon, you'll be able to help others on the team.

Also, increase your goodwill balance on the team. The more warmly disposed towards you that others are, the more likely it is they will be open to being your buddy on projects.

6. Take the Initiative

Some of the most productive engineers I have seen consistently pick up smaller or larger pieces of work which were not asked of them. This is called taking the initiative.

Many of these engineers research a new technology to use on a project, be it an internal system, or an open-source component. They talk with teammates, get involved in learning about other projects, and offer to help out with smaller tasks. They're often the first to volunteer for any opportunity that arises, from investigating an inbound bug, to giving a presentation to undergraduates.

Engineers who are perceived as reliable and productive go above and beyond the call of duty. The more autonomous the culture you work in is, the more important this trait becomes.

At fast-growing tech companies, it can be career-defining to take the initiative by getting involved in things not directly assigned to you. For example, at Uber, I observed a junior engineer become the go-to person for deployments after they set out to investigate and prototype a new microservices deployment system. The rest of the team was too busy to do this and didn't realize the new service would make their work much easier.

Approaches to taking the initiative

Here are ways you can take the initiative to help your team and yourself, without using up too much time.

- Document unclear things. Share this documentation with the team. Documenting will strengthen your understanding, show colleagues you're assisting the team, and it might help a teammate or new joiner in future.
- Volunteer for investigations. This could be trialing a new framework or technology, prototyping how to integrate a new service or component, and anything else. If you're less experienced, offer to pair with someone, or ask someone to pair with you.
- Investigate interesting tools or frameworks your team could use. Share learnings with the team. Between your work tasks, investigate tools and frameworks available at your company, or ones which other teams use. For example, this could be trying out a new frontend framework, a new documentation tool, a logging framework, a new build or deployment system, and much more. Give it a go, and make a demo for the team with your verdict. Even if the outcome is "we shouldn't use this," your team will see you're venturing beyond your role to learn more.
- Talk with your manager about upcoming projects. While doing so, express interest in work you're curious about. By asking your manager what's coming up, you'll get a better sense of priorities, and what's ahead, work-wise. You're more likely to work on projects of interest to you by informing your manager of this. You might also learn what to investigate in advance.

A word of warning, ensure you get your "expected" work done before taking on many new initiatives. New initiatives help others see you as a productive person, assuming you get your most important and assigned work done, first. If you must choose between doing something new or finishing your current work, I advise you to finish what's needed.

8

CODING

Writing code is the core of software engineering. As a software developer, you will likely spend around 50% of your time at work coding – potentially even more! In this chapter, we cover topics on how to get better at this skill. We cover:

1. Practice coding – a lot!
2. Readable code
3. Writing quality code

1. Practice Coding: A Lot!

Being a competent software engineer begins with being a good coder; it's the foundation of everything discussed in this book. Of course, there are many traits which solid software engineers possess, but coding is an area in which you need to gain strong proficiency. Why? It's vital to translate your thoughts and ideas into working code as efficiently and seamlessly as possible.

For this, you need to code often, learn a language in-depth, and keep solving real-world problems.

Code regularly

Developing your coding skills is a bit like sports training. You can read all the resources available on how to code well, and which techniques will make you faster, stronger, and better. But the biggest contributor to your progress is always how much you practice.

This holds for coding, too. Books and online resources can help get you started in expanding your knowledge. But ultimately, you must apply that knowledge by writing code – a lot.

Coding daily is a great habit to pick up because going from learning to code to being "alright" at it, takes a lot of time and effort. Therefore, aim to work on meaningful tasks and problems every day which you solve with code.

Early in your career as a developer, an almost universal expectation most tech companies have, is that you code daily. If you're not doing this for whatever reason, try to find ways to. This could involve picking up an extra project at work, moving to a team which does a lot of coding, or even working on a side project that sharpens your programming skillset.

You need to code daily to keep growing into a competent software engineer. I know of no substitute for this.

Ask for code reviews

Writing code that works is one of the foundations of coding proficiency. Another is writing code others can read and understand, and following common conventions. After you write your code, get feedback on it so you can further improve it. Do code reviews.

Most tech organizations do code reviews; in fact, you cannot push code to production at many places without first going through a code review. But when you're starting out, you might write a lot of code which doesn't go into production. For example, you might do prototyping, write a utility or a tool, do experimental projects, or find yourself working alone.

Aim to get feedback on all the code you write, even if code reviews aren't required. If more experienced people are around, you can ask them for extra feedback to help you grow faster. Most people are happy to spend a little additional time helping junior colleagues.

If getting additional code reviews is hard, you could ask a colleague to pair with you, so you can walk them through your code and ask which areas for improvement they see. And if there's nobody to work with, try finding someone from outside your team who's experienced with the technology or the domain, and can give meaningful feedback.

Artificial Intelligence (AI) tools are also useful sources of coding feedback. But be aware that not all AI-generated feedback is always accurate, and these tools will likely not consider additional context, which your teammates do. AI tools are better than nothing, but nothing beats a thorough peer review.

Learn from code reviews. Consider making notes on the feedback you get. If you see repeated comments, consider addressing them. For example, do reviewers regularly point out that your functions do too many things, or that you forget to add tests? Aim to refine how you code by addressing reviewers' comments, so you don't get identical feedback repeatedly.

If you don't understand the reasoning behind a comment, find out by talking to the developer who gave the review.

How do you deal with code reviews that feel harsh? The reality is that there will be code reviews that sting you: their tone will lack empathy, or you will disagree with what a more senior engineer suggests.

Angie Jones is VP of Developer Relations at Block, a Java Champion, and used to be a senior software engineer at Twitter – now renamed to X. She wrote the article, The 10 commandments of navigating code reviews[1], which answers this question in the most thorough way I've read. She writes:

> "In my years of developing software, I've come up with 10 commandments that I follow to navigate code reviews. They have worked like a charm on every team I've ever been a part of, so I hope they work for you.
>
>   1. Thou shalt not take it personally. ($\cdots$)
>
> I've been coding professionally for 15 years and decided long ago not to take code review comments personally. Trust me, I have certainly gotten my fair share of rude or patronizing comments when joining a new team. However, this never lasted long because I learned to navigate code reviews and change the tone of them, no matter what the underlying issue was. Wondering why I am getting rude comments only stresses me out, so I have made the conscious decision to give every reviewer the benefit of the doubt and assume the comment is directed at the code, not me."

Read as much code as you write

While your coding proficiency will grow fastest by writing code, reading code is equally important. If you only focus on writing code, you might develop styles and conventions nobody uses. And later, it may be hard to understand other people's code. Also, "bad habits" can be difficult to unlearn once embedded in our coding approach.

Often, the easiest way to read code is to get involved early in code reviews across the team or the codebase. Do this even when you're not an expert in the language, or very familiar with the codebase. Make it a habit to go through each change colleagues make, understand what it does, and make notes on the approaches taken. When something is unclear, talk to the person who wrote the code to learn more.

It's beneficial to read code written outside of your team or company. If you can access other projects in your workplace, start following code changes and code reviews by teams whose codebases you depend on. Teams and companies often follow conventions specific to their environment.

Reading open-source code is also an excellent way to see other people's code and get a sense of what's going on beyond your company. Try to find an actively developed open-source project which works with a similar language as you use. GitHub is the easiest place to do this. Check out a project, familiarize yourself with how it works, and then start following the changes. Try to make sense of what's happening, which type of code is being written,

---

[1]https://angiejones.tech/ten-commandments-code-reviews

and the feedback which code reviewers give.

Find a balance between writing and reading code without going overboard on either one.

Code some more

You can practice coding in additional ways, aside from doing work projects. Here are some ideas:

- **Build a side project**. A small side project that solves a minor problem for you, your friends, or your family, is a nice way of coding a bit more, and even picking up a new technology stack. A side project gives you the excuse to try new approaches as you wish. Your goal is to write code that works, but you can go crazy and complicate things by using parts of the language you never would, normally.
- **Complete a tutorial/training with coding exercises**. Tutorials and training provide structure, meaning you can just follow along and not think about what to do. Such training is great for going deeper into a specific language or technology. The biggest challenge of tutorials and training is getting the time and motivation to complete them. If your company supports or provides in-person training, take advantage of it. This opportunity is a useful way to dive deeper into a technology.
- **Do coding challenges**. Tackling coding challenges like those on Leetcode, Project Euler, or similar sites, is an opportunity to practice a language which you use, and they can also improve your algorithmic problem-solving skills.
- **Do regular code katas**. This helps to familiarize you with a language, and improve your problem-solving and algorithmic skills. Search online for daily code kata challenges. Code katas should be a short investment of time. Aim to do them regularly – ideally, daily – for a few weeks, until the katas stop being challenging.

Paying for resources can boost your focus. Learning a programming language in depth is time-consuming, and it's easy to put this task on the back burner when you become "good enough." There will always be real work to be solved for which you don't need fancy language features.

A trick I've found that helps me to stay focused and not stop midway through the learning process is to be invested in it by paying for the resources I want to study. This provides the knowledge that if I don't finish it, my money will be wasted. Many free resources are often of similar quality to paid-for ones, but making a financial investment is why I prefer to buy a book, online course, or in-person training. Parting with money gives me the motivation I need to not give up early and lose my investment.

2. Readable Code

Readability is one of the most important characteristics of all code. It's equally important as code that's correct and does what's expected.

However, it is harder to verify that code is readable than to verify that code is correct. This is because the correctness of code can be established by using tests: there's a binary "yes, it is correct," or "no, it's incorrect," answer. There is no equivalent approach to pinpointing hard-to-read code.

Incorrect code cannot hide for long, but unreadable code can go undetected for ages. It sits silently in the codebase until a developer tries to understand what it does while fixing a bug, or adding a new feature. They want to understand what this unreadable piece of code does and whether it needs to be changed.

If code is not readable, an engineer who makes changes later will spend a lot of time on what should be straightforward work. They might misunderstand the code and use it in unintended ways, and then spend multiple iterations on getting the change right. Or they might change the code, unintentionally breaking functionality elsewhere. This is only a minor annoyance if there are automated tests for the functionality. If not, this will mean more problems and more time spent on making the change correctly.

In some cases, a developer might spend so much time trying and failing to understand the code, that they may just completely rewrite it; deleting the original code and writing a new implementation. But not all edge cases may be covered by this rewrite; potentially resulting in more time spent on the rewrite than was on the original code.

The biggest risk of unreadable code is that it starts a low-readability spiral. An engineer making a change spends much time figuring out how the code should work. Instead of making the code more readable, they may make the smallest possible change, resulting in even less readable code. The next person will then spend more time understanding the code and might break the system, or just give up, delete the code, and reinvent the wheel.

Unreadable code is a major contributor to technical debt, which builds up for various reasons, including lack of automated testing, missing processes like continuous integration (CI) or continuous deployment (CD,) and poor onboarding and documentation. Tech debt is a significant contributor to teams slowing down.

This is why code readability and thorough testing are two of the most important principles for pragmatic engineers. Readable, well-tested code makes refactoring, extending, and modifying a codebase as easy as possible. Readable, well-tested code is the foundation of a solid codebase that gives engineers confidence to make changes.

What is readable code?

"Readable code" means slightly different things and varies between teams, companies, and programming languages. There are two important judges of how readable code is: yourself and everyone else who reads it.

Readable code begins with code you find easy to read. When finishing coding, take a break to clear your mind. Then, re-read the code as though seeing it for the first time, imagining you know nothing about the changes or why they were made.

Can you follow your code? Do the names of variables and methods help you understand what they do? Are there comments in places where the code isn't enough? Is the style of the code consistent across the changes?

Think about how you could make the code more readable. Perhaps you see some functions which do too much and are too long. Perhaps you find that renaming a variable makes its purpose clearer. Make changes until you feel the code is as expressive, concise, and presentable as possible.

The test of readable code is simple: can others understand it? Get feedback via code reviews. Ask how clear the code is. Encourage people to ask questions if something doesn't make sense. Code reviews – especially thorough ones – are the best source of feedback.

Readable code will attract few to no clarifying questions, and reviewers won't misunderstand it. So, pay attention any time someone misunderstands why you wrote something or asks a clarifying question. Each question and misunderstanding is a hint that the code could be more readable.

A good way to get more feedback about your code's clarity is to ask someone who is not an expert in the codebase. Ask specifically for feedback about how easy your code is to read. As your colleague will not be an expert, they'll focus on how much they can follow your code. Most comments they make will be about readability.

If you're happy with how clear the code is and other developers find it readable, then you're on the right track. There are many ways to make code more readable and clearer. But before going too deeply into that, focus on the essential of code that's easily read by yourself and colleagues.

Things to pay attention to

You should always write code with two main goals in mind:

1. The code should be correct, meaning it produces the expected result when executed
2. Other developers should find it easy to read and understand

Coding is a social activity. Your code doesn't exist in a vacuum, implementing a lone task. The code you write will be re-read by many other developers to understand or modify how it works.

The code you write needs to be easy enough for other engineers to maintain. This starts with the code being readable. A few things to pay attention to:

- **Naming**. Use self-explanatory, concise names. Stick to consistent naming approaches in line with the naming used on the codebase.
- **Well-structured**. The codebase is easy to navigate as functions, classes, and modules follow a logical structure. Formatting is consistent across classes and the codebase.
- **Keep the code simple (KISS)**. KISS stands for "Keep it simple, stupid!" The simpler code is, the easier it is to read and understand. With this in mind, aim for small functions and classes that don't grow too big. Avoid introducing complex coding solutions just for the sake of it, when you could get things done simpler.
- **Single responsibility**. Aim for functions to do just one thing, and for classes to have a main responsibility. A single focus makes it easier to test for correctness, and also for tests to be reusable.
- **The "DRY" principle**: Don't Repeat Yourself. Avoid copy-pasting code. Instead, if you find the need to reuse, consider refactoring the code so it follows the single responsibility principle.
- **Comments**. There are two schools of thought when it comes to comments; some engineers swear by the code always documenting itself, whereas others see comments as a necessary way of adding context which code cannot convey. Come up with your approach to commenting, keeping in mind the end goal: for someone else to make sense of the code you write. As a rule of thumb, explain the "why" on the code, not the "how" in your comments. This may be context like a business reason for why an edge case was added, or linking to an outage that promoted a seemingly odd code path.
- **Continuously refactor to maintain readability**. Codebases grow. As a simple class gains more responsibility, it expands in size and complexity. Readable codebases stay readable thanks to continuous refactoring. A new complex class might be broken into multiple parts or changed in other ways, in order to stay easy to read.

There are many books and other resources which go into greater depth on what readable code is, and how to make yours clearer. I recommend these:

- "Clean Code" by Robert Martin
- "The Art of Readable Code" by Dustin Boswell and Trevor Foucher

3. Writing Quality Code

As a competent software developer, you'll want to write code that uses the correct amount of abstraction and works reliably enough, accounting for potential error cases. This is, of course, on top of it being readable – which we covered right before this section.

Use the right level of abstractions

When you structure your code, you create classes that are abstractions. These classes abstract away implementation details from other parts of the code. For example, you might come across a class called "PaymentsIntent" which implements the following functionality in one file:

1. Makes an API request to make a payment
2. Takes the JSON response and evaluates whether it's valid by looking at the signature in the JSON. Transforms it into a PaymentsResponse object
3. Returns the PaymentsResponse response

This class doesn't do much, but you might decide it makes sense to abstract #2 – turning a JSON into a PaymentsResponse object – functionality into its own class. Then, PaymentsIntent would do this:

1. Make an API request to make a payment
2. Create a new PaymentResponse with the result, and return this object

Why would we abstract away the parsing of the payments response JSON? A few reasons:

- The same functionality from other parts of the code can now be used, without needing to copy logic. This conforms with the Don't Repeat Yourself (DRY) principle
- The responsibilities of the classes shrank, and each class has a single responsibility
- In future, it will be more straightforward to identify which code should be modified if the payments API responses change, as the parsing functionality lives in one place

In the book, "A Philosophy of Software Design," author John Ousterhout describes the benefits of information hiding:

> "Information hiding reduces complexity in two ways. First, it simplifies the interface to a module [or class.] The interface reflects a simpler, more abstract view of the module's functionality and hides the details; this reduces the cognitive load on developers who use the module.
>
> Second, information hiding makes it easier to evolve the system. If a piece of information is hidden, there are no dependencies on that information out-

side the module containing the information, so a design change related to that information will affect only one module."

Building a system with the "right" level of abstraction is something you improve at, the more you do it. After all, you don't want to break up a system into *too many* small pieces, as excessive numbers of tiny classes add unnecessary cognitive load.

Handle errors, and handle them well

In my experience, so many outages lead back to errors being handled incorrectly in some part of the code. As a software developer, when you write code you need to think about how things could go wrong, and spend sufficient time and effort on error handling.

Have a consistent error-handling strategy. What do you do when you come across a condition which could be an error? Do you throw an exception, log the error, do both, or something else?

You should be able to explain how you handle errors; ideally, consistently with how everyone on the team does. Logging errors is a sensible strategy, and you should aim to have a strategy for logging. One is provided in Part V: "Software engineering."

When in doubt, use defensive programming. This assumes inputs from other parts of the code are unreliable and potentially malicious. With this mindset, you tend to question and then validate inputs to a system, a class, or even a function.

Here are a few approaches for defensive programming:

- **Validate inputs, especially from users**. Assume malicious intent or accidentally incorrect information. For example, you expect that a string parameter in a function should be a positive number. But you still validate this to be the case, and throw an error when it's not.
- **Expect invalid responses**. When invoking a function, don't assume it will always return a "valid" value. Expect empty responses or odd values. For example, when invoking a function called `GetSalaryForEmployee()` which returns an integer with the salary for the given employee, it's good to validate that the returned value is not zero or a negative number and also isn't a value which is not a number.
- **Expect malicious inputs**. Expect that an attacker might try to deliberately send input that breaks the system. For example, attackers might try to submit strings that could be used for an SQL injection[2] attack. Or, on the web, an attacker might try to inject a malicious script using a cross-site scripting (XSS) attack[3].

---

[2]https://en.wikipedia.org/wiki/SQL_injection
[3]https://owasp.org/www-community/attacks/xss

- **Expect exceptions and errors**. When invoking functions, be prepared that they might throw an exception, or return an error.

There will be times when you don't need to use defensive programming. For example, when working with a class where all inputs have been validated by design. Also, you might need to worry less about defensive programming when working with strongly typed languages, or languages where functions declare which exceptions they can throw. The more constraints a language has for error handling, the more a compiler can warn of incorrect assumptions.

Be wary of "unknown" states

One surprisingly common issue is the mapping of API responses to success or failure codes, and what to do with "unknown" cases. For example, a payment API for requests to make a payment can return responses like "okay," "not enough funds," or "API temporarily unavailable." You need to map these responses in your code to "Success" or "Failure."

You know the payments API can add or remove responses later, and you want to build a robust enough system to handle future cases when the API might introduce a new code called "Needs User Action." Here are two common approaches for doing this:

Allowlists. With this approach, you create a list of successful responses (the allowlist) and assume everything else is a failure. So, the allowlist becomes the "OK" response, and everything else is considered a failure.

This approach is more defensive. A problem occurs when there's a response that's not strictly a failure, like "Needs User Action."

Blocklists. With this approach, you create a list of responses considered failures (the block list) and assume everything else is a success. This approach is more risky because the API could introduce new error codes which you'd map as successes.

Handling an "unknown" state can cause unexpected problems. Unfortunately, neither allowlisting or blocklisting works universally. If the API provider introduces a new type of response code you've never seen before, then it's an unknown. The best approach I know for handling unknown responses and codes is having a third state (besides "success" and "failure") that is "unknown," and raising an error, alert, or something else, to get an engineer to look at it.

Know that whatever decision you make with an unknown state or response could be based on a wrong assumption. Often, the correct way to handle these is to not handle them by leaving them alone.

9

SOFTWARE DEVELOPMENT

How do you become a developer who's seen as a competent, solid, and efficient professional, who "knows their stuff" about software development? In this chapter, we cover these topics:

1. Become proficient in a language
2. Debugging
3. Refactoring
4. Testing

1. Become Proficient in a Language

Learn a language really well. You hit a new level of comprehension, understanding, and competence when you truly know a language inside out. What does "inside out" mean? It is knowing how to use the language: constructs, operations, etc. It means knowing best practices and understanding why they are recommended. It means going deeper under the hood, and understanding how memory management and garbage collection work, how the code compiles, and what matters for performance.

Learn the fundamentals of a language

There are levels to learning a language in depth. First, it's about mastering the things the language provides. These include built-in data types, variables and data structures, operators, control statements, classes and objects, and standard ways of error handling. Understand and try out some of the more advanced parts of a language, like generics, parallel execution/threading, more complex data types, and additional features the language supports.

A good way to go through the basics of a language is to consult its documentation; find a good language reference, look at code examples, or study a book on its fundamentals. Video courses with coding examples work equally well – indeed, these are even better for some people. Find the format that works for you. Having reference material you can return to is handy, so I recommend investing in a book.

Go a level deeper

When you know how to use the language, try going a level deeper. Do this by asking questions, like:

- What really happens when you declare a variable, a function, or a class?
- How will the code be compiled to machine code, and which optimizations might occur?
- What is the memory footprint of the program? How can you observe the memory used?
- How is memory freed up? Assuming the language uses garbage collection, how does this work?
- If the language supports generics, are both covariance and contravariance supported?
- How is generic code interpreted, and how is it optimized under the hood?

Seek out books, videos, online courses, and other resources on the advanced parts of a language. AI tools offer shortcuts to answering some questions, but they will likely not be as in-depth as more detailed books, or online resources. When trying to answer questions like the above, don't forget these are complex and cover areas you might not know, or be able to tackle by yourself.

The way I learn languages in depth is by working my way through books about them, doing advanced courses, reading articles which dive into the nitty-gritty details, and – recently – asking AI assistants to summarize concepts and verify the correctness of answers. There are always multiple experts in any cutting-edge technology, who delve into the very depths of languages and share their discoveries. Search for in-depth resources and devote time to studying them.

Learn and use tooling to peek under the hood and get more information on how things work. Tools that help with this could be memory and CPU profilers, developer tools, and diagnostic tools. These not only help you understand more about the inner workings of a language but come in handy for more advanced debugging.

The intern who became their team's Go expert

At Uber, my team used Java, some Python, and some Node.JS on the backend. This mix of languages came about because our team needed to work with services written in those languages.

Go was a language that started to gain popularity within the company, and lots of new services were being built with this language. Our team liked to explore, so we built a new service using Go because it provided an excuse to learn the language.

An intern joined our team, who was really into Go. Even before his internship, he spent a lot of time doing tutorials, reading up on interesting parts, putting together pet projects, and experimenting with different language features. This intern immediately got involved in code reviews, and started to give tips to teammates on how to write things "the Go way." Engineers on the team started to involve him more; asking him to leave reviews on Go code, and pairing with him as they built the service.

This intern became the "Go expert" on our team. How did he do it? He put in a lot more time and effort than anyone else and kept going deeper into the language's workings.

This is a good reminder that even if you lack experience, you can still become an expert in a language, framework, or a specific area by putting in the time and effort to master it!

Learn the "main" framework you use with a language

These days, using only one language is rare, although you will most likely use your "main" language with a framework. For example, if you use JavaScript or TypeScript on the frontend, you might also use React, Next.js, or another opinionated fronted framework. If you write Ruby code, you might use Rails. If it's PHP, then this could be Laravel, and so on. When building products, opinionated frameworks allow faster progress and are popular.

Follow the same approach in learning a framework as when learning a language. Learn the fundamentals of the framework, then peek under the hood to go deeper.

An advantage of open-source frameworks is that you can look directly under the hood, even if its codebase initially seems overwhelming. This is an advantage you do not have with most programming languages.

Many developers are content with being "good enough" at their main framework, and so don't invest much time in diving deeper to understand how and why things work like they do.

If you take that additional step and invest more time in digging deeper into the framework, the knowledge you gain should be an advantage when debugging tricky bugs, making architecture decisions, or migrating to new versions of the framework.

Learn a second language

Once you're familiar enough with your first language, look for opportunities to pick up a second one. For example, if some team members are coding in a different language, it could be worth volunteering to join the effort, and being clear that you're interested in getting started with this new language.

Learning a second language has far more benefits than is often assumed:

- **It's easier to compare strengths and weaknesses**. When starting to use a second language, you'll find some things are harder to do, while others are easier. Assuming you learned your "first" language in-depth, you can immediately see where the new language works better, and where not.

- **Go deeper into your first language**. This may seem counter-intuitive, but learning a second programming language tends to help you become more expert in your first language. This happens when you try to figure out how to do something in your "main" language which the second language supports. This is often how you learn the limitations of a "first" language, discover new capabilities, or better understand concepts like dynamic typing, generics, and other advanced language features.
- **You shake the habit of only using your "main" language**. If you're proficient in only one programming language, you are likely to always reach for it. However, a single programming language is rarely the best fit for all projects and situations. You'll have cases when using a new programming language brings benefits – like libraries you can use, or better performance characteristics. Get into the habit of being unafraid to learn new languages by doing precisely that.
- **It's easier to learn more languages**. Your first programming language tends to be the hardest to learn. The second is still tricky, but then things start to become easier. The more languages you learn, the more you appreciate their different features and capabilities.

AI tools can greatly help in learning the syntax of a new language. Tools like ChatGPT and other AI assistants can "translate" code from one language to another. They can also answer questions like, "show me the different ways to declare a function in [insert language being learned."] Use these AI tools to speed up your learning. Just remember they can give wrong answers – so be sure to validate their output!

To go broad or go deep?

Competent software developers have a depth of knowledge to fall back on. This means they understand at least one language and framework really well. However, this language or framework might not be the first they learned.

I advise developers to "go deep" in at least one area, early in their careers. Follow the approaches we've discussed, like studying in-depth resources. Another good approach is pairing with someone who's an expert in an area and learning from them while asking for self-learning resources and completing them.

Another way of going deep is to study the "boring" but necessary things you come across, day to day. Software engineer, Ben Kuhn[1], calls this "blub studies." The term "blub" comes from an essay[2] by Paul Graham, cofounder of Y Combinator, in which "blub" is the name of a hypothetical language. In Ben's article, In defense of blub studies[3], he describes why it is useful to go into the seemingly boring, pointless details of frameworks and languages:

---

[1] https://www.benkuhn.net
[2] http://www.paulgraham.com/avg.html
[3] https://www.benkuhn.net/blub

"Suppose your blub of choice is React. You might worry that learning the gory details will be useless if you ever move to a different part of the stack, or even a different web framework. And, yes, some of them will. But the core idea of React—writing pure render functions, using reconciliation to make updates fast—is extremely powerful and general. In fact, it's now been copied by the next generation of UI frameworks on both iOS (SwiftUI) and Android (Jetpack Compose.) Learning the principles behind React makes it easier to learn those other frameworks. In fact, it can even be a useful source of ideas to "import" from one to the other.

Blub studies are surprisingly broadly applicable because even if you're learning about the details of some specific blubby system, that system's design will contain a juicy, non-blubby core of extractible general principles.

Blub studies also compound more than you'd naively expect, in two ways. First, knowing about one blub makes it easier to learn about alternative blubs that serve the same purpose—like the React/SwiftUI example above. Second, knowing more about one blub helps you learn blubs in adjacent parts of the stack more quickly."

It turns out you can go deep while also going broad, and blub studies – finding out how the tools and frameworks you use actually work – is a good example. As long as you spend time learning things outside of your comfort zone, then your depth and breadth of knowledge and skill will grow.

2. Debugging

When you write code to solve a problem, it won't always work as you expect. The less experienced you are, the more often this happens. So, how do you find out what went wrong? Inspect the code and try to go step by step through it, until the error is found. Basically, you debug.

Engineers who can debug quickly and efficiently, fix errors quicker, and iterate faster. And while some people seem to have a natural talent for debugging, all of it can be learned. So, how do you get better at debugging?

Know your debugging tools

Most integrated development environments (IDE,) such as VS Code, or JetBrains IntelliJ, come with powerful runtime debugging tools. But I've noticed less experienced engineers are often unaware of just how powerful these are. Inspecting the code while it is executing is one of the best ways to see what incorrect assumptions you made, and how the code actually behaves. A debugging tool can save hours, compared to a *"change and run and hope it works"* approach.

Start by discovering the debugging tools which come with the IDE you use. Set breakpoints and inspect the local variables. Step in/out/over functions and inspect the call stack. Look up documentation and tutorials on how to use more advanced features. Some debuggers may support helpful features, including:

- Modifying variables on the fly
- Evaluating expressions during debugging
- Conditional breakpoints and exception breakpoints
- Watchpoints (a breakpoint set on a variable, fired when it is changing)
- Dropping to a frame (restarting debugging from another part of the call stack)
- Skip between threads
- Modify source code while the debugger is running
- Modify environment variables
- Simulate sensory inputs (for hardware-based environments like mobile)

Tools like Visual Studio, JetBrains IDEs, and Chrome DevTools support almost all of the above features – as do modern development environments built with developer productivity in mind. If you've not tried them yet, now is a great time to.

Observe how experienced developers debug

An underrated way to improve at debugging is to see how developers do it who are very good at debugging. When you hear a fellow developer mention a tricky bug, ask if you can shadow them or pair with them as they debug it. Mention that you're interested to learn how they approach finding the root causes of bugs.

On your team, aim to pair at least once with every developer on a debugging session. You are guaranteed to learn new debugging techniques, and perhaps discover new debugging tools.

Learn how to debug without tools

Sometimes, you may not have access to a debugging tool – for example, when working on the command line – or you decide against using one. There are ways to discover what's gone wrong by debugging without tools. Such approaches usually require extra work, but you might learn more. Here are a few:

- **Log to the console**. This is the simplest approach. Start dumping messages when a function is called; print the values of variables and anything else that could be helpful. Then, rerun the code and try to figure out what is happening by looking at the console log.
- **Paper debugging**. Take a pen and paper, or use a whiteboard. Write up key variables

you care about and start to execute the code in your head, writing down how those variables change each time. More granular notes often help. If you get stuck, ask someone to follow along to ensure you're executing the code correctly in your head. This approach is especially powerful if you have access to a debugger. First, do paper debugging, and then run the debugger to check if you ran the program correctly in your head.

- **Write (unit) tests.** This approach is similar to test-driven development (TDD) and is especially useful when debugging functions. Write tests that specify the expected input and the expected outputs. When running these, check which ones succeed and which don't. Then, modify the code and quickly rerun the tests. This approach helps because once you have tests written, you can get rapid feedback on whether your modifications work or not. Besides, as we cover in Part III: Testing, tests are the basis of maintainable code, so you probably will need to write them, anyway.

3. Refactoring

Refactoring is an important, often overlooked part of coding. Getting good at refactoring is similar to learning to code. You can read all you like about a topic, but without doing it you'll never truly master it. To be good at refactoring, you must do it – a lot.

Practice refactoring as often as possible

Start by refactoring your own code after it's written. When you complete a task and your code works, read through all the changes with a critical eye. What could be done better, or more expressively? How could the code read more nicely?

When you see something you can improve, make the change. These will often be small changes that might not feel like refactoring but are a good start.

Get ideas for refactoring via code reviews – and act on them. When people review your code, or you check other code reviews, there will be comments pointing out things which could be improved at the codebase level. These comments might not be related to the code changed but to the surrounding code. Comments like this often highlight opportunities for refactoring other parts of the code.

If you see a comment which could be an opportunity for a code change, take it up and volunteer to do a refactor. Pair with someone who can confirm it's a good idea and review your refactor later. Do this refactor as a separate task or pull request to make it easy to review.

Read through the code. While reading code, make notes of inconsistencies and hard-to-understand parts. Getting ideas for refactor opportunities via code reviews can be hit and miss. A more focused way is to read the code and try to understand what it does. This helps in two ways.

First, you deepen your knowledge of the system. By reading the code, you'll better understand what gets done and where. You'll be able to debug better and reason about the code better. *See this chapter's "Read as much code as you write" section.*

Second, you will spot many inconsistencies. Things will be named differently, or seem like duplications, and much else. Some parts will be hard to understand; you'll scratch your head wondering what a method does, or why a certain class exists. And you'll see unreadable code.

Make notes of all these things. You could just put them into a private document, or you could use an extension for your IDE and record your own comments, with these comments stored in a local file and not committed or seen by anyone else.

Write up a list of things you'd like to refactor, then get feedback from others. As tempting as it is to jump into fixing everything you've spotted, it's not the best way to go. The team might already know some of your observations. In rare cases, they might have decided to trade off less readable code for other reasons, like performance or maintainability. Parts of the Kubernetes source code are a good example of this. You might also spot things to refactor that are actually conventions agreed by the team.

Instead, get a second opinion and talk through your observations with someone experienced enough with the codebase. Get their feedback and decide which refactorings make sense and which don't. With the new list, estimate the effort each one would take and put them together in a sequence of how to proceed. It's a good idea to put simpler refactorings first.

When you have a prioritized list, you can treat it as your "refactor backlog." If you work on a team where people record their planned work, you can create tickets. Start with one refactoring on the side of your regular work. You could do it when you have some downtime while waiting on code reviews, or between tasks. Try to complete this first refactor; get it reviewed, merged, and then seek feedback from others. Rinse and repeat, slowly but surely going through the list. When it's nearly finished, find new opportunities for improving the code.

In a healthy team, people will cheer you for doing this kind of work; especially those who gave feedback that they think the refactorings were a good idea. You get multiple benefits: not only do you practice refactoring, but you learn a lot more about the codebase, and build up the goodwill of teammates for doing cleanup work. And if you regularly ask for feedback before starting refactoring, you learn what colleagues think is important or unimportant, and why.

Know your IDE's refactor functionality – and use it

Many IDEs have built-in support for simple refactor operations, such as renaming variables, changing function signatures, extracting logic into its own function, and much more. Whichever IDE you use, invest time in learning the refactoring support it offers.

Simple refactoring tasks can be time-consuming and error-prone if you work by hand. Using a tool will mean you'll be faster and won't need to be concerned about whether it's worth the time it takes to refactor. It will only take the blink of an eye to do.

Refactoring is multifaceted. Start with simple refactors, slowly moving to more complex ones. A simple thing to refactor is the parts of a function; starting with renaming variables and then extracting functionality to other methods. The next level is refactoring multiple functions, for example, by removing duplication. Then, there's similar work at the class level. And finally, at the services/libraries/frameworks level.

The smaller the scope of a refactor, the easier it is to get it right and test that nothing broke. While any refactoring is good career experience, be careful not to bite off more than you can chew. If you've started a refactoring that is growing out of control, and you're finding it hard to keep track of all the changes, reduce the scope. Can you cut the refactor into smaller pieces, doing them one by one? If things get overly complex, it's a great opportunity to ask for help from people more experienced in the codebase, to understand how they approach the same problem.

Refactor the tests

One under-appreciated refactor opportunity is refactoring unit tests of a project. Often, this is code with lots of duplication and poor structure, which does not follow many best practices. People adding tests usually follow the established style and rarely improve it.

Refactoring tests can start with just one test, making it more readable, and then getting feedback via code reviews. From here, you can move to cleaning up a whole class. Extracting common functionality into their own methods, simplifying tests, and making them more readable is usually an easy win. You might also be able to facilitate a discussion on which style and practices to follow.

With some practices and conventions agreed at the team level, you can go on to refactor other classes. Refactoring tests are often seen as a thankless task, but I believe they're important. Also, you can practice being efficient at refactoring using IDE shortcuts. These tests have long-term effects: improvements you make will be followed by many other developers who write new tests, in accordance with your refined conventions.

Be very careful when refactoring poorly tested production code. It's key to have a safety net when refactoring frequently. This safety net is unit tests for the code. If you attempt to refactor code without automated tests, you will expend much more effort verifying that things work correctly.

There are exceptions when it's practical to refactor untested code. These are usually limited to parts of the codebase that the team deliberately did not test, such as the user interface (UI) layer. However, efficiency gains from quick refactoring are lost if you must manually verify every use case touched by the refactor.

Make refactoring an everyday habit

Strengthen your refactoring muscle. The ability to refactor without fear and with little effort is one you can only learn by exercising it frequently, making mistakes, and learning from them. For every few tasks you complete, make a point to do an important refactoring task, too.

4. Testing

Competent software developers are seen as reliable, which partly derives from being able to give good enough time estimates for work of reasonable complexity. The other, even more important thing is that reliable developers' code works as it should. How do these developers ensure this of their code?

They test code before requesting a code review or committing it. I'm not necessarily talking about automated testing. Reliable developers first and foremost manually test their code when the work is done, and before they request a code review, or push it to production.

They think about possible edge cases the code might encounter, and execute simple tests. If they build an API endpoint, they spin it up locally and make various requests to the endpoint to exercise the functionality. If they write a function which performs some logic, they make sure the function works as expected, even when invoking it with boundary conditions.

Reliable developers care deeply about edge cases. They go through potential edge cases, and confirm with stakeholders what should happen in such scenarios. For example, when building user input fields, a reliable developer confirms they need to validate the user's input, and what should happen if the user enters something different. Or, in an app for topping up a cash account, they'll consider edge cases like negative amounts, or non-numeric values.

Test cases, even manual ones, are things which reliable developers write down, even before starting development. They tend to extend this list as they go and find new, previously unconsidered edge cases. When the code is ready, they test for all cases and only commit the code when confident it works as it should.

Developers tend to introduce bugs by skipping consideration of edge cases and test cases, and when they check in code on the assumption it will work. Bugs that emerge will almost certainly be overlooked edge cases. A developer may think: "no big deal, it happens to the best of us." And yes, it does happen. But curiously enough, it doesn't happen nearly as often to reliable developers who spend time thinking about edge cases, and don't push their code until they've confirmed all assumptions.

Automated testing is a tool commonly used by competent developers. They have already defined the edge cases and test cases. Earlier in their careers, they probably manually tested all these cases. However, once familiarized with unit and integration testing tools, they won't go back to the slow, painful manual testing process.

Some give test-driven development a go. This is a method of creating unit tests upfront, and then writing code which passes these tests. However, most developers stick with writing code and doing meaningful automated tests simultaneously. We dive into the different types of automated tests in Part III: "Testing."

10

TOOLS OF THE PRODUCTIVE SOFTWARE ENGINEER

To be productive as a developer, you need a good understanding and control of the tools you use.

In some professions, formal training is given in the "tools of the trade." My father works in chemistry and he shared that, for a job in a chemistry laboratory, the first step is learning what the instruments are and what they do. Early days are spent as an assistant using simple instruments, under supervision. Once proficiency is demonstrated, there's access to more complicated tools and tasks. After a few years, it's possible for lab workers to operate complex instruments entirely by themselves and to train new assistants.

But in software, training like this is rare. Some companies are better than others at educating professionals on how their tooling, build, deployment, and other systems work. But often, you have to figure these things out yourself.

This chapter seeks to correct this. It's a summary of the tools and systems you need to use effectively, in order to be a reliable software engineer in many workplaces. We cover:

1. Your local development environment
2. Frequently used tools
3. Ways to iterate quickly

1. Your Local Development Environment

Master your coding environment; your interactive development environment (IDE,) or coding text editor. Get familiar with it and learn its capabilities!

Does your development environment support functionality like searching within certain files, replacing in a current file, extracting methods, and changing variable names? Can you build your project and run it with one click? IDEs are very powerful once you learn how to use them. Here are some capabilities you should find in a modern IDE:

- **Refactoring**. Can you refactor code more easily, like renaming variables/functions/classes or extracting methods? Look up the built-in refactoring capabilities of your environment.

- **Compiling**. Set up one-click building/compilation of a project. Which keyboard shortcut can you use to perform this step? Can you set up compiling or building every time you save a file?
- **Running the project**. How can you launch your compiled project to run with a single click or keyboard shortcut? This is especially relevant for frontend-facing applications like web apps or mobile.
- **Hot reload**. Is it possible to make a change to the code while it's running, and have this change be live after the file is saved and the environment reloads itself?
- **Debugging**. Get familiar with how to place a breakpoint, step into/step, over/step out. Where can you see the stack trace? How can you view local variables?
- **Advanced debugging**. Can you use conditional breakpoints? Can you ignore a condition N times before it breaks? Can you change variables when the breakpoint is hit?
- **Running tests**. How can you run automated tests, such as unit or integration tests? Can you do so with a single click, or with a keyboard shortcut?
- **Debugging tests**. How can you place breakpoints and debug a test? Can you debug a specific test by itself? If so, how?
- **Creating a pull request**. Can you do source control management, such as creating a pull request from within the IDE?

Figuring things out takes time. You'll make quicker progress by pairing with a more experienced engineer. Ask how they perform the actions above and learn from them! Understanding how to use your IDE effectively will shorten coding iteration cycles and speed up your work.

A rapid edit → compile/run → output cycle

If it takes more than a few seconds to make edits and see how they look, then you're likely losing time on context switching. With modern tools and decent hardware, there's little reason to wait more than a second or two to view changes, be they code refreshing in a web browser, unit tests running on the backend, or changes showing up in the mobile simulator.

Don't accept a slow cycle from an edit to the change being live in your environment. Ask teammates how they work, and copy the approach of someone who doesn't wait on their machine. If everyone has a slow coding iteration cycle, then search online and ask on forums – consult ChatGPT or other AI tools! – to figure out how to speed up this process.

Making iterations rapidly will boost your productivity, and keep you "in the zone" when working.

Configure your IDE and workflow

Once you have got the hang of development in your current environment and workplace, consider making your workflow more convenient. Here's how:

Set up shortcuts for frequent actions, such as running your project, running a test, searching the codebase, and so on.

If you repeat actions by clicking around in the IDE menu, figure out a shortcut or set up a keyboard shortcut. These are small efficiency wins which will help keep you "in the flow" as they become part of your "muscle memory."

Configure your color scheme. This is a minor detail for some people but makes a big difference for others. Choose a color scheme which makes your IDE easier to work with; it could be as simple as selecting dark or light mode, or something more involved like picking colors that match your terminal. Color scheme packs are available from editors, such as the "Dracula Color Theme," or "Colour Schemes" by Dayle Rees.

Set up code formatting and linting, if needed. When typing code, should brackets in an "if { }" statement be on the same line, or on the next line? How many spaces should be used when indenting? Or should indentation just use tabs?

If your team already has code formatting and linting rules in place, ensure these settings are applied to your local development environment.

If no rules are enforced, consider selecting a code formatter and linting style for your code. Enabling a code formatter means all code you write is consistent. Many of these tools can be set up to auto-format when saving the file, or with a keyboard shortcut. *When working in a team, it's helpful for everyone to use the same style. Consider discussing settling on one approach with teammates.*

If your IDE has a playground, use it. In some development environments, the IDE comes with a playground component for trying out things quickly; for example, XCode's Swift Playgrounds in iOS development. Get familiar with this environment and tinker with it, as it might be handy for quick prototyping.

Look into alternative development environments and playgrounds. There are many development environments. If your team has settled on one, prioritize learning that first. But also consider alternatives in case another tool works better in certain use cases. For example, coding playgrounds like JSFiddle could be a good choice for throwing together concepts quickly, when prototyping during web development.

2. Frequently Used Tools

Git

Get to know Git, as it's very likely to be in use as version control. Learn your version control tooling and the ideas behind Git, like:

- Branching
- Rebasing
- Resolving conflicts and merging
- Cherry picking.

Most importantly, find a Git client you're comfortable using.

Many developers swear by learning to use Git over the command line, instead of relying on a graphical user interface (GUI). If you do this, you won't depend on any one source control application. I encourage giving this a go and don't worry if the command line is less appealing than using a graphical interface. Git is just a tool; the main thing is that you can create pull requests and deal with conflicts, which are the most common actions.

The command-line/terminal

The command-line is a text-only interface and a powerful tool. It has different names on different operating systems:

- Mac: this is the "Terminal" application.
- Linux: the shell application. Linux has several shell applications available, like sh, zsh, csh, ksh.
- Windows: the Command Prompt or cmd, or the more powerful PowerShell command-line.

You'll also find the command line within IDEs. For example, in Visual Studio Code, it shows up under the "Terminal" tab. The command line is especially useful when working with remote machines when you might need to connect via SSH, and then use the command-line interface.

Familiarize yourself with common command-line commands like navigating directories, listing directory contents, running scripts – such as Python or Node scripts – searching within the contents of files, or setting the value of environment variables.

The best way to become familiar with the command line is to start using it for tasks. Find out how by searching "how to do X with the command line" – where "X" is the task you want to complete. The more comfortable you are with the command line, the more efficient your workflow is.

Regular expressions

Learn enough regex (regular expressions) because they may be helpful, especially when searching for certain files, or doing bulk editing/renaming. Learn the basic syntax of how they work and use them when searching files and replacing contents.

Find a tool that helps you test and verify regular expressions, which is to hand when needed. This tool could be a website or even an AI assistant.

SQL

SQL is the language for querying relational databases. When building a data-storing application or service, the data storage will be a relational database, or a NoSQL database. However, when querying any type of data, there's a good chance you'll use some SQL syntax.

So learn the basics of SQL: how to create a table, how to use the SELECT command with the FROM, WHERE, ORDER BY, GROUP BY, HAVING clauses, and also some more advanced aspects like joining tables, or using views. As a bonus, it's helpful to understand the performance of these statements and the importance of table indexes in executing more complicated queries, like joins.

Once you have a decent understanding of SQL, you can rely on this knowledge when doing data manipulation.

AI coding assistants

From early 2023, AI coding assistants exploded in popularity and efficiency. These assistants fall into two broad categories:

1. **Inline coding assistants**. These work like an "autocomplete on steroids," suggesting code to write based on existing code. Examples include GitHub Copilot, Sourcegraph Cody, Tabnine, and many others.
2. **Generative AI chat interfaces**. Many generative AI chat applications are trained on source code and programming concepts. These tools help to "talk through" coding-related topics and questions and are useful for generating code scaffolding, or larger pieces of code with multiple files. Examples include OpenAI, ChatGPT, Google Bard, and Phind.com.

Ask colleagues which assistants they use, try them out, and settle on ones that "click" with you. Figure out which prompts are helpful and save useful prompts in a file, for reference later.

AI coding assistants are just one more productivity tool, once you figure out how to use them well and understand their limitations. All tools have downsides, and a big one of AI tools is that they sometimes generate code that is not what you want. Or the code may have bugs, and models can hallucinate and make up APIs which don't exist. Being aware of the limitations lets you use these tools much more efficiently.

Development tools at your company

What are the internal – possibly custom – development tools that engineers in your workplace regularly use? As you onboard to your team and begin making your first few code changes, you will likely come across several.

For example, it's common at larger tech companies to have custom CI/CD systems, custom code review tools, custom monitoring and alerting tools, and custom feature flag and experimentation systems. Even if the tools aren't custom, different companies tend to use different vendors, so it's necessary to be familiar with them.

Ask fellow engineers which tools they use regularly. Make a list and figure out how to access them and how they work. Create your own "cheat sheet" on how to use them efficiently.

Your "productivity cheat sheet"

When I was at Uber – which possessed a huge volume of custom internal tools – I kept a document of useful links to internal tools and dashboards, and a list of commands, prompts, and queries. This document was useful for years!

Consider creating a personal "productivity cheat sheet." Start with a blank document, and add the names of tools with short descriptions of what they do, links, commands, and other notes. This small document can help a lot, especially during the first few months on a new team.

3. Ways To Iterate Quickly

Read existing code and understand what it does

The challenge of coding is often not how to write code, but what to write. This is especially the case when working within a more complex codebase. You'll be much more productive when you understand how things work, and can navigate the codebase. Here are a few things you can do.

Ask someone to walk you through the structure. Ask an experienced engineer to walk you through the parts of the codebase, which parts do what, and what to take note of.

Draw out classes/modules, and how they connect. Create a diagram by hand, or with a sketching tool like Excalidraw, LucidCharts, or similar. Draw parts of the codebase and note down your interpretation of their roles, and what they connect to.

Share your code map with teammates. Share the map you created with teammates and ask for feedback; it's often a good conversation starter. Frequently, it won't just be you who learns new things about the codebase; others may find pointers in your map to things the code should improve on, or relationships they didn't realize existed.

Create a cheat sheet. Take notes on where to find key parts of the code, and frequently used modules or classes. This could be as simple as a text file or a basic document. When you experience "a-ha!" moments of clarity, record them.

Know how to debug the CI/CD

CI stands for "continuous integration," and CD for "continuous deployment." Having a CI/CD system in place is commonplace at most tech companies and startups.

Every now and then, you might have problems with tests unexpectedly failing on the CI server, or when deploying with CD. These issues tend to be rare but can be challenging to pinpoint.

Understand how CI/CD works at your company and on your team. This understanding will develop your sense of what's happening behind the scenes. Which scripts run and in what order? How can you inspect the setup? Ask longer-tenured or more experienced engineers for pointers on this system. If there's a dedicated team maintaining the CI/CD system, talk to an engineer on that team.

How do you access CI/CD logs? They are key to understanding why some builds fail. Was it a CI/CD infrastructure issue, or could it have been a regression in a recent code change?

We cover more about CI/CD systems in Part V: Software Engineering.

Know how to access production logs and dashboards

Debugging production issues for users is challenging without access to details about what *might* have happened. So, figure out the options for accessing:

- Production logs, dashboards and metrics
- How to filter those logs to certain users
- How to query various relevant data sources for debugging
- How to access crash dumps, errors, and exceptions for specific users
- Processes to follow when debugging production logs. For example, if you access personal information when debugging production data, there may be a data protection

process to follow. Ask your manager and more experienced engineers

If you have a productivity cheat sheet, add details to it for quick reference later.

Make small code changes when possible

It's likely that you'll work in an environment where code changes are submitted as pull requests that describe them. This helps to avoid unnecessary changes being made, or ones that are illogical. Here are a few ways to make effective minor changes:

- Aim for small pull requests where possible. Break your changes into smaller steps, with each step doing a specific thing.
- Summarize the "why" and the "what." In the pull request, write no more than a few sentences about why the change is being made. Provide a short overview of what you changed. Remember, the pull request comment will be read by others in future to learn why your change was made, and it's more helpful to over-explain than under-explain it.
- Use images when UIs are changed. A picture is worth a thousand words, here. Attach an image of the "before" and "after" states.
- Mention edge cases covered and those not covered. Make clear which ones you accounted for.
- Be clear what's not in scope for a change, especially if there is expected to be follow-up work on further changes.
- Seek feedback on your pull request summaries. Ask more experienced engineers to go through your last few pull requests. Ask what they liked, what was confusing, and their advice for writing clearer, crisper summaries.

Run and write automated tests and checks

The most time-consuming thing about writing code tends to be precisely that: writing the code. It involves devising an approach, writing the correct code, and testing that it works. The next most time-consuming activity is fixing the things your newly written code broke!

The best way to write code that is bug-free and doesn't cause regressions is to test it. Naturally, you should manually test your code after making changes. However, there's a more efficient way: run automated tests already in place in the codebase and write new automated tests which exercise your code and can catch future regressions.

We go into more detail about why testing is important and common approaches, in Part III: "Testing." For now, here's a short summary of tests it's good to be familiar with:

- **Unit tests**. The simplest type of tests which are the baseline of testing in most environments. Assuming your team already uses unit tests, join in and learn how to write good tests. Get feedback from your team.

- **Integration, screenshot, and end-to-end tests**. These tests are more complicated to write and test a broader range of functionality. In backend development, integration tests can be more relevant. For web and mobile development, screenshot, and end-to-end tests might be more common. Find out if your team uses any of these tests and learn how to contribute to writing and maintaining them.

Don't just wait for code reviews: ask for them

Waiting for too long to get code reviews can slow your pace. When you send your code for review, consider that it could be helpful to let more experienced devs know that a code review would help you progress further.

The best way to go about figuring out if and when you should request such reviews is to ask other devs on the team: when you have code reads, would they mind if you ping them about this? Is there a team channel where people announce reviews?

More experienced developers will understand that providing a quick enough code review greatly helps developers move faster, and will prioritize doing so. But in the case they don't yet do this, ask how you can best let them know that you need their help to get unblocked, and get that much-needed review.

Get frequent feedback

The two fastest ways to grow into a reliable software engineer:

- Build things: solve problems by writing code and ship that code to production.
- Get feedback: does your solution work as expected? Does it do what you intended with no side effects?

Get feedback by shipping to production. The most straightforward way to get feedback on your work is to ship it to production and then confirm that it works as expected. The beauty of this approach is that if your code has bugs or issues, there's a good chance you'll get feedback really quickly from customers.

Of course, the downside of getting feedback from production is that you can break things. Fortunately, there are safer sources of feedback which it's smart to utilize.

Ask for feedback on your work. Sometimes it's more effective to ask for direct feedback on specific work from a peer whom you trust, or your manager.

The best time to seek feedback is when you finish a task or wrap up a project. This is when people will give the most specific, most helpful comments. The next time you complete a piece of work, consider pulling aside a more experienced engineer and asking what they thought you did well, and where you could improve.

If you have 1:1s with your manager, ask for direct feedback on specific work or projects. Your manager might not be able to give immediate feedback if they don't work closely with you, but they're in a good position to gather feedback from teammates and summarize it with you.

Plenty of engineers are poor at giving feedback, not because they don't care about giving good feedback, but because they don't know how to give specific and actionable feedback. Don't take it personally If you get feedback that sounds judgmental, or isn't helpful, like "you could have done it faster," or "you asked for a lot of help." Instead, probe more to translate this into something more actionable, and ask if those actions would address the feedback. For example, feedback that you could have done something faster might be a poor attempt to say that you didn't share when you encountered a delay. Actionable feedback would be to communicate a roadblock more clearly in future.

Compare your output with teammates' outputs. Work isn't a competition, but it's helpful to get a sense of where you are in terms of output and iteration speed, compared to your peers. Observe how frequently teammates submit pull requests, push code to production, and finish tasks.

The goal is simply to get an idea of how you're doing compared to the team's normal pace of work. Once onboarding is complete, it's a standard expectation that engineers get up to a reasonable speed for their level. It's helpful to have your own data points for figuring out how you're doing, even before explicit feedback from others.

Takeaways

Competent software developers get things done in projects of reasonable complexity, given their experience level. There is plenty to learn in order to be able to reliably complete well-defined tasks and smaller projects which call upon your tech skills, expertise, and experience.

"Practice, practice, practice" is the single best advice for growth. Beyond building software, things which can speed up your professional growth, include:

- Working in a team where you can learn from fellow developers
- Having access to mentors or buddies to whom you can turn with questions
- Being able to pair with developers
- Having enough time to dive deeply into a technology
- Working on projects and assignments for long enough that you become proficient in the technology, but are able to switch frequently enough in order to keep learning

Many developers are in a rush to reach the next rung on the career ladder. This is understandable, as titles carry weight, the promise of better compensation, and superior career opportunities.

However, building a solid foundation of knowledge and experience in software development practices; such as learning how to spot when you're stuck, how to unblock yourself, and acquiring the habit of continuous learning, all take time and will ultimately benefit your career. Time is not 'wasted' at junior levels if you keep learning and growing.

For further reading, check out the online, bonus chapter for Part II:

Getting Things Done as a Software Developer: Exercises

pragmaticurl.com/bonus-2

Part III

The Well-Rounded Senior Engineer

From this chapter onward, we discuss "software engineering" and not "software development." For this reason, the title "software engineer" replaces "software developer." This change is purposeful, even though software development and software engineering are frequently used interchangeably. In my personal usage, software development is a subset of software engineering. Also, software engineering involves thinking about software products across a longer time frame than is the case with software development.

Software development vs software engineering

Software development refers to the process of building software, such as:

- Outlining a basic plan
- Coding
- Testing
- Deploying
- Debugging

It's not uncommon for software developers to be given well-defined tasks, and for their work to be limited to implementing these tasks. At more traditional, non-tech-first companies, the breakdown of work is done by product managers, business analysts, project managers, or architects – but not software developers.

Software engineering is a lot broader than only development. It also involves:

- Gathering requirements
- Planning a solution and analyzing tradeoffs between approaches
- Building the software
- Shipping to production
- Maintaining the solution
- Extending the solution to new use cases
- Migrating to other solutions

A software engineer should be invested in the long-term impact of their work, as well as the short-term. Another reason we use the term "software engineer" is to emphasize that at senior-and-above levels, software engineers should consider longer-term impact and not confine themselves solely to the problem at hand, like fixing a persistent bug. Common long-term impacts to think about:

- How to ensure a bug will not recur? One solution could be automated testing.
- How to make sure a similar issue is detected quickly? Monitoring and alerting could be a solution.
- How can the fix be easy to maintain in future? Options could include readable code, documentation, or coding decisions that make code extensible for future use cases.

Starting this chapter, we adopt a longer-term mindset when discussing activities and advice. Looking beyond the immediate impact of code written and work done is an important distinction between software developers and software engineers.

In their book, "Software Engineering at Google," Hyrum Wright, Titus Winters, and Tom Manshreck, argue that software engineering is software development (or programming,) over a much longer time frame:

> "We propose that 'software engineering' encompasses not just the act of writing code, but all of the tools and processes an organization uses to build and maintain that code over time. What practices can a software organization introduce that will best keep its code valuable over the long term? How can engineers make a codebase more sustainable and the software engineering discipline itself more rigorous? (⋯)
>
> Software engineering can be thought of as 'programming integrated over time.' What practices can we introduce to our code to make it sustainable—able to react to necessary change—over its life cycle, from conception to introduction to maintenance to deprecation?"

Different senior expectations across tiers of companies

In Part I: "Career paths," we discuss the three tiers of companies, based on compensation:

- Tier 1: bench-marking against the local market
- Tier 2: top of the local market
- Tier 3: top of the regional/international market

Compensation for senior engineers at Tier 3 companies tends to be several times higher than at Tier 1 employers. This difference in compensation results in Tier 3 companies having higher expectations of their senior engineers.

In this chapter, we cover areas in which Tier 2 and Tier 3 companies hold reasonable expectations of senior engineers.

Typical senior titles

Titles for software developers vary across companies. Here's the most common:

- Senior software engineer/senior developer: most of Big Tech and many startups/scale-ups
- Software engineer: at some companies that dislike revealing levels externally, such as Meta
- Senior Member of Technical Staff (eBay and VMWare), Principal Member of Tech-

nical Staff (Oracle)

Title inflation is something that can be particularly observed at lower-tier companies. At Tier 3 employers such as Meta, Google or Uber, it takes two promotions to get to the senior engineer level. At Microsoft, it takes 4 promotions: entry-level engineers begin at L59 (software engineer 1) and the Senior engineer level starts at L63.

However, there are plenty of companies where the first promotion from entry-level software engineer is to senior engineer. Consultancies are a case in point; it's common enough to observe these places describe developers with 2-3 years experience as senior engineers, while engineers with 5-10 years experience at Big Tech can still be at the software engineer 2 level – just below senior.

Of course, title inflation is not confined to the senior engineer level, but this level is the first time that differences in expectations between employers become visible. That titles have different expectations from senior onward in different workplaces, also explains why a "principal" title at an – often lower tier – company, may be equivalent to senior-level expectations at a higher-tier working environment.

Typical senior engineer expectations

So, what exactly do tech companies typically expect of senior engineers? Below is a summary. *Keep in mind each company is unique, and no two have identical expectations.*

Area	Typical expectation
Scope	Medium-sized or more complex projects
Guidance	Works independently in most cases
Getting things done	Unblocks themselves
Taking the initiative	Expected to take the initiative for work within their scope
Software engineering	Follows team practices and sometimes improves them. Helps others to understand their value
Software architecture	Designs the architecture for projects they lead and seeks feedback
Engineering best practices	Follows those in place and introduces practices which help the team
Collaboration	With other engineers and stakeholders on the team
Mentoring	Can mentor less experienced engineers and also seek mentorship
Learning	Possesses hunger to learn
Typical years of industry experience	5-10+

Common expectations of senior software engineers

Senior as a terminal level

At some companies, the senior engineer level is considered a "terminal level." This means there is no expectation for engineers to progress further. It also signals that getting promoted to the next level is far rarer and much more challenging, than reaching senior level is.

Why do many companies decide to make the senior level "terminal?" It's because senior engineers are expected to be autonomous and to solve complex projects and problems by themselves. Plenty of teams and projects require no more expertise. We cover more on the terminal level concept in Part I: "Promotions."

11

GETTING THINGS DONE

More inbound requests, context switches, and more complex work in general, distinguish a senior software engineer's workload from more junior positions.

Becoming seen as an engineer who "gets things done" goes beyond what's discussed in Part II: "Getting things done." Of course, many approaches from that section apply here, such as:

- Focus on the most important work
- Unblock yourself
- Break down the work
- Find mentors you can learn from

But at the senior level, there are extra insights and useful approaches that we delve into now. In this chapter, we cover:

1. Getting things done: perception and reality
2. Your own work
3. Your team
4. The big picture

1. Getting Things Done: Perception and Reality

Which one of you do you think your manager would describe as the engineer who "gets things done?" Yourself, or the peer who seemingly lives on Easy Street?

It may be clear to you that you're getting things done, but how much of this does your manager see? If you do a poor job of communicating your work, but your peer is excellent at this, then the chances are your manager thinks they are better at getting things done.

Perception and reality may differ

The prescription to "get things done" can be distinct from the process of doing so by solving hard problems. Your manager doesn't see what goes into meeting a given deadline for an important project; such as those steps you took to track down and fix a tricky bug, or the creative workarounds and shortcuts you employed. Sometimes, there isn't a knowledgeable colleague to pair with who can observe and assist your efforts, so you work alone to get things done.

Two things are necessary to be seen as a senior engineer who gets things done:

1. Ability to solve complex engineering problems in a pragmatic way
2. Communication of work to peers and managers; including progress, roadblocks faced, solutions to roadblocks, and the complexity of the work.

Communicate what you do

Communicating about your work becomes increasingly important with seniority. Don't assume your peers or manager understand what's "easy" or "difficult" about it. Instead, be explicit about this during status updates, in 1:1 discussions, and at team meetings. For example, if you solve a complex problem, tell your team during the weekly meeting:

> "Last week, I came across a challenging edge case for our planned backend migration. I worked with another team to fix it. It took a bit longer than expected, but it's now done, and we're ready to migrate."

It's okay, but this is a low-information description. It doesn't explain the work, or why it was challenging, its importance, or how your efforts measured up to the task's complexity and outcome. Here's a better update that conveys all of this:

> "Last week, as I was doing more validation for our migration script, I noticed our shadow outputs were different from what was expected for payment requests for around 2% of users. The differences were down to currency conversion in Brazil. If we rolled out this change, we'd overcharge customers there.
>
> As I looked into the reason for the difference, it turned out that the new currency conversion system was missing several countries, Brazil included. I worked with the team on building this system to add these countries and also helped them set up alerting in case a currency is requested for which there is no conversion set up. I expect this work will greatly improve the reliability of the new service.
>
> Although we do not own the new currency service, I helped make the change using Go, and reviewed code from this team. After we made the change, I built two integration tests that exercise this functionality.
>
> By spending an additional day or two on it, we now have a safety net – with unit tests and two integration tests – and we helped the new currency service be more reliable than before.

I have been monitoring the shadow and the production systems, and there are no more differences in output: we had 100% identical responses in the past 4 days."

Under-promise, over-deliver, over-communicate

One of the best ways to be perceived as someone who gets things done is to deliver as much – and sometimes more! – than agreed, and to do so consistently.

This requires good judgment in figuring out how much you can definitely commit to, and to avoid promising too much. This could mean committing to certain dates or deadlines for well-understood work, or taking on difficult projects, bugs, and investigations which you have the capability and capacity to get done.

Don't forget to tell your peers and manager when you over-deliver. It can be a fine line, but this is not about boasting; it's about informing people when you go above and beyond expectations. For example, when finishing a project and building a neat utility that could be helpful later, you can say:

> "I got the PayPal integration done. I also created a utility that can be helpful later."

Here's a better version:

> "I got the PayPal integration done last week, in line with the week-long estimate. However, as I was building it, I found myself spending too much time manually testing if it was working, and thought: 'can we automate some of this?'
>
> So, I built a simple script that verifies if a payment method works, using UI automation. I built this for PayPal at first, and doing so actually made development faster, as testing was easier. Now we have this utility, it's pretty easy to change it to test other types of payment methods, like bank cards. Here's a wiki page on how to use this tool, and how to modify it."

Communicate roadblocks early and offer tradeoffs

The nature of software development is that unexpected problems occur all the time; like a library not working as expected, a strange bug that takes ages to fix, a new dependency appearing from nowhere and blocking you, and countless other things.

Engineers perceived as unreliable often don't communicate new roadblocks. Instead, they try to solve them by themselves and frequently struggle, only making progress after another engineer steps in to help.

In contrast, productive engineers are good at unblocking themselves – as discussed in Part II: "Getting Things Done" – and also recognize when a roadblock will delay a project.

When unexpected work appears from nowhere, share this with your team, manager, and project lead. But don't only share the roadblock. Offer tradeoffs on what else you could do, instead of just delaying the work. For example:

- Cut the scope of the project so you don't need to work on the roadblock, now.
- Put a hack or shortcut in place which solves the roadblock in the short term, then do a proper fix later. Basically, you're advocating taking on tech debt in order to move faster now.
- Have somebody solve the roadblock: for example, can a platform team or a third-party vendor make a change that solves the problem?

Get creative with tradeoffs. By forcing yourself to consider alternatives, you might get closer to solving the roadblock in a smarter, faster way.

2. Your Own Work

Deal with inbound requests efficiently

Senior engineers get a higher number of inbound requests, such as:

- "Could you join this planning review next week?"
- "We need you for an interview tomorrow as cover for an engineer who's sick."
- "Can you please be my peer reviewer for performance reviews?"
- "We have a university recruitment event next month. Could you be a speaker?"
- "I need your help with a strange bug in a component you created two years ago. Would you have a few minutes to take a look with me?"

These are all legitimate requests for which your experience is useful. On the other hand, they're also distractions that pull you away from more important work.

Inbound requests and asks from others will always arrive. Over time, the volume of these can get overwhelming. There's no single best way to deal with them, but here are some approaches I've observed experienced engineers use with success:

Block out time for uninterrupted, deep work. Allocate time when you don't help others in order to focus on your work. Mark this in your calendar and reject meetings and other interruptions. Treat it like a high-priority meeting. Of course, don't overdo blocking out!

Say "not right now" when in the zone. When you are in the zone and making good progress, push back on interruptions. Turn off chat notifications and tell people you'll get back to them later if they approach you directly.

Timebox how long you spend helping with something. When someone asks for assistance, limit how much time you spend on it, to say, 5-10 minutes. This forces you to be more efficient by giving the colleague pointers, instead of diving in to solve the problem for them.

Turn sync requests to async ones. For example, instead of attending a meeting where you would have little input, ask to be sent the meeting summary to read in your own time. This turns a synchronous request – the meeting – into an asynchronous one – meeting notes that you can review later. You can channel many requests for your time in a sync way, to give feedback in an async way.

Redirect requests to a colleague who'd benefit. Letting less experienced engineers take on some requests might boost their growth, while lifting some of the load from your back. **Know your "#1 priority work" at all times**. If you can only get one thing done today, what will it be? If you only ship one thing this week, what's the most important thing? This is your #1 priority project. Know what it is and ensure you have enough time and space to get it done.

Prioritize requests. Use the "urgent/important" matrix to assess how needed – or otherwise – your input really is:

	Important	Not important
Urgent	Do: now	Pass on or say no
Not urgent	In backlog	Say no!

One way to prioritize inbound work

Treat tasks differently by urgency and importance:

- **Urgent and important**: do at once, or when you're no longer in the zone. Tasks could include helping with an outage (where there's context,) or unblocking a team mate.
- **Important but not urgent**: record it and do it later, like giving feedback on a design document, a much-needed refactor, and so on. Tasks with deadlines may become "urgent and important" over time.
- **Urgent but unimportant**: This is work you don't necessarily need to do. Examples include a code review which others have already signed off on, mitigating an outage in which enough people are already involved, or responding to new emails – which can usually wait. If it's not important, resist the urge to act at the expense of distracting yourself from your "main" work. Is it possible to pass these tasks to someone else, or to just say "no"?
- **Not urgent and not important**: Just say no. Examples could include attending a meeting in which you have little input and don't care about, reading status update emails for projects you have no connection with, and so much more. Note, there is value in getting involved in work like this, but do so because there's a benefit, not just because you've been asked.

Create a system for capturing important but not urgent work. One repeat challenge you'll face is recording important but not urgent work. Find a method that works for you. This could be:

- In a simple document
- In a to-do list
- In your favorite editor or note-taking tool
- In a physical notebook
- In the Notes app of your phone

Experiment with which approach works best for you, and don't be afraid to switch things up.

For anything unimportant, say no. There are ways you can do this politely, such as:

- "I'd love to help, but unfortunately I have to compete #1 priority work and so cannot."
- "I already have too many things on my plate, unfortunately, and I cannot take this on." If you have a list of projects you're working on, it's worth showing!
- "I don't think I'm the right person to help: I'd suggest to ask add name"
- "I don't think you need me to solve it: here's a pointer to how you can figure it out yourself." Provide a resource.

Purge your to-do list, every now and then. Many engineers feel a sense of defeat when clearing their to-do list of "not urgent, but important" tasks. On the other hand, I'd recommend this as a way to reset things.

The reality is that what's important to you changes over time. Any list you create of important work will eventually go stale. When this happens, there's two options:

1. Go through the existing list and remove work that's become unimportant
2. Start from scratch and make a shorter list of "really important, right now" tasks

The second approach is faster and forces you to re-prioritize work by only recording the most significant tasks. It also reduces stress about the other ones, and reduces mental load, going forward. Just don't forget to update relevant colleagues whose requests don't make your new, leaner list.

Know that it's normal to feel overwhelmed. A common complaint senior-and-above engineers have is that no matter which approach they take, they still end up feeling overloaded, and without enough time to do their "important" work. This is common. Here are a few things that can help, should you encounter this:

- Collate everything you should be doing, and talk the list through with your manager and mentor – if you have one (if not, consider changing that.) What are the things you really need to do? What can be given to a teammate? Which tasks can you just say "no" to, with your manager's support? Chances are, your manager won't be aware of everything you've been doing, and will help you prioritize what's truly important for the team.

- Say "no" to new requests until your list shrinks. Alternatively, only take on new requests if you can strike something else from your list. See what happens when you decline for the reason that you're overloaded at present.
- Take a day or two off work. When you return, clear your list and start anew. *If you do this too regularly, consider one of the alternatives.*

3. When it's done, it's properly done

There's something to say about software engineers who get things done "properly." There's no shortage of engineers who can seemingly complete work quickly, but it later emerges the code they shipped has issues like bugs, uncovered edge cases, or UX that was cobbled together in haste.

Engineers seen as productive are not necessarily the fastest at getting things done. But their work is fast *enough*, and crucially, the end result works as it should.

Ask yourself if any of these apply to your work:

- After shipping a feature, bugs are sometimes found
- You rarely write a testing plan for your feature, which goes through scenarios to validate before shipping
- When your feature is finished, you don't always list unsupported edge cases with known bugs
- Automated testing, monitoring, and alerting are not always done when you ship a feature

It's rare to find engineers to whom none of the above applies. This is because it's natural to move fast, ship to production, and fix things later if needed. Since many people operate this way, other engineers stick out more when they don't ship issues to production, and who are well aware of edge cases and resolve these before the code goes to production.

So how can you be the engineer who gets things done properly, and whose work your peers and stakeholders can trust is properly done? A few approaches:

Have a written specification. Many bugs in products are misunderstandings between what stakeholders expect, and what software engineers build. Avoid such misunderstandings by insisting on a specification which describes how the feature should work, edge cases, and what's out of scope. Work with your product manager and business stakeholders before the implementation phase, to clarify all this.

Push back on starting work until you have a full understanding of how things should work from the product and customer points of view. Write this down to avoid misunderstandings.

A product spec doesn't have to be lengthy, and the product manager doesn't need to write it. If there is no spec, discuss how the feature is expected to work with the product person or business stakeholder, and summarize this in a page or two with bullet points, then confirm with them that this is how things should work. This hour-long exercise could save days of work.

There's also a fair chance the product person will point out errors, missing details, or edge cases, if you show them a written spec.

Have a testing plan. Before jumping into implementing a non-trivial feature, do some planning and sketch out your approach, such as which components you'll create and modify, how the architecture will be modified, tradeoffs on approaches, and which one you choose.

How will you test that your implemented feature works as expected? Which manual test cases will there be? What parts will you automate with unit, integration, or end-to-end tests? Which parts can only be tested in production, and how will that testing be done before the feature's declared ready?

Many engineers skip test planning upfront, because it's more exciting and motivating to jump straight into implementation. However, the best time to think about how to test and what to test is at the planning stage, before getting carried away with implementation.

When you have a test plan, share it with the product manager, business stakeholders, other engineers, or QA folks, for feedback. You'd be surprised by which edge cases were missed, or alternative testing approaches they suggest!

Include testing, monitoring, and alerting as part of estimations. Testing and monitoring should be part of "getting things done properly" when working on larger codebases, or building features for products where mistakes can have serious business impacts.

However, many engineers forget to add automated tests and monitoring/alerting to a feature, or they don't "bake" this work into their estimation. The problem with treating this part of the work as separate is that product folks and business stakeholders will often want to skip it, as they see it as an opportunity to save time and move faster.

There's a connection between getting things done properly and ensuring your work is tested and monitored in production. Skip testing and monitoring, and your work will be much less reliable. For that reason, don't negotiate over this part; just do it.

Don't "throw it over the fence" to QA. If you are lucky enough to have a dedicated quality assurance (QA) person/team in your workplace, don't just throw your work "over the fence" to them. An anti-pattern I've observed is that some engineering teams who work with QA folks tend to assume that testing and quality assurance is purely the responsibility of the QA team. So, they tend to build things and then pass them on for testing – throwing it over the fence – without giving much thought to edge cases, or how to test things, or without doing simple, manual tests.

Unsurprisingly, this means things take longer. QA finds obvious issues – which any engineer could identify by doing bare-bones testing – and sends it back to engineers, who fix these issues, then hand it back to QA, again. QA then finds more nuanced bugs, which might have escaped engineers' attention, and hands them back for fixing. Finally, after engineering resolves them, QA does another testing round – the third! – and declares things work as expected.

If this is you, then you're doing yourself a disservice.

Involve QA folks during planning and work with them to create a test plan from the start. QA engineers tend to have a good sense for exotic edge cases and hard-to-catch bugs, so learn from them, understand how they "stress test" systems, and utilize their expertise in making a more robust test plan.

And don't just throw things "over the fence." Work side by side with QA, so you don't spend time sitting idle and doing nothing while waiting for QA to test things.

Also, don't take QA for granted. Many engineering teams don't have dedicated QA folks. So, if you work with QA, collaborate with them, learn from them, and you'll grow your QA expertise. There's a fair chance that in your next team or role, there will be no dedicated QA, so having this skillset will help you ship higher quality work.

Work in short iterations

How long does it usually take from coming up with an idea, to having a prototype up and running to show others? How long does it usually take from picking up a bug, to having a fix in production? If the answer to both is weeks and not hours or a day or two, then you're likely not seen as a very productive engineer. In the best case, you're likely perceived as "slow and steady." In the worst case, delete "...and steady".

Ship something every day. Productive software engineers can (and do) ship code almost every day. I've observed this at small companies where it's easy enough to do, and at larger ones, all the way up to places with thousands of software engineers. At Google, where 20,000 software engineers work, an average of two code changes are shipped to production per engineer, per day. This includes automated ones, but they're not the majority.

The only way to ship so frequently is to work in short iterations, which means:

- Breaking down work into smaller, stand-alone chunks. These might be small iterations that are shippable as they are, or logical steps that split large pieces of work into smaller ones, such as: scaffolding ⊠ first piece of business logic ⊠ other edge cases ⊠ cleanup
- Produce small-enough code changes/pull requests. These are easier to create, easier to review, faster to review, and therefore faster to ship
- Incentivise your teammates to do the same. Smaller changes mean not getting stuck for hours on a single code review

Long stretches of work

There are reasons to do longer iterations. Iterating fast is a great approach for making rapid, stable progress, but speedy iteration is not the answer to every type of problem. Here are some examples:

- Research. When researching a new technology, framework, or library to use, the aim is to share learnings, and recommend whether or not to adopt it. This research can be time-consuming, but shorter iterations often make little sense.
- Improving tooling or infrastructure. Improving the tools your team uses often takes research, and then prototyping or building a new approach. For example, deciding to containerize development is a large undertaking involving a longer research phase, a prototyping/proof-of-concept phase, and a rollout phase. It's usually sensible to do research and prototyping as longer stretches of work, and to iterate on the rollout.
- A major refactor. Some refactorings simply can't be done in chunks. An experienced engineer might make drastic but necessary changes to a complex refactoring task. Most large refactors can be split into smaller pieces to show more visible progress – *if* you intend this.
- A rewrite. Similar to a refactor, except that rewrites usually have specific goals like addressing a performance problem. While rewrites can be done in chunks, it's almost always faster if an engineer does the whole change in one go. *Just be aware of the risks of rewrites; they are very expensive and might not bring the benefits you want.*

A long stretch of work under the hood, tends to be a set of shorter iterations for which an engineer decides not to create individual pull requests. Perhaps it's because during these iterations, parts of the product are deliberately broken, or because the engineer thinks short iterations would break their flow. Whatever the reason, there's always a method to this type of work.

Long stretches of work mean less feedback. A big downside of long stretches of solo work is that there's much less feedback:

- If you don't raise individual pull requests for code reviews as you go, the final one will be so complex that most peers will struggle to give comprehensive feedback, and even miss major issues

- If you don't share the outline of each step, people won't be able to give feedback, point out what's been missed, or identify that you're on the wrong track. If this feedback arrives at the end, a lot of work may need to be redone

Doing long stretches of work makes sense when you don't need feedback. Such situations include building a new company, a new product, or a prototype that proves a point. However, most situations involving teamwork and consulting others like product folks, business stakeholders or customers, do involve feedback.

4. Your Team

Break down and estimate projects

As a senior engineer, your focus will often be at the project level. Ensure you understand what work needs to be done for the entire project, and that it is broken down to the necessary level.

This work overlaps with a tech lead's responsibilities, so we go in-depth on ways to do this in Part IV.

Document for others

When explaining something to a teammate, consider writing down the key message, so that when the next person asks, you can point to a note or diagram. If your team already has a wiki or internal knowledge base, then add documents to it. If one doesn't exist yet, create it and lead by example in adding to it.

We cover more on documentation in Part III: "Software Engineering."

Unblock your team

By now, you should be good at unblocking yourself by noticing when you're blocked and getting support to be unblocked. As a senior engineer, you should try to spot when colleagues are blocked and help unblock them.

Pair with others. When you see a colleague stuck on a task or a problem, offer to pair with them. If your team holds regular status update meetings like daily standups, this can be easy enough to identify. If an engineer has been hung up on the same problem space for several days, then they are probably stuck.

When helping to unblock someone, resist the temptation to walk them straight to the fix

– assuming you know it. For example, if it's a bug and you can see the exact line of code responsible, don't just point it out. Instead, help them learn how to unblock themselves. Try coaching them by asking questions that guide them to the offending line of code, perhaps after showing them a new debugging method.

Lead by example in resolving external blockers. Some blockers are external to your team, like waiting on another engineering team to review a planning document, or waiting on a platform team to make a change to their API. If members of your team have external blockers they cannot resolve themselves, consider injecting yourself into the situation and resolving it, and explaining the process for this.

Doing this will involve communicating with stakeholders and teams external to your own. If you have a network within the company – basically, that you know people on the blocking team – then resolving the issue will be easier. And if not, then reaching out could be the way to sort the blocker and meet new people, which could be the start of a good relationship.

Become better at thinking "outside the box"

Productive engineers can "think outside the box," and offer unconventional yet effective solutions to problems. For example, at Uber, the mobile platform team noticed that the number of memory leaks in the Android app kept slowly increasing and degrading the app experience. Their theory was that these leaks were degrading business metrics, but had no proof of this. Fixing these leaks one by one would have been challenging because most leaks were in feature code: and platform engineers would have struggled to understand the business logic. Even if they did and managed to fix leaks, new leaks would have surely crept back into the codebase.

An engineer on the platform team suggested a less conventional way to tackle this problem; why not turn the fixing of memory leaks into a competition and make it a way to educate engineers on how to spot, fix, and avoid memory leaks? This engineer rallied a few others, and key members across several platform teams decided to do something. This group identified a list of the "top" memory leaks, and hosted an external speaker for a tech talk to inspire and educate engineers on solving Android leaks. Also, the mobile platform team hosted office hours to help teams debug. To measure the impact on the product, all memory leak fixes were put behind a feature flag and rolled out in experiments to measure their impact on business metrics. It turned out the aggregate of these fixes did make a difference to the business!

How do you get better at "thinking outside the box?" Here are some approaches:

- **Broaden your experience**. Get hands-on with domains outside of your own. Much "outside the box" thinking simply applies a common approach from one domain to another. For example, if you are familiar with common – or uncommon – practices for building frontend applications, perhaps some could work for backend development!

- **Go deep**. Become an expert in a few areas, and dig deep into understanding them entirely. It could be a language, framework, or a codebase. Once you have a full understanding of how things work, "thinking outside the box" will simply be offering the solutions that experts tend to do.
- **Come up with more than one potential solution to a problem**. When facing a problem, you'll likely come up with one way of tackling it. For example, when an important bug on the backend needs fixing, the obvious solution is to simply make a code change which does this. However, when an obvious solution is to hand, challenge yourself to find alternatives. For example, could the bug be fixed by making configuration changes without shipping code? If shipping a code change to the backend, can the fix be verified in a canary release, first? Could the fix be shipped as an A/B test, to observe if it improves the metrics it should positively impact?
- **Meet and observe engineers who solve problems creatively**. Ask how they do it, where their ideas come from, and how they know an idea might work.

5. The Big Picture

Become product minded

The most productive engineers aren't always the fastest coders or those who best understand computer systems. What they frequently are is engineers who are good enough at engineering, but excellent at understanding the product, customers, and the business. This helps them find smart tradeoffs and build less complex engineering solutions faster, as well as offer solutions that solve the customer's real problem.

We go into more detail on this topic in Part I: "Thriving in different environments." To recap, become a product-minded engineer by considering these approaches:

- Understand how and why your company is successful
- Build a strong relationship with your product manager
- Engage in user research, customer support, and related activities
- Bring well-backed product suggestions to the table
- Offer product/engineering tradeoffs for projects you work on
- Seek frequent feedback from the product manager

Understand the business

As software engineers, we are not paid to write code. What we're really paid to do is to **solve problems for the business** – frequently by writing code. Understand what the business cares about, and how the software you build helps the company achieve its business goals. We offer approaches for this in Part V: "Understanding the business."

12

COLLABORATION AND TEAMWORK

When working alone, coding is almost always the most challenging part of building software. When in a team, working with colleagues can be equally challenging. Many things matter in a collaboration: ensuring the agreed approach is followed, agreeing which coding patterns to employ, how to do testing, which naming conventions to follow, and more.

And when you work as part of a larger group – for example, when several teams build a product – you need to ensure you're pulling in the same direction as everyone else. This could be making sure a new API endpoint which you expose, works the way another team expects when they use it. Or telling a team that they're blocking you because they need to make changes to their service.

Communication, collaboration, and teamwork are baseline expectations for well-rounded senior software engineers at most companies. In this chapter, we address the most common collaboration situations and dig into how to excel at them.

We cover:

1. Code reviews
2. Pairing
3. Mentoring
4. Giving feedback
5. Working with other engineering teams
6. Influencing others

1. Code Reviews

A good code review examines a change and how it fits into the codebase. It inspects the clarity of the title and description, and the "why" of the change. It covers the correctness of the code, test coverage, functionality changes, and confirms everything follows coding guidelines and best practices.

A good code review points out obvious improvements to make, such as hard-to-understand code, vague names, commented-out code, untested code, or overlooked edge cases. It also notes when too many changes are crammed into one review, suggests keeping code changes as single purpose, and breaking down the change into more focused parts.

Better code reviews also look at a change in the context of the broader system, and check that changes are easy to maintain. They might ask questions about the necessity of a change and how it impacts other parts of the system. They look at abstractions introduced and how these fit into existing software architecture. They note maintainability observations, such as complex logic which could be simplified, test structure, duplication, and other possible improvements.

The tone of the review

The tone of voice in speech and writing influences morale within teams. Reviews with a harsh tone create the impression of a hostile environment and can be seen as micro-aggressions. Opinionated language can make people defensive and spark heated discussions. In contrast, a professional, moderate, and positive tone can contribute to an inclusive environment in which people are open to constructive feedback, and code reviews trigger healthy, lively discussion.

Good code reviews ask open-ended questions, over making strong or opinionated statements. They offer alternatives and workarounds that might be superior. These reviews assume the reviewer may miss something, and so seek clarification before making a correction.

Better code reviews are also empathetic. They recognize that the person who wrote the code spent a lot of time and effort on the change. These code reviews applaud nice solutions and are generally positive in tone.

Requesting changes before approving

Good code reviews don't approve changes while unresolved questions remain. However, they make clear which questions or comments are non-blocking or unimportant, and often refer to these as "nitpicks" – or "nit." They are explicit when approving a change, such as giving a "LGTM" (looks good to me.) They are equally clear when requesting a follow-up, and use the code review tool or team convention to communicate this.

Better code reviews don't approve changes while there are important questions that need to be addressed. These reviews are firm on principle but flexible in practice; sometimes, comments will be addressed by the author in a follow-up code change. For urgent changes, reviewers try to make themselves available for quicker reviews.

Talking to each other

Good code reviews ask as many questions as needed, and if the revision does not address them, a good review will note this. When a conversation turns into a lengthy back and forth, reviewers reach out to the author in person, in order to not use up more time on the code review tool.

The presence of many comments suggests misunderstandings which are easier to identify and resolve by talking things through. Effective engineers know that in-person contact saves time and avoids hard feelings.

Nitpick comments

"Nitpick" refers to a comment about a minor change that doesn't significantly impact the quality of the pull request; such as an alternative name for a variable or function, claiming variable declarations should be in alphabetical order, or that indentation could be improved.

Good code reviews make it clear when querying a change is nitpicking and usually don't contain too many of these. Excessive nitpicking can be frustrating and a distraction from more important topics.

Better code reviews realize too many nitpicks are a sign of a lack of tooling, or standards. Reviewers who come across these frequently will look at solving the problem outside of the code review process. For example, most common nitpick comments can be solved via automated linting. Those that cannot, can usually be resolved by the team agreeing to certain standards and following them, and perhaps eventually automating them.

New joiners and code reviews

Good code reviews apply the same quality bar and approach to everyone, regardless of job title, level, or length of tenure. They have a moderate, supportive tone, and are clear which changes they request be made prior to approval.

Better code reviews pay attention to making new joiners' first few reviews a great experience. They're empathetic that a new colleague might not know all coding guidelines – especially unwritten, informal ones. Reviewers are also well aware a new joiner is still ramping up with the codebase, and won't be up to date on which conventions the code follows.

Better code reviews also put extra effort into explaining preferred approaches and offering pointers on where to learn more. They're positive in tone, celebrating the first few changes to the codebase a new joiner makes.

Cross-office, cross-timezone reviews

Good code reviews account for timezone differences in distributed workplaces, where possible. Reviewers aim to review code during overlapping office hours when both sides are at work. For reviews with many comments, reviewers offer to chat directly, or on a video call.

Better code reviewers notice when they repeatedly run into timezone issues and look for a systemic solution, beyond the code review framework. Solutions to this kind of problem are often not simple and could involve refactoring and creating new services/interfaces, or tooling improvements. Solving dependencies like this makes life easier for both teams and progress more efficient.

For more advice on how to do good code reviews, see:

- Code review developer guide[1] by Google
- Code review guidelines[2] by GitLab

2. Pairing

For a less experienced engineer, pairing is a fantastic way to get difficult things done, learn more, and level up. But pairing is equally useful when you're more experienced. You will inevitably face situations where you get stuck, and when pairing with someone can help unblock you. Getting stuck is especially common when working with a new codebase or technology. Pairing with experts in that codebase or technology on your team or a neighboring team can help you overcome issues quicker. You also learn from someone else and create stronger professional relationships.

Pairing can be pair programming, or simply pairing up to solve a problem.

Pair programming, when done in person, this usually involves sitting next to each other and working on the same screens, taking turns with the keyboard, or using two keyboards and two mouses. In a remote setting, it's usually done on a call and with screen sharing, or more commonly, with a collaborative editor which you can each input text into, in parallel.

Pairing up means sitting next to each other or whiteboarding when it's in person. When the pairing is remote, it usually happens on a call with tools like screen sharing or collaborative editing, as needed. I use the term 'pairing' for both activities, going forward. Pairing is the simplest, most efficient form of collaboration between two people to solve a problem.

Situations where pairing can be useful

For software engineers, these are the most common problems that pairing can solve:

- **Onboarding to a new team, codebase or system**. When new to a team or codebase, hitting the ground running is easier when pairing with someone who goes through

---

[1]https://google.github.io/eng-practices/review
[2]https://docs.gitlab.com/ee/development/code_review.html

key, must-know information, sets up things for the first time, identifies known problems, and so on. It is by far the most common use of pairing.

- **Implementing a feature**. When an engineer is unsure how to implement something, pairing up with a more experienced developer in the domain educates them on how to do it, and gives insight into the more experienced colleague's thinking.

- **Debugging a tricky bug**. There are times when you cannot figure out why something isn't working, even though you try debugging the issue in several ways. Pulling in another pair of eyes can be very useful, and the person you pull in doesn't even need to be more experienced. Often, just explaining what your suspicion is and all the things you've tried, can help identify a solution.

- **Planning and architecting**. Before starting to build a complex project involving coding for a few days, it's smart to talk through your approach with another developer. Sketch out your ideas, tell them approaches you considered but ruled out, and outline how you plan to build, including details about the technology, language, frameworks, and libraries you'll use, existing components you'll reuse or modify, the class structure you'll put in place, and how you'll test and validate your solution.

- **Confirming you're doing things correctly**. When you implement a functionality or feature, you might want to talk your approach through with someone and show them the decisions you made. As with debugging, they don't necessarily need to be more experienced.

- **Understanding how something works**. When working with a new system, service, or component that's difficult to understand, it can be faster and more educational to pair with someone who is an expert – or who built it! – for a rundown on how things work.

- **"Cheat" by observing and learning how another developer works**. A huge benefit of pairing is that you see how people really work. You talk with them and get a sense of how they think, see their IDE, which shortcuts they use, how they write and test code, and more. Pairing with someone for the first time was often an eye-opener for me, and I "borrowed" tools and approaches I liked.

Beyond transferring knowledge, pairing also helps build a personal relationship with the engineer you are pairing with. Regardless of who's more experienced, you'll learn from each other by solving a problem together.

Approaches when you're more experienced

When you are the more experienced in a pairing, there's ways to make the session more efficient:

- **Define the problem**. Ask your pair partner to explain the problem they need to solve. There will be times when an engineer comes to you seeking to pair but isn't clear about what they need help with. The session will be more focused if you start by clarifying this. Is it about getting a basic implementation of a feature running? Is it about helping them understand how a component works? Be specific, and don't start the session until the topic is clear.

- **Get a sense of the urgency.** There's a big difference between someone wanting to pair with you to mitigate an outage impacting thousands of customers per minute, versus pairing on a non-time-sensitive matter.
- **When there's time pressure, solve first while explaining, then follow up.** When time's of the essence, don't be afraid to take the lead. Explain what you are doing to solve the issue, and why, and how you verify that your changes work. Once the problem is fixed and there's no more time pressure, go back and teach the person how to do what you did.
- **Aim to teach your pair partner something, not just give answers.** It is a low-leverage task if you quickly solve your pair partner's problem as efficiently as possible, then return to your work. Why? Because the next time they have a similar problem, they still won't know how to solve it and will come back to you. However, pairing becomes a high-leverage activity when you spend time teaching a colleague how to solve the problem. Then, next time they have a similar issue, they can solve it themself.
- **Avoid immediately giving answers, even if you can.** When a developer says there's a bug they cannot fix that's driving them up the wall, and you know exactly what the problem is, it's tempting to tell them immediately. However, do you remember how you figured out the problem, and which approaches you used to rule out other causes? Coach them so they go through the same learning process you did!
- **Give the other person enough space to talk and type.** You're the more experienced one, and there's a good chance you can solve the problem faster. But don't forget that a great pairing session teaches the other person something. So, give your pair room to express their thoughts, and if you start coding up a solution, pass it to them to finish.
- **Try to learn something from your pair partner.** As the more experienced in this pairing session, you might think you'll teach and lead the session, and have nothing to learn. But this might not be the case! If you coach the other person and ask open-ended questions, they might surprise you with approaches you didn't think of, or experiences you didn't know they had.
- **Give compliments when due.** When your pair completes a part of the work well, give them positive feedback. It will mean a lot and reinforce the behavior.
- **It's natural to go off-track sometimes.** It's common to get sidetracked when pairing, and veer off from solving the main problem. This can especially happen when there's no time pressure. This is okay and natural. Pairing is part problem-solving, part learning from each other, and part getting to know someone better. And it's also fun; so if you get to explore an interesting area, do so.

Approaches when you're less experienced

Don't be afraid to ask someone if you can pair with them! While this feeling is more common for less experienced engineers, I've even observed senior engineers worry that asking a staff or principal engineer to pair with them would be an admission that they can't do the job. But it is not: asking to pair is a great way to get things done quicker and learn.

When you ask someone to pair with you, respect their time and be flexible if they have something urgent to finish. If this person is helpful, thank them for making time for pairing. Consider doing this in front of others. It's a nice thing to say, and can also encourage teammates to make their own pairing requests after seeing that you did it, and benefited from it.

Pairing is an approach that seems underutilized and undervalued, especially in remote working contexts. I suggest you use pairing to help others around you by offering to help a developer who seems stuck and pairing with colleagues who could unblock you.

3. Mentoring

As a senior engineer, there will be plenty of opportunities to mentor colleagues. It can also be a good idea to have more experienced mentors to learn from.

Informal mentorship

Mentorship doesn't need to be formal in order to be a valid learning experience. And mostly, it isn't formal. Mentoring happens naturally when developers work together and collaborate.

Code reviews, or working on a project in a team, are common cases of informal mentorship. There's no structure in place; just engineers working together, giving and getting feedback, and learning from each other.

Having informal, 1:1 sessions with other engineers, and simply talking about what keeps them occupied, can also be a kind of informal mentorship – even if doesn't feel like it! It's still informative and often provides ideas for different approaches to try.

Formal mentorship

The rarer form of mentoring for developers is the formal type. This is a setup where a more experienced colleague agrees to mentor a junior engineer, kicks things off, and holds meetings at a regular cadence, helping the mentee grow. But why bother with the effort of formal mentorship, if informal mentoring happens all the time? There are a few reasons:

- You might not be working with experienced enough people and want someone to learn more from.
- A more formal mentoring relationship can help you grow faster and in a more focused way, as you spend dedicated time on professional growth.

There are two places where it's easy to get started with formal, focused mentorship: more structured tech companies, and online communities. Some tech companies have mentorship programs, but these are rarely advertised. Uber, PayPal, and Amazon all have internal programs that make getting focused mentorship easy.

Online communities of mentors are also welcoming and easy to get started in. There's an ever-growing collection of sites: search "developers mentoring other developers," for resources.

I would have grown faster with formal mentorship during my developer years. For that reason, I made a point of setting up mentoring relationships between less experienced and more experienced engineers on my team, when I transitioned into engineering management. It was no surprise that junior engineers ended up growing faster, as a result. What I didn't predict was how much senior engineers benefited from formal mentorships with staff or principal engineers.

So, how do you set up formal mentorship? As with any project, a good kickoff helps to get everyone – in this case, the mentor and mentee – on the same page.

Kicking off mentoring: the introductory meeting

The best way to start formal mentorship is with a kickoff. I often suggest people approach potential mentors and say: "You're someone I look up to. Can I set up a time to talk about areas I'd like to grow in and how you could potentially help, as a mentor?" It's good to dedicate time to this, share some background, and see if you are each willing and able to commit to mentoring.

Come prepared with a list of topics to discuss at the kickoff, such as:

- **Background**. It's nice to share backgrounds to "break the ice."
- **"What's in it for me?"** What do you hope to gain from this relationship, and how would you like to grow? Ask the other person the same. The best mentorships are two-way relationships, from which both people get something.
- **Topics to cover**. What are you interested in? Where would you like to grow? Is there something more pressing to discuss?
- **Cadence**. How often to follow up, and when? Most developers catch up once every two weeks for between 30-60 minutes, at a time that works for both parties.
- **Communication between catch-ups**. Is the mentor open to random pings? What's their schedule like?
- **Short-term wins**. What is an area you'd like to grow in during the next month? Start by focusing on that.
- **Evaluating progress**. Which criteria would assess how effective the mentorship is?
- **Challenges**. It's nice to set these out. For example, it's okay to share with a would-be

mentor that you have no clue how mentoring works. Or your mentor might say they have a crazy next month and will be swamped by work.

Don't forget, if you're asked to be a mentor, it's always okay to say "no." As a mentee seeking a mentor, I had several potential mentors politely decline. For some, it was a lack of time, while others felt they didn't have the expertise I sought. Don't let rejection derail you; ask for any recommendations they might have for other potential mentors. You'll find a match sooner rather than later.

When you're the mentor

Here are approaches to being an effective mentor.

Be clear on expectations from the start. Clarify how much time you can commit, and also what you expect from the mentee. If you'd like them to have a list of things to talk through, say so. Keep it casual if that's your style, and tackle things as they come. Discuss this approach.

Listen to what the mentee has to say. This is the most important role of a mentor. Yes, a mentee wants actionable advice, but talking about what's going on and how they are feeling is just as important.

Try starting the conversation with questions they can engage with, like "what's on your mind?", "what are you struggling with?", "what are you working on?", "what are your goals for the week?" Listen for areas you might be able to help them with.

Avoid serving up answers on a silver platter. Being an efficient mentor is not about solving other people's problems. It's about helping them grow so they can solve their own problems. When mentoring, you want to delay sharing solutions for as long as possible.

Instead, ask questions, offer alternatives, and resist telling people what to do. Taking a patient, coaching-first approach empowers junior developers and accelerates their learning.

Discuss specific situations to dive deeper. These can be raised by the mentee, or be things the mentor notices. Topics may be communication, cultural issues, deep technical questions, code reviews, and much more.

Provide context and perspective for specific situations. You've probably been in the industry longer and know the situations the mentee is struggling with. If you work at the same company, you probably know how things work a lot better than they do. Reflecting on how you struggled with a challenging situation back in the day, can help the mentee feel less anxious when it happens to them.

Leverage your network to help your mentee. Mentors are usually better connected than mentees, which is powerful if you work at the same company. A mentor can put a mentee in touch with colleagues who can help. Making introductions and inviting others to spend some time with the mentee goes a long way.

If you work at different companies, there might still be opportunities to connect them with others or offer to help with an introduction.

Let your mentee know you're on their side. People who approach you for mentorship are not only looking for advice but also support. The less experienced they are, the more likely they feel like an impostor, and the more your support can help. Encouraging words go further than you'd think:

Every mentor I worked with ended our conversations with a "you got this!" or "you can do this!" or similar. Only words, but damn, they meant the world to me.

More tips on how to be a great mentor:

- **Aim to learn something new from your mentee**. Be curious about the problem they want to solve and understand their viewpoint. Even if you know the right answer, you might learn something new, and see a problem through a fresh lens.
- **Help mentees come up with multiple solutions to problems**. Also, help them articulate tradeoffs. Explain concepts over solutions and help mentees understand solutions are rarely either/or. This is especially true for technical topics and also holds for most non-technical problems.
- **Tailor your approach for technical vs non-technical topics**. Technical questions are usually easier to deal with. You can give mentorship by asking which avenues they've tried already, and guide them with questions towards something that works. Listening is key for non-technical topics like communication, conflict, etc.

When you're the mentee

With a cadence in place and regular catch-ups, how do you keep getting value from a mentorship? I'm a firm believer that as a mentee, you need to invest time and effort in mentorship to get value from it.

Set clear expectations at the start. Come prepared to catch up with your mentor and make good use of their time. Bring challenges, wins, and topics about which you'd like their input. Have a list of topics to discuss. As you get advice and ideas, commit to actions and follow them through. Let your mentor know how it goes.

It can be helpful to keep a running doc to share with your mentor. You can drop notes in it between catch-ups about topics to raise next time, such as:

- **Key events**. Tell the mentor briefly about significant things that have happened. Keep it short.

- **Reflections on action items / guidance / discussions, from last time**. If you did something based on a discussion at the previous meeting, share the results. This is useful for you both.
- **A recent challenge**. Describe a challenge, talk it through, and brainstorm an approach to solve it.
- **A recent success**. Describe a situation which went well and why it did, asking the mentor to share their opinion. Nine times out of ten, their feedback will make you re-evaluate how to handle things.

Long-term benefits of mentoring

Mentoring offers major long-term benefits for all parties. The software industry is surprisingly small, so the junior person you mentor today, will become more senior over time, and you may reconnect later in a different setting. If you were a supportive mentor, they'll likely remember this. Who knows how a good relationship may be beneficial at some point in future.

There's no one pattern for mentorship. For most people, it's a mix of informal knowledge sharing and regular catch-ups. Mentees often reach out to mentors with one-off questions. Some prefer in-person mentoring, and other mentorships don't go beyond the reviewing of code. Every mentoring relationship is different; what's important is that it works for both mentor and mentee.

4. Giving Feedback

As a senior engineer, you notice when other developers do great work, and when they could do better. In each case, you can choose to say something, or stay quiet. My take is that it's a wasted opportunity to not give feedback, as long as it's done respectfully and with the intent of helping the other person grow.

Better ways to give positive feedback

Giving positive feedback is easy, right? After all, it's complimenting someone. But there are ways to make feedback more effective:

- **Make it concrete**. Don't just say, "good job." Point out specifics such as, "I liked how you handled all four edge cases in your pull request and wrote tests for all of them. We need more of this kind of thoroughness; keep it up!"
- **Make it sincere**. Don't fall into the trap of saying nice things you don't mean. It can work in the short term, but over time people notice insincere feedback. If you think someone did an okay job, don't tell them it was excellent. Instead, find the detail that

was excellent and highlight it. Give constructive feedback on everything else.

Giving constructive or negative feedback

Ask questions before jumping in with feedback. This is especially true if you're unfamiliar with the other person's work, or they didn't explicitly ask for feedback.

For example, say you notice a pull request from a new joiner is missing unit tests, but the guidelines mandate them. You could jump in and give feedback on the missing tests. However, a better strategy might be to ask: "have you thought about how to test this change?"

Framing it as a question gives them the opportunity to share more context, and also to correct the omission. In the above case, the person might respond in a few ways:

- "Of course. I'm aware we usually do tests, but this is an urgent fix to resolve an outage. The tests are coming in the next pull request!"
- "Wow, I totally forgot. Thanks a lot for asking. Let me do it right now, and I'll make sure to not miss them next time."
- "Tests? What tests? I didn't know you did that here?"

Notice the absence of negative sentiment in these responses. That's the beauty of asking questions before giving feedback.

Deliver corrective feedback empathetically. Share your observations, then ask questions to guide them to the right conclusion. Once they have it, give positive reinforcement.

The more trust you have with the person receiving your feedback, the more "raw" you can be without offending them. Use your judgment about what's appropriate. Don't forget, the goal of feedback is to help the other person improve. As long as you offer feedback that's encouraging and not discouraging, you help them grow.

Being good at giving feedback is a massive advantage. The single best resource that helped me in this area was these two books:

- "Radical Candor" by Kim Scott
- "Crucial Conversations" by Joseph Grenny, Ron McMillan, Al Switzler and Kerry Patterson

5. Working With Other Engineering Teams

There are many reasons why you might work with another engineering team, such as:

- Trying to understand code written by – or last modified by – an engineer on another

team
- Modifying parts of the code owned by another team
- Having questions about how to use a service or component owned by another team
- Planning modifications to code which another team owns, and wanting to follow conventions
- Another team needs to unblock your work on a system they own

If your workplace has an internal open source model – meaning you have access to most of the code and can create pull requests for it – then engineers on another team may block your changes when you make a pull request. This is usually because the team owns that part of the code, so it's wise to consult them before making changes – especially for large teams.

At small companies with a handful of engineers, it's easy enough to get to know developers and find out what they do. For example, in a workplace with six engineers, including yourself, you'll know Bob and Suzy are backend, Sam and Kate are web, and Tom is mobile, so you know who to approach for questions. The same goes for a company with five engineering teams: Platform and Core are mostly backend, while Web Core, Customer Support, and Customer Experience are a mix of web, mobile and backend engineers.

However, at companies with more than a dozen engineering teams, it becomes tricky to figure out which ones your team has relationships with. Often, the best pointer for whom to talk to is checking who changed a relevant line of code last time, and reaching out to them.

Draw a map of teams

Draw up a map of engineering teams connected to your team, and which ones your team has connections with. List:

- Engineering teams your team depends on. Teams whose APIs or services your team uses
- Engineering teams that depend on your team. Tip: look through outages that impacted your team, when the change was made by another team. There's a good chance that is a dependent team
- Teams building similar features with potential for functionality overlap, especially for customers
- Teams on the same screen as your team's features, if your team owns user interfaces
- Infrastructure teams your team uses, even indirectly

Once you have the map, show your peers and managers to find out if there's any blanks.

Introduce yourself to other teams

Make yourself known to engineering teams with whom you have a connection. Use the map of teams connected to your own, to meet at least someone on each. You may already be working with some of these teams. But if not, here's a suggestion; set up a short introduction meeting with an experienced engineer or the team manager. Tell them your goal is to understand a bit more about their team, and to put a face to the name. If there's relevant documentation, read it beforehand.

At the meeting, introduce yourself and share briefly what your team does and ask the other person about theirs. How long have they worked there, what's their role on the team, what does the team do, which technologies do they use, and what are their challenges?

The goal of an introductory meeting is two-fold:

- Gather information about a team that can speed up your work, later. For example, when planning to build a new feature, you may realize this other team will need to make a change in their system. You could immediately talk to the engineer you know on that team about this.
- Build a personal connection. The larger an organization, the more that personal connections with other teams matter.

Through an introductory meeting, you learn more about another engineering team, which is always interesting! There's a good chance you'll learn something new, or get inspired to try a different engineering approach that they use.

6. Influencing Others

As a senior engineer, your "influence" within the team and company matters. The more respected, well-known, or influential you are within a group, the more your voice is heard, and the easier it is to guide things in what you believe is the right direction.

So, how can you become more influential as an engineer? Here are some approaches.

Ship great work

What "great" looks like depends on your environment. Ensure your work has the right balance of quality and speed. At startups, "great" might lean towards shipping things quickly, while at larger companies, "great" might mean well-tested, clean code, or code changes which are straightforward to review, or maintainable solutions.

Get familiar with what "great" means in your engineering organization, and gather regular feedback from peers and managers for a sense of how your work matches up. When you build a reputation as someone who does great work, others will trust you.

Get to know other people

Specifically, people outside the engineering organization. Try to make time to break out of your engineering bubble. Talk with product people, colleagues in design, data science, other non-engineering functions, and on the business side.

Do this with the aim of understanding more about the product direction and the business strategy. Consider setting up a regular 1:1 with your product manager – say, once a month – to get a better understanding of what product does, why, and how you can help.

Join calls with engineers on other teams whom you work with. When working in a distributed environment or with remote teams, the chances are that most work is done via emails, chat, documents, and coding.

Don't keep things fully asynchronous; consider hopping on a video call, to talk "face to face" with colleagues you collaborate with. Make an excuse to talk with someone you work with asynchronously. During the call, try to get to know them better. How long have they been in their team? What other stuff do they work on? What's going on in their part of the world?

There are several benefits of talking with people, as opposed to just focusing on the work. First, you'll each get a feel for who's behind those emails and pull requests. Second, you'll gather a lot more context about how they work. Finally, you might make an unexpected connection, via similar views, personal interests, or something else.

Take part in cross-functional projects

Get involved in RFCs / design docs / cross-team planning. If your company utilizes RFCs, design docs, or ADRs, start reading other teams' plans, and get involved when your expertise can help.

When I joined Uber, a new world opened to me, thanks to its transparent RFC culture. I learned a lot about how other teams worked, just from reading their RFCs, and forged connections with teams by getting in touch with them via an RFC, when I had the expertise and interest to contribute. Your influence and your network are connected; there are few more fun ways to grow your network than by contributing to interesting planning docs, learning something new, and helping fellow engineers along the way.

Take part in cross-team projects. If the only people you collaborate with are teammates, then your influence will be limited to your team. To build trust with people beyond your team, work and build relationships while expanding your understanding. When you're comfortable on your team, seek opportunities to get involved in projects with different engineering teams and non-engineering teams.

I've found that one of the best ways to network is by not "networking" at all. Instead, just work on a shared problem. For example, at Uber, some of my strongest connections were built by working on projects which involved talking daily with other engineers, managers, product managers, or designers, to get something important done.

'Promote' your work – without boasting

Make sure your peers and manager know when you do great work. I'm not suggesting to be pushy about this. However, if you have team meetings where people showcase what they do, then why not present your progress and wins, too? If your team presents at a larger meeting, volunteer to talk about areas you've worked on.

Keep track of work you do and share it with your manager, every now and then, via a format like the work log we cover in the "Owning your career" chapter.

Aim to build a strong personal brand. Leonard Welter is a product manager at Bloomberg. He observed that engineers have "personal brands." Here's his advice:

> "The concept of 'building a personal brand' can be seen as a negative type of politics, especially when it reverts to style over substance. However, it is important to reflect on how you are perceived in the organization. Thinking about your 'brand' is again something I wish someone took me through, early in my career. Is your 'brand' someone who is seen as getting things done? Or someone who has strong opinions, but rarely rolls their sleeves up? Results are not the only things that matter when it comes to this kind of brand."

13

SOFTWARE ENGINEERING

Software engineering starts with coding and ends with practices which guarantee the long-term maintainability and extensibility of the systems you build. In this chapter, we cover areas in which well-rounded, senior engineers are competent:

1. Languages, platforms, and domains
2. Debugging
3. Tech debt
4. Documentation
5. Scaling best practices across a team

1. Languages, Platforms, and Domains

It's expected that a well-rounded senior engineer has a solid grasp of a few programming languages and a few platforms – platforms like frontend, backend, iOS, Android, native desktop, embedded, and so on –, and mastery of at least one. We cover more on how to master a language in Part II: "Software Development."

However, an effective engineer doesn't stop at being proficient in a few technologies; they continue to broaden their knowledge of frameworks, languages, and platforms.

When you know a programming language, learning another one is much easier. This is because most languages are pretty similar – at least on the surface. For example, if you know JavaScript, then learning TypeScript begins easily enough. Likewise, knowing Swift means you can understand a lot of Java, Kotlin, or C#, just by reading them.

Of course, each language has its own syntax, idiosyncrasies, strengths, and weaknesses. You discover all these details by using the language and comparing it to others you already know, well enough.

Learn an imperative, a declarative, and a functional language in depth

There are three distinct types of programming languages:

1. **Imperative**: the most common type of programming language, wherein the computer

is given step-by-step instructions on what to do, as a set of commands. For example: "If X, then do this. Or else, do that." C, C++, Go, Java, JavaScript, Swift, PHP, Python, Ruby, Rust, TypeScript, and most object-oriented languages are imperatives.

2. **Declarative** programming specifies the expected outcome of the program but doesn't give instructions on how to achieve this. SQL, HTML, and Prolog languages are examples.

3. **Functional** languages are a subset of declarative languages that are distinct enough to merit their own category. These treat functions as first-class, meaning functions can be passed as arguments to other functions, or returned as values. Examples include Haskell, Lisp, Erlang, Elixir, and F#. Functional languages tend to provide immutable states and pure functions with no side effects.

Your first – or even second – programming language is most likely an imperative one. Learning additional imperative languages is useful, but picking a different type of language will help you grow more as a professional.

Imperative, declarative, and functional languages each require different ways of thinking. It can be challenging to switch from an imperative language to a functional or declarative one, but you expand your understanding and "toolkit" by doing so.

For example, functional programming is widely applied within imperative languages, because following a functional model guarantees an immutable state. A good case is the Reactive programming pattern[1], which takes functional programming ideas and offers a more functional pattern to languages like Java (RxJava), Swift (RxSwift), C# (Rx.NET), Scala (RxScala) and others[2].

After you master a language from each category, you will have little trouble picking up more languages. This is because there are more fundamental differences between an imperative and a functional language like Go and Elixir, than between two imperative or two functional languages, such as Go and Ruby, or Elixir and Haskell.

Get familiar with software development platforms

It's common for a software engineer to specialize in a platform, like:

- Backend
- Frontend
- Mobile
- Embedded platforms

---

[1] https://reactivex.io
[2] https://reactivex.io/languages.html

When your team is building a new feature or solving a problem, there's a good chance work will take place across platforms. For example, shipping a new payment flow will surely mean changes on the backend, the frontend, and perhaps even the mobile side. Debugging in the mobile app will mean investigating whether the issue derives from the mobile business logic, the backend, or perhaps at the intersection of backend APIs and the mobile business logic parsing the API response.

If you have no idea what happens on neighboring stacks, you'll have trouble debugging more complex, full-stack issues, and leading projects to build and ship full-stack features.

Become more full stack

"Full stack engineering" is increasingly a baseline expectation of senior engineers across the tech industry. This is because product folks and business stakeholders don't really care about the distinction between embedded, backend, and frontend/web. From their point of view, the distinction is an engineering decision.

A well-rounded senior engineer can take any problem and figure out how to break it down between different platforms. To do this, expertise in your domain is needed, along with enough competence in other domains.

So, how do you build this understanding? There are plenty of approaches:

- **Get access to other platforms' codebases**. For example, if the team you work on owns mobile, web, and backend codebases, then get access to those which aren't your "primary" platforms. If you're a backend engineer, check out the web and mobile codebases and set them up for compiling, running tests, and deploying them locally on your machine.
- **Read code reviews by team members on other platforms**. Follow along with code reviews, by reviewing those on other platforms, or by asking to be added as a non-blocking reviewer. Reading code is much easier than writing it, and most code changes are related to business logic, so you should have little trouble understanding the intentions of changes. You might even be able to spot business logic issues or missing business logic test cases!
- **Volunteer for small tasks on the other platform**. The best way to get more familiar with another platform is to work with it. Pick up a non-urgent, unimportant task you can complete at your own pace. Ask advice from other engineers on the team.
- **Pair with an engineer working on another stack**. Pair programming is an efficient way to pick up a new stack. Ask to pair with someone who is more experienced on the stack you'd like to pick up; you'll speed up the learning process. You could start by shadowing this person – and as you become more hands-on, ask to lead the session and for the other person to give feedback on your approach.
- **Do an "exchange month" of working on another platform**. An even better way to

learn more intensively is to switch platforms for a period of time. This could be a few weeks, or months. The downside is that your velocity will drop in the short term, as you'll be learning the basics of another platform. However, in the mid to long term, your velocity will increase as you'll have the expertise and tools to unblock yourself.

AI helpers can make the transition quicker

AI helpers can aid the transition between languages. With tools like ChatGPT, Bard, GitHub Copilot, and other AI assistants, it's much easier to pick up new programming languages. These assistants can do things, like:

- Translate a piece of code from one language to another
- Summarize how functions and variables are declared in a language
- Summarize differences between two languages

Keep in mind that many AI assistants suffer from hallucination: they sometimes make up things that aren't true. Therefore, it's necessary to verify their output. But for the purpose of getting familiar with a new language, AI assistants are helpful and can speed up the learning process.

2. Debugging

The difference between a senior and a non-senior engineer is pretty clear in debugging and tracking down difficult bugs. More experienced engineers tend to debug faster and pinpoint the root causes of more challenging problems – seemingly with ease. They also have a better sense of where the issue might come from, and where to get started in debugging and resolving it. How do they do this?

Part of it is practice and expertise. The longer you write code, the more often you come across unexpected edge cases and bugs, and so you start to build a "toolkit" of the potential root causes of problems.

Over time, you also expand your debugging toolkit. In Part II: "Software development," we touch on how to get better at debugging, covering:

- Get to know your debugging tools
- Know how to debug without tools
- Familiarize yourself with advanced debugging tools

The ability to debug efficiently tends to set experienced and less experienced engineers apart. Below are more approaches for improving at debugging.

Know which dashboards and logging systems to look at

Especially at larger tech companies, your ability to debug production issues is heavily dependent on knowing where to find production logs and production metrics, and how to query these metrics. Even so, it usually takes months for senior engineers to appreciate the importance of locating these systems.

Finding the right dashboards and logging portals can be especially challenging at companies where teams own many services, and each uses different ways of logging things, recording information in various systems, or using different logging formats.

Upon joining a company, make it a priority to learn where the production logs are stored, and where to find systems' health dashboards. These might be living in systems like Datadog, Sentry, Splunk, New Relic, or Sumo Logic. Or within in-house systems built on top of the likes of Prometheus, Clickhouse, Grafana, or other custom solutions. And they might be in a mix of places. Figure out where they are, get access, and learn how to query them. Do this for systems your team owns, and also related systems which you interact with.

Make debugging easier for others

As a senior engineer, you should know which dashboards and logging systems to look at. But if they are not in place, then you're in a position to put them in place and make them easy to use.

We cover more on this topic in Part V: "Reliable Systems."

Understand the codebase

Understand smaller codebases inside out. When working with a decent-sized codebase – typically no larger than 100,000 lines and written by no more than 20 people – there's no excuse for not understanding *exactly* where everything is located. Look through the structure of the codebase, read a lot of code, and map out how the different parts of the code are connected.

Draw up architecture diagrams based on reading the code, and ask people on your team to confirm if your understanding is correct. Get to the point where you know which part of the code owns what functionality.

With large codebases, it's good to understand their structure and how to find relevant parts. At larger companies, codebases are common with well over 1M lines built by hundreds of engineers. It's unrealistic to understand a codebase of this size deeply, but it is reasonable to aim for a *broad* understanding so you can go deep into the parts of it you need to work on.

At companies that use monorepos, get a sense of their structure and what different parts of the monorepo are responsible for. How are various parts of the system built? How are tests run?

At companies using standalone repositories, seek access to these. Aim to understand how systems work at a high level relating to your team. It's a good exercise to check some of these out, build them, run tests, and run the service or feature locally.

Find out how to search the whole codebase, and learn useful shortcuts. Most companies have some kind of "global code search." This might be a custom, in-house solution, or a vendor like GitHub's code search, or Sourcegraph. Find out how to use the global code search tool and which features it supports. For example, how can you search a specific folder of the code? How can you search for test cases? What about searching only the codebase that your team owns?

Even at large companies where engineers can access most of the codebase, some parts of the codebase may be off-limits. This is often for compliance, regulatory, or confidentiality reasons. In most cases, it should make no real difference to your day-to-day work. But if it slows you down, you could ask for access.

Know enough about the infrastructure

Some production issues are caused by infrastructure problems. Figure out how services are deployed into production, how secrets are stored, and how certificates are set up. Look into how the infrastructure is managed, and where infrastructure configurations are stored.

If you work at a company with a dedicated infrastructure team, it can be tempting to skip the learning process and turn to the infra team, when you suspect an infrastructure issue. However, this approach will ultimately slow you down. Besides, learning how infrastructure works under the hood is not only interesting in itself; this depth of understanding is table stakes for well-rounded senior engineers.

Learn through outages

Debug outages as they happen and reread old outage investigations. A great way to improve your debugging skills is to debug when it *really* matters, as outages happen. If your team has an outage, offer to help investigate and find what caused it so that the cause can be mitigated.

Debugging outages requires learning to access and analyze production logs, locating the code responsible for certain business logic, making changes to the code, validating changes, and rolling them out. All of this happens in urgent situations when timely action matters.

There are ways to improve debugging skills for outages other than waiting for a bug to strike your system. Check out postmortems of former outages, if your company publishes them.

As you read, try to "debug" by locating the logs which pinpoint issues, and finding the code behind the outage. Researching historical outages is a great way to learn about new dashboards and systems you don't know well, and to discover new outage mitigation steps.

3. Tech Debt

"Tech debt" is a term that experienced software engineers are all too familiar with. It describes the incremental cost of software development on systems over time. Tech debt is what happens when code builds up and makes things more complex.

The characteristics of tech debt are similar to taking on a loan. Used smartly, debt can accelerate progress. But when used poorly, it can become expensive to maintain. And bankruptcy via tech debt is real: it is the point at which it's cheaper to delete and rewrite an entire codebase than to continue maintaining and fixing it.

Here are typical phases of the relationship between tech debt and software engineers/engineering organizations:

- Unawareness. When a software engineer starts to build software, there's a period – usually short – when they're not aware that tech debt exists.
- Denial. As an early-career engineer, it's easy to assume you could never be the cause of tech debt, or that tech debt which you notice is not a big deal, and so it won't hurt to ignore it.
- Acceptance. Soon enough, most engineers realize that writing code and introducing tech debt often go hand in hand, especially when there's insufficient time to do things "properly." The better a company's engineering culture, the better engineers and engineering leaders are at acknowledging tech debt.

While tech debt is a given, it accumulates much slower when certain healthy engineering practices are followed for maintainability and ease of code modification. Such practices include writing readable code, testing, code reviews, CI/CD, documentation, sane architecture decisions, and more.

Paying down tech debt

With small tech debt, just fix it as you go. Follow the scouting rule of leaving a place – in this case, a codebase instead of a campsite – cleaner than you found it.

For larger pieces of tech debt, take an inventory and quantify the impact it makes and the effort needed to remove it. When there's lots of tech debt, you won't be able to tackle it all.

Without data about larger pieces of tech debt, it's hard to make good decisions on how to deal with it. If it includes things that would take weeks or months to fix, a team must prioritize.

How does the value of paying off tech debt compare to doing work with a business-facing impact?

To tackle tech debt purposefully, propose projects with clear impacts. Are there pieces of tech debt begging to be resolved because their impact is so obvious? Reliability, cost savings, faster development cycles, and fewer bugs, are common types of impact I've seen people cite in pitches to remove larger tech debt, or get migration projects done.

For example, take duplication of logic as a form of tech debt, with parts of the code copy-pasted to different places. What would be the impact of moving duplicated code to a shared library, and at what cost? The impact will be far greater on a codebase that's frequently used. On the other hand, a soon-to-be deprecated codebase might mean a large effort for small reward.

Or take the example of slow build times. If a build is run frequently by many engineers, then the impact of paying off tech debt could be large. Just multiply the time wasted per build by the number of times an engineer runs this build per day, times the number of engineers doing this.

Couple tech debt removal with high-impact projects. Here's the secret of being an engineer who's seen as productive, and who also removes tech debt: not asking permission. Instead of seeking approval to remove tech debt, productive engineers just bundle tech debt-removal with a high-impact project and remove it as part of that project.

The highest priority projects are usually ambitious, with high visibility. And to ship them, systems with the most tech debt are frequently touched. If you need to touch a system that is heavy with tech debt, it means your work will be slower. Therefore, if you're spending time making changes to systems laden with tech debt, it's sensible to make the case for reducing tech debt while you're at it.

Reduce tech debt accumulation

Instead of spending time and energy on paying down tech debt, it's sensible to spend much less time and energy in preventing – or slowing – the accumulation of tech debt in the first place. Here are some practices for this:

- **Write code that's easy to read**. Code which is easier to read is easier to understand. If understandable code is the target, it's less likely engineers who touch it later will add "hacks" to work around parts they don't understand.
- **Make time to clean up the code**. Some tech debt makes its way into code because redundant things are not cleaned up. Remove concluded experiments, unused feature flags, code paths no longer executed, and unfinished code additions.
- **Build systems with extensibility in mind**. A lot of tech debt is introduced when a system needs to be extended – like adding a new use case – but when there's little time

for this. Try to cater for future use cases when building the system and create obvious ways to extend your solution. This is where using well-understood design patterns like the Strategy pattern, Decorator pattern, or Factory pattern is helpful, as well as things like configuration files to specify behavior.

- **Note tech debt and don't seek permission to remove small pieces**. As you work in the codebase, you'll notice things that slow you down. Make a note, and tackle them when you have time.

"Just enough" tech debt

Is there such a thing as too little tech debt? If you pay off enough tech debt, you will at some point realize that yes, there is. It goes by the name of "premature optimization" – and can slow down teams and companies at critical times.

Take the example of a startup. Upon launch, speed and fast iteration are key to survival and winning. At this time, do you worry about clean APIs and nice data models, or just dump everything in an unstructured JSON, which any developer can modify? The startups I've worked at which grew to be successful, all had a tech debt-heavy approach during the early days.

Ride-sharing app Uber was one such startup. When I joined, there was a lot of leftover, early tech debt, and short-term decisions haunted parts of the codebase. But that tech debt served its purpose, as it allowed Uber to move fast when speed mattered most in getting a product-market fit. Afterward, Uber invested in cleaning it up.

Tech debt is something you want to have in early-stage projects, for throwaway prototypes, minimum viable products (MVPs), and when validating a startup's business model. Tech debt can be fixed by throwing time and developers at it later like Uber did. Most late-stage startups that are growing fast are usually busy paying off early tech debt on the side – because by this later stage, these startups usually have more people – and time! – to address this issue. Likewise, if a team that owns a mature product is not keeping tech debt in check by investing here and there in keeping it at bay, then something is also probably off.

Pragmatic engineers don't see tech debt as a bad thing; they see it as a tradeoff between speed and quality. They see it as the characteristic of a system. They put tech debt in the context of a project's goals and don't try to pay off more than needed. They also keep track of the debt and step in to reduce it before it mounts up – and being creative where needed.

4. Documentation

"Documentation" can refer to a few areas, and not all types of documentation are relevant for every project. Here's a list of common types of documentation which engineers write, and when it's helpful to write and maintain them.

Design documents/request for comment documents

These provide a high-level view of a system. They might contain diagrams and the reasoning behind technology choices and tradeoffs.

Design documents have the most value when written before coding starts, and when circulated for feedback, as the goals of these documents are to help build the right thing, and to surface misunderstandings early.

Test plans, rollout plans, migration plans

When project planning is complete, there are documents which help ensure the system will be of high quality, such as:

- **Test plan**: how will the system be tested? Which edge cases are essential to exercise? Will these tests be one-off, manual, or automated? If there is a list of manual tests – often called "sanity tests" – then the list will need to be kept updated.
- **Rollout plan**: how will the system be rolled out? Which feature flags will be used, how will the experiment run, and to which regions or user cohorts will it roll out? This document usually needs input from product or data science folks.
- **Migration plan**: when migrating from one system to another, what is the approach? How will it be validated that the new system works correctly before traffic is moved to it? What are the phases of the migration?

There's plenty of value in writing these documents at the start of a project. There's usually little value in maintaining them once the project has been rolled out, or a migration finished.

Interface and integration documentation

API or interface documentation. When developing an API or interface for use by other software engineers, this documentation explains things like:

- How to use the API
- The list of endpoints, the input each one expects, expected outputs
- Error codes and messages returned
- Code sample on using the API

API documentation is something you'll want to keep up to date when changing parts of the code. Explore ways to do this automatically – for example, generating the documentation using comments.

SDK (software development kit) documentation and integration or plugin documentation, are similar to API documentation, as these guides help other teams use your SDK, integration, or plugins.

Release notes

This practice seems unfashionable, but some engineering teams still compile release notes for each major release. Writing release notes is usually straightforward, and doesn't take long. Just summarize which customers will notice the impact of your work, or collate the impacts of all features shipped. This can make it much easier to update API, SDK, and integration documentation.

Release notes offer a great way to reflect on the work. They're also an excellent reference to share with stakeholders such as other engineering teams, or even non-technical teams.

Onboarding documentation

How can new engineers learn how a system works which your team owns? The answer is good onboarding documentation, which includes:

- A high-level overview of how the system fits into the bigger picture: its responsibility, other systems it interacts with, etc.
- How to modify the system: checking code, how to make changes.
- How to test and validate changes by running tests, or inspecting certain parts.
- How to deploy it to production, deployments which might be automatic via CI/CD.
- How to monitor the production system
- How alerting works and how to tweak it, if needed
- Tips on how to debug the system in case of production incidents

Onboarding documentation is very valuable for new joiners, and sometimes for existing team members, too! Unfortunately, there's usually little incentive to write or maintain it, especially if no new engineer is joining the team.

I suggest investing in putting this documentation together, for when a new colleague joins, and updating it for each new joiner. Why not ask the new recruit to edit the documentation, fix incorrect details, and add missing parts, as a task near the end of their onboarding?

A team "handbook"

How does the team operate? How does the team's mission tie into business objectives? A team handbook answers these questions and also covers areas like:

- How work gets prioritized
- How team members go about raising issues, and picking up the next thing to work on

- Processes the team uses
- Team values

If your team does not yet have a handbook, talk with the lead or manager, and suggest putting one together. If you have enough trust with the team, you could simply start such a handbook, and ask others for input.

Oncall runbook documentation

What are the steps to take when the oncall engineer is paged with an alert from a system? Where can they find relevant dashboards and logs? Which dependencies does this system have on other systems? Good oncall runbooks answer these questions.

User manuals and guides

If the software you build has end users working with it, then they need manuals that explain how it works. They will need different programming languages to describe the system, while screenshots and visual cues will be very useful.

Even if these guides already exist, ensure to flag when you change parts of the system that change its behavior for users. If possible, update the user guide personally; after all, you made the change and understand it best!

Documentation is a high-leverage activity

Writing documentation can be time-consuming at first, but it's a very high-leverage activity. Also, once a document is written, keeping it up to date is more straightforward. Good documentation, such as for onboarding, can help greatly reduce tech debt by providing education on how systems work.

Scaling Best Practices Across the Team

As a senior engineer, strive to deliver quality work and help your team do the same. An obvious way to do this is with best practices.

What is a "best practice?" It's a proven engineering approach which is very effective in the environment you work in. Individuals and teams following best practices usually get things done quicker, with fewer defects, and produce more easily maintainable code.

However, the term can be misleading as each team and company is different in its skillsets and dynamics. A practice which works very nicely for one team might be less efficient for another.

"Software engineering practices" is a term I suggest as an alternative to "best practices."

Tried-and-tested software engineering practices have applications for several parts of the software engineering process, such as:

- **A written planning process**. Before starting to code non-trivial projects, a plan is written and circulated for feedback. This plan could be a Request for Comment (RFC,) an Engineering Requirements Document (EDD,) a Design Doc, or an Architectural Decision Record (ADR.)
- **Automated testing**. The writing of unit, integration, end-to-end, performance, load, or other types of tests. This approach usually increases quality and maintainability, often resulting in quicker shipping of software by flagging regressions more rapidly. *We cover more on testing in the next chapter.*
- **Test-driven development**. A subset of automated testing where tests are written before the code is.
- **Code reviews**. Other engineers review and sign off code before it's committed.
- **Post-commit code reviews**. Code reviews are done after commits are made. This approach typically increases iteration speed, while keeping some code reviews in place. A tradeoff is that more regressions can make their way to production. This practice works best with very small or highly experienced teams.
- **Testing environments**. Shipping code to intermediary environments for further testing, not straight to production. The upside is higher confidence that the code is correct. The downside is it takes longer to ship things to production and maintaining testing environments is more work.
- **Staged rollouts**. Releasing new features in stages and then gathering feedback, instead of releasing them to customers all at once. Feature flags, experimentation, and A/B testing are all tools for staged rollouts. *We cover more details on these in Part IV: "Shipping to Production."*
- **Testing in production safely**. Shipping to production, instead of using testing environments and employing safe methods of testing, utilizing things like tenancies, feature flags or staged rollouts.

Which practices should you put in place for your team? Actually, this is the wrong question to start with. Instead, ask what the biggest challenges are to shipping things on your team.

Is the challenge that too many bugs make it to production? Consider whether practices like TDD, testing environments, or testing in production, would help. Is it that code reviews take a long time? Consider whether a practice could help with this: for example, dedicating time for reviews, fewer reviews, smaller code changes, or something else.

The more familiar you are with engineering practices, the more you can recognize when a specific practice can help your team. One way to get familiar is by learning them. Another way is to get input from people with first-hand experience. The most educational way of all is to acquire personal experience by trying them out!

14

TESTING

Testing is a healthy software engineering practice and a sizable enough topic to merit its own chapter in this book.

How do you ensure a piece of software works as expected? You test it. Broadly speaking, there are three ways:

- Manually verify all scenarios and edge cases. For example, manually testing use cases as part of declaring a feature complete
- Automatically verify all scenarios and edge cases. For example, run these tests as part of the continuous integration/continuous deployment pipeline
- Monitor how the software behaves in production and detect malfunctions. When a gap is found, teams build automated tests and add them to the CI/CD system

Testing is a core part of any tech company's engineering culture. The question is not whether an engineering team tests; it is how do they test, and which tests are used.

When it comes to automated tests, there's a variety of ways to create them. In this chapter, we cover:

1. Unit tests
2. Integration tests
3. UI tests – aka end-to-end tests
4. Mental models for automated testing
5. Specialized tests
6. Testing in production
7. Benefits and drawbacks of automated testing

1. Unit Tests

The simplest of all automated tests. These test an isolated component, aka the "unit". Most mobile unit tests exercise a class, a method, or a behavior of a class.

As the codebase grows, unit testing classes with many dependencies becomes challenging and slow, unless you introduce dependency injection to the codebase. Doing this may seem an overhead at first, but is worthwhile because it makes the codebase unit testable. It also makes class dependencies explicit and the application's architecture more modular.

The larger the codebase, the more important it is for unit testing to have these characteristics:

- **Fast**. Are the tests quick to execute, and require as little setup as possible? Do they use lightweight mocks over expensive-to-instantiate implementations?
- **Reliable**. Are the tests deterministic and non-flaky? Do they depend on no local configuration or regional settings to run in the same way?
- **Small**. Are tests atomic, as in they test as little as possible? Focused tests are fast and easy to debug, which should keep them reliable.

There is a compounding benefit of unit testing code, which grows as the system and its development team do. The tests help validate code changes, force you to separate concerns, and help to document the code's behavior. They also help reduce accidental regressions in the codebase and act as a safety net when refactoring parts of it.

The senior engineer who wrote zero unit tests

I once worked on a team where one of the most senior developers didn't believe in writing unit tests. Let's call them "Sam." He was a C++ wizard, who had worked in the video games industry for a decade and had shipped major, hit titles, and was responsible for coding the most complex parts of game engines. Sam insisted his code almost never had bugs, and even when it did, the bugs were undetectable by unit tests. On that basis, Sam declared unit tests of any kind a waste of time, and that he was better employed on more productive tasks.

This caused our team to split in two; people who wrote unit tests, and those who sided with Sam in believing unit tests were not worth the trouble.

Things went fine until Sam carried out a major refactoring of the codebase. When he checked in the changes, all hell broke loose. The app started breaking everywhere and it took two days to fix all the breakages. Sam claimed these breakages were inevitable and not his fault; indeed, his code changes had *surfaced* existing issues. Despite this, more of us were skeptical about his "*no bugs from me*" claim.

Over the next few months, Sam's code had more and more bugs. Then another senior engineer – let's call them "Jess" – stepped up. Jess covered their code in tests. The team did not yet have a CI system, so these tests only ran when executed locally. Jess paired with Sam on a task that involved changing much of Jess's code. She let Sam make the changes; he was happy with them and wanted to check them in. Jess asked Sam to run the unit test suite before doing this.

The unit tests broke because Sam's changes introduced several regressions. As Jess and Sam walked through the reasons for the changes, every one of them was a code change by Same. Reluctantly, he fixed these regressions one by one and checked in the code when the test suite succeeded. Jess told Sam the obvious conclusion she'd reached: "*It seems you do make mistakes in code, and that unit tests can, indeed catch them. When they're written, that is.*"

After this event, Jess put a CI system in place that ran the unit test suite, and the team decided engineers would write unit tests for their code. Jess was soon promoted to team lead, thanks to the quality improvement she drove across the team, with the number of bugs dropping, and Sam's changes no longer breaking the main branch as often.

I took two lessons from this episode. First, it is possible to write good software without unit tests. Sam *did* ship successful games for a decade with no tests. However, at game development studios there were manual testers and other, gaming-specific advanced testing methods like AI which played the game. Basically, there are environments where unit tests make less sense, and regressions are caught differently.

The second takeaway is that not having unit tests makes it difficult to refactor a large codebase without introducing bugs. If Sam had written unit tests from the start and when refactoring, there would've been a safety net to validate that the code worked as expected. Much time would've been saved and frustration avoided.

2. Integration Tests

Integration tests exercise multiple units at once. They are more complex unit tests, often spanning several classes, exercising how they work together.

Integration tests include testing two or more "units" working together, such as testing both the business logic "unit" and the database "unit." It could mean testing that two services interact correctly while mocking out other dependencies outside of those services.

Integration tests sit between very simple unit tests, and much more complex end-to-end tests. As such, some teams write integration tests using the same libraries as for unit tests – except they do not mock out all dependencies of the tests. And some teams use frameworks also used for end-to-end tests when integration testing, except they mock some components for the test.

3. UI Tests

UI tests – often called "end-to-end" tests – spin up the application and then exercise it as if a user were entering input. They don't use any mocking; the test runs the web or mobile application and uses UI automation to simulate user input, such as taps, clicks, text input, and other actions.

The biggest upside of UI tests is that they come closest to simulating real usage of an application, by going through the same flows that users experience. However, there is a tradeoff of this more powerful capability: more brittle tests, and slowness.

- More brittle tests: UI tests tend to be the most brittle, between unit and integration tests. This is because end-to-end tests can break for minor reasons, like a button's text changing and the test being unable to locate it.
- Slowness: the tests have more latency because they have to wait for the network. Also, some scenarios can be difficult to simulate; for example, having the server return certain error messages.

Some engineers build end-to-end tests which aren't fully end-to-end and simulate the network layer. This is done to speed up the tests and make it easier to test edge cases with special network responses. Some teams will refer to such tests as integration tests, while other teams stick with the UI test naming. My view is that the name is less important, so long as the team is clear about what they mean by integration and UI testing.

4. Mental Models for Automated Testing

Here are *common* characteristics of unit, integration and end-to-end tests:

	Unit	Integration	UI or end-to-end
Coverage	Very narrow	Narrow	Broad
Ease to write	Easy	Medium to hard	Medium to hard
Time to maintain	Little time	Some time	A lot of time

Common characteristics of three common types of automated tests

Note that this is a generalization and specifics can differ by platform, language, and environment. For example, there are end-to-end frameworks in certain platforms that make writing and maintaining end-to-end tests much easier, and comparable to writing or maintaining unit tests in some environments.

Still, assuming the table is accurate, what is a good ratio of unit, integration, and end-to-end tests? There are two popular mental models for this.

The testing pyramid

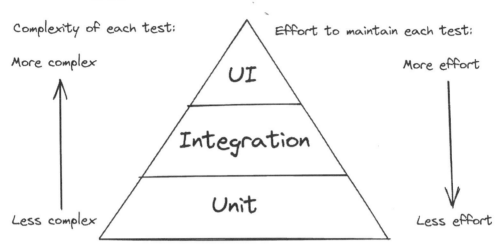

The testing pyramid: a mental model suggesting it's worth writing simpler, cheap-to-maintain tests, like unit tests

The testing pyramid was introduced by Mike Cohn in his 2009 book, "Succeeding with Agile." The idea of the testing pyramid is to cover as much of the testing surface as possible with unit tests, as little of the surface as possible with UI tests, and somewhere in between for integration tests. This model quickly caught on and became the most common model for testing in the software engineering industry.

The testing pyramid approach tends to work pretty well for backend systems with little to no UI. It also holds up for some native mobile applications for which end-to-end testing and integration testing are difficult.

An area in which the testing pyramid is less useful is frontend development. When building for the frontend, unit testing tends to be less useful, and integration testing much more so.

The testing trophy

The testing trophy is a phrase coined by software engineer, Kent C. Dodds, in 2019. The idea was inspired by[1] this insight from Guillermo Rauch, founder and CEO of Vercel: "Write tests. Not too many. Mostly integration."

This is what it looks like:

[1] https://kentcdodds.com/blog/write-tests

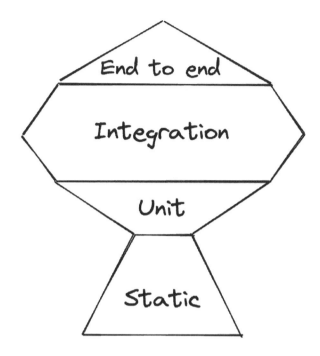

The testing trophy. First shared on the blog of Kent C. Dodds

Why did the testing trophy emerge? It's because in the years since the test pyramid appeared, many things have changed, especially in frontend development:

- Code has become much more modular, so many bugs occur between components
- Testing frameworks have become more powerful and tests easier to write
- Unit testing frameworks can be used for integration testing with relative ease
- Static analysis tools have evolved and can indicate runtime errors

It's true that for frontend development, integration testing offers the best "bang per buck" in terms of time spent writing them and the breadth of what they cover. It's increasingly true for full-stack applications, too. Read more about the testing trophy in the article The testing trophy and testing classifications[2] by Kent C. Dodds.

There is no single best approach for how to invest in tests. The testing pyramid and the testing trophy are mental models for thinking about categories of automated tests. But instead of trying to make your testing approach fit a model, do it the other way around.

Ask what would be great automated testing on your system. Then choose your approach and keep refining it. If it doesn't mirror a model, don't worry. It's more important the automated

---

[2]https://kentcdodds.com/blog/the-testing-trophy-and-testing-classifications

tests achieve their goal of ensuring quality even as teams move fast, than that they conform to a mental model.

When seeking guidance on how to approach testing, it can be helpful to reach out to engineers working at companies at a similar stage as yours, or in a similar industry. For example, Meta is a company that has historically invested less in automated testing, but more in monitoring and automated rollouts, thanks to having billions of users using its products. Banks and more traditional companies with less frequent releases often invest more in manual testing, and much of Big Tech like Google or Uber, invests heavily in unit and integration testing.

5. Specialized Tests

Beyond generic categories of unit, integration, and UI tests, there are several other automated tests with more niche usage which can be handy in specialized cases.

Performance tests

These tests measure the latency or responsiveness of a system. Performance tests can be used in many cases, such as verifying that a code change:

- Did not introduce a UI performance regression to a mobile app
- Has not increased latency on a backend endpoint

Automated performance tests are tricky to do well because there's a lot of nuance in capturing an application's performance, such as other processes impacting the performance of the target code being measured, non-deterministic events impacting the measurement, or the measurements running on different machines which makes results hard to compare.

Load tests

Load tests ensure a system performs adequately under a specific load. For example, an e-commerce company knows it will get about 10x the normal traffic on Black Friday, and wants to test that its backend systems respond with a reasonable latency. For this, a load test is conducted.

Load tests are specific to backend systems and there's several ways to do them:

- Dedicated testing infrastructure that sends test requests to systems to be tested. In this case, a testing infrastructure needs to be set up which generates the request.
- Batching existing production requests. In this setup, production requests are delayed on purpose. After enough batching, all production requests are sent at an increased rate to the production systems. This approach works with non-time-sensitive requests.

- Production testing with smaller infrastructure. Instead of testing whether the current infrastructure can handle 10x traffic volume, a valid test is to check if 1/10th of the infrastructure can handle current traffic volumes.

Chaos tests

Around 2008, Netflix moved its architecture from a monolithic setup, to one spread across hundreds of smaller services. Running so many services helped reduce a single point of failure, but it led to seemingly random outages where a small service misbehaving or going down, took down other seemingly unrelated parts of the system.

The Netflix engineering team came up with an unconventional way to simulate these outages. A 2010 blog post explained:

> "One of the first systems our engineers built in AWS is called the "Chaos Monkey." The Chaos Monkey's job is to randomly kill instances and services within our architecture. If we aren't constantly testing our ability to succeed despite failure, then it isn't likely to work when it matters most — in the event of an unexpected outage."

Netflix has since open-sourced its Chaos Monkey implementation[3] and it's popular at companies running a large number of services. Infrastructure teams implement a similar approach of shutting down services, or deliberately degrading them, to observe how the system responds.

Snapshot Tests

Snapshot tests compare the output of a test to a pre-recorded output. They are most frequently used in web and mobile development, and the "snapshot" is an image of a screen. The test compares whether or not a webpage or mobile application looks exactly like the snapshot.

Snapshot tests for UI validation are especially popular for mobile apps. They're cheap to write, and fast to run compared to mobile UI tests. They are also easy to debug: when a test fails, you can compare the image the test generated to the reference image, and see the differences immediately.

A major downside of using snapshot test suites for UI validation is that reference images used for comparison, can quickly grow too large to keep in the same repository as the test code. It's common enough for companies with a large number of snapshot tests to store the reference images outside of the code repository.

---

[3]https://netflix.github.io/chaosmonkey

Application size/bundle size tests

For mobile applications and web applications, the size of an application or the initially loaded bundle, can be a focus. There are teams that put monitoring in place to alert when the size of a mobile app or a web bundle increases above a given size.

Smoke tests

The term smoke testing comes from electronic hardware testing. In the book Lessons Learned in Software Testing by Cem Kaner, James Bach, and Brett Pettichord, this is how they define the origin of this term:

> "The phrase 'smoke test' comes from hardware testing. You plug in a new board and turn on the power. If you see smoke coming from the board, turn off the power."

Smoke coming out from a circuit board is bad as it means that the board is melting down. The idea behind smoke testing is to run simple tests – almost always automated ones – that can verify if there is something obviously wrong with the product.

Smoke tests are the subset of the full test suite and are meant to be executed frequently and before any production release. A few examples of more common smoke tests are these:

- Does the application launch, without crashing?
- Does a page load in an application, without errors?
- Does basic connectivity work: does the application successfully connect to the back-end or to a database?
- Does a core functionality work: such as logging in, or navigating to a frequently used part of the application?

Manual tests and sanity tests

Sanity tests are a collection of manual tests that should be run to confirm an application works as expected before every major release. These tests might be executed by the engineering team or a dedicated quality assurance team.

Sanity tests tend to have detailed instructions on what to execute and what to observe as output. Thanks to such detailed instructions, when teams have more bandwidth to invest in automation, these tests can be a prime candidate to partially or fully automate as UI, or end-to-end tests.

But why are all sanity tests not automated? It might be because the team didn't get around to it. In some cases, automating could be impractical – for example, if certain sanity tests are rarely run, the team may decide it's not worth the effort to build and maintain automated tests. And there are tests that can be challenging to automate, such as looking at a user interface and confirming that the layout looks good.

Other tests

Automated testing is an ever-evolving field. The main thing is that an automated test helps validate the correct functioning of a system. It's less important what it's called; what matters is that they're in place to exercise the system.

A few other types of automated tests include:

- **Accessibility testing**. Especially relevant for mobile applications, web applications, and desktop applications. This type of test might be tricky to automate.
- **Security testing**. Some of these could be automated, and others might need to be performed manually.
- **Compatibility testing**. Verifying that software works as expected on various hardware or operating systems.

6. Testing in Production

Where do you run your automated and manual test suite? The answer for a long time was in dedicated test environments, such as a staging environment, or a User Acceptance Test (UAT) environment.

Today, an increasingly popular place to test software is in the production environment which end users also use. While this approach is riskier, it has significant upsides to testing in a dedicated environment – when done right.

How do you test in production, safely? A few approaches:

- **Feature flags**. To test a new feature in production, put it behind a feature flag. Once deployed to production, turn on the feature flag for automated tests and manual tests to be completed. When the team is confident this approach is working, roll the feature out to more users. We cover more on feature flags in Part IV: "Shipping to production"
- **Canary deployments**. Roll out production changes to a small number of servers or users (the "canary" group.) Run tests here, and monitor observability results. If there are no alarming signals, continue the rollout to all users and servers.
- **Blue-green deployments**. Maintain two different environments: a "blue" one and a "green" one. Only one environment is live at any one time. Deploy the changes to the idle environment, run all tests, and once you're confident about the changes, switch traffic to that deployment.
- **Automated rollbacks**: combining canary deployments or blue-green deployments,

with an automated monitoring setup. If the system detects an anomaly upon rolling out the feature, the changes are rolled back automatically for the team to investigate.

- **Multi-tenancy environments**. The idea behind tenancies is that the tenancy context is propagated with requests. Services receiving a request can tell if it's a production request, a test tenancy, a beta tenancy, or another. Services have logic built in to support tenancies and might process or route requests differently. Uber describes its multi-tenancy approach in this blog post[4] .

The biggest benefits of testing in production:

- **Confidence**. Tests are run in the production environment, so you can be far more confident they work as expected.
- **More straightforward debugging**. If you spot an issue to debug, you should have the tools to do it in production. Once you've identified the issue, you can then write a test case for it using production data!
- **Fewer environments $\rightarrow$ less infrastructure complexity**. Testing in production reduces the number of test environments to maintain. Maintaining a test environment is expensive in both hardware costs and time invested to ensure the environment represents production closely enough.

There are plenty of challenges to testing in production, though:

- **Infrastructure investment**. There is a lot of legwork which teams must do to ensure safe testing in production. For example, moving to a multi-tenancy setup can be a long, painful process. Similarly, building a system with canarying that does automated rollbacks is a complex, time-consuming mission.
- **Compliance and legal challenges**. Testing in production does not mean engineers should be able to access sensitive user data, such as personally identifiable information (PII.) Tooling might need to be built to ensure relevant privacy regulations are followed when debugging and testing in production.

7. Benefits and Drawbacks Of Automated Testing

Writing automated tests involves a pretty big time investment. So, what are its benefits to a team? Here's the most common:

- Validating correctness. The immediate benefit of any automated test is validation the code works according to what the test specifies. If writing tests before the code itself –

---

test-driven development (TDD) – then the expectation is specified upfront, and the code is written to satisfy the test.

- **Catching regressions**. With automated tests, regressions can be caught early. This happens before code is merged, if the automated test suite is integrated to the CI system. If integrated to the CD system, then regressions can be caught before shipping the code to production.
- **Documentation**. Tests can help establish what the code intends to do, and how it should behave for edge cases. But documentation becomes dated, so the test suite needs to be up to date, or the tests will fail.
- **A contract**. Tests can be a way to validate formal contracts, like how an interface or API should behave, to ensure it behaves exactly as described to users.
- **A safety net when making large changes**. Codebases with thorough automated test suites provide engineers with an extra safety net. Large code changes like major refactors can be done with more confidence thanks to the test suite.

Automated tests have downsides, too:

- **Time taken to write**. The biggest, most obvious downside is that tests take time to write, which can feel wasted on code you assume is already correct. Of course, the benefit of the test is only partly to verify your work. The other upside is that a test can catch regressions.
- **Slow tests**. A test suite can become slow to run over time, due to a large number of automated tests, or them being slow to run. A sluggish test suite can slow down the cadence of development.
- **Flakey tests**. Some test types are more prone to flakiness and failing when the application works correctly. For example, UI tests can break when there's a network delay, but the application works fine. Flakey tests introduce noise and degrade the test suite's usefulness.
- **Maintenance cost**. When changing code, the related tests must also be updated. This is straightforward for simple tests like unit tests. But changing more complex tests so they work as expected, can be more effort than writing the code!

Testing is a core part of software engineering and always has been since the very early days of software development. Writing code is only the first part of development; validating how it works, shipping it to production, and maintaining the code, all follow. Automated tests help in all phases after the code is written.

For software that's maintainable and can be supported across a longer timeframe, automated tests are a baseline requirement, and also for making iteration faster on the codebase. For that reason, embrace testing and try out a variety of approaches. This way, you build up a broad testing toolset, and use the best type of test for your current project.

15

SOFTWARE ARCHITECTURE

Software architecture involves design principles and decisions which are usually made early, during the planning phase of a project. These design decisions have an outsized impact on how a system is built, how easy it is to extend and maintain, and how easily new engineers can onboard to the codebase.

The terms "software architecture" and "software design" are interchangeable. I like "architecture," for its connection to the practice of making physical buildings. Developing a property has two distinct phases: the drawing up of plans (architecting,) and the work of constructing it. These are linked: an original plan can be tweaked as construction progresses, should assumptions made during planning turn out to be less valid.

However, there's a major difference between architecting buildings and software. The architecting of a property is heavily constrained by laws of physics, which isn't the case for architecting software. With software, the constraints on what can and cannot be done are much fuzzier. Physical laws govern software engineering much less: skillsets and dynamics on teams, and the constraints of technologies tend to be more important considerations.

Essentially, there is not one approach for doing software design well. But there are approaches that are pretty common across many companies. In this chapter, we cover:

- Design documents, RFCs, and architecture documents
- Prototyping and proof of concept
- Domain-driven design
- Software architecture that ships

1. Design Documents, RFCs and Architecture Documents

Many tech companies and startups utilize design documents often referred to as RFCs (Request for Comments,) as part of the planning process, including Uber, Airbnb, Gojek, GitLab, LinkedIn, MongoDB, Shopify, Sourcegraph, Uber, Zalando, and many others[1].

---

[1]https://blog.pragmaticengineer.com/rfcs-and-design-docs

Here, "RFC" is used to refer to design documents, to emphasize that they are a way to gather feedback which improves a design. RFCs are created by engineers for non-trivial projects before they start the meaningful work. There are usually no hard rules; they exist to share context and the suggested approach, tradeoffs, and to invite feedback.

The goal of RFCs

As mentioned, the overall objective of writing and distributing an RFC is to shorten the time it takes to complete a project, by getting key feedback early. It's up to engineers working on the project to decide how an RFC fits into their workflow. Here are a few approaches:

- **Prototype, then RFC, then build**. This is typical for projects with many unknowns – like building on a new framework – which can be discovered by prototyping. The RFC shares a partially completed plan, perhaps with gaps. The team gets feedback, and then builds.
- **RFC, wait for feedback, then build**. For projects with lots of dependencies or teams that are dependent on what's being built, progress may ultimately be faster if feedback from all stakeholders is gathered first.
- **RFC, then build while awaiting feedback**. For projects of some complexity about which there are unlikely to be many questions, it's pragmatic to start building when the RFC is distributed. The team can easily incorporate feedback, and not lose much time if changes are needed.
- **Build, then RFC**. Engineers build what they need to and then write an RFC which documents decisions taken. This may be because the project was more complex than planned, or to comply with internal rules on RFCs. This approach can get awkward, as the RFC is seen as a "tick box" exercise, and the team doesn't welcome actionable feedback. But the document is useful for archival purposes, and getting feedback at this point is still better than later after people move on to new projects. *In my experience, this approach is fairly common.*

Benefits

Writing an RFC and distributing it for feedback has some major benefits:

1. **You clarify your thinking**. How many times have you rushed into coding up a solution, only to realize halfway through that you're on the wrong track? If only you'd clarified what you're trying to do, then this could have been avoided. A design document forces you to explain your thinking in a way that makes sense to you and others.
2. **Get important feedback, faster**. If you just go and code up a solution and present it to your team, you'll often get feedback which creates extra work. For example, a teammate might point out missing edge cases, or the product manager could say the wrong use case is being solved for. A document via which people can give feedback

before coding starts, helps minimize misunderstandings and additional work.

3. **It scales your ideas**. If you don't create a design document, the only way for another engineer to understand your thinking is by talking with you, directly. If five engineers want to understand your approach to building the system, then all five need to grab time with you. By writing the plan down instead, they can read it and ping you with questions.

4. **It promotes a writing culture**. If teammates see value in your design document, they're more likely to do the same for their projects. This is a win for everyone, including you, as sharing documents usually leads to better feedback, quicker.

Reviewing RFCs

Reviewing RFCs is obviously key to getting the feedback they contain. The most common ways to get feedback are:

- **Asynchronous feedback**: via comments in the document. Google, GitHub, and Uber gather feedback this way.
- **Synchronous feedback**: organize a meeting to discuss an RFC in depth. Amazon, the online retail giant, prefers this type of process.
- **Hybrid**: a document is distributed to gather feedback asynchronously. A meeting is called if the project's complexity warrants it, or there are many comments.

The best format depends on the project. You need a different approach for a project which impacts twenty teams who all give feedback, than when you're building a service that only your team and a single partner team will use.

Don't forget the *true* goal of the RFC process. It's to reduce the time it takes to ship a project, by getting feedback early. Ask yourself which approach saves the most time.

Architecture documents

Architecture documents differ slightly from RFCs, in that they are written to record decisions made, with little intent for feedback – which is unlike RFCs. Architecture documents come in a few popular formats, and each company tends to have a favorite:

- **ADR**[2] (Architecture Design Record) is probably the most popular format due to being created for use with Git as Markdown files, and its simple structure.
- **C4 model**[3] is a more involved, diagramming software architecture, defining four diagram levels for use: context, containers, components, and code. It was created by independent consultant and author, Simon Brown.

---

[2]https://adr.github.io
[3]https://c4model.com

- **Arc42**[4] is an approach that comes with an opinionated template of 12 sections, including "Context and scope," "Solution strategy," "Building block view," and "Cross-cutting concepts."

2. Prototyping and Proof of Concept

How do you build a complex system that works as expected? Thorough planning is one approach. An alternative – often underrated – is to not start with planning. Instead, start by showing how it could work, and build a quick-and-dirty prototype for demonstration purposes.

The issue with complex projects is that there are unknowns, and the planning stage involves debate about these unknowns. Building a prototype can address some unknowns and show an approach could work well enough.

I recall being part of a project to architect a new, complex payments system, which would replace two existing payments systems. It involved around 10 engineering teams. Initially, all teams planned their own approaches. For two months, hundreds of pages of RFCs were produced and circulated. But the project didn't achieve a consensus about how to proceed.

Then the group changed tack and brought one representative from each team together, and this new team spent two weeks prototyping a barebones approach. There were no planning documents and no comments were sought; it was just people in one location writing code and demonstrating ideas through prototyping.

Within two weeks, the group built a prototype and addressed many sources of conflicts and unknowns. This prototype was thrown away later, but served as the scaffolding for different systems' ownership, and how they talk with each other.

Prototyping for exploration

Many software engineers whom I consider great software "architects" build throwaway prototypes to prove a point and showcase their ideas. After all, it's a lot more productive to reason about *concrete* code than abstract ideas.

When there are many unknowns or moving parts, use prototyping as an exploration tool. It's a fantastic fit for problems about which there isn't enough information to make a plan with high confidence. For example, if you need to integrate with a third-party API but aren't sure how, build a throwaway prototype that does third-party API calls and provides a suggestion for how it could work.

---

[4]https://arc42.org

I'd argue that if you're *unable* to prototype architecture ideas, then you're no longer hands-on with development, or an idea is over-complicated. Otherwise, you could demonstrate how it works with a prototype!

Build with the intent to throw it away

Build *throwaway* proof of concepts and make it clear they're *not* for production. The point of prototyping is to prove something could work, and to then start building it properly, after validation. You'll learn a lot by building a proof of concept to show people, and have productive conversations about something concrete and specific.

You can move faster by being clear that what you build is throwaway, so there's no need for code reviews, automated tests, or code that can be maintained later. Seriously, you don't need *any* of these things because it's throwaway!

The danger with any proof of concept is that someone higher up, like a product manager, says it looks good and to ship it. But it's a prototype which was hacked together, and none of the practices for production code have been applied. Shipping in this state would be a bad idea! In this case, stand your ground and refuse to ship a prototype. Build a proper version from scratch, instead. This should not be so difficult with a working prototype.

If there's too much pressure to ship prototypes, use the trick of purposely building the prototype on top of non-production technologies. For example, if your team uses Go on the backend, write the prototype in Node.js which is *obviously* only used for prototyping, and won't be shipped.

To develop better architecture approaches, use prototyping to build proofs of concept as a tool. The more you do this, the more productive you'll become and the better the architecture you build will be.

3. Domain-Driven Design

Domain-driven design (DDD) involves starting by creating a business domain model to understand how the business domain works. For example, when building a payments system, start by understanding the payments domain, business rules, and context of the payments domain.

The term "domain-driven design" was coined by Eric Evans in his book, "Domain-Driven Design: Tackling Complexity in the Heart of Software." Its components are:

- **A standard vocabulary**. The first step is to ensure everyone involved in the design speaks the same language. DDD calls this the 'ubiquitous language.' To develop this shared vocabulary, sit down with business domain experts and define the terms and jargon to be used. This might seem a simple task, but software engineers and payment compliance experts may define things very differently; even a term as seemingly clear as "making a payment."

- **Context**. Break up complex areas into smaller parts, which DDD refers to as 'bounded contexts.' Each of these contexts has its own standard vocabulary. For example, when designing a payment system, contexts could be Onboarding, Paying in, Paying Out, and Settlement. Each context can be modeled independently and broken down further.
- **Entities**. An entity is something defined primarily by its identity, which has a life span. Many named things, like the parts of a system, people, and locations, tend to be entities. For example, an accounting entry would be an entity in a payments system.
- **Value objects** describe entities and are immutable, meaning they don't change. For example, the currency of an accounting entry is a value object.
- **Aggregates** are clusters of entities treated as a single unit.
- **Domain events** are things that happen which other parts of the domain should be aware of and may react to. Domain events help to make triggers – and reactions to triggers – more explicit. For example, when a payment comes into a payment system, the account balance increases by the sum of the payment. However, when introducing a domain event like a PaymentMadeEvent, this formerly implicit logic becomes explicit: the Account now reacts to PaymentMadeEvents, not monitoring of Payment objects that arrive.

The biggest benefit I've seen of applying DDD principles to a software engineering project is that it forces software engineers to understand the business context. You need to talk with business folks and let them describe how their world works. Thanks to shared vocabulary (see above,) the software you build will resemble the "real world" more closely.

A few benefits of DDD approaches:

- **Fewer misunderstandings between engineering and business**. So many software projects are late because software engineers build something different from what the business expects. With DDD, there's plenty of communication with business stakeholders from the start, so the chance of misunderstandings greatly reduces.
- **A better handle on business complexity**. Business rules can be surprisingly complex, and DDD helps capture this, and tame it using Bounded Contexts.
- **More readable code**. Thanks to a well-defined, shared vocabulary, the code is clearer. Class and variable names are more consistent and easier to understand. The code will be cleaner, as a whole.
- **Better maintainability**. Thanks to easier-to-understand code and a defined vocabulary.
- **Easier to extend and scale**. When new business use cases need to be added, this extension can be first inserted into the existing domain model. Once the logical ex-

tensions are made, implementing the change at code level is easier. Scaling a codebase by adding a large number of new business use cases is much easier and less messy.

To learn more about applying DDD, I recommend these books:

- Learning Domain-Driven Design[5] by Vlad Khononov (2021)
- Domain-Driven Design[6] by Eric Evans (2003)

4. Software Architecture that Ships

I've talked with plenty of experienced software engineers who were frustrated that their architecture ideas for improving systems were hard to ship, due to pushback received while circulating their idea. So, how can you get helpful ideas shipped to production?

Verbalize the business goal

Take a step back and consider what the business goal of this change is. How will it help your product or company? Which business metrics would it improve, like revenue, costs, user churn, developer productivity, or other things the business cares about? Once you have an idea of the business impact, it should be easy enough to make a case for prioritizing this change.

If the business impact is much smaller than that of ongoing projects, ask if it's pragmatic to spend time working on a relatively low-impact project. Of course, it's sensible to work on projects with smaller business impacts if they help the engineering team. But when there are higher-impact projects, it's reasonable to do lower-import work on the side, or to fit it around the other projects.

Get buy-in from stakeholders

For architecture changes, you often need buy-in from other teams, senior-and-above engineers, and sometimes, from business colleagues. For this, you'll need to present your idea and win the support of key people. A few ways to do this:

- Meet the key people and describe your approach. *This is pretty time-consuming, and it can be hard to reference specifics later.*
- Write a proposal, send it around, gather comments, and get people to sign off on your idea. *This approach scales better, and makes decisions less ambiguous.*
- Start by writing things down, and end by talking to key people who are "on the fence"

---

[5]https://learning.oreilly.com/library/view/learning-domain-driven-design/9781098100124
[6]https://www.domainlanguage.com/ddd

about your idea. Then, update your proposal with modifications after those conversations. *This is a hybrid approach and should work in the majority of cases for getting support.*

An underrated way to get key people to agree to a written proposal is to seek their input *before* you write the proposal. So, take time to present your idea to a select few stakeholders. Whiteboard your ideas, ask for feedback, and incorporate it into your document. Then let those people know their input was taken into consideration, and they will almost certainly support your approach. Early support could make it easier to win over the rest of the group, too.

As you seek buy-in, don't forget the goal of your work is to support the business, but you may get feedback from people who think the work will not do this. Don't dismiss this feedback: there's times when not doing something is the right choice for the business. It's not personal.

Beat decision paralysis

There are times when architecture decisions get stuck because a group is divided on which path to take. Here are some ways to break the deadlock:

- **Specify capability requirements**. These dictate the outcome, not the implementation. They can be system-level constraints you need to adhere to, like expected latency, or acceptable consistency requirements. They can also be constraints on the UX side, such as response times of no more than 500 ms, or business constraints such as double charging is unacceptable. Once outlined, you can inspect suggested solutions through the lens of capability requirements. Outline these before coming up with solutions, and remove solutions bias, which means jumping into "solution mode" before you understand the problem.
- **Appoint a decision maker before the discussion**. Agree on a decision maker in case of a conflict. Doing this in advance of a discussion is best, because introducing a decision-maker during a conflict tends to create friction, by raising the question of how neutral they are. For example, if a participant pulls in their own manager to be the decision maker, that person will likely support their team member.
- **Who will do the coding, is the tie breaker**. The simplest and fairest way is to leave the decision to the person who does the coding. After all, they will also have to take on the maintenance burden of the solution.
- **Prototype**. When things are stalling, go ahead and build a prototype of your idea. This is guaranteed to get things moving and people will talk about the prototype, not the deadlock.
- **Get sponsorship from your product counterpart**. Product managers have a vested interest in building the right solutions for the business, in both the short-term, and also for long-term maintainability costs. Product sponsorship is a very effective way to avoid deadlocks. But most software engineers don't utilize it nearly enough!

Roll out changes properly

Once the changes are built, devote enough time to a proper rollout, because there's more chance something could go wrong if you're not meticulous about the rollout.

- **Quantify what the rollout means**. Find metrics that indicate if the new architecture works as expected. This could be tracking usage of the "old" system versus the new, performance metrics, business metrics, and so on.
- **Have a rollout plan**. Define the phases of the rollout. How will you validate that a rollout phase is "healthy," and the next phase can start?
- **Define the right 'time to bake.'** When shipping major changes, take time to validate that all parts of the system work as expected. Use generous enough time frames for the new system to "bake" in production, before declaring the project a success. And be sure to measure key system health metrics during the baking phase.
- **Have a rollback plan**. How can changes be undone if something goes wrong during rollout? It's more challenging if the rollout includes changes to data, or the data schema.
- **Do a 'pre-mortem' exercise**. If a rollout fails, what could the causes be? Map out possible scenarios, then figure out how to detect such failures, and prevent them from happening.

No decision is final in software engineering

There's no doubt you will have disputes in which the sensible approach is to concede, in favor of an approach you don't fully support. This outcome may not be as bad as it sounds. No decisions are final when it comes to software!

Almost every decision can be reversed later, including technology changes, architecture approaches, and business rules added. The cost of reversing a decision varies and some are very expensive to reverse. So long as the decision is pretty easy to reverse, then going with one choice beats being stuck in a deadlock!

Architecture changes with rollback plans are pretty easy to reverse, should they not work as expected. For changes involving a migration, there should be a way to migrate back to the original state.

When you roll back a decision, capture the learnings on why the approach didn't work and share them, typically as a document, distributed to relevant people. It could be sent via email, shared over chat, or presented in a meeting.

Even if a team decides on a given architectural approach, then builds and rolls it out, there's nothing stopping someone from introducing a different approach with new upsides and downsides, later. After all, this is exactly how software systems evolve to keep up with ever-changing business requirements and the real world.

Reflect on your architecture decisions

When a project is shipped, it's common for the team to hold a retrospective to discuss what went well, what could have been better, and what will be different next time.

When was the last time you reflected on your architecture decisions? One issue is that new architecture needs time to "bake" and prove itself. Also, to get a sense of how well an approach works, you need to be hands-on enough to observe how the architecture holds up when engineers maintain and extend it.

You need to give your newly shipped architecture enough time to observe how decisions play out across a longer timeframe. And then, you need motivation to gather feedback from users.

This isn't always easy. Here are some sources of motivation for making the effort to gather feedback on how well the system (and therefore the architecture) actually performs:

- **Share your learnings**. Commit to sharing your learnings about the architecture.
- **Performance reviews/promotions**. How will your management chain know how useful your work on a given system was? Gathering feedback could help your work gain more recognition.
- **Help others with your learnings**. You might mentor engineers who are looking to design similar systems as you. Go back and get feedback to reflect on how your design decisions worked out – and what could've been better.

When gathering feedback on your work, it can be tempting to only focus on the positives. It's great to hear your work is well received, but this doesn't help you grow as a software engineer nearly as much as a valid critique does. As you collect feedback, find out where your architecture decisions didn't work as well as expected, and build on these very valuable lessons. Too few engineers do this proactively!

Takeaways

To be a role model senior engineer, it's necessary to master the craft of software engineering, but this alone isn't enough. In fact, at senior level, coding-related activities are the less challenging work; collaborating efficiently with others, and helping the team get stuff done, is much more difficult.

It is at the senior level where the impact of your work is more important than the effort you put into it. For that reason, finding smart ways to work can yield large dividends.

Separately, mentoring somebody is an underrated way to help them become a more efficient engineer, and it also helps you grow as a professional. Similarly, seeking mentorship from more experienced engineers can broaden your outlook, and help you get increasingly complex work done.

The term "senior engineer" is often a bit vague across the industry. There are places at which it is a mid-level engineering role (usually lower tier companies, as we covered in Part I: "Career Paths",) but in some businesses, it refers to something like the tech lead level. Meanwhile, other companies have expectations that are more common for staff and principal engineers.

However broad or narrow the definition of 'senior' is, it's a reasonable expectation that a relatively complex project will be accomplished when a senior engineer is involved. If issues come up, it is the senior engineer who finds ways to unblock things. And if they get stuck, they flag this, ask for help, and bring options to the table.

For further reading, check out the online, bonus chapter for Part III:

Getting Things Done as a Senior Engineer: Exercises

pragmaticurl.com/bonus-3

Part IV

The Pragmatic Tech Lead

The tech lead position is a particularly interesting one because being a tech lead is more frequently a role than a formal title.

Being a tech lead implies you're an experienced, usually senior-or-above engineer. You are also the lead on a project, or the go-to person in your engineering team during all projects. There are teams with multiple tech leads; one for each initiative, and others with only one tech lead, who's usually the most experienced, or longest-tenured engineer on the team.

Typical tech lead titles

At companies like Google, Meta, Amazon, Microsoft, and Uber, there's no title called "tech lead." After the senior engineer level is the staff engineer level. But at these companies, there is frequently a tech lead role within a team or project. In contrast, some companies do have a formal tech lead position.

At companies where the tech lead is a formal title, the most common titles for this position are:

- Tech lead
- Lead engineer / lead developer

Typical tech lead expectations

Expectations of tech leads are usually similar to those of senior engineers, with the addition of leading projects. At some companies, tech lead expectations are closer to those of a staff engineer. See the introductions of Part III (Senior) and Part V (Staff) for common expectations of those levels.

Additionally, expectations of a tech lead can overlap with those of an engineering manager. Tech leads are not responsible for managing people, but they tend to take on the management responsibility of helping people to better align. This is an area engineering managers typically own, until they have tech leads to delegate it to:

Where do you typically spend most of your time, between these three activities, in each role?

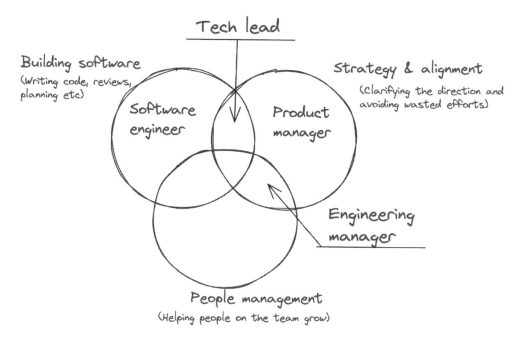

How software engineers, tech leads, and engineering managers tend to spend most of their time. Tech leads start to do more strategy and alignment activities that are typical of engineering managers

Where the IC and manager paths diverge

A high-performing tech lead who is usually a prime candidate for an internal engineering manager promotion, or transition. At the same time, tech leads often have the opportunity to stay on the individual contributor path, and grow into staff+ positions.

At fast-growing companies that need to hire several engineering managers, it's common for tech leads to have the option to move into a manager position. The manager role is different to the software engineer one, and this transition is outside the scope of this book. For advice on navigating the transition into manager, here are books I recommend:

pragmaticurl.com/engineering-management

16

PROJECT MANAGEMENT

At high-growth startups and in Big Tech it's common for engineers of all levels to lead engineering projects. As an engineer, building up the skills for this is important in order to grow into senior and staff roles.

As a tech lead or an engineer acting as one, leading projects is a regular task. So, how do you do this efficiently and with confidence?

In this chapter, we cover:

1. Companies where engineers lead projects
2. Why do we do project management?
3. Project kickoffs and milestones
4. "Software project physics"
5. Day-to-day project management
6. Risk and dependencies
7. Wrapping up projects

First, let's talk about projects which are good to lead as a tech lead.

1. Companies Where Engineers Lead Projects

Which tech companies empower software engineers to act as engineering leads for projects, even if they're below the senior or tech lead levels? Quite a few, actually.

At most places, each team decides how it operates, and no particular working style is mandated. Below are companies which I've confirmed have several teams where engineers lead projects, with support from managers and more experienced engineers:

- **Shopify**: this role is called 'IC Champion' (individual contributor champion)
- **Amazon**: non-senior engineers often lead projects which are good fits in complexity terms
- **Atlassian**: a common role fulfilled by mid-level engineers, called Feature Lead
- **Microsoft**: many product teams operate like this
- **GitHub**: calls this role the DRI (Directly Responsible Individual)
- **X**, formerly Twitter: several product teams call this role the PTL (Project Tech Lead)
- **DAZN** (sports streaming scaleup) calls this role the Project Captain

- **Klarna** has teams experimenting with this approach
- **Trivago** calls this role the Tech Driver.
- **Skyscanner**: many teams have less experienced engineers shadow projects, and then lead one.
- **Thought Machine** (a FinTech scaleup) has project teams led by engineers, while engineering managers lead "component teams."
- **Big Tech**: several teams at Meta, Google, Apple, and Uber use this approach.

Apple merits a separate mention, as its co-founder Steve Jobs believed individual contributors (ICs) do the best job of managing. He said in an 1985 interview[1]:

> "You know who the best managers are? They're the great individual contributors who never, ever want to be a manager, but decide they have to be a manager because no one else will do as good of a job as them."

2. Why Do We Do Project Management?

"Project" is the word many organizations use to coordinate efforts which move the needle of a specific business goal. They may take as little as a couple of weeks, but often last months from start to finish, while long-term efforts could span years. However, at tech companies with healthy engineering cultures, engineers ship business value multiple times a day, and ship projects considered "complete" every few months.

But could we just get the work done without any form of project management? If you are working by yourself and depending on no other teams – and none depend on your work – then go ahead! You can sketch out a plan for the functionality you want to build, code it, ship it, and it's done. You probably don't need any tools mentioned in this chapter.

However, when more people are working together there's a need for:

- **Goals**: being clear what problem you are solving with this project
- **Planning**: having some high-level idea of how to solve this problem. In some cases, a more formal specification could come before the plan itself.
- **Coordination**: being clear who does what.
- **Keeping everyone on the same page**: as work progresses, keeping all team members informed about how things are going.
- **Managing risks, changes, and delays**: building software is full of risks because we often build solutions in new, untried ways.

Project management approaches offer tactics for all of the above, and help to answer the

---

[1] https://pragmaticurl.com/steve-jobs-interview

question many engineers dread: "how long will it take?"

Dates and deadlines are important for projects, whether or not we as engineers like this. This is especially true in environments where the business uses dates to coordinate and communicate between functions. Most of Big Tech and most high-growth startups are date-driven enterprises. As I write in the article, Yes, you should estimate software projects[2]:

> "Estimates matter because most people and businesses are date-driven. Publicly traded companies plan and budget based on quarters. They also decide how much to invest in projects and people after asking, "how long does it take to launch?" Private, venture-funded companies try to get new features out in time to help with the next fundraising round.
>
> Yes, some businesses are not very date-driven, but they are rare. Private, profitable lifestyle businesses and public bodies are perhaps the best examples of entities that don't care as much about dates."

What we cover in this chapter applies to more complex "work units" in any framework, and is not necessary for simple, well-defined pieces of work. Any sizable piece of work involving the coordination of people and working across several dependencies is a project which can benefit from the approaches covered here.

3. Project Kickoffs and Milestones

I've observed that a major reason why projects fail is by starting with misaligned expectations. This often only becomes apparent near the end of a project, just when the engineering team thinks they're done.

Kickoffs help ensure there's no misunderstandings at the outset, which can later cause large chunks of work to be thrown out, or redone entirely. I think of kickoffs as events where big questions are clarified with relevant stakeholders:

---

[2]https://blog.pragmaticengineer.com/yes-you-should-estimate

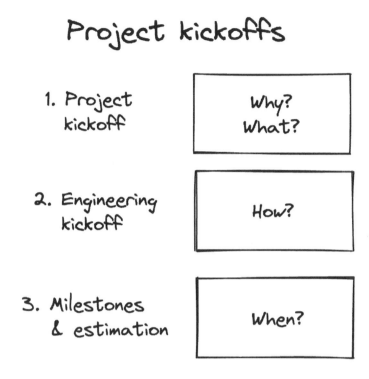

Topics a project kickoff can clarify

The best way to de-risk any project is to do a kickoff, in which all project stakeholders confirm they understand the goals and approach of the project, and endorse the high-level plan.

How you prepare for a kickoff depends on the complexity of the project and the number of stakeholders. In my view, a written document is essential, to circulate beforehand for people to add comments to. This approach is a must in any organization where teams work remote or partially remote.

A Product Requirements Document (PRD) is a common format for describing a project's "why" and "what." While engineering should be involved to some extent, it's not about engineering details at this stage. Rather, it's about aligning all product, engineering, design, data science, and business stakeholders. See examples of PRDs at various tech companies[3].

---

[3] https://www.vindhyac.com/posts/best-prd-templates-from-companies-we-adore

The project kickoff

The project kickoff aligns everyone with the "why" and "what." This kickoff is when people go through the plans and tackle questions. A successful kickoff is one in which the project lead asks, "are there any questions about what the project is, why we're doing it, or how we are approaching it?"

Ideally, everyone answers that all is clear, based on the information available. In practice, I've seen a room erupt with questions – which proves the kick-off's value. It's better to settle questions before the team starts building, than afterward when changes might mean previous efforts are binned.

I recommend the kickoff to be a meeting. Dedicate ten minutes to reading the proposal document, or for the project lead to walk attendees through it. If running an online meeting, consider asking participants to turn on video, so the meeting facilitator can get visual queues and spot when people could be disagreeing, and when a little nudge could help those people speak up.

As counter-intuitive as it sounds, I recommend inviting all stakeholders with a relevant say to join the kickoff. This means inviting everyone from the business, including customer support. More people in a meeting makes it more expensive time-wise, but this is okay because it's an opportunity to capture misunderstandings early and avoid wasted effort later.

The engineering kickoff

The engineering kickoff follows the project kickoff. Its goal is to align engineers on the "how," and involves the engineering team and relevant engineering stakeholders, like the data science, machine learning or infrastructure teams. Once the business goals and high-level approaches are clarified, engineers dive into planning exactly how this approach will work.

This varies, some teams do whiteboarding – sometimes virtual. Most of Big Tech and many startups kick off with engineering planning documents that are circulated like RFCs (request for comment,) ERDs (engineering requirement documents,) or ADRs (architecture decision records.)

I'm a big fan of writing down the agreed engineering approach because it has so many benefits. It forces engineers to clearly describe a proposed approach, thereby limiting misunderstandings. The plan can be circulated for comments, broadening its reach. And the planning document will be available later for those working on the project, to aid their onboarding and understanding of decisions made.

Establishing milestones

The goal of this step is to align the engineering team with the "when." Several engineering teams combine their planning with the project's milestones and estimations. But I prefer these two to be separate. The reason is that if you set engineering's dates and milestones at the planning stage, there's a high chance the team will immediately add shortcuts and make decisions that create tech debt. By doing the engineering planning separately, the team should devise a plan that makes the best possible decisions for the long-term health of the systems and services – not just for the project.

With an engineering plan in place, it's time to get a sense of shippable milestones. The more granular these milestones, the better. This is because all estimates will be off by some degree, and the only way to really know by how much, is to hit a milestone. Also, these have the intrinsic value of bringing the project's final goal a step closer, with each one hit.

Once milestones are agreed, the team does a breakdown of the work each one needs, with a rough time estimate. Some teams use T-shirt sizes as units of time, others prefer to do the Planning Poker approach with Fibonacci numbers as estimates for complexity (1, 2, 3, 5, 8, 13, etc.,) while others prefer engineering days. In the end, whichever method you choose at a date-driven company, you'll have to give a rough date estimate for when this milestone should be achieved.

I prefer milestones to be small enough to be achieved in no longer than a few weeks. If milestones involve lengthy chunks of work, I'd challenge the team to set intermediary milestones that capture smaller parts.

Ensure estimates aren't binding

Software projects are full of unknowns and risks, and the most anyone can reasonably ask of a team is for a rough idea of how long things should take, based on the best information. As a project progresses, risks and challenges will pop up which add more complexity and change the estimates.

The business will, of course, want to know the final shipping date. As project lead, there are several ways you can go about sharing this estimated deadline. Many leads add padding or inflate the estimates by adding time, then communicate this externally.

I always prefer to add some padding, but also to educate the business that there's no such thing as a "fixed date." Commit to the business that they will get regular updates, and then as the project passes its milestones, you can give dates with increasing confidence.

In this sense, software engineering and construction work are similar. Anyone who's contracted house building or renovation knows that dates and budgets are estimates at best. It almost always ends up taking longer than expected. Software projects are no different.

Of course, there are times when the dates are fixed. For example, some companies have upfront communicated, fixed release dates. Within finance and banking, deadlines to make changes and comply with new regulations are tied to dates. In such cases, the date is not negotiable: but, in turn, the scope of the work could be reduced. In such scenarios, it's especially important to understand what matters for the business – see Part V: Understanding the business for more on this topic.

4. "Software Project Physics"

While the software we build is virtual, there's a "law" of software physics which I've found is strikingly accurate:

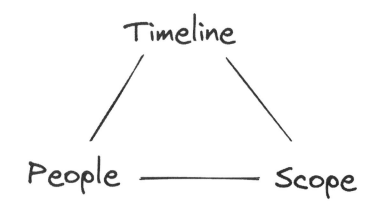

The triangle of "software physics." The timeline, scope and people on the project are all connected.

If this triangle looks familiar, it's probably because it resembles the project management triangle[4], which is a commonly used model to describe the connection between cost, time, scope, and quality. For teams in Big Tech and at high-growth startups, I've found quality is

---

[4]https://en.wikipedia.org/wiki/Project_management_triangle

rarely up for negotiation: timeline and scope are much more so.

The engineers who work on the project, its timeline and scope, are all connected. If one changes, at least one other needs to change in turn.

When scope increases

When the scope grows, then the timeline needs to also increase, or more people need to be assigned to the project. The first option of the timeline growing in line with scope is straightforward, but the business usually doesn't like it.

For the second option of adding more people, the extra hours and overtime increases the "people" component of the project triangle. Note, the number of team members doesn't have to increase, and can be the same as before, if existing teammates work more hours. One upside is that they have full context and don't need onboarding. But make no mistake, more labor hours are now going into the project than was planned.

Adding more people to a project without slowing it down is challenging, but is possible in rare cases. Whenever I say this, Brooks' law is regularly quoted at me. It's from the book, The "Mythical Man Month," by Fred Brooks:

> "Adding manpower to a late software project makes it later."

I would not treat this as a universal truth. It's not correct for projects where onboarding takes little time, the work is broken down and can be parallelized, when people with domain understanding are pulled in, and where you add few people, relative to team size.

Pulling in engineers familiar with the codebase to pick up standalone work, can speed up projects. I've also succeeded in delivering projects which increased in scope relative to the original timeline, by adding new engineers.

However, this always involves hard tradeoffs in onboarding time and communications overhead. Onboarding takes time and can take the focus off the team. The easier the onboarding – e.g., by using an internal open source model – and the more domain knowledge new joiners have, the less expensive it is. The lower the communication overhead is, with clear documentation, a clean codebase and asynchronous processes, then the lower the impact of onboarding is.

The reality is that for most projects of expanding scope, pulling in extra engineers isn't possible, as they'd need to come from another team or project, and it's rare that there are idle engineers waiting around on standby. And for many projects, the work might not be sufficiently parallelizable for new joiners to simply pick it up.

Be aware of different ways of getting more people, how overtime equals more labor power, and to recruit engineers with domain knowledge only if they'd speed up a specific project. To state the obvious: doubling the number of engineers won't cut the time to completion in half, but if they have domain knowledge and the work can be split up, then it can reduce the timeframe if done smartly.

When the project timeline changes

If the project's deadline is moved closer, something needs to give. The likelihood is that the scope is cut. What's less obvious is that the "people" dimension almost always increases in this situation, as with a tighter deadline, people often start to do longer hours or are asked to put in more time. So, the project's total "people hours" increases without additional people.

What about adding more engineers to a project with a shortened timeline? This is possible, but the time to onboard a new member can make it impractical, unless the deadline is months away.

When fewer people can work on a project

Unexpected issues may mean fewer people work on a project, such as team members being pulled away to other work, illness, etc. When there are fewer people, the scope needs to decrease, the timeline should be increased, or more people added.

Changing the scope or timeline is easiest, here. Adding more people hours can be done by pushing the reduced team to do more hours. However, this approach can backfire if overtime becomes a regular occurrence and people burn out. Pushing overtime on a team often increases mistakes as people work longer and ship more bugs, often without noticing. Don't forget, one exhausted person can have a net negative effect on a project by introducing avoidable regressions which they would not, had they gotten enough rest.

It's useful to be aware of the relationship between scope/timeline/people, and know that if one component changes, then at least one other should also change. As the project lead, this mental model can help you negotiate more realistic tradeoffs with the business.

When people working on the project change

A less intuitive case is when a new person joins the team. Does it affect the timeline, for example by making it shorter because more people are on the project?

Frequently, the timeline will not change, or it could even be extended! If a new team member is also new to the company, the onboarding could take long enough to distract team members and slow the project down. If onboarding is quick and the new joiner hits the ground running, then they could speed things up. There are companies where new joiners ship to production by the end of day 2, but at some places, it takes 1-2 months to get the first change into production. The faster a new joiner's onboarding is, the more likely it is that adding them will speed up projects.

Similarly, if team members are replaced – for example, when someone transfers out of the project, and someone else transfers in — the length of onboarding will influence whether or not timelines are impacted. There are teams where this is minimal, but on other teams it is a major hit. Take offboarding and onboarding time into account, and communicate that the scope or timeline of the project could change as a result.

5. Day-to-Day Project Management

There are a couple of widespread project management approaches that many engineering teams utilize:

- **Scrum**: usually for sprints lasting a week or more. A team usually does planning and estimation sessions, regular grooming sessions to prioritize the work in preparation for the next sprint, and sprint retrospectives. A big benefit of Scrum is structure, but this approach may be too rigid for experienced teams.
- **Kanban**: an approach where the next piece of work is the one that's at the top of the backlog, and a team puts in place some kind of planning and prioritization sessions. A major benefit of Kanban is flexibility and it's not an issue if priorities change. The downside is a lack of structure which less experienced teams might prefer is in place.
- **Scrumban**: a mix of approaches from Scrum and Kanban, using approaches from each as appropriate. This usually means a less rigid approach to sprints and more flexibility in picking up high-priority work.

I don't believe in being proscriptive on how to run projects. One approach I recommend is to experiment with different ways of doing things. If the software engineering field taught me anything over the course of two decades, it's that an effective approach for one team probably won't work so well somewhere else.

Try out approaches you think will work, including ones you're unsure about. Try opinionated project management approaches, different standup formats – including having none at all – and new ways to estimate or track work. There are few better ways to learn than by doing.

My suggestions of things to pay attention to, whatever approach you take:

- **Is everyone on the same page?** Ensure there's a way to check this. Few things better indicate a project is failing than when the answer is "no."
- **Keep the team and yourself accountable to what's been agreed**. Few things promote accountability better than writing things down, and people signing it. This is

why a weekly status email signed on behalf of the whole team works very well for accountability. Expect – and encourage! – team members to speak up if they feel they don't want to sign up.

- **Delegate generously as a project lead**. Delegate upwards to your manager, and sideways to people supporting you. Consider delegating to team members, and offering leadership opportunities they want to take on.
- **Iterations and feedback**: the more frequent, the better. The waterfall model of software development fails because feedback comes years after planning started. The more frequently you can get feedback on the true status of a project, the more likely you are to stay on track. This is why having short iterations, small milestones, and frequent feedback, is a solid framework for success. Retrospective meetings every few weeks can help identify what works well, what to improve, and how.
- **Expect the unexpected**. Call out risks as soon as you notice them – more on this below. Cut corners when needed and use your judgment about when this is necessary.
- **Never forget the big picture and the project's ultimate goal**. The goal isn't to write code, complete tickets, or output work at a certain velocity. The goal is something related to the business, so state it frequently and focus on achieving it, instead of doing busywork that doesn't get you closer to completion.

Taking decisions, as a tech lead

The tech lead role – or even the project lead role – has the downside of being ambiguous. It's clear a team manager can and does make team-level decisions, and it's equally clear engineers make some decisions of their own. But what about the tech lead; do they need to make project-level or team-level decisions, and if so, when? Do they go ahead and make them, or consult with their manager and defer to them?

For example, a project is two weeks away from the shipping date when an engineer discovers the framework they were planning to use is missing a key feature. So, either the feature needs to be changed – making it more limited – or you need to build a bunch of custom code, but doing this will push back the project's timeline. The engineer looks to you as the Tech Lead, to make a decision: one choice impacts the scope, the other impacts the timeline. Can you make this decision alone, or do you need to consult stakeholders like your manager, the product manager, or the business?

Don't forget to consult the rest of the team, before deciding. Less experienced tech leads often assume that if a decision needs to be made, they should make it. But are they in the best position to do so?

Consider empowering the person with the most information to decide. In the above example, the engineer suggesting the two workarounds might already have a suggestion they think is the best option. Help them verbalize which one it is, and then support it, while deciding whether to inform or consult stakeholders.

Inform stakeholders. When making a decision which impacts a project's timeline, scope, or people, always consider informing stakeholders. This means sharing:

- The situation aka the problem
- Potential solutions on the table, with tradeoffs
- The approach the team has chosen, which you support

Can you decide, or should you consult first? As a tech lead, you're expected to move things forward, and not defer to stakeholders – or your manager – about every decision. Use your judgment for whether it's fine to make a decision on the spot, or if it's better to consult stakeholders or your manager first.

Over time, you'll build up trust with stakeholders, and be able to predict when a decision is small enough in scope to merely inform others of it, and when its impact means you should consult others.

6. Risks and Dependencies

As mentioned earlier, building a new piece of software and constructing a new apartment complex have parallels. Both often take longer than planned and run over budget. No two projects are identical: materials and technologies vary, as do constraints and challenges.

Construction and software engineering also share in common that some risks are only revealed after work begins, which you need to respond to as you go. Let's go through the eight most common types of risks in software projects, and how to mitigate them:

1. Technology risk
2. Engineering dependencies
3. Non-engineering dependencies
4. Missing decisions or context dependencies
5. Unrealistic timeline
6. Not enough people or bandwidth
7. A surprise midway through the project
8. No idea how long something will actually take

Technology risk

When you have not used a framework, library, language, or service before, and there are "unknown unknowns" – which are risks you're not aware even exist.

How to mitigate:

- Prototype. Spend a day or two building something related to what you need to do.

As you prototype, you'll discover gaps, risks, and unknowns.
- Review the roadmap and tooling. Go through tooling, resources, and feedback. Are there breaking changes ahead, how stable is this technology, and how much maintenance/investment does it have?
- Evaluate "unstable" frameworks and tools. You may be tempted to use an unstable version of libraries, frameworks or APIs, so evaluate how risky this instability is. There will be cases when the risk is acceptable because using the latest, stable-enough version means you won't have to update to it when it becomes more stable.
- Consider alternatives to something that's bound to change a lot. This is a tradeoff between using something new, interesting and innovative, versus something guaranteed to reliably work.

Engineering dependencies

When you cannot make progress until an engineering team makes a change to a service, library or framework they own.

How to mitigate:

- Talk with the other team for a sense of what needs doing.
- Offer to do the work yourself, assuming there's an internal open source model. Don't underestimate the time this will take, as you need context on their services and to take constraints into account. Expect to have lots of constraints if a platform team owns what you need to modify. Platform teams need to ensure their changes don't break any customers.
- Mock around this dependency to unblock yourself and make progress while the other team builds.
- Remove this dependency from the critical path, e.g., by building your own, simpler version, and remember you will need to maintain what you build. Carefully consider the maintenance burden if you choose this path.
- Swarm as a team. Get the whole team involved in solving the problem. This can work wonders on truly hard problems, and unite the team.
- Pull in help from above by escalating to managers to help prioritize work on the other team's roadmap. Before doing this, I suggest always trying engineer-to-engineer communication.

Non-engineering dependencies

This is when you cannot make progress without information or signoff from a non-engineering team.

How to mitigate:

- Talk with the team and outline what you need, why, and what the impact will be if they don't take action.
- Can you work around this team? For example, if it's a design dependency, can you mock up something as a placeholder?
- Pull in help from above if needed, such as the PM or EM. But share the right context and recognize the difficulties or constraints the team has.

Missing decisions or context dependencies

When you're unsure how or what to build, or the "why" of the work is unclear.

I know only one way to mitigate this risk: refuse to start work until you understand the context, or have the decisions. Tell stakeholders what exactly you need from them before you can progress. It's doing a disservice to the team, the company and yourself, to start work on something about which fundamental questions remain unanswered. Ensure you have a clear picture of what to do, and why. Start work only when this is clear.

Unrealistic timeline

This typically happens when a completion date is handed down from above without input from the team, with a short timeline you're uncomfortable committing to.

How to mitigate:

Break down with rough estimates the work that needs to get done, so you have something to discuss. Offer tradeoffs that help meet the timeline, reduce scope, and consider adding more engineers to the project. Don't be afraid to think outside the box. Examples of how to approach managers with such suggestions:

- "Instead of a functional chat, we could ship a button that captures a message and opens a Zendesk ticket, using basic automation. Then we can meet the deadline."
- "Well, if we can hit pause on all the other projects my team is doing, AND get two senior Android engineers to shift over for the next two months, AND pause retiring the Zeno service so we don't need to migrate to Athena, then and only then, we might have a chance of making this deadline. Alternatively, we leave things as is, and push the timeline back by two months, or cut the scope so that we don't ship chat."

Refuse to accept top-down deadlines. If you're a manager, protect your team and have them come up with a time pressure-free estimate. Be clear what you can and cannot do with your constraints.

Not enough people or bandwidth

With all the other work going on, the team cannot realistically take on another project, but leadership says there's no choice.

How to mitigate:

- Be clear on how many efforts/projects your team can handle at one time. Basically, clarify what your typical output is.
- Offer to drop other, currently top priority projects, but be clear on the impact. Take this response as an example: "Look, if you convince the Chief Product Officer that we can stop working on Project Zeno, we can take on this other project. However, even if we do so, stopping work will be a blow to team morale and the context switch will add several weeks to the Zeno work. I need the CPO personally telling me she is okay with the team dropping this work, taking the hit to morale, and adding four weeks to Zeno."

A surprise midway through the project

Building software is full of surprises and things come out of the blue unexpectedly and unpredictably.

How to mitigate:

- What type of risk is it? See if any of the above mitigation approaches work.
- Can it be worked around or ignored? It might be a false alarm, so investigate.
- Should the timeline be extended? This is the most sensible approach, and the answer is more often 'yes' than many people expect.
- Can you take on tech, architecture or process debt in doing a quick fix, and only do a proper fix at the end of the project? The risk here is that the fix never gets done, so take responsibility for it getting prioritized.

No true idea how long something will actually take

This is a common risk, however it's one that's often invisible to leadership because all they see is the estimate, which is often a stab in the dark.

How to mitigate:

- Figure out what type of risk this really is. In most cases, it's a technology risk; something you've not used or done before.
- Can you break it down into smaller pieces, splitting off well-understood things from unknowns?
- Prototype, or get more information on the underlying challenge. You could also time-

box this as a research activity, sometimes referred to as "doing a spike."

Discovering new risks and building software in new ways, go hand in hand. Instead of trying to eliminate risks, accept they will exist. Learn to differentiate between major and minor risks, and keep your cool when you find new ones. Keep the "law of software project physics" in mind, and if the new risk increases the scope, then know you have to either cut the scope, lengthen the timeline, or find a way to add more labor to the project.

7. Wrapping Up Projects

I've seen many great project kickoffs, but far fewer good wrap-ups. Failing to properly wrap up projects has drawbacks:

- The team often doesn't get credit for good work they've done. Also, there's no celebration.
- Team members get pulled in to work on other projects, and the final stage of the project – typically the rollout – is done ad-hoc.
- Without a wrap-up there's no reflection on how the project went, and team members don't get learnings.

A proper wrap-up for a project is just as important as a good kickoff. It's a win for everyone: project stakeholders – even those unaware of the project – the team which owns the project, everyone working on it, and the project lead too. What does a good wrap-up look like?

- **Clarity on what "done" means**. This is where the kickoff is important; "done" should be clear from the start. With clarity in place, it's easy enough to decide when to declare completion.
- **Consider doing a retrospective with the team**. At the end of the project it's good to reflect on what went well, talk through what could have been better, and collect learnings. Choose a retrospective format that resonates with you. If you're a project lead, you can run this retrospective, or support someone in facilitating the discussion to help them grow.
- **Write a final project update for a wider group**, including any team which might have an interest in the project, as well as project stakeholders Write a concise summary of why people should care, what the impact – or expected impact – is, summarize the work, highlight key contributors, and link to details.
- **Get feedback on this final update from others, before distributing it**. For example, show the document to your product manager, ask them to point out what's unclear, and for one improvement suggestion. You could solicit similar feedback from other engineering managers or product managers, or someone in the company who you've read good status update emails from. People interested in the project should find your

final update easy to read, so follow the advice in the issue Becoming a better writer[5], and get feedback, pre-publication.

- **Time the final update for release soon after the project group disbands**. There are projects where you need to wait weeks or months for concrete results. I suggest writing a final update not long after the project team moves on to other things. Use your judgment, but I've found raising awareness that a project is going live and offering ways for people to track its results, is more efficient than waiting until the final update.
- **Spotlight all team members and anyone who meaningfully helped**. A final project update email is the place to praise people by name, and in the chat channel as well. Also, if there's the chance to present the project at a company talk or event, do the same thing there. Make sure not to omit key contributors, which is why pre-publication feedback is good.
- **Celebrate with the project team**. This is a great opportunity to let off steam and bond as a group. It could involve going out for dinner as a team, or to a fun event. For remote teams, celebrating is more tricky, but could involve shipping gifts to people, sending a virtual gift card, or doing a remote toast with everyone on a call.

What about projects which fail more than succeed?

Sooner or later, you'll work on a project that is objectively a failure.

For me, this was when we got all the way to beta testing when we had to admit we could never ship the project as it was, and that addressing problems would be a bigger task than the project itself. Nonetheless, we did a wrap-up to recognize our work and ended on a positive note. Here's what we did:

- **Close positively**. Yes, we failed to achieve the business objective. However, we succeeded in building and shipping a version of the project. We started the wrap-up by acknowledging it was complete and that we'd done the work we signed up for.
- **Share learnings**. The project did not move the needle in the way the business needed, but we learned several reasons why not. We shared these learnings after a long retrospective and period of reflection. Part of the wrap-up email was a summary of learnings.
- **Share small wins**. There's a high chance the work contains partial successes, and that there were some wins along the way. In our wrap-up, we highlighted these and thanked team members for their work.

You cannot fully control the business outcomes of any project, but as project lead you have a big influence on the wrapping up of an unsuccessful project. Learn the lessons, and acknowledge the good work and wins you all shared on the journey. Ensure you apply those learnings, next time!

---

[5]https://newsletter.pragmaticengineer.com/p/becoming-a-better-writer

17

SHIPPING TO PRODUCTION

As a tech lead, you're expected to get your team's work into production quickly and reliably. But how does this happen, and which principles should you follow? This depends on several factors: the environment, the maturity of the product being worked on, how expensive outages are, and whether moving fast or having no reliability issues is more important.

This chapter covers shipping to production reliably in different environments. It highlights common approaches across the industry and helps you refine how your team thinks about this process. We cover:

1. Extremes in shipping to production
2. Typical shipping processes at different types of companies
3. Principles and tools for shipping to production responsibly
4. Additional verification layers and protections
5. Taking pragmatic risks to move faster
6. Additional considerations for defining a deployment process
7. Selecting an approach

1. Extremes in Shipping to Production

Let's start with two "extremes" in shipping to production:

YOLO shipping

The "you only live once" (YOLO) approach is used for many prototypes, side projects, and unstable products like alpha/beta versions. It's also how some urgent changes make it into production.

The idea is simple, make a change in production and check if it works in production. Examples of YOLO shipping include:

- SSH into a production server → open an editor (e.g. vim) → make a change in a file → save the file and/or restart the server → see if the change works.
- Make a change to a source code file → force land this change without a code review → push a new deployment of a service.
- Log on to the production database → execute a production query to fix a data issue

(e.g. modifying records with issues) → hope this fixes the problem.

YOLO shipping is as fast as it gets when shipping a change to production. However, it also has the highest risk of introducing new issues into production because there is no safety net. For products with few to zero production users, the damage done by introducing bugs into production can be low, so this approach is justifiable.

YOLO releases are common for:

- Side projects
- Early-stage startups with no customers
- Mid-sized companies with poor engineering practices
- Resolving urgent incidents at places without well-defined incident handling practices

As a software product grows and more customers rely on it, code changes need to go through extra validation before production. Let's go to the other extreme: a team obsessed with doing everything possible to ship zero bugs into production.

Thorough verification through multiple stages

This is an approach used for mature products with many valuable customers, where a single bug can cause major problems. This rigorous approach is used if bugs could result in customers losing money, or make them switch to a competitor's offering.

Several verification layers are in place, with the goal of simulating the real world with greater accuracy, such as:

- **Local validation**. Tooling for software engineers to catch obvious issues.
- **CI validation**. Automated tests like unit tests and linting on every pull request.
- **Automation before deploying to a test environment**. More expensive tests such as integration tests or end-to-end tests, before deployment to the next environment.
- **Test environment #1**. More automated testing, like smoke tests. Quality assurance engineers might manually exercise the product, running manual tests and doing exploratory testing.
- **Test environment #2**. An environment where a subset of real users – such as internal company users or paid beta testers – exercise the product. The environment is coupled with monitoring and the rollout is halted upon sign of a regression.
- **Pre-production environment**. An environment in which the final set of validations are run. This often means running another set of automated and manual tests.
- **Staged rollout**. A small subset of users get the changes, and the team monitors for key metrics to remain healthy and checks customer feedback. A staged rollout strategy depends on the riskiness of the change being made.
- **Full rollout**. As the staged rollout increases, at some point changes are pushed to all customers.

- **Post-rollout**. Issues arise in production, for which monitoring and alerting are set up, and also a feedback loop with customers. If there's an issue, it's dealt with by the standard oncall process. *We discuss this process more in Part V: "Reliable software engineering."*

A heavyweight release process is used by:

- Highly regulated industries, such as healthcare, aviation, or automotive.
- Telecommunications providers, where it's common to have 6 months of thorough testing of changes before major changes are shipped to customers.
- Banks, where bugs could cause financial losses.
- Traditional companies with legacy codebases with little automated testing. These places want to keep quality high and are happy to slow down releases by adding verification stages.

2. Typical Shipping Processes

Different companies tend to take different steps in shipping to production. Below is a summary of typical approaches, highlighting the variety of processes:

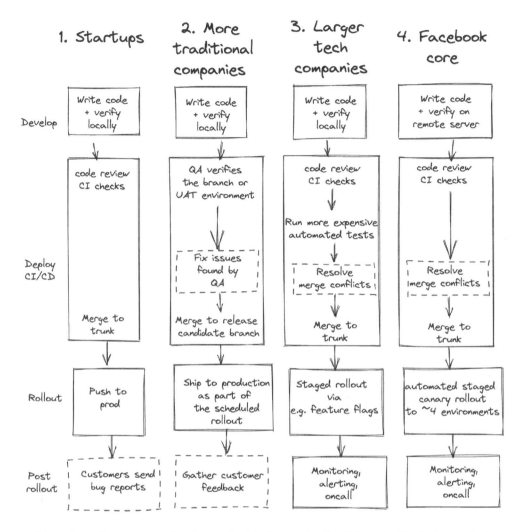

How do various companies typically ship to production? An admittedly imperfect attempt to visualize the common approaches – and their differences. Dotted boxes mean "often, but not always."

Startups

Startups typically do fewer quality checks. These companies tend to prioritize moving fast and iterating quickly, and often do so without much of a safety net. This makes perfect sense if they don't have customers yet. As customers arrive, teams need to find ways to avoid regressions and the shipping of bugs.

Startups are usually too small to invest in automation, and so most do manual QA – including the founders being the 'ultimate' testers, while some places hire dedicated QA folks. As a company finds its product-market fit, it's more common to invest in automation. And at tech startups that hire strong engineering talent, these teams can put automated tests in place from day one.

Traditional companies

These places tend to rely more heavily on QAs teams. Automation is sometimes present at more traditional companies, but typically they rely on large QA teams to verify what is built. Working on branches is also common; it's rare to have trunk-based development.

Code mostly gets pushed to production on a weekly schedule or even less frequently, after the QA team verifies functionality.

Staging and UAT (User Acceptance Testing) environments are more common, as are larger, batched changes shipped between environments. Sign-off is required from the QA team, the product manager, or the project manager, in order to progress the release to the next stage.

Large tech companies

These places typically invest heavily in infrastructure and automation related to shipping with confidence. Such investments often include automated tests which run quickly and deliver rapid feedback, canarying, feature flags, and staged rollouts.

These companies aim for a high quality bar, but also to ship immediately when quality checks are complete, working on trunk. Tooling to deal with merge conflicts becomes important, given that some places can make over 100 changes on trunk per day. *For details on QA at Big Tech, see the article How Big Tech does QA*[1].

Meta's core product

Facebook, as a product and engineering team, merits a separate mention, because this organization has a sophisticated and effective approach few other companies use.

This Meta product has fewer automated tests than many would assume, but on the other hand, Facebook has an exceptional automated canarying functionality, where the code is rolled out through 4 environments, from a testing environment with automation, through one that all employees use, then through a test market that is a smaller geographical region, and finally to all users. At each stage, the rollout automatically halts if the metrics are off.

---

[1] https://newsletter.pragmaticengineer.com/p/how-big-tech-does-qa

3. Principles and Tools

What are principles and approaches worth following for shipping changes to production responsibly? Consider these:

Development environments

Use a local or isolated development environment. Engineers should be able to make changes on their local machine, or in an isolated environment unique to them. It's more common for developers to work in local environments. However, places like Meta are shifting to remote servers for each engineer. From the article, Inside Facebook's Engineering culture[2]:

> "Most developers work with a remote server, not locally. Starting from around 2019, all web and backend development is done remotely, with no code copied locally, and Nuclide facilitating this workflow. In the background, Nuclide was using virtual machines (VMs) at first, later moving to OnDemand instances – similar to how GitHub Codespaces works today – years before GitHub launched Codespaces.
>
> Mobile development is still mostly done on local machines, as doing this in a remote setup, as with web and backend, has tooling challenges."

Verify locally. After writing the code, do a local test to ensure it works as expected.

Testing and verification

Consider edge cases and test for them. Which obscure cases does your code change need to account for? Which real-world use cases haven't you accounted for yet?

Before finalizing work on the change, compile a list of edge cases. Consider writing automated tests for them, if possible. At least do manual testing. Coming up with a list of unconventional edge cases is a task for which QA engineers or testers can be very helpful.

Write automated tests to validate your changes. After manually verifying your changes, exercise them with automated tests. If following a methodology like test-driven development (TDD,) you might do this the other way around by writing automated tests first, and then checking that your code change passes them.

Another pair of eyes: a code review. With your code changes complete, put up a pull request and get somebody with context to look at your code changes. Write a clear, concise

---

[2]https://newsletter.pragmaticengineer.com/p/facebook-2

description of the changes, which edge cases are tested for, and get a code review.

All automated tests pass, minimizing the risk of regressions. Before pushing the code, run all the existing tests for the codebase. This is typically done automatically, via the CI/CD system (continuous integration/continuous deployment.)

Monitoring, oncall and incident management

Have monitoring in place for key product characteristics related to your change. How will you know if your change breaks things that automated tests don't check for? You won't know unless you have ways to monitor health indicators on the system. For this, ensure there are health indicators written for the change, or others you can use.

For example, at Uber most code changes were rolled out as experiments with a defined set of metrics they were expected to improve, or not have an impact on. One metric which should be unchanged was the percentage of customers successfully taking trips. If this metric dropped with a code change, an alert was fired and the team making it had to investigate whether it degraded user experience.

Have oncall in place, with enough context to know what to do if things go wrong. After a change is shipped to production, there's a fair chance some defects will only become visible later. That why it's good to have an oncall rotation in place with engineers who can respond to health alerts, inbounds from customers, and customer support.

Make sure the oncall is organized so that colleagues on duty have enough context on how to mitigate outages. In most cases, teams have runbooks with details about how to confirm and mitigate outages. Many teams also have oncall training, and some do oncall situation simulations to prepare team members.

Create a culture of blameless incident handling. This is an environment in which the team learns and improves from incidents. I'm not saying to follow all these ideas, but it's a good exercise to consider why you would not implement these steps. We cover more on this topic in Part V: "Reliable Systems."

4. Additional Verification Layers

Some companies have extra verification layers for delivering reliable code to production. Here are 10 of these safety nets:

1. Separate deployment environments

Setting up separate environments to test code changes is a common safety net in the release process. Before code hits production, it's deployed to one of these environments, which might be called testing, UAT (user acceptance testing,) staging, pre-prod (pre-production,) etc.

At companies with QA teams, QA often exercises a change in this environment and looks for regressions. Some environments are for executing automated tests, such as end-to-end tests, smoke tests, or load tests.

These environments have heavy maintenance costs, both in resources, as machines need to operate to make this environment available, and even more so in the keeping of data up to date. These environments need to be seeded with data that's generated or brought over from production.

2. Dynamically spin up testing/deployment environments

Maintaining deployment environments tends to create a lot of overhead. This is especially true when doing data migrations[3] for which data in all test environments needs to be updated.

A better development experience involves investing in automation to spin up test environments, including the seeding of the data they contain. This opens up opportunities for more efficient automated testing, easier validation of changes, and automation which better fits your use cases. At the same time, putting such test environments in place can be a significant investment. As a tech lead, you need to make a business case for building such a solution, or buying and integrating a vendor solution. For example, some cloud development environment vendors offer ways to spin up these environments. *We touch on cloud development environments in Part V: "Software engineering."*

3. A dedicated Quality Assurance (QA) team

An investment many companies make to reduce defects is to hire a QA team, usually responsible for manual and exploratory testing of the product. Most QA teams also write automated tests, such as end-to-end tests.

My view is that there's value in a QA team doing only manual testing. In productive teams, QA often becomes a domain expert, or people code automated tests; and frequently both:

- QA is a domain expert: QA folks help engineers anticipate edge cases and do exploratory testing of new edge cases and unexpected behaviors.
- QA rolls sleeves up and writes automation: QA folks shift to become QA engineers, as well as manual testers. They start getting involved in the automation of tests, and have a say in shaping the automation strategy, to speed up getting code changes into

---

[3]https://newsletter.pragmaticengineer.com/p/migrations

production.

I worked with dedicated QA engineers at Microsoft, in 2013. Back then, this role was called software development engineer in test (SDET,) and these engineers brought a real testing mindset to the table, on top of writing automated tests. For more details on the evolution of the SDET role at Microsoft, see my article How Microsoft does QA[4].

4. Exploratory testing

Most engineers are good at testing their changes to verify they work as expected, and at considering edge cases. But what about testing how retail users utilize the product?

This is where exploratory testing comes in.

Exploratory testing involves simulating how customers will use the product, in order to reveal edge cases. Good exploratory testing requires empathy with users, an understanding of the product, and tooling to simulate use cases.

At companies with dedicated QA teams, it's usually they who do exploratory testing. At places with no QA team, it's down to engineers, or the business may recruit vendors specializing in exploratory testing.

5. Canarying

This term derives from the phrase "canary in the coal mine," which was a practice by miners of taking a caged canary bird with them down a coal mine, to detect dangerous gas. The bird has a lower tolerance for toxic gasses than humans, so if it stopped chirping or fainted, it was a warning sign that gas was present, and the miners evacuated.

Today, canary testing means rolling out code changes to a small percentage of the user base, then monitoring this deployment's health signals for signs that something's wrong. A common way to implement canarying is to route traffic to the new version of the code using a load balancer, or to deploy a new version of the code to a single node.

6. Feature flags and experimentation

Another way to control the rollout of a change is to hide it behind a feature flag in the code. This feature flag can then be enabled for a subset of users who execute the new version of the code.

Feature flags are easy enough to implement, and might look something like this for an imaginary feature called "Zeno:"

---

[4]https://blog.pragmaticengineer.com/how-microsoft-does-qa

```
if( featureFlags.isEnabled("Zeno_Feature_Flag")) {
        // New code to execute
} else {
        // Old code to execute
}
```

Feature flags are a common way to run experiments involving bucketing users in two groups: treatment group (the experiment) and control group (those not subject to the experiment.) These groups get different experiences, and the engineering and data science teams evaluate and compare results.

Stale feature flags are the biggest downside of this approach. With large codebases, it's common to see feature flags "polluting" the codebase because they weren't removed after the feature was rolled out. Most teams tackle this issue by having a reminder to remove the flag after rollout – for example, adding a calendar event, or creating a ticket – while some companies build automated tooling to detect and remove stale flags. The Piranha tool[5], open sourced by Uber, is one such example.

7. Staged rollout

Staged rollouts involve shipping changes step by step, and evaluating the results at each stage. They typically define the percentage of the user base which gets a new functionality, or the region in which this functionality should roll out, or both.

A staged rollout plan may look like this:

- Phase 1: 10% rollout in New Zealand (a small market for validating changes)
- Phase 2: 50% rollout in New Zealand
- Phase 3: 100% rollout in New Zealand
- Phase 4: 10% rollout, globally
- Phase 5: 25% rollout, globally
- Phase 6: 50% rollout, globally
- Phase 7: 99% rollout, globally (leaving just a very small "control" group for more verification)
- Phase 8: 100% rollout, globally

Between each rollout stage, a criteria is set for when it can continue. This is typically defined as when no unexpected regressions happen and the expected changes occur (or do not occur) to business metrics. Canary releases are fundamentally a simpler type of staged rollouts – and canarying is usually much quicker than a staged rollout process.

---

[5]https://github.com/uber/piranha

8. Multi-tenancy

An approach growing in popularity is using production as the one and only environment to deploy code to, including testing in production.

While testing in production sounds reckless, it's not if done with a multi-tenant approach. In this article[6], Uber describes its journey from a staging environment, through a test sandbox with shadow traffic, to tenancy-based routing.

The idea behind multi-tenancy is that the tenancy context is propagated with requests. Services receiving a request can tell if it's a production request, a test tenancy, a beta tenancy, and so on. Services have logic built in to support tenancies and might process or route requests differently. For example, a payments system getting a request with a test tenancy would likely mock the payment, instead of making an actual payment request.

9. Automated rollbacks

A powerful way to increase reliability is to make rollbacks automatic for any code changes suspected of breaking something. This is an approach Booking.com uses; any experiment which degrades key metrics is shut down and the change rolled back[7].

At companies which invest in multi-staged automatic rollouts with automated rollbacks, engineers rarely fear breaking production and can move quickly with confidence.

10. Automated rollouts and rollbacks

Taking automated rollbacks a step further by combining them with staged rollouts and multiple testing environments, is an approach Meta has uniquely implemented for its core product.

Note that while it's common for teams to use some of the approaches mentioned here, it's rare to use them all at once. Some approaches cancel each other out; for example, there's little need for multiple testing environments if multi-tenancy is in place, and testing in production already happens.

5. Taking Pragmatic Risks

There are times when you want to move faster than normal, and are comfortable with taking more risk. Here are pragmatic approaches for doing so.

---

[6]https://www.uber.com/blog/multitenancy-microservice-architecture/
[7]https://twitter.com/mangiucugna/status/1528715664860622850

Decide which process or tool it's not okay to bypass. Is force-landing without running any tests an option, can you make a change to the codebase without anyone looking at it, can a production database be changed without testing?

It's down to every team – or company – to decide which processes cannot be bypassed. If this question arises at a mature company with a large number of dependent users, I'd think carefully before breaking rules because it could do more harm than good. If you decide to bypass rules in order to move faster, then I recommend getting support from teammates first.

Give a heads up to relevant stakeholders when shipping risky changes. Every now and then, you'll ship a change that's less tested than is ideal. This makes it a riskier change. It's good practice to give a heads-up to people who could alert you if something strange happens. Stakeholders worth notifying in these cases can include:

- Teammates
- Oncalls for teams which depend on your team, and whom you depend on
- Customer support
- Business stakeholders with access to business metrics, who can notify you if something trends in the wrong direction

Have a rollback plan that's easy to execute. How can you revert a change which causes an issue? Even when moving fast, have a plan that's easy enough to execute. This is especially important for data changes and configuration changes.

Revert plans used to be commonly added to diffs at Facebook during its early days. From Inside Facebook's Engineering Culture[8]:

> "Early engineers shared how people used to also add a revert plan to their diff to instruct how to undo the change, in the frequent case this needed to be done. This approach has improved over the years with better test tooling."

Inspect customer feedback after shipping risky changes. Check customer feedback channels like forums, reviews, and customer support tickets, after you ship a risky change. Proactively check these channels for customers with issues stemming from a rolled out change.

Track incidents and measure their impact. Do you know how many outages your product had during the past month, or past three months? What did customers experience, and what was the business impact?

If the answer to these questions is "don't know," then you're flying blind and don't know how reliable your systems are. Consider changing your approach to track and measure outages,

---

[8]https://newsletter.pragmaticengineer.com/p/facebook-2

and accumulate their impacts. You need this data to know when to tweak release processes for more reliable releases. You'll also need it for error budgets.

Use error budgets to decide if you can do risky deployments. Start measuring the availability of your system's SLIs (Service Level Indicators) and SLOs (Service Level Objectives,) or by measuring how long the system is degraded or down.

Next, define an error budget[9]. This is the amount of temporary service degradation that's deemed acceptable for users. So long as this error budget isn't exceeded, then riskier deployments – which are those more likely to break the service – might be fine to proceed with. However, once the error budget is used up, pause all deployments that are considered risky.

6. Additional Considerations

In this chapter, we haven't gone into detail about some parts of the release process to production which any mature product and company must address. They include:

- **Security practices**. Who's allowed to make changes to systems, and how are these changes logged for audit? How are security audits on code changes done to reduce the risk that vulnerabilities make it into the system? Which secure coding practices are followed, and how are they encouraged or enforced?
- **Configuration management**. Many changes to systems are configuration changes. How is configuration stored, and how are changes to configurations signed off and tracked?
- **Roles and responsibilities**. Which roles are in the release process? For example, who owns the deployment systems? In the case of batched deployments, who follows up on issues, and gives the green light to deployments?
- **Regulation**. When working in highly regulated sectors, shipping changes might include working with regulators and adhering to strict rules. This can mean a deliberately slow pace of shipping. Regulatory requirements could include legislation like GDPR (General Data Protection Regulation,) PCI DSS (Payment Card Industry Data Security Standard,) HIPAA (Health Insurance Portability and Accountability Act,) FERPA (Family Educational Rights and Privacy Act,) FCRA (Fair Credit Reporting Act,) Section 508 when working with US federal agencies, SOX compliance (Sarbanes-Oxley Act, important in finance,) the European Accessibility Act when developing for a government within the European Union, country-specific privacy laws, and many others.

---

[9]https://sre.google/workbook/alerting-on-slos/#low-traffic-services-and-error-budget-alerting

7. Selecting an Approach

We've covered a lot of ground and many potential approaches for shipping reliably to production, every time. So how do you decide which to choose? There's a few things to consider.

How much are you willing to invest in modern tooling, in order to ship more iterations? Before getting into the tradeoffs of various approaches, be honest with yourself about how much investment you, your team, or company, are willing to make in tooling.

Many of the approaches we've covered involve putting tooling in place. Most of this can be integrated through vendors, but some must be purchased. At a company with platform teams or SRE teams focused on reliability, there might be lots of support. At a smaller company, you may need to make the case for investing in tooling.

How big an error budget can your business realistically afford? If a bug makes it to production for a few customers, what's the impact? Does the business lose millions of dollars, or are customers mildly annoyed – but not churning – if the bug is fixed quickly?

For businesses like private banks, a bug in the money flows can cause massive losses. For products like Facebook, a quickly-fixed UI bug will not have much impact. This is why the Facebook product has less automated testing in place than at many other tech companies, and why Meta has no dedicated QA function for pure software teams.

What iteration speed should you target as a minimum? The faster engineers can ship their code to production, the sooner they get feedback. In many cases, faster iteration results in higher quality because engineers push smaller and less risky changes to production.

According to the DORA metrics[10] – which stands for DevOps Research and Assessment metrics – elite performers do multiple on-demand deployments per day. The lead time for changes – the duration between code being committed and it finally reaching production – is less than a day for elite performers. I'm not the biggest fan of only focusing on DORA metrics, as I think they don't give a full view of engineering excellence, and that focusing only on those numbers can be misleading. Nevertheless, these observations of how nimble teams ship to production quickly do match my experience. *For more of my thoughts on developer productivity, see this two-part article, co-authored with Kent Beck*[11].

At most Big Tech firms and many high-growth startups it takes less than a day – typically a few hours – from code being committed to it reaching production, and teams deploy on-demand, multiple times per day.

---

[10]https://dora.dev

[11]https://newsletter.pragmaticengineer.com/p/measuring-developer-productivity

If you have QA teams, what is the primary purpose of the QA function? QA teams are typical at companies that cannot afford many bugs in production, or lack the capability to automate testing.

Still, I suggest setting a goal for what the QA organization should evolve into, and how it should support engineering. If all goes well, what will QA look like in a few years' time? Will they do only manual testing? Surely not. Will they own the automation strategy, or help engineering teams ship code changes to a deployment environment on the same day? What about allowing engineers to ship to production in less than a week?

Think ahead and set goals which lead to shorter iteration, faster feedback loops, and catching and fixing issues more quickly.

How much legacy infrastructure and code is there? It can be expensive, time-consuming, and difficult to modernize legacy systems with some modern practices like automated testing, staged rollouts, or automatic rollbacks. Take an inventory of the existing tech stack to evaluate if it's worth modernizing or not. There will be times when there's little point investing in modernization.

Consider investing in advanced capabilities. As of today, some deployment capabilities are still considered less common because they're hard to build, including:

- Sophisticated monitoring and alerting setups, where code changes can easily be paired with monitoring and alerting for key system metrics. Engineers can easily monitor whether their changes regress system health indicators.
- Automated staged rollouts, with automated rollbacks.
- The ability to generate dynamic testing environments.
- Robust integration, end-to-end and load testing capabilities.
- Testing in production through multi-tenancy approaches.

Decide if you want or need to invest in any of these complex approaches. They could result in faster shipping, with added confidence.

18

STAKEHOLDER MANAGEMENT

Stakeholders are people and groups with an interest in a project's outcome. Internally, they may be product folks, the legal team, engineering teams, or any other business unit. Stakeholders can also be external to the company, in the form of users, customers, vendors, regulatory bodies, and others.

The best time to figure out the key stakeholders in your project is as soon as possible. The worst time is when you are ready to ship, as an important-enough person could then appear seemingly from nowhere and take a proper look at your project for the first time, and declare major changes are needed. In this case, it would have been better to consult this key stakeholder earlier.

In this chapter, we cover ways of identifying stakeholders and working with them.

1. The real goal of stakeholder management
2. Types of stakeholders
3. Figuring out who your stakeholders are
4. Keeping them in the loop
5. Problematic stakeholders
6. Learning from stakeholders

1. The Real Goal of Stakeholder Management

As a tech lead, why do you need to manage stakeholders? Why identify them and give them detailed enough, frequent enough updates? Is it to maintain a good relationship with them? This is nice to have, but isn't the real goal.

The point of stakeholder management is for the project to succeed by keeping everyone on the same page. So many projects fail because the people involved have different ideas of what to do and how to do it. This means that when engineering announces a project is done, business stakeholders often say that what has been built is not what the business needs.

Stakeholder management involves various approaches to ensure everyone with a meaningful say in the project knows what's happening, knows about new risks and changes to the project, and is aware of – and does not object to – key responses to changes in a project. It is just a tool to help a project succeed and to ensure everyone agrees what success looks like.

I worked on a project with several teams involved, in which the project lead sent weekly, pages-long status updates to all team members and posted updates on chat. Yet it felt like everyone was pulling in different directions, and it was unclear what the real focus was, beyond finishing our assigned engineering task. In the end, the project seemed like a failure and left a sour taste in everyone's mouths.

On another, similarly complex project, the goal was much clearer and updates were sparser, but the project felt more united. And when we shipped, the business stakeholders surprised the engineering team with a bottle of champagne as a thank-you. The difference between this project and the previous one? The project lead communicated much more with product folks and business stakeholders.

Good stakeholder management is highly collaborative. For the latter, successful project, the tech lead did far less "formal" stakeholder management in terms of emails and written updates. What they did was talk with business stakeholders in person and on video. And the tech lead became familiar enough with the business domain that they used good judgment in seeking input from the business when an engineering risk meant potentially changing the scope of the work.

2. Types of Stakeholders

For most engineering projects, stakeholders typically fall into these groups:

- **Customers**: users of a project's outputs. For engineering teams building B2C (business to customer) products, these are the end users. For B2B (business to business) projects, they're the product's users. And for internal-facing projects – frequently built by platform teams[1] – these are internal teams.
- **Business stakeholders**: internal, non-tech groups at a company with skin in a project, such as Legal, Marketing, Customer Support, Finance, Operations, and others. My take is that a good kickoff is needed so that engineering is aware of who all the business stakeholders are, which we cover in the "Project Management" section. Why? If a business stakeholder is out of the loop, it can delay a project.
- **External stakeholders**: teams at other companies with an interest in a project, such as vendors, or other engineering teams at a partner organization.
- **Product stakeholders**: product managers, design, data science, and other groups in tech that work closely with product managers. Most of them collaborate with business stakeholders and the engineering team.
- **Engineering stakeholders**: internal engineering teams which are upstream or downstream dependencies for a project, defined below.

---

[1] https://blog.pragmaticengineer.com/platform-teams

Categorize stakeholders by dependency

Bucketing stakeholders into one of the following categories can be a useful mental model. For this, visualize a flowing river, with teams building dams in different places, both downstream and upstream, from your team.

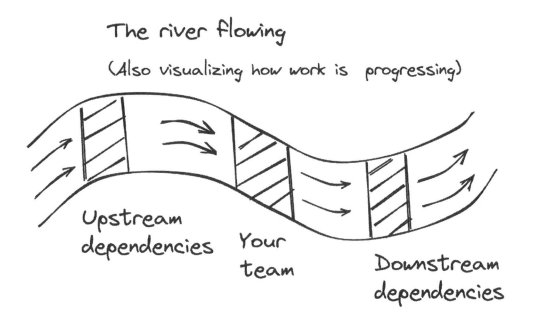

The river flowing

(Also visualizing how work is progressing)

Upstream dependencies

Your team

Downstream dependencies

Upstream and downstream dependencies, visualized.

- **Upstream dependencies** are teams whose work you depend on. They must do a specific task in order for your team to do its work, and for the project to get done.
- **Downstream dependencies** are teams that depend on your work. Downstream teams come after yours, meaning your work must be done before they can complete their part of a project.
- **Strategic stakeholders** are people or teams you want to keep in the loop, who can often help unblock upstream dependencies.

This categorization helps make it clearer which stakeholders to communicate with in certain situations. For example:

3. Figure Out Who Your Stakeholders Are

As a tech lead, knowing your key stakeholders is vital because not knowing can easily harm a project in the forms of wasted work and delays. I have personal experience of this. On one project, my team forgot to share the engineering plan – the RFC – with an engineering team whose service we needed to modify. When we got to making this modification, the engineering team in question blocked it because our approach made no sense for their system. We eventually found a solution, but not knowing the team was a stakeholder delayed the project by two weeks.

In another case, I observed an engineering team work for a month on a project, only for the legal department to intervene and block it, unexpectedly. Legal had not been in the loop, even though they should have been. They reviewed the proposed changes, said the project was too risky to ship and wouldn't budge from this judgment, so the project was canceled. The engineering team would have saved themselves much wasted work had they involved the legal team earlier.

So, how do you find out who your stakeholders are? This question is especially relevant at large companies with dozens – or hundreds – of engineering teams, and large numbers of product/design/data and business folks. There's the hard way, as detailed above, and there's the easy way:

Just ask! Consult people who definitely are stakeholders about who else could be a stakeholder. For example:

- Ask your product counterpart which business colleagues could have an interest.
- Talk with data science folks, as they often collaborate with other data scientists to ensure experiments don't overlap.
- Ask experienced tech leads which teams they identified as stakeholders for previous projects. Could any of them be your stakeholders, too?

Look at architecture changes and the code. Finding engineering stakeholders can often be done just by understanding which parts of the code and which services will be modified by your project. Reach out to teams who own those parts of the code and services.

The concept of upstream and downstream stakeholders is useful when modifying services. This is because a common enough conflict is when an engineering team modifies a service, which breaks a downstream user of it. This can be avoided by identifying the downstream user as a key stakeholder early. Then the engineering team could get feedback sooner, and modify their plans so as not to break that team.

Identify the "usual suspects." There are some teams whom it's safe to assume have an interest in your project. At midsize and larger companies these tend to be:

- Engineering
- Product
- Design/user experience
- Data science
- Security and compliance

- Infrastructure, DevOps, Site Reliability
- Legal
- Marketing/growth/user acquisition
- Customer support/helpdesk
- Operations
- Sales/business development
- Finance

Make a list of the usual stakeholders at your company, then figure out if they have an interest in your project.

4. Keep Them in The Loop

"Stakeholder management" is a fancy phrase for ensuring everyone who needs to know what your team is doing, does know. Poor stakeholder management is leaving key people and teams out of the communications loop. This can cause frustration, trigger complaints, and delay a project.

Once you've identified your stakeholders, it's helpful to ensure they don't get taken by surprise by decisions your team makes. Given there are usually several stakeholders, it's impractical to use one-to-one communication, and it is more efficient to update stakeholders as a group.

I've observed three common ways to keep stakeholders updated:

1. **Meetings**: recurring or ad-hoc. In a meeting, the project lead shares progress, decisions made, blockers, and invites input from stakeholders.
2. **Asynchronous updates**: such as emails or chat messages. The content is the same as in a meeting, but less time-consuming. A downside is stakeholders might miss a message, and tend to focus more during meetings.
3. **Hybrid**. When stakeholders are expected to have significant input, organize a meeting. Milestone demonstrations and major project changes may warrant this. Otherwise, stick with asynchronous communication.

It's helpful to understand your organization's culture; how do tech leads and product folks keep stakeholders updated? Do stakeholders prefer certain formats for updates? If so, it could be sensible to use familiar formats in the first few projects you lead.

Proactively written communication on how a project is progressing is always useful. An approach I've seen work well is sending regular update emails about progress, risks and how they're being mitigated, timeline changes, and confidence about deadlines. Here's an example of an update email:

Project Zeno Update - week ending 22 Jan

Home | Tracking | Roadmap | Status | Subscribe to weekly reports

Project goal: enable a one-tap shopping experience for 2M customers in Brazil.

Executive summary: 2 weeks delay compared to the original timeline.

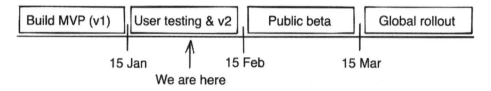

Milestones	ETA	Status	Comment
MVP (v1)	15 Jan	✅ Complete	
User testing (v1)	15 Feb	🔄 In progress	100 users onboarded.
V2 features	15 Feb	⚠️ 60%	Delayed from 1 Feb. See details below.
Public beta rollout	15 Mar	Not started	Depending on legal signoff. See details below.
Global rollout	15 Apr	Not started	

A status update email proactively sharing the project's status, risks, and mitigation. Template source: Software engineers leading project / The Pragmatic Engineer[2]

A nice thing about an email is that it acts as a "master" status update and useful reference in meetings and other catchups with stakeholders. Meetings can be necessary for stakeholders who are demanding or tend to have lots to say about a project. However, as a tech lead the more you can get stakeholders to treat regular status update emails as the 'source of truth,' the easier it will be to ensure all stakeholders are quite literally on the same page.

5. Problematic Stakeholders

You will encounter problematic stakeholders as a project lead. But what does "problematic" mean? This depends on whether they are a downstream, upstream, or a strategic stakeholder:

- Downstream problematic stakeholders are teams or individuals you see as unreliable,

---

[2]https://newsletter.pragmaticengineer.com/p/engineers-leading-projects-part-2

or have issues collaborating with, or trusting them.
- Upstream problematic stakeholders often bug you about when you'll be ready, and try to push you and the team.
- Strategic problematic stakeholders continuously seek updates, or give you a hard time about emerging challenges.

In each case, the biggest issue tends to be communication and trust. Below are some approaches to improve things that apply to all the above groups.

Talk face-to-face

Instead of communicating via chat or email, consider talking in person with problematic folks. Get on a video call, or meet in the workplace and lay out the issues you're observing. Discuss what can change to improve things. For example, if an upstream stakeholder keeps nagging you about whether your team can ship a milestone sooner, walk them through the progress to date and what's left to do, give feedback that being nagged isn't helpful, and reach an agreement on how to work better together.

Be transparent and educate them

For upstream stakeholders and strategic stakeholders – both typically impatient – explain what needs to be done and why, and where you are right now with it. It's easiest to do this in face-to-face meetings.

Update emails are another way to be transparent and educational. Regular, honest updates about progress helps to calm nerves, which is another reason I'm a fan of them. If you write these, there's a good chance that simply adding problematic stakeholders to the mailing list will resolve the problem.

Ask for support

There may be times when talking directly and being more transparent doesn't help. If you're getting nowhere, it's time to pull in your management chain or project leadership chain for assistance. Ask for help and advice from people with more authority than you.

6. Learning from Stakeholders

If you do a good enough job of managing stakeholders, you'll reduce the risk of unexpected delays caused by a stakeholder who's not in the loop. However, if you focus solely on managing stakeholders, you miss out on one of the best parts of working with the people invested in your project: learning from them!

As a tech lead, you'll likely interact with people in different teams, and stakeholders working across various disciplines. This is a fantastic learning opportunity. Explore their professional area, their discipline, and their part of the business. As we cover in Part V, understanding the business is table-stakes at staff+ levels. Tech leads have the chance to learn on the job by working with stakeholders day-to-day.

Here are some approaches to make the most of working with stakeholders and learning from them:

- **Ask about their part of the business**. What are they responsible for, how does their area contribute to the company, what are their team's goals, any recent wins?
- **Ask about their challenges**. What is a difficult problem they have, even if it's unrelated to the project you're collaborating on? You can learn a lot from someone sharing their biggest challenges.
- **Ask what they do outside of the project you're collaborating on**. Which other projects do they have? What was the last product they contributed to?
- **Small talk**. Get to know them better as a person, especially if working together for an extended period. What did they do before joining the company, what are their hobbies, do you have shared interests at work, or outside of it?
- **Consider grabbing coffee or lunch**. In some cases, it could be easy enough to catch up over lunch, and take the opportunity to discover more about them.
- **Ask if you can shadow their team meeting as a one-off**. As a tech lead, there are two major benefits in shadowing another team's meeting. First, you get new ideas about how to run such meetings, and observe the dynamics in the room. Second, you'll likely hear a lot you don't fully understand. This is a chance to learn more about what another team works on, why it matters, and to expand your knowledge and understanding.

A benefit of learning from stakeholders is that it makes you better at handling them at work. When you understand what they do, their domain, and their challenges, it's easier to be empathetic and to express details about your project in terms they understand.

Learning from stakeholders is much easier in person than in a remote setting. When working remotely, it helps to be much more upfront about your intentions and to schedule more focused sessions. Here is an approach that worked well for software engineer and engineering manager, John Crickett[3]:

"If you're remote, send people an invite. Mine is this:

'Hi X – I'm John, I've recently joined [Org] and would love to meet you to understand more about your area of the business. I'd really appreciate 15 minutes

---

[3]https://www.linkedin.com/in/johncrickett

of your time if you can spare it. I've picked a free spot in your calendar, but please suggest an alternative if it's inconvenient. Many thanks, – John'

"The area or areas and the project name, could be appropriate details to add. So far, no one has ever said no! And most people are okay with this catchup overrunning or offering a longer slot.

I make sure I am on the call on time and have a list of questions for them to help move the conversation along. Typically it's general questions like:

- What is your team working on?
- What's the biggest challenge you have right now?
- How can I/the team I've joined, help you?"

19

TEAM STRUCTURE

As a tech lead, you can have an outsized influence in shaping your team's dynamics and processes. But how do you use this influence to create a structure that's healthy and functions well?

In this chapter, we cover:

1. Roles and titles
2. Team processes
3. Boosting team focus

1. Roles and Titles

How does your team work, and who has which responsibilities? Ultimately, the manager of the team is responsible for ensuring these are clear. As a tech lead, you need to understand how roles are defined and divided across the team for your own role and fellow team members.

The difference between titles and roles

Titles confer reasonable expectations upon its holder. For example, a software engineer with the title "new grad software engineer" is unlikely to be expected to spot hidden risks in projects. But someone with a "senior engineer" title is expected to be able to identify such risks. For staff engineers, it's usually a baseline expectation.

Roles on the team are often temporary positions like "project lead" for a piece of work, or the owner of a certain feature, or a meeting facilitator.

"Tech lead" can be a title or a role

In some workplaces, tech lead is the title and career level after senior engineer. Leading key initiatives across a team, and being the point of contact for other engineering teams, is often an expectation. At other companies, "tech lead" means the same as "project lead" or "engineering lead." In such places, it's a role more than a title and is used in long-running projects, or for parts of a product. For example, the tech lead of Checkout is most likely the engineering lead.

Roles can be implicit or explicit

When roles are explicit they're directly communicated to team members to avoid confusion. It's clear who is the lead for which project, who's the point of contact for a feature, and who's taking the weekly oncall.

A team with explicit roles could define them like this:

- Project Zeno Lead: Sam
- Support engineer for the week: Bob (rotates weekly)
- Oncall engineer for the week: Eva
- Point of contact for project stakeholders: Sarah

In practice, roles are often implicit. It's common for engineers to simply pick up a role, and this may not be widely communicated. This approach works fine in teams with good communication, but implicit roles cause confusion in some scenarios. For example:

- Two team members think they own the same role, such as leading a project.
- Team members think they're the point of contact for a feature or project, and make decisions without consulting others.
- Team members assume someone else owns an area like pre-release load testing, so nobody does this important work.

Decide which roles are explicit

As a tech lead, figure out which roles are explicit and which are implicit in your team, starting with your own. At the very least, be clear what your manager expects of you.

Exercise: Map out and list the roles on your team by talking with your manager and team-mates. Who has which role, do the roles overlap, is there confusion about roles, do some overlaps cause conflicts?

One approach I've seen consistently works well is making the project lead role explicit to the whole team, no matter how small a project is. It creates accountability for the person leading the project, and provides clarity to others. On teams with many projects, there's scope for everyone to lead a project.

2. Team Processes

Which processes should a team have in place?

This is actually the wrong question to start with. Processes are not the reason why teams exist; they exist to get things done. Processes can aid this, or they can get in the way.

As a team grows, lessons are learned about how to operate better, ship faster, more reliably with higher quality, and how to iterate quicker. Some learnings lead a team to put in place practices and processes which help engineers achieve goals, which are almost always related to speed, quality, reliability, serving customers, and the business.

There are processes that help engineering teams, just as there are common engineering practices which usually make sense, like code reviews and testing. But not all processes are helpful.

The best way to know if a process – such as an oncall rotation – really solves a pain point, is personal experience. Below is a selection of common team processes worth knowing and trying out. Once they're in your toolbelt you can decide which to deploy as needed.

Planning

- Brainstorming sessions
- Involving engineering in planning with other disciplines, such as design or business stakeholders
- Project kickoffs
- Design documents/requests for comments (RFCs)
- Architecture decision records (ADRs)

Building

- Prototyping
- Code reviews
- Automated testing
- Continuous integration
- Documenting decisions

Releasing

- Continuous deployment
- Release plans
- Feature flags and experimentation
- Signing off with stakeholders, such as product, compliance, security
- Gathering feedback from customers
- Canaries and automated rollbacks

Maintaining

- Oncall process
- Support engineering
- Incident reviews

- Improving infrastructure and platforms
- Periods of non-product development, such as fixing tech debt, improving infrastructure

Engineering productivity

- Team retrospectives
- Handling tech debt
- Investing in efficient tooling like CI/CD, helpful scripts, etc.
- Reducing frequency of meetings
- No-meeting days

Team health

- Team events and offsites
- Spontaneous team events like getting ice cream. For remote teams, organizing events where everyone gets together, or virtual, fun events
- Celebrating team and individual achievements

Remove processes, don't just add more

Most teams introduce new processes over time. After all, a team makes mistakes, learns from them, and puts new processes in place to avoid the same mistakes in future. As a tech lead, you are among the best-placed people to champion the removal of redundant processes. This matters because efficient engineering teams are nimble and tend to be low on process, by default.

When you see a process with questionable value-add, consider removing it. If there's a process that consumes time and effort, can it be automated partially or fully? Remember, processes are never the goal. Don't ask which processes your team should have in place, ask how the team can get stuff done better and faster!

When making changes to processes, you might need to get buy-in from your manager. Part of being a tech lead is creating space for everyone to work better, so your manager will likely support such an initiative. Just explain to them the productivity and morale boosts that derive from decluttering.

3. Boosting Team Focus

As a tech lead, one of your main roles is helping teammates focus on the right thing. If people are working on the wrong thing, or keep getting distracted, they won't execute as expected.

To help the team focus, be clear what their priorities are, or what a project's priorities are, what the most important thing to get done is, what comes next, and so on.

A way to ensure you focus on the right thing is to write it down and confirm it with your management chain, every now and then.

Keep reminding your team of the focus because repetition is often helpful. For example, during a weekly standup, summarize the focus of the current phase. Even more frequent reminders can be helpful for new joiners, less experienced colleagues, and easily distracted people.

Push back on sudden changes of focus

Resist abrupt changes to your team's top priorities, even if these come from above. A team that switches focus frequently can easily become unhealthy and good tech leads protect their teams from it. There's a few ways you can push back when your manager or a stakeholder wants to change a team's top priority:

- **Impact**. Ask about the impact of the new work. If the impact is unclear, refuse to start it. After all, why would your team work on something of dubious value, or whose impact is less than the team's top priority?
- **A written spec**. Ask for a specification of the work which answers the "why" and "what". This could be a Product Requirements Document (PRD,) or a summary, and it should include the impact. If the person seeking to interrupt the team cannot coherently explain the problem, then there's a good chance your team would be disrupted for no good reason and would spend days figuring out what to do. If there's no spec, refuse to start the work. Alternatively, you could offer to co-write a spec, but be clear that no work will start until all stakeholders sign it off, as skipping this step risks wasted work later.
- **Engineering planning and feasibility**. Assuming the spec is clear and you know why the new work is important, what its impact is, and what you're being asked to do, still don't start work until the team does some basic engineering planning and estimation. There might be risks which make the work impractical. Also, a project intended to take just a few days could last months after planning is done.
- **Make the cost of context-switching painfully clear**. When a stakeholder, another team, or your manager asks your team to start working on something new, *right now*, they're often unaware of the actual cost of a full context switch. If the team stops working on what they're doing now, it will take time to wind down and ramp up to the new work. This usually takes days, but could be more depending on the current work's complexity. Team morale will certainly drop if people are told to throw away work.
- **Offer alternatives to get the work going without disrupting the whole team**. Assuming that impact, and the "why" and "what" are clear, and engineering effort is

roughly estimated, offer alternatives which don't involve the whole team stopping what they're doing. Could someone who's winding down on the main project pick up the new work, or could the work begin nearer the end of the current project? Does the new work need more user feedback, or for stakeholder disagreements to be sorted, first?

My experience is that if your manager or a stakeholder comes with urgent work to be done at once, then that work is likely to be too vague, with unclear impact, and unwarranted urgency. As a tech lead, do your due diligence and be cautious about allowing the team to be distracted from their current work.

You might rationalize that one interruption is fine. But there will be another, and another, and another after that. It's a slippery slope, so the sooner you set boundaries for protecting the team, the better off everyone will be.

20

TEAM DYNAMICS

As a tech lead, you have broad scope to shape the team's dynamics, such as improving health and morale, and solving conflicts. But how do you use this influence to create a healthy, well-functioning team?

In this chapter, we cover:

1. Healthy teams
2. Unhealthy teams
3. Teams with growing pains
4. Improving team dynamics
5. Relationships with other teams

1. Healthy Teams

What makes a team healthy? Here are characteristics I've consistently observed in teams which perform well.

Clarity

In a healthy team, it's clear why the team exists, what its goals are, and how to achieve them. Clarity starts with the leadership; the tech lead, engineering manager, and product manager. They provide clarity by consistently communicating with team members.

One easy way to know if there is clarity is to ask engineers what the team's goals are, and why these goals exist. If everyone gives roughly the same answer, there's clarity. If not, it's worth asking why people give different answers.

Execution

The team "gets things done." This means shipping projects, features, products, and services, in a way that's visible to stakeholders.

We have dug into what it means to "get things done" as an engineer, and how it's a combination of good work and communicating this work to others. The same applies to healthy teams. As a tech lead, you tend to play an outsized role in helping the team do good work, and ensuring organizational stakeholders know about it.

Good morale

Healthy teams have good morale and people feel positive about coming to work. A few indicators of good morale:

- Engaged teammates: people are invested in their work, contribute ideas, and help one another.
- Mutual support: there's camaraderie and it's common for team members to help a teammate, when needed.
- Low attrition: few team members leave the team, even when there's an opportunity.
- Positive atmosphere: there's good energy within the team, and members are motivated to get things done.

Healthy communication

Civilized and constructive communication is a baseline for healthy teams. People are respectful of each other, even in difficult situations. Communication is open and respectful, and there's mutual trust between engineers, the engineering manager, product manager, and other core members.

Every team has conflicts, but on healthy teams these are handled constructively. There's no real "drama" – at least nothing that's not quickly resolved.

People are open in challenging each other to create better solutions, and do this respectfully and constructively. For example, code and design reviews contain useful, non-judgmental feedback.

An engaged team

Everyone contributes to the team and takes part in planning, and the work itself. Nobody is left out or does significantly less than others. Junior members and new joiners are invited to participate. Team members feel safe being themselves and are comfortable enough to be vulnerable in front of others.

2. Unhealthy Teams

Unhealthy teams are by definition the opposite of healthy ones. Indicators that a team is unhealthy include:

- Lack of clarity
- Poor execution
- Unconstructive conflict handling
- Absence of communication and trust

- Unconstructive feedback
- Lack of psychological safety
- Not all team members contribute

Let's look at common reasons why teams become unhealthy.

Why teams are unhealthy and how to address this

Poor management. This is often subjective but can involve a manager neglecting team dynamics for too long, having favorites, being inconsistent in their expectations of team members, letting their biases overly influence them, micromanaging, and much more.

It tends to be easy enough to notice poor management, as team members frequently discuss irritating practices among themselves. Changing this, of course, is hard. If the manager is open to feedback, then as a tech lead you could have success in sharing constructive ways for the manager to get on top of things. However, tread carefully because it's ultimately the responsibility of the team manager to put healthy management practices in place.

A "brilliant jerk" on the team. One experienced engineer who's a "bad apple" can be one too many, especially if the manager protects them because they worry about losing the expertise this "jerk" brings. However, a brilliant jerk tends to damage team morale and dynamics.

As a tech lead, if you notice this situation, it's advisable to handle it and not let it fester. You can try giving feedback to the "jerk" team member in question. If this doesn't succeed, you'll likely have to approach their manager because they have more tools than you for dealing with this issue, including performance management approaches.

Lack of skills on the team. A team can have poor output when team members lack the skills or experience to execute. It could be a missing technology skillset; for example, working on a Go codebase when most team members lack experience in this language.

As a tech lead, you can invest in guiding and mentoring others, or make training suggestions. If you lack a needed skill, there's little excuse for not acquiring it as an experienced engineer. Time may be an obvious impediment to this, but if it's critical that the team has expertise, then making time to acquire the skill during working hours may be a large enough priority for you to do proactively without getting permission, first.

Lack of feedback or empty feedback. On a team whose members don't share feedback, people will be unaware of how their behavior affects others. The same is true when feedback is overly generic, and avoids pointing out problems to be addressed.

I've worked on a team with a "brilliant jerk" whom everyone avoided. Later, I learned nobody gave them feedback about this. When a peer told this person, their behavior changed. While there's no excuse for a manager to not give feedback to their direct reports, as a tech lead you can consider providing constructive feedback which helps people recognize when their actions negatively affect the team.

Unclear direction. A team whose direction and goals change frequently or are unclear, tends to be a confused, less healthy team. As a tech lead, you should ensure the direction of the team and project are clear, and aim to minimize disruption.

Treading water. There are teams which work really hard but still get barely anything done. They are usually busy putting out fires, and have to do a huge amount of work just to keep the lights on (KTLO.) Team stakeholders get irritated and assume the team must be slacking, when the opposite is true!

As a tech lead, if you observe your team treading water, bring this up with management and put a plan in place to break free from KTLO. This could mean stopping product work for a short amount of time and addressing the root cause of the "busywork." It could mean passing on ownership of systems that should no longer reside with the team. It could mean many things, so sit down with the team's engineering and product leadership, and find a way to break the cycle.

One efficient solution for when a team is treading water is to limit the work in progress. In the book "An Elegant Puzzle," engineering executive Will Larson suggests this:

> "When treading water, the system fix is to add processes to consolidate the team's efforts to finish more things and reduce concurrent work until they're able to begin repaying debt (e.g. limit work in progress.) Tactically, the focus here is helping folks transition from a personal view of productivity to a team view."

Excessive context switching. A team in which almost everyone works on several things at once, tends to get few things done and even does these poorly. This is a subset of treading water, but is easier to spot.

As a tech lead, learn what people are working on. If you observe most teammates balancing several important things at once, offer them help with prioritizing, and provide cover so that team members can work on the highest-priority task. Finishing something before starting anything new is a helpful approach.

Too much process. If a team operates with too much red tape, it can feel like a huge effort to get simple things done, such as changing code or using a new tool. This can pull down team efficiency and morale, and cause more attrition.

As a tech lead, you're in a strong position to push back on unnecessary processes and cut down on red tape. You're also in a position to educate team members on which processes are important to follow. But who says those processes cannot be simplified or automated? Challenge tedious, time-consuming manual processes. Consider that some of the largest tech companies in the world don't annoy engineers with poor processes. Apple, Microsoft, and Amazon, invest plenty of time, effort, and money in automating a bunch of their engineering processes, so perhaps you can push for initiatives that replace processes with automation!

Lack of structure. Too much process is rarely a good thing, but zero process can be challenging for teams with inexperienced engineers. If you find yourself on such a team, putting up basic guardrails could be a good idea, with the intent to remove them as the team matures.

Automated guardrails are easier to follow and more durable than manual ones, but manual guardrails are easier to put in place. For example, if most people on the team skip writing tests and bugs keep creeping in, then as a first step you could implement automated tests for all code that changes the business logic.

Alternatively, you could add automation to the CI system which checks the code coverage of pull requests and adds an automated warning when test coverage decreases with a pull request. Reviewers might ignore the warning, but this automation will make it harder to neglect testing, assuming the team wants this area to be a focus.

Plagued by tech debt. If tech debt goes unaddressed for too long, even simple things like modifying a feature or making a seemingly small change to a system, can take longer or break the system, resulting in more time spent fixing things. A team with too much tech debt will start treading water and get bogged down in dealing with increasingly fragile systems.

Structural reasons teams struggle

There are times when a tech lead can do little to change the circumstances which make a team unhealthy, including:

Too much attrition. Too many people leave in a short period, or people with key knowledge and skills depart and leave a gap. Reasons for attrition are numerous, including bad luck, or deep problems at company-level or in engineering management. The most sensible thing to do when attrition spikes is to re-negotiate expectations because the team can't deliver the same quantity or quality of work as before.

Too many new joiners. Counter-intuitively, when a team has an influx of new joiners, execution can slow down due to onboarding. If new joiners enthusiastically get involved in projects, then the pace could well pick up, but the output temporarily drops while they learn the nuts and bolts of systems, often by making mistakes and learning from them.

Junior-heavy teams. A team lacking experience in execution suffers. As a tech lead, you can do plenty of things to increase the team's skillset and experience, but not overnight.

Things that tend to help are pairing with engineers, reviewing their work and giving feedback – code reviews tend to become important – pulling in more experienced engineers for a short time to help uplevel the team, or getting mentorship for engineers whom you don't have time to support.

A sudden change in direction. When the team unexpectedly changes direction, the pace of execution usually drops. Changing direction means the team needs to wind down old work, and start planning the new approach. All of this is normal; as a tech lead, you need to set the expectation with stakeholders and leadership that the team needs a breather to realign itself, after which execution will be back on track.

3. Teams with Growing Pains

There are teams that look healthy but have growing, unseen problems. If these aren't addressed, they could pull down the team to become unhealthy. Growing pains include:

Silent conflicts and Chinese whispers

It appears a team has no conflicts among members and that communication is civilized. However, below the surface silent conflicts are playing out, and cliques are being formed. The manager of the team – and even some team members – may be blissfully unaware of this. The longer that conflicts brew, the more they can hurt productivity.

As a tech lead, if you notice this it's helpful to alert your manager, who has the best tools for dealing with it. But don't rely exclusively on them; attempt to clear the air with the parties involved by using your judgment and leveraging the trust they have in you.

Silently-growing execution problems

The team is executing well, but doing so is becoming harder. This could be due to tech debt mounting up fast, operational work taking over product work, people nearing burnout, and other reasons.

As a tech lead, don't wait until these problems spill over and hamper team performance. Try to ease the problems by starting with the most pressing ones.

Good work going unnoticed

Some team members do great work, often outside the team. However, their manager is unaware of it, and not only do they not recognize this additional work, but they think these team members are less productive than their teammates

As a tech lead, aim to get a good understanding of work that people on the team do. Have this good work recognized, even if it's outside the team. You're in one of the best positions to shine a light on unnoticed work, so use your influence to do so!

Growing attrition risk

It's not uncommon for team members to know when a teammate is trying to leave the team, but for the manager to be clueless about this. If you find out, what do you do: tell the manager, or stay silent?

This is a delicate situation, as there's a chance the person in question won't depart. It's worth talking to them to understand the root cause of them seeking opportunities elsewhere, and if possible, to try and address the reason. If their motive is financial, there's not much you can do as a tech lead. But if they feel close to burning out due to continuously putting out fires, this is something you can help with, for this person and the whole team.

A senior-heavy team without enough challenges

A rarer situation is when a team has lots of seniority but too few challenges. Such teams can have "too many cooks spoiling the broth," and conflicts arise over opportunities to work on impactful, interesting projects. Dynamics can get especially complicated if engineers have the same promotion ambition as each other, which is tied to delivering projects and being able to claim impact.

Performance management is rarely your responsibility as a tech lead, but it's sensible to raise such concerns with the responsible manager.

4. Improving Team Dynamics

As a tech lead, you are probably in the best position among individual contributors on the team to improve team dynamics. You're likely one of the more experienced people and already have responsibility for some projects, which means you have some informal authority. Here are approaches for using your position to improve team dynamics.

Observation

Start by observing the dynamics of the team. Don't jump into "fixing" anything immediately, especially if you're new to the team. Get a sense of how the team is doing. Which areas feel unhealthy, and what are the unhealthy parts?

As an exercise, make a list of healthy and unhealthy characteristics from earlier in this chapter, and apply them to your team. What do you see? Record the three best things about your team, and three areas for improvement.

Alternatively, consider running a team exercise where everyone reflects on areas they think are going well, and those which could be improved.

Talk privately with team members for a better feel of things. Engineering managers regularly use one-on-one meetings to talk with their direct reports and to get a sense of how things are really going. People tend to be more candid in private settings.

Consider doing one-on-ones with team members, not necessarily regularly like managers typically do, but at least as one-offs. When in private, ask what they think works well, and what the biggest issues are. Listen to their challenges and how they see things.

It's a lot easier to do this by building up trust, first. There's no shortcut, but having the backs of teammates, helping them out in selfless ways, and not eroding trust, all go a long way.

Improving team dynamics

Reduce negative interactions in group settings, when possible. In meetings and other group settings, how do the dynamics play out? Do some people dominate discussions while others take a back seat, and does conflict happen in the open, or in private?

When negative dynamics are at play, consider actions to remove negative interactions from group settings. For example, if an argument between two team members gets heated, consider cooling it down by helping to lower heightened emotions, and focus on solving the problem at hand. After all, you have seniority and so if you act as a bystander to unprofessional behavior, you effectively endorse it.

Get team members involved in relevant discussions. I've observed two types of engineering teams:

1. Team A: experienced engineers make decisions without involving other team members. They then present these decisions as the plan to follow.
2. Team B: experienced engineers come up with a proposal, but involve other team members, or present their reasoning and give teammates the chance to make suggestions or challenge decisions.

Which team works more efficiently? You could argue that when time is short, Team A will probably move faster by spending less time discussing topics on which less experienced engineers will have less input.

But which team has the better dynamics? I'd argue that a team in which everyone, including inexperienced engineers, feels included and has their voice heard, has healthier dynamics.

As a tech lead, you'll have the opportunity to shape the team's culture to be like Team A or Team B. Balance the need for efficiency with involving less experienced engineers, so they see how decisions are made and can contribute to decision-making.

Solve the most pressing health problem, or escalate it to your manager. Once you have a feel for how things are going on the team, you'll recognize the most pressing issues.

These could be an overly-dominant team member, a lack of direction, or anything else. Attempt a solution by using the trust and authority you have on the team. In some cases, you'll be able to solve things by talking with people or giving feedback. Leading by example can also help.

But there will be times when you can't solve a pressing problem. Your manager is ultimately responsible for team dynamics, so escalate to them when you don't have the tools to fix something. As a tech lead, not every problem is yours to solve. For example, a colleague with performance issues isn't your problem; that's on your manager.

Suggest solutions to your manager, rather than presenting a list of problems. Also, try to not surprise them with problems from nowhere. If you have regular catchups, flag issues you notice early, so they don't grow into bigger problems.

5. Relationships with Other Teams

A healthy team is not just healthy on the inside, it has healthy relationships with other teams, too. As a tech lead, you are influential in helping shape these relationships. Put simply, if you have a productive relationship with engineers, product folks, and stakeholders on other teams, then you'll be much better able to help your team get things done.

We cover tactics for working better with other engineering teams in:

- Part III: "Collaboration and teamwork"
- Part V: "Collaboration"

On top of the advice in those sections, also consider the approaches below for building healthy relationships with other teams.

Catch up with engineering project leads on other teams. Make time to grab lunch or have a catchup meeting – in person or on a call – with project leads, who could be fellow tech leads, or senior or staff engineers. Discuss how things are going at their end; what's going well and what challenges they have. Share information about what's happening on your team, and offer to help with their challenges, if possible.

Speak to engineering managers or product managers on other teams. Every now and then, it's helpful to get to know managers on teams which you frequently work with. Follow the advice in the Stakeholder Management chapter: "Learning from stakeholders" subsection.

Consider verbal, not written communication for problematic situations. Your team will undoubtedly face problems related to other teams. For example, you could be frustrated that a promised API change has not materialized, or that the team rejected a pull request which changed a part of the codebase they own.

When such conflicts arise, take the opportunity to get in touch with another engineer on that team in person, or via a video call. By talking, you can avoid the misunderstandings that plague written communication channels like chat or email. Also, talking with someone you don't know will help resolve the problem at hand, and also build a more personal relationship. When it comes to strengthening relations with other teams, it really is good to talk.

Takeaways

In the tech lead role you need to balance several things at once:

- Leading a project or an engineering team
- Empowering team members, as well as helping remove blockers
- Keeping in the loop stakeholders, product, and perhaps even your manager
- Being a role model when doing individual contributor (IC) work like coding, code reviews, and being oncall

All this is not easy to balance; it takes time, practice, and some trial and error.

Lead by example. In the tech lead role, the rest of the team will expect you to lead by example, even if this expectation isn't explicit. As a tech lead, you should be hands-on enough to take part in planning, writing code, doing code reviews, and joining the oncall rotation if there is one.

Keep in mind that if you take shortcuts like shipping code with no automated tests, or move fast – but regularly breaking production – this will set the tone for the team. If you want to maintain a high quality bar across the team, the best way is to lead by example and produce high-quality work. The same applies to fostering a culture of getting things done and unblocking yourself, or talking to customers and solving their problems.

Also, in the tech lead position, there are additional responsibilities which means less time to do IC work. So when you can do IC work, make it count. Let your output set a high quality bar for getting things done on your team.

The best tech leads don't think they are superior to other engineers. One reason why many companies don't use the title "tech lead" is that the word "lead" denotes a leader of followers. But the most productive teams I've worked in all had in common that everyone felt they had a valid say, and job titles didn't get in the way of suggesting how to do things better, faster, or with higher quality.

As a tech lead, strike a balance between taking the lead when needed, and creating an environment where all engineers have a voice and the confidence to take the initiative and make decisions. Don't forget your goal as tech lead is not to "lead," with people always turning to you and following your decisions. The goal is to help the team and project to succeed, and for people to work as efficiently as possible.

A team in which people are more independent will almost always be more efficient than one where everyone waits for the tech lead to decide.

For further reading, check out the online, bonus chapter for Part IV:

Working Well with Product Managers as a Tech Lead

pragmaticurl.com/bonus-4

Part V

Role-Model Staff and Principal Engineers

Previously in this book, we discuss "tech lead" being more commonly a role and not an explicit title or career level. So at companies with no tech lead career level, what comes after the senior position? The first level above senior engineer is frequently called "staff engineer" or "principal engineer."

At Google, after the senior engineer level (L5,) is the staff engineer level (L6,) followed by senior staff (L7,) then principal engineer (L8,) distinguished engineer (L9,) and fellow (L10.) Several Big Tech companies follow a similar approach of senior → staff → principal → distinguished. Uber and Databricks are cases with similar career paths. Netflix and Dropbox also have similar levels, except those companies did not employ a "distinguished engineer" level at time of publication.

However, tech companies tend to have slightly different takes on how they think about titles beyond the senior engineer level. For example, Microsoft, Amazon, and Booking.com have no concept of staff engineer; the next career level after senior engineer is "principal." And there are companies that use titles like "architect" (Oracle,) "principal member of technical staff" (eBay,) or "lead consultant" (ThoughtWorks,) as the level after the equivalent of senior engineer.

Why do titles vary so much between companies? It's because expectations vary. It's worth looking at the title a company uses and asking:

- What is the *full* career ladder at a given company? This gives a better idea of the seniority that certain staff+ titles hold. A good resource for mapping out which career levels companies have beyond the senior engineer level is the website Levels.fyi[1]. Just be aware it's harder to compare the scope of two positions than the website may depict, as the devil lies in the details.
- What are the engineering and business impacts of an engineer in a given position? There's a difference between a staff engineer owning a system generating $1M/year in revenue that's used by a handful of customers, and another staff engineer owning a system generating $500M/year in revenue, which millions of customers use.
- What is the blast radius of a given position? How many engineers are directly impacted directly, typically? For example, at a smaller company, the blast radius of a principal engineer might be around 10 engineers. In a large workplace like Uber or Google, it could be 100 engineers or more. These two positions are identical in title, but very different in expectations!

Typical staff+ engineer expectations

"Staff+ engineer" is the term this book uses to refer to levels beyond senior engineer, referencing staff, principal-and-above titles.

---

[1] https://www.levels.fyi

Staff+ roles vary greatly by title and expectations. Here is my attempt to summarize common expectations across much of Big Tech and larger scaleups. Keep in mind that expectations might be higher than listed for senior positions like principal engineer at companies where principal comes after staff, distinguished, or fellow positions.

Area	Typical expectation
Scope	Complex projects within their group and the company
Guidance	Works fully independently and guides others around them
Getting things done	Unblocks themselves and teams they are on
Taking the initiative	Takes the initiative to solve problems, and finds problems worth solving
Software engineering	Establishes and improves best practices across their group
Software architecture	Makes practical technology and architecture choices to solve problems at their group's level. Designs systems even when requirements are vague or dependencies are numerous
Engineering best practices	Leverages industry practices and introduces those which help the group execute better
Collaboration	With product folks, other engineering managers, and software engineers. Common to collaborate with business stakeholders as well
Mentoring	Mentors senior engineers and less experienced engineers
Learning	Keeps up with their domain, the industry, and keeps learning
Typical number of years of industry experience	10+

Common expectations of staff+ software engineers. At staff+ level, expectations vary by the company you work at, and are typically more demanding at higher staff+ levels

Staff+ is a partner of EMs and PMs

At most Big Tech and scaleups with a dual-track career ladder for individual contributors and managers, staff engineers are usually on the same career level as engineering managers (EMs,) or senior product managers (PMs.) This is not only symbolic; it also acknowledges staff-and-above engineers are expected to be partners of EMs and PMs. The same is true for more senior staff+ career levels. For example, at Uber the principal engineer level (L7) is the same career level as the director of engineering (also L7.) Also at Uber, principal engineers are expected to be partners to directors of engineering and product. *We cover dual-track career paths in Part I: "Career Paths."*

This expectation is oftentimes unspoken, and it's down to the staff+ engineer to put in the work and invest in strengthening this partnership. As with any collaboration, the key to making it work is trust; EMs and PMs put in the work to get things done that matter and communicate openly.

21

UNDERSTANDING THE BUSINESS

As a staff+ engineer, there is often more work on your plate than you can easily handle. So how do you figure out what to focus on in the interests of the business? In order to answer this question, it's necessary to understand the business.

It's possible to grow in your career to staff level without paying too much attention to the business side, but it's very difficult to thrive in a staff+ job and grow further, without this knowledge. Other parts of the role like software engineering, long-term planning, and collaboration, are also important and are skills you've likely strengthened during your career journey.

In this chapter, we cover:

1. North stars, KPIs and OKRs
2. Your team and product
3. Your company
4. Public companies
5. Startups
6. Your industry

1. North Stars, KPIs, OKRs

The concepts of North Stars, KPIs, and OKRs are things most software engineers find boring and irrelevant. A CEO talking about OKRs, or a product manager discussing KPIs, tend to be uninteresting to software engineers because we prefer specifics. Rather than talk about OKRs and KPIs, we like to focus on which project to do and why.

For a single engineering team, it's easy to talk about the specifics of projects and their impact. But with more teams, you can't just list what every team plans to do; it's necessary to step back and look at the bigger picture. And this is where North Stars, KPIs, OKRs, and roadmaps come in. As a staff+ engineer, you need to understand why these concepts are important and what they mean, and translate this for engineers on your team, so they understand what to care about and why.

One more reason these concepts are so important is that most staff+ engineers are partners to engineering managers (EMs) and product managers (PMs) in defining the team's strategy and roadmap. To speak the same language as EMs and PMs: North Stars, KPIs and OKRs are helpful.

North Star

This is the vision of a team or product; it's what guides these things to where they need to get to. For example, the North Star of an internal Payments team could be: "enable any team at the company to integrate payments into their product in a day or less."

The North Star is usually ambitious and not trivial – or even possible! This is intentional because it is aspirational and intended to keep team members motivated and focused. A good example is the North Star of spacecraft engineering company SpaceX: to get humans to the planet Mars. By focusing on this grandiose goal that's currently unachievable, the company makes incremental improvements that bring it closer, step by step. This is the purpose of a North Star for any team or company.

North Star metrics are measurements which capture progress made towards it, such as numbers of customers, daily users, and similar.

KPIs

KPI stands for Key Performance Indicator and is a quantifiable measure for progress in an area. Most North Star metrics are captured in KPIs. Here are some common one:

- Gross merchandise volume (GMV.) At Uber, this refers to total revenue comprising customer spending. Similarly, for a payments processor like Stripe or Adyen, it refers to the total amount of money the company's customers process with the payments processor.
- Revenue: the amount of money a product or team earns. In the case of Uber, this tends to be about 10-20% of GMV because the remaining sum is paid to drivers, restaurants, and couriers. In the case of Stripe or Adyen, this is much lower, at 1-3% of GMV.
- Number or customers: this is straightforward and is commonly used by B2B (business-to-business) services.
- DAU or MAU: a product's daily active users, or monthly active users.
- Incremental numbers: incremental GMV, incremental revenue, incremental DAU/-MAU.
- Churn percentage: the percentage of customers who do not recur in a given period, as a share of the total customer base. The period is usually a month or a quarter, for up-to-date feedback.
- Uptime: the amount of time the service is fully operational as a share of total time.

The challenge is defining what "fully operational" means, and how to measure it.

- Percentage of customer support tickets: at large companies, it's common to capture the percentage of customer support tickets for areas which teams own. A spike in this metric may indicate quality issues.
- Net promoter score (NPS): Customers are sent surveys with questions about how much they would recommend the product to others. The questionnaire creates an average score, which is tracked.

There are countless other KPIs, like customer lifetime value (CLV,) customer acquisition cost (CAC,) the number of reported bugs, and potentially anything else you can think of. A good KPI is measurable, unambiguous, and helps indicate progress and flag up problems. A good KPI is also very hard to "game:" to make the metric go in the right direction without real improvement happening.

OKRs

Objectives and Key Results (OKR) is a very popular approach for setting and measuring goals at tech companies, which Google introduced in 1999 when the company was a year old, with around 40 employees. The approach was suggested by investor John Doerr, who later wrote the book, "Measure What Matters," about it and its success.

Businesses operating with OKRs set them at company level, organizational level, and all the way down to team level. An OKR has two components:

- Objective: a high-level goal that is qualitative, meaning not necessarily measurable
- Key results: measurable outcomes that help determine progress toward achieving the objective

An OKR always has one objective but can have multiple key results. Some examples:

#1: Objective: "Improve the reliability of our service"

Key Results:

1. Increase system uptime from 99.8% to 99.9%
2. Reduce by 20% the p95 latency for API responses
3. Reduce by 30% unhandled exception errors

#2: Objective: "Improve the security of our web and mobile applications"

Key results:

1. Complete a third-party security audit and address major issues raised
2. Build and ship two-factor authentication for all customers

3. Respond to 90% of security issues raised within 2 business days

#3: Objective: Optimize infrastructure costs

Key results:

1. Increase the median CPU utilization of virtual machines to 25
2. Retire or migrate all services still running on the unsupported and resource-intensive Python 2

If your company uses OKRs, understand which objectives and key results the leadership cares about, by starting at the top. Figure out how your team contributes to which objectives.

Work with your product manager and engineering manager to craft OKRs for the team that make sense for the business and that engineers understand. You might have to step in to translate some of this from corporate jargon, as well as the definitions of key results and objectives.

Don't obsess too much about OKRs. They're a tool to help a team focus, similar to how tools like ticketing systems can aid efficiency. However, as with any tool there's a risk of over-using OKRs, and becoming fixated on achieving a certain result, rather than building the right thing for customers.

Are the right things being measured?

A noticeable difference between standout engineering teams and average ones is that on standout teams, engineers question KPIs and even OKRs from product folks. For role model staff-and-above engineers, I consider this practice to be a given.

Question every single measurement brought to the table and investigate it from several angles:

- **Are we measuring the right thing?** If a metric is improved, will it yield the expected business result? For example, if a KPI is about the latency of an endpoint, is reducing latency going to make a noticeable difference for customers and the business? Or would reducing the error rate be more significant?
- **How can this measurement – or measurement target – be gamed?** Measurements can be "gamed" – aka manipulated – in creative ways. For example, at Uber my organization mandated all endpoints to have 99.9% reliability. What followed was several teams with reliability well below this target simply changed their measurement of reliability to hit the new target. They made no code changes. Another time, the target was to reduce 500 server response codes, and a team simply changed existing 500 (failure) response codes to be a 200 response code, moving the error message to the body of the response.

- **What other things should be measured as "countermeasures?"** As any measurement can be gamed, it's good to have a couple of additional metrics to capture for a more balanced overview. For example, a goal might be to increase median CPU utilization from 15% to 25% because this is a proxy metric for superior resource usage. However, how will you measure that there are no code changes which make the code less efficient, and use more CPU? You'd want to put some performance benchmarks in place to measure baseline code performance over time; and perhaps also measure the latency of the endpoints (the p50 and p95 values) to ensure that higher CPU utilization doesn't noticeably degrade user experience.

Don't forget the bigger picture. Measuring a system's characteristics is much easier than measuring customer satisfaction, customer frustration, or why customers convert or churn. These crucial details risk being lost by focusing only on very specific measurements.

2. Your Team and Product

The best place to start figuring out how the business works, is with the product you and the team are working on. Understand how this product works, why customers use it, what the competition is, and how it contributes to the company's bottom line.

Put on a product manager hat

Does your team have a dedicated product manager? If yes, fantastic; this is someone you can – and should! – partner with. If not, the product manager role still needs to be filled, so consider doing that.

It's especially common for internal-facing engineering teams like a platform team building a technical product to have no product manager. *We cover more on platform teams in Part I: "Thriving in Different Environments."*

However, even on these teams, there are product-related activities someone should pick up in order for the team to be efficient, including:

- **Identify and understand customers**. Who exactly are the customers, which problems do the team's services or product solve for them, and what are some "customer personas" that can help developers empathize with customers?
- **Measure customer satisfaction**. How happy or unhappy are customers with the service they receive? Especially on platform teams with no product manager, there's often a knowledge gap because the team doesn't measure this via surveys, or by talking to customer teams.
- **Get input from customers for the team's roadmap**. If your team is building a service or product for other internal teams, it would be silly to not get their input for the

roadmap. To do this well, someone needs to engage personally with these teams.

In the absence of a dedicated product manager, put on your product manager hat, and get to work on the activities mentioned above. And if you do have a dedicated product manager, partner with them. Perhaps you can help with these activities.

Put yourself in the customer's shoes

Why would you want to spend a lot of time and effort to understand customers? It's because understanding how customers operate is how you can find customer problems that need solving.

A key difference between senior and staff+ engineers is problem-solving vs problem finding. Both senior engineers and staff+ engineers are expected to solve challenging problems: but staff+ engineers are also expected to find problems that are worth solving. Putting yourself in the customer's shoes is one of the most obvious ways to do so.

If you are not a regular user of the product you're building, try and become one! This is much easier to do with consumer products, especially ones that solve a problem. For example, when I joined Skype I was using the video-calling service for contacting friends, so was already a user. However, this can be trickier with certain types of products:

- **B2C (business-to-consumer) products**. When building a product for which you are not a target customer, sign up and attempt to use the product like customers do. Learn about the target demographic and always consider how people use the product.
- **B2B (business-to-business) products**: Putting yourself in a customer's shoes isn't easy. Still, it's worth trying. For example, at Shopify, many developers set up their own store on the platform and list some digital products no external users see, in order to experience the set-up process as a user. They also test things like the purchase flow from the merchant side.
- **When customers are internal**: try using test accounts, or other ways to observe the customer experience. This is great for building empathy and getting closer to customers.

Get involved with customer support. This is one of the best ways to put yourself in the customer's place. Read customer support tickets and listen to customer support calls. Even better, talk to customer support folks who can summarize users' most common issues and share how customer sentiment changes over time.

Know why customers use your product

"Why do customers use us?" is an obvious question, and it's surprising how often engineers don't have an answer. As a staff+ engineer, you cannot afford to not know this. So find out! Here's how to:

- **Talk to customers**. Especially for niche products like B2B products, it helps to talk to customers, or join sessions where sales, product, customer support, or other user-facing functions, talk with customers.
- **Observe user research sessions**. If your company runs interview sessions with customers and runs plans by them, then join in! This is a fantastic way to learn what users care about.
- **Read reviews**. Go through user reviews, which are subjective personal opinions, and also analysts' reviews for better-known products, and also media articles which may contain information about competitors.

Who are your competitors and how do they work? What do they do differently, do better, and do worse than you?

Tracking competitors is often the responsibility of product folks, but I believe it greatly benefits a staff+ engineer – and your product! – to do this research. You are likely to spot things a product person misses, and might find glaring gaps in your product that competitors don't have, and which metrics overlook.

If possible, sign up to a competitor's service to evaluate it as a user. This is straightforward for consumer products but might be a lot harder for business ones. Talk to product folks about how they evaluate the competition, and see if you can use existing accounts to assess competitors' products.

A great way to share your observations is to create a "comparison document" featuring your product and the competition. This can help spread knowledge to the rest of the team. Particularly useful comparators include:

- A UX comparison of user flows, such as signing up and executing similar actions, captured in images or video.
- Comparison of features and capabilities listed next to each other.
- A strategy comparison, sharing insights about competitors' strategies and how these compare to your company's.
- Comparison of user feedback about your product and competitors' products.

Understand the product's business value

Why does your company invest a pile of money and effort into building your product, and what is the return on investment? The easiest way to answer these questions is to ask your product manager, or engineering manager. Don't accept shallow answers and dig deep to understand why the business invests in your product and team.

Products can generally be split into two categories, by their contribution to the business:

- **Profit centers**: products the business perceives as creating wealth for the company, such as products that directly generate revenue like the Ads division in a social media company, or the front office teams at an investment bank.

- **Cost centers**: products which are necessary parts of the business, but don't generate income, such as compliance, legal functions, and customer support.

We cover more details on profit centers and cost centers in Part I: "Career Paths."

Here are some questions for identifying which of the two categories above your product fits into, and how it relates to business value:

- What are the KPIs and OKRs of your product, how do they map to the company's revenue, growth, and cost metrics?
- How much revenue/cost savings does this product directly generate today, and in future?
- How much revenue/cost savings does this product indirectly generate; for example, by other functions using it?
- To how much customer growth does your product contribute?
- Does your product reduce customer churn, or increase retention? If so, how, and by how much?

Create a SWOT analysis of your product

SWOT stands for Strengths, Weaknesses, Opportunities, and Threats. It's a planning document which describes a product and the business environment it exists in.

Research these four areas, put it into a document, and share it with your product counterpart and team for feedback. This exercise forces you to think like a business owner and understand the competition. You'll view your product in a more strategic way after you complete the exercise.

3. Your Company

Being inside your company is the best way to start to understand the business. There are plenty of ways to get a sense of how things work:

What is the business model?

How does your company generate wealth; how does it turn revenue into profit, and manage costs? If it doesn't yet turn a profit, what's the plan to achieve this?

At startups, it's common to make a loss for a longer period of time and to take years to reach profitability. It's still worthwhile understanding what the unit economics are, and where they need to get to, in order for the company to turn a profit. Unit economics refers to the cost of producing a single unit of product or service that the business sells. For example, in the early days of Uber, the per-unit cost of a trip in a new city could be double the revenue it brought in.

For publicly traded companies, the quarterly business results are public domain and provide a picture of recent performance. At these places, you can usually get a recording of the latest earnings call – or a transcript – after the event. Evaluate these sources to understand more about the business model of your company, and where the current focus is.

To understand how the company makes money, it's useful to familiarize yourself with areas such as:

- Marketing, sales, and consumer behavior, especially at B2C companies.
- How enterprise sales works, and how it differs at B2B companies.

Have 1:1s with product people

Product managers are the "glue" between a business and its product. They need an excellent understanding of the business, and how their products affect performance and growth. To get a better "business sense," talk to these people! Consider starting with a one-off meeting with a product person, and ask them how the business works, and how their products relate to it.

Talk with people outside of software engineering and product

A mistake some staff+ people make is to only connect with engineers and product people while ignoring the wider business. Don't do this; expand your outlook.

Consider talking with people from:

- **Other tech disciplines**: such as design, data science, UX research, technical program management (TPM,) and similar areas. Infosec/security is highly relevant for most products, while legal is helpful for open source licensing queries.
- **Business areas your team supports**: the business teams that rely on your products. These could be customer support, marketing, finance, HR, etc, depending on your product's connection to the business.
- **Corporate communications/public relations (PR)**: at larger companies, this group is useful to know for publicity-related matters like blogging, talks at conferences, and presenting your team's work publicly in any way.
- **Groups unconnected with your team or product**. As counter-intuitive as it sounds, it can be useful to occasionally talk with people within the company who have no connection with your product, in order to understand what they do, how they help

the business, and what their connection to engineering is. For the most part, this type of conversation has no benefits in the short to mid-term. However, it can help broaden your perspective, and to make a personal connection with someone in a very different part of the business. Basically, it's a form of networking and a learning opportunity.

Have 1:1s with business stakeholders

Product managers are often colleagues who talk directly with business stakeholders with an interest in the product you build. Product folks capture requirements and expectations and also set expectations with business stakeholders on what is realistic, and communicate with these people about what is being built.

As a staff+ engineer, do you need to talk with business stakeholders? If you have an amazing product manager who captures details and has strong connections with these people, then the answer might be "no." The product manager may have things under control, and another person (you) talking with the business stakeholder would only create overhead.

However, it's often the case that meeting business stakeholders and giving them your undivided attention in a 1:1, is an incredibly high-leverage activity you should do because:

- Without this relationship, you are fully dependent on your product manager, and cannot stand in for them if needed
- As an engineer, you get more of the unfiltered business context and less watered-down detail via a product manager
- By reaching out directly, business stakeholders are more likely to ping you when they see engineering-related problems and issues which a product manager may filter out and not share with the engineering team

As a staff+ engineer, you need to be a partner to the business. But how can you be a great partner, if you don't even talk to business colleagues? In my experience, business people at tech companies jump at the chance of a 1:1 with a staff+ engineer. This is because they often believe their area gets little to no direct attention from engineering, even though their results heavily rely on engineering work. Basically, it's in stakeholders' interest to build a connection.

Which business areas are useful for you to have conversations about? Here are a few:

- Business teams that are active users of your product, or for whom you build
- Customer support and operations teams that get feedback from users
- Marketing and sales teams which might use your product to close customers, or market the business
- Finance teams that generate reports based on your product's metrics

Identify these teams – your product manager could help with this – and set up 1:1s with the right people by reaching out and saying you're interested in learning about their business area, and how engineering might be able to help them. I have yet to see any business unit turn down an engineering representative who wants to help and seeks information for this.

Pay attention to leadership's communication

When leadership holds all-hands, town halls, or sends emails to large groups, pay attention to what is said. If this is delivered indirectly, try to figure out what the real message is.

At staff+ level, you may be used to leadership communicating in an indirect way and using language to deliver sensitive messages in ways which require interpretation. For example, a CEO will rarely say an area is to get a lower priority in the coming period, even if it will. But this fact can deduced from clues, such as:

- The area is absent from key investment areas listed by the CEO
- They casually mention that colleagues in an area should prepare to do more with less
- They mention a cost-saving initiative, adding something like, "this is just the first, and I hope more follow"

After big announcements, talk with product managers and engineering managers to confirm you understood the "real" message. As a staff+ engineer, it's necessary to translate corporate language used by leadership, which is a skill that comes with practice.

Talk and listen to customers

If your customers are consumers or external businesses, find ways to hear from these people. A few methods:

- B2C companies: get access to customer feedback. This could be on social media, app store reviews for consumer mobile apps, and customer feedback channels.
- B2B companies: ask to sit in on sales calls.
- Volunteer to do customer support, helping triage incoming issues and to fix some of them. This is an underrated way to understand what is frustrating customers. Also, your offer will most likely be welcomed because few engineers are enthusiastic about support, in general.

Get involved in strategy discussions

As a staff+ engineer, there should already be a seat at the table for you in engineering strategy and planning discussions. However, you probably won't be invited to product strategy and business strategy discussions.

But attending these meetings is an excellent way to broaden your understanding of the business. So make this happen and shadow some meetings. Talk to your manager or product manager, and ask to attend a session where you can listen and learn. They're unlikely to reject such a request!

Work on cross-functional projects

The easiest way to get a broader appreciation for the business is to work on projects involving collaboration with a variety of engineering and business teams. As a staff+ engineer you are more likely to be assigned to work on these kinds of projects.

However, if you're not working on such initiatives at staff+ level, it's helpful to seek them out. Here's how:

- **Talk with your manager.** Tell them your goal is to help the company and your team to execute better, meaning you put team projects first, and that if there are cross-team initiatives your team can help with, you'd be thrilled to. Depending on how much trust you've built up with your manager, you could share that working on cross-team projects could help you grow professionally, increase your understanding of the business, expand your network, and ultimately help your team execute better.
- **Talk with people on other teams.** Talk with fellow engineers, product managers and engineering managers on other teams to broaden your understanding and network. There might be opportunities to get involved in their projects.
- **Look out for projects you can help with.** If your company has a culture of RFCs or design docs, monitor them and offer to help out in areas you have expertise in. Talk with other managers and engineers and offer to help part-time when there's a project for which your expertise is useful.
- **Mentor others.** If you mentor engineers on different teams, you will get insights into challenges they face. Mentees working on cross-functional projects will likely face challenges, and you'll have insight into problems from their perspective. Of course, you're not guaranteed to be paired with such people, but mentoring is such a large growth area, that as a staff+ engineer it's sensible to take this activity on, anyway.

Have 1:1s with your manager and leadership chain

During 1:1s with your manager, ask questions about parts of the business you don't fully understand. Your manager will be able to clarify things, or they can give you guidance on where to look. It's in their interest and your own to get a clearer understanding of the business, even if some less experienced engineering managers don't yet know it.

Have 1:1s with your skip-level, and other engineering leaders. When I worked at Uber, a VP of Engineering who headed the developer platform – an organization I worked with, but was not part of – visited our office, and I had a 1:1 with them to understand more about what their team was working on. It turned out this VP wanted to hear more about developer tooling pain points on my team. I learned a lot about how developer tools work, and ways to help each other. As a follow-up, I asked the VP to do a 1:1 with a staff engineer on my team, and they happily agreed. The staff engineer on my team got a lot of value from that one conversation.

Later, when an experienced staff engineer joined our organization, they set up such conversations proactively, without waiting for their manager to do it. Indeed, they had 1:1s with pretty much their whole management chain, and the peers of their skip-level managers, in an effort to understand the business, and what mattered to engineering's leadership. Unsurprisingly, this staff engineer identified "low-hanging fruit" projects to get involved in, and figured out which projects to prioritize.

Carve out dedicated time to read PRDs

Within Big Tech and in many scaleups and tech companies, product managers write product requirements documents (PRDs) as a way to capture business ideas to turn into features or products. These documents usually capture the business goals and the proposed functionality of the product.

Spend time reading PRDs relevant for your business area: and ask questions when you find something unclear. Doing this regularly will help you stay connected with what the business direction is. Knowing about this direction will help with making architecture decisions: for example, on how to evolve the infrastructure to support a couple of related product initiatives that are already captured in various PRDs.

If your company does not have a culture of PRDs or of product managers capturing specifications in writing: you'll have to find alternative ways to keep a sense of product direction: for example, by talking with product people.

Create conditions for serendipitous meetings

It can pay off to meet and talk with colleagues whom you don't know, especially if it doesn't consume much time. Here's a couple of ideas:

- If working in an office, sit next to someone at lunch whom you don't know, and strike up a conversation about your jobs. You can also do this when grabbing a coffee.
- When attending training sessions, make the effort to get to know other attendees.

In these situations, I've found it interesting to get to know which areas people work in, what makes that area special, and what their challenges are. Plus, I was always interested to hear how they worked with tech and engineering, and if there was anything I could help with.

I've found meeting people from different parts of the business is an eye-opening experience, especially in how differently they work from software engineering, and how a "major challenge" means something completely different.

Serendipitous meetings will often not result in much that's immediately actionable. But as long as they don't take up too much time, they should be interesting. A meeting like this could sow the seed of a future collaboration, or form a connection with a different part of the business.

Why do few engineers meet business stakeholders?

My experience of working at larger tech companies, and talking with peers elsewhere, is that it's pretty rare for engineers to take the initiative and reach out to business stakeholders. Why is this? Common reasons I've observed include:

- **"My manager doesn't, so why should I?"** In many cases, engineering managers don't talk directly with business stakeholders, and assume this is product folks' job. Therefore, there's little incentive. At more "political" companies where there's not much trust between managers and engineers, it could even be seen as "rocking the boat" to reach out to the business if your manager does not.
- **They've never seen a fellow engineer do it**. For engineers who haven't worked with peers who proactively talked with business stakeholders, there is no "role model" for doing so, even as these engineers become more senior.
- **Product leadership doesn't encourage it**. When engineering managers, product management, or the company's leadership doesn't encourage engineers to work directly with the business, or fails to highlight cases of such collaboration, it's little wonder engineers don't think of doing so.
- **Engineering doesn't work closely with the business**. Some companies claim engineers are product-focused or customer-focused, but a divide exists which means the business has no real way to interact with engineering, and vice versa.
- **The company culture encourages silos**. Plenty of companies run a more "traditional" management style which favors information being collected and distributed by key people, usually managers. There may be informal and formal structures which mean individual contributors have less access to information, and few opportunities to distribute it. Most Big Tech companies don't work like this, but I've observed a surprising number of startups do so as they grow, due to leadership not being deliberate about building a culture of transparency, and empowering engineers to make decisions.
- **Engineers don't have autonomy**. In companies where engineering is treated as a "feature factory" and engineers are expected to do as they're told, there is little to no autonomy. Within these companies, engineers are discouraged from talking with business stakeholders because it's seen as a waste of time. Product managers and project managers already do this, after all!

4. Public Companies

If you work at a publicly traded company, there is an opportunity every three months to find out how the business is doing. This is the quarterly reporting cycle, which includes an earnings call with interested parties after the publication of the latest financial results.

Publicly traded companies must disclose key information in quarterly reports, as part of which the leadership answers questions by analysts and journalists. These calls are usually for investors, stakeholders, and the media, but as an employee you can often find information which isn't communicated internally.

Useful information in quarterly reports and investor calls:

- **Numbers**. How is revenue trending, and what about profitability or lack thereof?
- **Investment areas**. Which products, teams, and areas does leadership choose to highlight?
- **Questions from analysts**. Expect these to probe the leadership on sensitive areas. What are these areas, and does the leadership have good responses?
- **Forward-looking commitments**. What could be the impact on your product or area of forecasts for targets like revenue generation and spending reduction?

Understanding the meanings of terms like debits and credits, net revenue, cash flow, and EBITDA, provides a strong sense of a company's financial situation. This is universal knowledge that might help you in future if you start your own business, or get the chance to take an executive position.

A good resource for getting started is Accounting for Developers[1] by Modern Treasury. A book that's helpful for understanding how to think about the business is, "The Personal MBA" by Josh Kaufman.

5. Startups

Unlike publicly traded companies, startups do not report quarterly on their financial situation, nor face awkward questions from analysts. However, startups often have far greater internal transparency. So use it!

If your startup is transparent by default, you should have access to business metrics, and a sense of how things are going, growth areas, and challenges. If not, ask about them. There should be little reason to not share such details with a highly experienced engineer. After all,

---

[1] https://www.moderntreasury.com/journal/accounting-for-developers-part-i

this information helps improve decision-making about what to work on.

Take advantage if your startup is small enough that you have access to the founders. Hold catch-ups with the founders every now and then, and get a sense of how they think about the business, and what their priorities and business goals are. Ask about relations with investors, and what the priorities of investors and the board are, for a picture of how things are going.

If your startup is raising a new round of funding, ask if you can see the pitch deck. It will describe where your startup is at, and where it hopes to get to. Knowing those goals will make it easier to decide which work to say "yes" to, and what to deprioritize.

6. Your Industry

As a staff+ engineer, it is invaluable to understand the industry or sector in which your product or company exists. Understanding an industry is a huge undertaking, which is effectively never-ending because industries are enormous, complex, and always change. But here are some approaches that can help:

- **Map out key players and key products**. Which companies and products are the market leaders, and which are "up and coming?" Data from industry reports, such as from Gartner or similar sources, can help with this.
- **Find and read trade publications**. For each industry, there are dedicated publications like websites and magazines. For example, in the travel industry, Skift is an in-depth online magazine many insiders read. For the creator economy, The Information's "Creator Economy" is a popular source. Find relevant publications and decide which to follow. Many quality publications are paid-for, so consider making a business case to your manager for buying a subscription to keep up with developments in your industry, which could pay dividends for the team and company.
- **Follow industry news**. Is a competitor releasing a new feature that customers are excited about, or is another competitor retiring a product which could be a chance to onboard their frustrated users? Keep on top of industry news, especially that which relates to your product area. After all, products aren't built in a vacuum, and your product and team must adapt to changes as they happen. By keeping up with industry news, you might be able to react faster and to capitalize.

22

COLLABORATION

As a staff+ engineer, much of the work involves collaborating with fellow engineers, managers, product people, business stakeholders, and others. In many cases, it isn't you who initiates a collaboration, people come to you.

The most challenging projects are rarely hard because of the code to be written. Often, the main pain point is working with others, and the feeling this creates of "herding cats" – referring to a task that's difficult or impossible to organize.

As you collaborate with colleagues, it's inevitable you will get involved in internal politics to some extent, or be perceived as involved in it. Why? Because people are "political animals" by nature, according to one piece of ancient Greek wisdom. Collaboration involves people in your network, while your influence creates opportunities for engineers in your team. It's a differentiator in career success, which is why we're focusing on it. In this chapter, we cover:

1. Internal politics
2. Influencing others
3. Collaborating with managers
4. Collaborating with staff+ peers
5. Expanding your network
6. Helping others

1. Internal Politics

Internal politics – aka office politics – has a bad reputation among many software engineers. If an individual contributor (IC) or manager is known as "political," it almost always has a negative implication. It usually means someone makes few to no technical contributions and uses others to get what they want, sometimes employing manipulation for personal ends.

What about being seen as "influential;" is this so different from being political? Influence usually describes a colleague with strong technical skills, who also excels at gathering support for initiatives that benefit their team or organization, and not primarily themself.

In reality, politics and influence often go hand in hand, even though we perceive a "political" colleague and an influential one differently. Influence is a "good" form of internal politics. That's why if you want to support your team and progress your career as a software engineer, it's helpful to be seen as influential, but not political.

The "wrong" type of politics

The label "political" gets a bad rap because it often describes activities seen as self-serving and for the benefit of one person or group at the expense of others. It's worth avoiding being seen by colleagues as making their lives more difficult in order to benefit yourself, or your "in group."

When success depends mostly on informal soft skills and networking ability, this feels wrong. Most developers I know – myself included – believe software engineering should be objective and based on the merit of ideas, which is why many engineers disdain internal politics.

Perception matters. You may do something selfless, but if colleagues don't have the full context, then your motivation could be misunderstood and interpreted as self-serving.

Take the case of a staff engineer who's on a promotions committee which decides a senior engineer's compensation package, who's on the staff engineer's team. The proposal is rejected after the staff engineer fails to endorse it.

Did the staff engineer act selfishly by not sticking their neck out for their teammate, and what was their motive; was it political? And who benefits? Certainly not the senior engineer getting no pay rise. Surely the staff engineer must be the beneficiary in some obscure way? Questions like these which are hard to answer without being in the room where a decision is made, can lead people to assume their colleague is playing the "wrong" type of politics.

In reality, it's perfectly possible that committee members had to recuse (omit) themselves from voting in cases of conflict of interest. And it's perfectly likely the staff engineer did this, by not having input into a decision about their team member.

However, it's easiest to assume the staff engineer sabotaged the proposal by not voting for it, for some reason. This gets the all-important question of motive wrong in this case: the staff engineer acted in the higher interest of impartiality by declining to take part in a decision in which they had a direct interest.

This example shows why it's hard to make an accurate judgment without the full context. In practice, people fill knowledge gaps with assumptions. That's why perception and context matter!

Problematic perceptions

Being self-interested. If someone's perceived as caring only about their own projects and work, then they will make few friends due to appearing fixated on personal advancement. Who wants to work with – or help – someone who gives nothing back and uses others to benefit their personal ambition?

Elbowing colleagues out of the way. Even worse than being nakedly self-interested, is to be seen as someone who actively pushes others aside in order to climb the career ladder. For example, an engineer who hogs a project and blocks contributions from others so they can get all the credit, should not be surprised if teammates perceive them negatively.

Being inflexible. Engineers who show no flexibility when discussing proposals and just push their point of view, can be seen as pursuing a personal agenda. This is especially true if they pull rank rather than use rational arguments, with words to the effect: "I'm a staff engineer and this is how it should be because I say so."

Being two-faced. Saying different or contradictory things about a topic to different people can create an impression of being manipulative and of pursuing a personal agenda. Once there's a perception that somebody behaves like this, colleagues' trust in them typically plummets.

Bulldozing their will through. One frequently applied leadership principle at Amazon is "have a backbone; disagree and commit." This encourages colleagues to disagree while a decision is being made, but to commit and bury disagreements after it's made. This "disagree and commit" mentality exists at many companies. However, this approach can become weaponized, when someone forces a commitment in the absence of agreement. Forcing through initiatives can be efficient in the short-term, or when in "wartime" mode. But it's an approach that rarely wins friends.

Distrusts other engineers. Some experienced engineers delegate engineering work to less experienced engineers. This is great! However, if they find the less experienced engineer is doing things unconventionally, then they take this work back from them. Doing this fosters a perception of a lack of trust in colleagues, and can create a negative perception, meaning less experienced engineers may avoid seeking advice and guidance from their highly experienced colleague.

All talk, no coding. A special breed of political animal is the experienced engineer who never codes. This is a tricky perception because engineers are expected to do far less coding as they climb to staff-and-above levels. They simply don't have time to be hands-on, due to working on other priorities.

Still, staff-and-above engineers who never touch the codebase, are never oncall, and push through changes which impact engineers in ways they disagree with, will often be seen negatively; as aloof and hands-off in decision-making.

Giving feedback on "bad" politics

Feedback matters because its absence usually makes things worse. It's unlikely a software engineer arrives at work thinking, "I'm really looking forward to behaving selfishly, being out of touch, and manipulating my colleagues." And yet, some people generate precisely this impression. So, what's happening?

Missing out on feedback is a common reason why engineers behave in ways that others perceive as political. And they often have no idea they're perceived like this!

But it's often challenging to give this kind of feedback. However, I'd argue that as a team-mate there is plenty you can – and should! – do to help someone see how their actions are perceived:

- **If you're a peer of a political person**: give feedback directly to them, or to your manager. Your choice will depend on your relationship with the person in question. My suggestion is to give direct feedback where possible, but this can be challenging if there's a lack of trust.
- **If you're senior to the political person**: give them direct feedback. Aim to describe specific actions or events, and get their side of the story. Suggest how they might change their behavior if their intentions were different from how they were perceived.
- **If you're junior to the political person**: give feedback to your manager, as it might not be appropriate to give direct feedback. But it's your manager's job to hear your observations, and then decide how to proceed.

2. Influencing Others

It's wise to avoid creating the perception of being overly political. Nonetheless, the ability to influence engineers and managers is often important, while being a form of "good" internal politics itself. Here are a few situations where being influential can help:

- **Getting proposals accepted**. You have a proposal for a new system with lots of upsides versus the current setup. You're convinced this proposal will be a large benefit to the organization if only others could see it.
- **Pushing back on an initiative damaging to your organization**. A mandate comes from above to move to a new system. However, you see the new system has too many gaps, meaning your team would have to do a huge amount of additional work to fill them, or customers will lose functionality. Neither option is acceptable, so you have to tell the decision-makers.
- **Making a case for your teammate's proposal**. A member of your team has a really good proposal that's not winning support, including from your manager. You think the proposal has merit and should be discussed at team level, given its positive business

impact. You could leverage your influence for your colleague's idea.
- **Working on important projects**. You learned about a new project that another team has kicked off, where your expertise could help them progress faster. The right thing for the organization would be for you to spend time on this new project. However, you cannot get your current work done and spend enough time on the new project. So it's necessary to convince your manager that shifting your focus is the right thing for the organization.

A strong organizational network and the ability to influence people in the organization are indivisible. In general, people listen to you because they trust you, meaning you already put in the work to build that trust. But how do you earn trust so that people listen to you? In Part III: "Collaboration and teamwork," we cover approaches that are helpful at senior engineer level. Here, we discuss approaches for the staff+ level.

Earn "trust capital"

Much rests on "trust capital." What are the sources of this asset in your organization? They're likely to be:

- **Title/authority**. People pay attention to colleagues with titles which convey expertise or authority, like principal engineer, distinguished engineer, director, VP of engineering, and so on.
- **Tenure**. If someone has been in the organization for a long time and is known to possess deep understanding, then people will take their opinion seriously, even without a title or authority.
- **Expertise**. If an experienced React Native engineer joins an organization, people will most likely go to them with React Native problems, even if they lack tenure or authority. This applies to any technology area.
- **Track record**. People with less tenure and less authority can still have outsized influence if they have a track record for getting things done.
- **Visibility of work**. If you do a great job but nobody knows it, did you do a great job? A mistake software engineers tend to make is assuming their work will speak for itself. This is often not the case. The hard truth is that good work matters less when your manager and teammates don't know what it was, how it was done, and what its impact is.

The obvious way to build trust capital is to get things done over a long period of time, during which you develop a track record and tenure. Below are some approaches which might help to speed up the trust-building process.

Another helpful way of thinking about trust comes from Anne Raimondi, former product director at eBay. She defines trust as the sum of credibility, reliability, and authenticity; divided by the perception of self-interest. She shares more advice for increasing trust in the article Use this equation to determine, diagnose, and repair trust[1].

Ask questions and be an active listener

Invite colleagues to share their views and expertise so you can learn from them. This is especially useful if you lack information or expertise, such as when joining a new company.

A senior VP of engineering whom I worked with at Skyscanner onboarded with this approach. Bryan Dove told colleagues he was objectively the least knowledgeable person in the room, setting the expectation that he'd ask many questions. He did so, and listened actively to the replies; asking follow-up questions and adding comments. Bryan went on to become the CTO, and then CEO of Skyscanner.

My observation is that the approach of asking lots of questions early on, helped Bryan learn faster and also to build trust with engineers who saw him as a curious, down-to-earth leader, and not an aloof, bossy, know-it-all.

Explain your point of view

Once you get the hang of how things work, try to get into the habit of expressing to peers what you think about problem areas. This could be for pull requests, during standups, architecture/design discussions, in planning documents like RFCs, or similar. *Read more about RFCs, design documents and ADRs*[2].

For pull requests, get into the habit of summarizing a problem you solved, notable edge cases, and things out of scope. If the change is visual, consider using images.

For initial proposals, get into the habit of outlining:

1. The problem as you see it
2. Your preferred solution
3. "Known unknowns" and tradeoffs

Consider following the sequence of starting with a problem, and ending with the tradeoffs. You'll want to get people aligned with the problem first, then get buy-in for a solution, given the known unknowns and tradeoffs.

Follow this approach and you'll build credibility and trust. It's less important whether the solution is one you suggest or if it comes from someone else. The main thing is to choose what works best. Indeed, you can often build more trust by not going with your proposal, but encouraging or championing another option by someone else that's a better fit.

---

[1] https://review.firstround.com/use-this-equation-to-determine-diagnose-and-repair-trust
[2] https://newsletter.pragmaticengineer.com/p/rfcs-and-design-docs

Take sides in design discussions and explain your reasoning

When your team is debating design or architecture choices, engage in this process. Rather than staying silent like a disinterested arbiter, why not voice your preference and reasoning? Doing so makes you an active participant and is a great learning exercise in explaining your thinking. Of course, you need to be in the room where these discussions happen. Get invited by talking with team members, your manager, or both.

Roll up your sleeves and get things done

To build trust with peers you need to do the work, as well as listen and explain. The work will differ by role, level, and expectations. Aim to clarify these expectations and ensure your output matches or exceeds them.

Make your work visible

Share the work you do with your manager, and also with teammates and stakeholders. Consider starting a work log document[3] to make notes of tasks you do, and share it with your manager during 1:1s. Get comfortable with sharing the business impact of your work, its challenges, and learnings.

If you're a leader, consider giving weekly 5-15 updates[4] to your manager chain and team. This means spending 15 minutes writing a document which takes five minutes to read and summarizes the above things. In larger organizations, you'd be surprised how useful these notes can be in bringing visibility to your work and getting feedback.

Take the lead and ship initiatives

As you familiarize yourself with the organization, step up by seeking opportunities to help your team, org, and company. Evaluate why an opportunity matters, make a plan, and involve people who support it.

You will likely find yourself leading projects[5]. With every successfully led and shipped project, you build more trust and acquire trust capital.

Support others selflessly

It's hard to build trust with others if you focus only on your own work. It's equally important to support others, even when there appears to be nothing in it for you.

---

[3] https://blog.pragmaticengineer.com/work-log-template-for-software-engineers
[4] https://lethain.com/weekly-updates
[5] https://newsletter.pragmaticengineer.com/p/engineers-leading-projects

When you support something a peer is doing or trying to win support for, help them during discussions, planning, and provide positive feedback. You don't need a senior title to do this; just be honest.

Of course, there's a place for corrective feedback when you disagree with an approach, but tread lightly and avoid negative feedback in public, if possible. Constructive feedback can build trust when delivered the right way when it's clear you mean well and want to help someone and the team.

Become a better writer

Especially at larger organizations, writing becomes critical at staff-and-above levels because written messages are read by more people, and writing is the way you reach, converse with, and influence engineers beyond your immediate group.

In big workplaces, writing is essential to make your thoughts clear and decisions durable. For people to read and absorb what you write, it must be written well. You need to grab people's attention and explain your thoughts clearly and concisely.

By writing well, you scale your ability to communicate effectively with multiple teams and organizations across the company. And the ability to communicate and influence beyond your immediate team is table stakes for staff+ engineers.

So how do you get better at writing? This topic is outside the scope of this book, but you can find practical examples in this bonus, online chapter:

Becoming a Better Writer as a Software Engineer

pragmaticurl.com/bonus-5

3. Collaborating with Managers

Staff+ engineers tend to have a unique relationship with engineering managers. This is because a staff+ engineer and an engineering manager usually have similar spheres of influence, but slightly different focuses. Here's a visualization of how staff+ engineers and engineering managers typically allocate time:

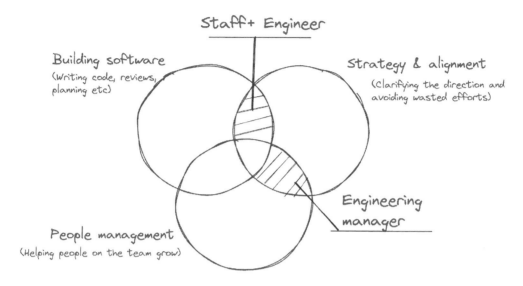

Where staff+ engineers and engineering managers typically spend their time

Staff+ engineers and engineering managers spend a good amount of time on strategy and alignment. So it's only logical to aim to partner with engineering managers, especially ones whose teams you support!

Be clear with engineering managers that you're on their team. It should be obvious to managers whose teams you support – including your own manager! – that you work with them to support their teams. So take time to talk with them, understand how they work, and figure out how you can collaborate.

Avoid treading on engineering managers' toes. Both staff+ engineers and engineering managers help align teams, and you could be in situations where your decisions override another manager, or feel that a manager is overriding yours. If so, do what you would do if this happened with a peer staff+ engineer; take the discussion private and talk through how the two of you can "row in the same direction." It's smart to avoid these differences playing out in front of less experienced engineers.

Build up trust with other managers. You want to get to the point where other managers treat you as a partner, and vice versa. Achieving this involves building trust and proving people can rely on you.

Start building trust with your own manager. Have a frank discussion about responsibilities, and figure out where you can take on some of their workload, be it coordinating an engineering effort, leading a project, or unblocking the team with a tricky dependency. Tell your manager that your goal is to be a true ally in engineering-related matters.

4. Collaborating with Staff+ Peers

To be an efficient staff+ engineer, you need to work well with your team, business stakeholders, and other managers, but also with your peers: fellow staff+ engineers.

Get to know staff+ folks, face-to-face. If you can introduce yourself in person, do this! Learn about what they do, tell them about yourself, and discuss how you can help each other. These kinds of personal relationships can go a long way. If you are in a remote setting, aim to do the same in a video call.

Join a staff+ community – or create one! In some companies, there are staff+ communities where you can interact with peers regularly. For example, Amazon famously has a strong principal engineering community and in the early years, all principal engineers met at an annual offsite, had weekly lunches, and a company-wide tech talk series.

If your company does not yet have a staff+ community, consider organizing one for your immediate peers, at least. This could be as easy as a regular discussion session. Such a community is helpful for all staff+ engineers because this role raises as many questions for other folks in the organization, as for you. Get ideas for activities you could organize from Amazon[6].

Be aware that collaborating with "staff+ archetypes" is different. Engineering executive and author, Will Larson, who wrote the books, "Staff Engineer" and "An Elegant Puzzle," identified four staff engineer archetypes[7]:

- **Tech Lead**: guiding the approach and execution of a particular team
- **Architect**: responsible for the direction, quality, and approach within a critical area
- **Solver**: someone who digs deep into complex problems and finds a path forward
- **Right hand**: borrows their engineering executive's scope and authority to operate in complex organizations

Collaborating with a tech lead who leads projects is different from working with an architect or right hand. So figure out what staff+ archetype you might be, and which fellow staff+ engineers you could align with. '

---

[6]https://pragmaticurl.com/amazon-principal-engineers
[7]https://staffeng.com/guides/staff-archetypes

5. Expanding Your Network

Your network of people with whom you share mutual trust makes a difference in how efficient you are at finding allies and wielding influence. Here are some ways to grow your network.

Find yourself a mentor in the organization

Even as a staff+ engineer, you should still seek people to learn from, who can be advisors or allies when you need to get things done. These people don't have to be engineers, they could be engineering leaders, product people, or even executives like the CTO.

Mentorship can be informal; for example, by working on a project with a more experienced colleague. Some organizations run formal mentorship programs.

Work on cross-team projects

The best way to network is to not "network," but just spend extended time with people in other teams. This happens naturally when working on shared projects. As a staff+ engineer, such projects often come with the job. If not, seek ways to get involved!

When working with others, try to make time to get to know them better, as you might build a connection which lasts much longer than any project.

Attend internal training

At larger companies, internal training is an underrated way to build a network. This is especially true for managers' managerial training, and in-person training events.

When I was at Uber, I met a good number of managers from non-tech areas at training sessions, and talking with them opened my eyes to how other parts of the business worked. I also made connections whom I could reach out to later, and share ideas with. In general, internal training brings together people with similar interests, and provides a shared experience which is a springboard for further conversations.

Meet people outside your team

Talk to colleagues at company events and offsites, or even when just having lunch if you work in an office. Utilize employee resource groups, and take part in cross-organizational initiatives. The more people you meet beyond your team, the more likely you'll build lasting connections. These are increasingly important as you climb the career ladder.

Network and influence are connected

In order to influence people, they must first trust you. This is achieved by getting things done and helping colleagues.

Your network helps your career well beyond your current workplace. People you share trust with can provide introductions and referrals at other companies in future, or help you get interviews for positions not listed publicly, or skip introductory interviews.

The challenge of a strong network is that it takes years to build. It's made of accumulated goodwill, trust, and hard work invested into professional relationships, over time. The best way to build a strong network today is to help people, do good work, and build a reputation as someone who gets things done, helps those around them, and uses influence positively.

6. Helping Others

As a staff+ engineer, you are one of the more experienced engineers in the organization. You have the knowledge and influence to meaningfully help colleagues. So do this!

Mentor others

Mentoring is about guiding someone, sharing your knowledge, and helping them grow. As a staff+ engineer, you have plenty of experience which can help others grow faster. Mentoring doesn't need to be formal, it can be as easy as offering to help new joiners get up to speed.

By getting into the habit of helping others grow – while expecting nothing in return – you will improve your ability to teach and explain. If you keep mentoring and helping others over time, you're likely to build up a reputation as someone whom senior-and-above engineers can seek out for advice.

We cover mentoring in Part III: "Collaboration and teamwork," and also in the article, Mentoring software engineers[8].

Sponsor others

Sponsoring takes things a step further than mentoring; it means advocating for someone and leveraging your position to benefit their career.

As a staff+ engineer, your influence reaches managers and business stakeholders. You can – and should! – use it to sponsor engineers whose careers you can help. Sponsorship can involve:

---

[8]https://blog.pragmaticengineer.com/developers-mentoring-other-developers

- **Bringing visibility to great work**. You see an engineer doing outstanding work and going beyond the call of duty, but their manager seems oblivious. You opt to sponsor this person and bring visibility to their work; for example, by inviting them to present their project at a group meeting.
- **Lending support for promotions**. You believe someone you sponsor is operating at the next level, but it seems they won't be considered for promotion. You can talk with their manager – and fellow managers – to highlight that this person is ready for the next step and give your support for this.
- **Bringing people "into the room."** You're involved in a complex project in its planning phase. You could handle this yourself, but recognize it's a fantastic opportunity for a colleague whom you sponsor. Invite them in and collaborate.
- **Advocating for projects**. When your manager is discussing which engineer should lead which project, you can advocate for the person you sponsor to take a leading role. If the manager pushes back, try offering to get partially involved yourself.
- **Speaking up**. As a staff+ engineer, you may attend closed meetings like performance calibrations. In these meetings, ensure the work and achievements of the people you sponsor aren't overlooked.

Mentorship and sponsorship often overlap. It's common for an engineer's mentor to become their sponsor over time, but it's also possible to sponsor individuals without being a mentor.

23

SOFTWARE ENGINEERING

As a staff+ engineer, your role incorporates that of a senior engineer, plus a whole lot more. It's common to be responsible for your team's pace of engineering work and its quality, as well as your own – and often the outputs of other teams, or a whole group.

Due to your seniority, you're likely expected to improve the execution speed and engineering quality of the teams you work with. In this chapter, we cover approaches that help with this, including:

1. Coding you still do
2. Helpful engineering processes
3. Engineering practices to iterate quickly
4. Tools to make engineers more efficient
5. Compliance and privacy
6. Secure development

I want to say there are no "silver bullets" in software engineering or approaches that universally work in every setting. But some approaches do tend to work well across the board. As a staff+ engineer, the best you can do is to become experienced in using these approaches, broaden your toolset, and learn when to deploy which approach at the appropriate time when it helps your team.

1. Coding You Still Do

How much time should a staff-or-above engineer spend coding? There's no single answer, but one thing is for sure: there are plenty of other things to do. Yes, you should make time for coding, but less of it.

Code in bursts

Accept you cannot code as often as you'd probably like to. But book out times – ideally across a few weeks – when you get hands-on with it. Coding in bursts can work well if it aligns with the start of a project, or another key phase. Stay focused on this priority by being involved with reviews and giving feedback when not coding.

Bursts are also a good reminder of why it's useful to push back on some non-coding commitments, to make time for coding.

Pair during coding bursts

Don't hesitate to pair, especially if it could benefit other developers. When pairing, don't lead things, and instead nudge your pairing buddy in the right direction. This approach takes longer than taking the lead and doing things the "right" way, but nudging helps level up your buddy – thereby improving the team's skillset. This is what makes pairing a high-leverage activity.

Use coding as an opportunity to mentor, coach, and lead by example. When you write code and get "in the zone" doing it, you may well enjoy it being just you and the computer, at last. This is a great feeling, but if you spend this time rushing through the code, and put up a sloppy, half-baked pull request with no tests, then your teammates will likely see it. This can happen if your skills are a bit rusty, or you're in a rush and want to move fast.

Don't forget, code you write will most likely go through code review, which is often a learning experience for engineers. For this reason, pay attention to creating a well-documented, clear pull request, that's a model of what a good one looks like.

The quality of code you write matters because junior colleagues often look to staff+ people to set the bar for quality, whose code is an example to follow and take inspiration from. If the team sees the quality bar is lower in your work, then this legitimizes lower standards elsewhere. After all, if the staff+ engineer can get away with it, why not everyone else?

This is why it's worth coding properly. This means that when something's done, it's done – as we cover in Part III: "Getting things done." Leading by example helps to improve the team's engineering culture.

Jump into struggling projects

If you're stretched by working across teams, you could focus on putting out fires, which means getting involved with coding, pairing, and code reviews on teams which need help the most.

A team that needs help could be one at risk of slipping with a key project, or falling behind. This approach is reactive but sometimes is the most impactful, so long as the team doesn't see your intervention as a case of "seagull management" where someone from above intervenes in a team and "poops" on its work, for example by committing code that's a hack and not a sustainable fix, and who then departs as quickly as they arrived.

Adapt your style to the team

There's a fair likelihood of working with several engineering teams, or being asked to join one to help ship an important project. By now, you will likely have an opinionated way of working; preferred coding styles, processes, naming, and tooling. When not deeply embedded in a team, aim to adapt to it rather than reshape it around you.

Colleagues will respect you more if you adapt and help them improve practices. Ideally, these should come from team members themselves, who feel empowered by your support to make sensible changes.

Be strategic

Choose wisely *which* work you pick up when writing code. As one of the most experienced engineers around, who knows several ways to be strategic about coding, you have various approaches to choose from, such as:

Pick up challenging parts of coding tasks and lead by example in solving them; balancing efficiency, quality, and maintainability.

You might encounter more complex work and problems requiring in-depth domain expertise, such as understanding how related systems work, or something for which there's a lack of in-depth technical expertise on the team, like low-level performance optimization.

Take on coding work with a wider impact. Some coding tasks are more strategic than others. Here are a few examples which can have a wide impact:

- A pull request to add a new framework, and the first few pull requests to demonstrate its use. Examples of how the framework is used serve as proof that it works as expected, and are a template for colleagues to follow.
- Adding a new type of automated test; for example, adding the first few integrations or UI tests. Adding these probably involves writing them and configuring the CI/CD system to run them on every pull request and deploy.
- CI/CD changes or improvements. For example, adding a linter to run on every pull request, or changing the CI server to add a warning when a pull request has low test code coverage.
- Improving the engineering team's tooling. This could involve building and sharing a tool that automates a tedious but necessary development task, like rolling out a feature flag, making a deployment, or rolling back a change.

Get involved in the early coding phase of a project, then make space for others. The early stages of a project are when the right decisions are most critical, like setting up the architecture, putting the code structure in place, ensuring tests are written as agreed, and that monitoring and logging is done in line with agreed parameters.

It's often a sensible approach to be very hands-on by writing code, pairing, and giving feedback via code reviews.

Use time constraints to do more creative coding. It's wise to make time for uninterrupted periods of coding, as you need this time to get "in the zone." However, it's also smart to gather context on the most productive way to spend your limited time on coding. Are there ways to improve the team's efficiency? Is there a complex blocker to tackle? Would pairing be more helpful?

There's rarely as much time to code as you'd like, so make the most of the time you have!

2. Helpful Engineering Processes

What are ways to improve a team's quality of software engineering? As ever, there are no "universal" methodologies that work for all teams, regardless of skillset, experience, or constraints. However, some approaches and processes often help, such as these:

Define "done"

What does "done" mean? It sounds like a simple question, but do all team members have the same answer? In many cases, the answer is that everyone has a slightly different definition of what "done" means. Are automated tests part of what "done" means or are they a bonus, what about the accessibility of a user-facing feature, and is updating documentation part of this criteria?

On a team perceived as shipping low-quality work, clarifying what "done" means and reaching agreement on this, can lead to visible improvements. When working on such a team, or helping to improve its execution, consider this exercise:

Facilitate a discussion where teammates describe what "done" means to them individually, and then discuss a shared definition for it. You can do this by using post-it notes, a digital whiteboard, or people taking notes. Just ensure to start by setting the goal of the session to be agreement on the bare minimum criteria of "done" in quality work. Give everyone a say and push for an agreement. Once "done" is defined, put it in writing. Congratulations; team members have now set their own bar and there's a target for them to hold each other accountable to.

This is often called the "Definition of Done" (DoD.) It evolves as a team does, and can change with projects. The DoD will be different for a proof-of-concept, when there's pressure from an external deadline, or a project being built for long-term maintainability.

Coding style guidelines

On inexperienced teams, clear coding style guides can avoid arguments about how to format code, and which conventions to follow. Guidelines need to be set, with a way for members to suggest modifications.

The clearest way to "enforce" coding style guidelines is to configure a linter to check for them, then wire up this linter to the continuous integration (CI) system. When linting rules aren't followed, consider blocking a pull request from being merged.

Several companies open source their coding style guidelines. Below are examples for inspiration:

- Google's style guides[1]
- Airbnb: JavaScript style guide[2] and Swift style guide[3]
- GitLab: frontend style guides[4]

Code reviews

A good code review process in which feedback is timely and reviews are helpful, tends to promote quality and enables a team of mixed seniority to move faster, overall, as reviews catch issues before code makes it into production.

As one of the most experienced engineers, you're in an excellent position to get a sense of the dynamics of code reviews. In Part III: "Collaboration and teamwork" we cover the features of good code reviews. Look out for these dynamics and find ways to nudge engineers to do better code reviews. An obvious way is to lead by example. Another approach is to give feedback on other code reviews; praising the good parts and pointing out how engineers could improve them.

Post-commit code reviews

For highly experienced teams, blocking code reviews can reduce productivity. These are teams where code reviews tend to say less about the code and focus more on sharing understanding of the changes made.

Obviously, post-commit code reviews happen after code is committed. Software engineer Cindy Sridharan details her experience with post-commit code reviews in the article, "Post-

---

[1] https://google.github.io/styleguide
[2] https://github.com/airbnb/javascript
[3] https://github.com/airbnb/swift
[4] https://docs.gitlab.com/ee/development/fe_guide/style

Commit Reviews[5]":

> "In many ways, post-commit reviews offer the best of both worlds: developer velocity is not sacrificed at the altar of waiting for approval, and reasonable concerns get addressed in short order by the developer in follow-up commits.
>
> While there are a number of caveats to post-commit reviews [...] preponderantly favoring post-commit reviews can allow developers to rapidly iterate on features they're developing while also keeping their changes small."

Post-commit code reviews don't necessarily mean a review happens post-deployment, though. In fact, post-commit code reviews tend to work well in teams where deployments are not necessarily continuous, but occur as regular build cuts. They tend to work best in high-trust environments, which are often – but not always! – teams of long tenure and a high degree of seniority. Teams invested in automation which catches obvious issues also tend to benefit more from this approach.

Let's end this section with more from Sridharan, a long-time practitioner of post-commit code reviews:

> "Walking the tightrope between developer productivity and high-quality code is always going to be a challenging undertaking, requiring smart choices and tradeoffs. The iteration speed of developers can be improved by either flavor of post-commit reviews.
>
> As with all good things, it requires time and investment to get right, but for teams or organizations trying to improve developer productivity, it's certainly an avenue worth exploring."

Automated testing and testing in production

Automated testing is table-stakes at most tech companies. Its upsides almost always justify the effort put into them. Look at the approach to testing of teams you work with, and consider if investing effort in testing would help them move faster with higher quality. If so, you're in the right position to drive improvements to the testing approach.

We go into more detail on automated testing approaches, including testing in production, in Part III: "Testing."

---

[5]https://pragmaticurl.com/post-commit-reviews

Scaffolding new services and components

How do engineers set up an application's new services or components? One approach is a robust scaffolding system, which can deliver a major productivity boost. The absence of one can be a drain on productivity, as engineers keep reinventing the wheel, and each service gets slightly different configurations, dependencies, and coding styles.

There's a reason why most developer portals have the functionality to define software templates or skeletons: it's because easy-to-do scaffolding is such a big developer productivity unlock!

If you observe engineers regularly setting up services or components from scratch at the start of projects, consider defining a way to scaffold them. This can just be a project template linked to a wiki page, or be as sophisticated as a code generator that can create scaffolding for a wide range of use cases.

Rollouts and experiment hygiene

How are rollouts done on teams you work with, and how safely are configuration changes made? Are there rollback plans in place for major rollouts, and are some of these rollbacks automated?

If rollouts are a source of mistakes and outages, then planning for rollouts, rollbacks, and automated rollbacks, can make them more reliable. For example, if a team experiments frequently by using feature flags, stale feature flags, and stale experiments, then this can become a source of tech debt. A codebase with many feature flags – many of which are redundant – is harder to navigate and riskier to make changes to, than one where pointless feature flags are removed.

Experiment hygiene means removing feature flags that have served their purposes. But how are teams you work with doing this? Some create follow-up tasks and remove feature flags after an experiment concludes. But this is a task that's easy to overlook. Another option is to build automated tooling that captures inactive feature flags. Taking it a step further, you could even put tooling in place that creates automated pull requests for review by an engineer that suggests stale feature flags to be removed. An example of this is Piranha[6] by Uber, which automatically refactors code based on how a flag is expected to permanently behave.

---

[6]https://github.com/uber/piranha

Systems health dashboards

How healthy are the systems which your team owns and operates? The most straightforward way to answer this is a dashboard that visualizes the team's key business and systems metrics. An engineer should easily be able to understand whether their systems are healthy or unhealthy.

Do teams you work with have dashboards? If not, ask why not. There are no rules about how a dashboard should look; it should just make sense to the team. Of course, it's a bonus if stakeholders can also understand it, but not a requirement. If there's no dashboard, get to work on putting one together!

The "Reliable Software Engineering" chapter in Part V of this book, has suggestions for defining what to monitor.

3. Engineering Practices to Iterate Quickly

As a staff+ engineer, your goal should be to improve the efficiency of the engineering team you work with, and other engineering teams in the group. There are several tools and processes which efficient engineering groups can use. Here's a selection:

Continuous integration (CI)

Continuous integration (CI) refers to frequently integrating your code back to the main branch, via pull requests. Every opened pull request kicks off an automated build which typically has these steps:

- Compile and build the project
- Run static analysis tests and linting
- Execute unit tests, integration tests, and other automated tests
- Execute further automation, like security checks or custom rules

The benefit of CI is rapid feedback and detection of regressions much sooner than without it.

One of the biggest challenges for all CI systems is getting the running times of automated tests down, ideally to minutes. If an engineer opens a new pull request but must wait more than 30 minutes for feedback, this isn't a timely feedback cycle.

The challenge of making CI automation execute fast is especially tricky on large codebases, and when there are high numbers of tests. A few approaches can help speed things up:

- Modularize the code and cache build artifacts which are unchanged

- Split up the test suite and run it in parallel on several machines
- Only run a smaller part of the test suite for CI, and run the full test suite later
- Only run tests that exercise code that changed during CI, and run the full test suite later

Continuous deployment (CD)

Continuous deployment (CD) takes CI one step further and deploys approved code changes straight to production. CI and CD typically go hand-in-hand, as there is little point in CD if there's no CI set-up in place.

Advanced automated deployment practices tend to be of value to larger systems, including:

- **Automated staged rollout of changes**. Rolling out changes to larger systems can be risky, even if all automated tests are passed. For backend systems, a canarying approach can be used to deploy new code to a fraction of servers. The CD system monitors health metrics and continues a rollout only if they're healthy.
- **Automated rollback**. When the system detects unhealthy metrics post-rollout it automatically rolls back the latest deployment and sends an alert for teams to investigate.

CI and CD systems offer rapid feedback for engineers, and reduce errors by automating testing and deployment steps. CI/CD is a very common practice across most tech companies.

However, there are downsides to CI/CD systems:

- Time taken to set up. The initial setup takes time and effort, which can be non-trivial
- Slow builds and tests: if these are sluggish, then engineers spend a lot more time waiting for tests to run, which isn't a good developer experience
- Maintenance cost: a healthy CI/CD system needs to be maintained. Builds and tests get slower as more code is added. If test suites are time-consuming, they can slow developers down.

Trunk-based development

This is a common strategy at many tech companies where all engineers work on a single, shared branch (often called the 'main' branch) of the codease. This is the opposite of working in a long-lived branch, and merging to a release branch infrequently.

Trunk-based development has several advantages:

- A single source of truth: the 'main' branch is the code that runs in production and all engineers develop on it.
- More frequent commits: to stay in sync with the main branch, engineers commit frequently to it.

- Continuous integration: it's necessary to set up CI for trunk-based development to ensure the main branch is healthy.
- Feature flags: teams will still want to do staged rollouts of functionality in a trunk-based environment. In the absence of long-lived branches where this functionality could live, feature flags tend to be an obvious option.

The biggest downside of trunk-based environments is that more investment is needed in build tooling and CI/CD. Merges into trunk are more frequent, as are builds, which can put a strain on the build system so that it becomes necessary to improve build throughput and reduce build times.

It's common enough for companies with trunk-based development to have a platform team which is at least partially responsible for build tooling. The larger the engineering team working on a codebase, the more complex this is.

Feature flags

A common way to control a rollout is to hide it behind a feature flag in the code. This feature flag can be enabled for a subset of users who execute the new version of the code.

Feature flags are easy enough to implement and might look something like this for an imaginary feature called 'Zeno':

```
if( featureFlags.isEnabled"("Zeno_Feature_Flag)) {
        // New code to execute
} else {
        // Old code to execute
}
```

Feature flags are especially common in these contexts:

- Trunk-based development: feature flags are the most viable way to commit not-yet-production-ready functionality into the codebase
- Native mobile and desktop applications: these ship binary code to the end user. Feature flags can toggle which parts of the code to execute.
- Companies with a culture of experimentation. Feature flags are a preferred approach for guarding and controlling experiments and feature flags.

We touch on feature flags in more detail in Part IV: "Shipping to Production."

Monorepos

A monorepo refers to when all the source code across a platform lives in a single, large repository. For example, there might be one monorepo for all Go code, one for all iOS code, and so on. This is the approach of large tech companies like Google, Meta, and Uber.

The size of a monorepo is its biggest downside, as the repository can become so large that checking out the codebase on a single developer machine is time-consuming or even impossible for very large codebases. Tooling is another challenge; most source control vendors offer better support for more reasonably sized repositories.

However, with dedicated tooling, developing in a monorepo tends to be much more efficient. This is because dependencies are clearer, refactoring is simpler, and it's easier to write integration tests that span multiple components in the repository. It's also easier for engineers to navigate all of the codebase once they understand its structure.

Most tech companies start by having desiccated repositories for each major project. As companies grow, there is a natural push to consider moving to a monorepo, to improve developer productivity and experience.

Microservices vs monoliths

Microservice architecture structures applications as a collection of loosely coupled, independently deployable services. These can be small and are called "microservices." Monolithic architecture is the opposite: all features are within a single codebase and run as such.

There is an eternal debate whether a monolithic application design or a microservices architecture, serves a company better. There are tradeoffs to both approaches and also examples of companies employing each one successfully. For example, Shopify famously sticks with a monolithic application design with more than 2 million lines of Ruby code powering[7] the core of the company, while Uber went down the microservices route and operated well over 2,000 services[8].

Modular monoliths and microservices with a more modular structure seem to be the pragmatic middle ground between both approaches. As a company grows, the pain points of both become more pronounced:

- For monoliths, the codebase becomes large and it can get harder to make code changes, given the tight coupling of all parts of the codebase.
- For microservices, their numbers explode and it can become easier to accidentally break other services that have implicit dependencies on those being modified

Companies that follow a monolithic approach eventually modularize their monolith, so engineers can work on smaller parts of it which are more independent. This is the approach Shopify takes[9].

---

[7]https://shopify.engineering/shopify-monolith
[8]https://www.uber.com/blog/microservice-architecture
[9]https://shopify.engineering/shopify-monolith

Companies employing the microservices approach eventually introduce guidance on structuring and organizing them in a more logical architecture. This is the approach Uber took, structuring thousands of microservices into a few dozen collections called "domains."

4. Tools to Make Engineers More Efficient

Several tools can make engineering teams more efficient, especially at larger tech companies. It's useful to know these tools as they ease developer productivity pain points.

Services catalog

At companies where teams build services or microservices, service sprawl becomes a problem. As the number of teams and services increases, it gets harder to answer questions like:

- Is there a service that does X?
- Who owns service Y and where is the oncall rotation?
- How do I onboard my team to this service?

The most obvious way to start answering these questions is with a services catalog. It's a portal where teams can register their services, and engineers can search for them. Several larger tech companies build their own services catalog, but an increasing number adopt developer portals which offer them as a feature.

Code search

How easy is it to search the whole codebase? Does your company's codebase search method offer:

- Searches of the entire codebase
- Support for regular expressions
- Support for cross-references for clicking through to classes for their definitions
- Speed

Consider that for more than two decades, Google has had a team dedicated to building and maintaining an advanced code-search tool. The search giant realized that efficiently searching the codebase is a major productivity boost for engineers, and its "Code Search" products support all the use cases above and more.

Version control vendors such as GitHub and GitLab support code search to some extent. Sourcegraph is a better-known vendor that aims to build code-search tooling as capable as Google's.

Given how valuable it is to be able to efficiently search source code, it's a bit strange that some companies give this no thought. As a staff+ engineer, it's worth understanding where your company stands on this, and consider if improving code search would boost engineering efficiency, overall.

Developer portals

The best-known open-source developer portal is "Backstage," developed by Spotify. It was built as a way to address pain points the company experienced as it expanded to hundreds of teams, as many services, and an increasingly fragmented way of scaffolding projects.

Backstage consists of several components:

- A software and services catalog to track services, websites, libraries, APIs, and other resources. Teams can register their resources in the catalog for engineers to find.
- Software templates to scaffold a new API, website, service, or another component. Engineers can create easy-to-find templates, so complex actions can be executed in a few clicks.
- Tech docs: a wiki for engineering documentation.
- Plugins: the portal is modular and plugins can be installed from a central catalog. Engineers can also build new plugins.

Large tech companies like Google, Meta, Amazon, and Uber, have custom developer portals. Elsewhere, it's becoming common to adopt existing developer portals.

Cloud development environments

The default way to develop software has been to do it locally, and not using the cloud. Here are the steps for using a local development environment:

1. Install the given integrated development environment (IDE) you use
2. Check out the code
3. Install dependencies
4. Install additional tools or IDE extensions for a project
5. Compile, test, and locally deploy the code, perhaps with custom steps
6. Locally run and debug the code. Custom steps are also an option

As a codebase grows, developer productivity can drop at large tech organizations in a few ways, such as:

- Checking a codebase takes longer than 10 minutes due to its size.
- Building the code takes too long
- Running tests takes more than 10 minutes
- Setting up the development environment is a complicated, error-prone process

- Every now and then, a software engineer has trouble building/testing/deploying because their local environment is different from most others
- Relatively simple git operations like git status take well over 10 seconds

When things slow down, cloud developer environments (CDE) can become an interesting option. CDEs offer benefits which local environments don't, including:

- **Shorter feedback loops**. Builds are faster and so is the running of tests. For example, when Uber built a cloud development environment, complicated builds got 2-2.5x faster.
- **Consistency and reproducibility**. Engineers use the same environment, so it's easier to reproduce bugs, and less time is spent tracking down issues across different environments.
- **Sharing of environments**. Developers can share cloud development environments for things like debugging. Environments can be also shared with business stakeholders, or customers for demonstration purposes.
- **Simpler security auditing**. Instead of monitoring each developer's local environment for security threats, cloud environments can be equipped with security tools to detect and mitigate threats. Cloud environments are also a smaller attack surface.
- **Faster onboarding**. Cloud environments tend to offer much faster onboarding than local development environments for new engineers to get up to speed with a new codebase.

A cloud-based environment has downsides, too:

- **May not solve an important bottleneck**. "If it ain't broke, don't fix it" is a pretty pragmatic approach to follow for most engineering teams. Where are the productivity bottlenecks? If slow build/test times, lengthy onboarding, and inconsistent developer experience aren't among the top bottlenecks, then a CDE might not help much. So why spend time and money on one?
- **Initial set up and maintenance**. Setting up and maintaining a cloud development environment takes time and effort, no different from investing in a CI/CD environment. Just ensure to budget for this cost during planning.
- **Cost**. Operating CDEs could cost more than the engineering team's laptops. This is down to vendors and usage, but it doesn't come cheap to spin up really powerful machines in the cloud. Large tech companies like Uber, Slack, and Pipedrive, can justify increased costs because the "developer infrastructure cost" per software engineer is a fraction of a senior engineer's compensation.
- **The maturity of CDE solutions**. These evolve rapidly, so you might not find exactly what you want. There could be pieces missing from the tech stack, customization options, and so on.
- **Vendor lock-in**. Some CDE vendors operate a software as a service (SaaS) model, and make it hard to drop their product. Exercise caution when choosing such a CDE

vendor.

Cloud development environments make a lot of sense for large organizations, but much less so in smaller groups. Midsized teams and companies should identify the engineering team's productivity bottlenecks, and decide accordingly.

Experimenting is always an option. It can be daunting to persuade a whole engineering organization to trial a CDE. But do you really need to do this? It can be much more efficient to trial a CDE solution on one or two teams, and gather feedback. Does the CDE result in faster builds and tests? Do engineers feel more productive? Do they spend less time fixing their environment? Collect data to inform your team whether to keep this setup in place. This could help the wider organization decide whether to onboard to a CDE.

For more details on CDEs, see my article, Why are cloud development environments spiking in popularity?[10]

Artificial Intelligence (AI) coding tools

AI coding assistants are on the rise, and adoption of them accelerated from 2022, with the release of ChatGPT. The first widely-adopted AI coding assistant was TabNine (2019,) followed by GitHub Copilot (2021,) and many others in 2023 – like Sourcegraph Cody, Replit Ghostwriter, Amazon CodeWhisperer, and more.

AI coding assistants improve developer productivity, and we're still in the early days of utilizing this technology to its full potential. A few things to consider with AI assistants:

- The performance of the underlying model seems an important indicator of how helpful the assistant is. Some machine learning models perform better at coding than others.
- Training the coding assistant on the codebase can be beneficial, especially for large or unique code bases. But there seem to be benefits without this training.
- Data ownership and retention are important for most tech companies. Is data for the model also shared with the vendor? If so, could this sensitive data – the company's source code! – possibly leak or be retained in unintended ways?

AI coding tools that can be built, will do more than coding assistants. Obvious applications of AI and large language models (LLM) include:

- **Code reviews**. The AI tool critiques a submitted code review and points out obvious issues.
- **Writing automated tests**. There are plenty of engineers who think a tool should not

---

[10]https://pragmaticurl.com/CDE

write tests, but the reality is writing automated tests can be tedious. AI tools can generate test cases, which engineers can tweak before committing them.

- **Refactoring**. Refactoring tools in IDEs are already advanced and make things like renaming methods or classes straightforward. But AI tools can take things further by executing refactoring across a project based on text inputs like "rename all Company-NameXXX references to NewCompanyNameXXX references."
- **Stale feature flag removal**. A specialized and very useful use case for refactoring.
- **Compliance and security reviews**. AI tools can point out how a code change might raise regulatory or security flags.

Tech companies are already building for some of these use cases, and I reckon it's only a matter of time before vendors offer more advanced AI-assisted tooling.

Buy, build, or adopt?

When acquiring one of the above tools there are typically three options:

- **Build it**. This is the approach which large tech companies tend to take, as most vendors don't support their scale, and big companies can afford to avoid being locked into a single vendor.
- **Buy it**. This is the fastest way to get started if a vendor offers the tool and capability you need. In the short term, it's usually the cheapest because building and adopting require dedicated engineers.
- **Adopt it**. If there's an open source project for your needed tool or capability, you can adopt this project and operate it yourself. It's much cheaper than building. However, you will need to pay for infrastructure resources and maintenance. Plus, the tool may need customizing for your company's use case.

As always, there's no universal rule on whether building, buying or adopting is the best option. Vendors will say buying is the cheapest option, long-term. Engineers have a bias for building, and this or adopting a solution are activities that tend to be recognized more positively during performance reviews and promotions. Also, building is a lot more fun and educational than negotiating terms with a vendor.

Conventional wisdom says you should maintain full control over the core capabilities of your company, and buy other things. This sounds good in theory, but some of the most successful tech companies repeatedly ignore conventional wisdom and follow the path that works for them.

If you're in a position to influence or make buy/build/adopt decisions, follow a similar process as with any major engineering choice. Gather information and fill in the gaps; for example, by prototyping alternatives for a sense of what they involve.

5. Compliance and Privacy

There's a high likelihood that the software engineering process at your organization needs to adhere to certain compliance and privacy guidelines.

Larger tech companies tend to have a compliance or legal team that determines which regulations, processes, and guidelines to follow. Some companies have in-house compliance, privacy, and security teams, while others hire external consultants. Compliance violations are costly, both reputationally and financially. Part of a staff+ engineer's job is ensuring the company takes this area seriously.

Regulations

PII (Personally Identifiable Information) should not be accessible to anyone but those who should have access. No software engineer, customer support person, or other employee, should be able to access this information.

GDPR (General Data Protection Regulation) is a significant piece of European Union (EU) regulation that has expanded the scope of PII, which can only be stored and processed for lawful, legitimate purposes.

Industry-specific compliance guidelines may apply to your organization. A non-exhaustive list of these includes:

- **PCI DSS** (Payment Card Industry Data Security Standard) for handling credit card information
- **HIPAA** (Health Insurance Portability and Accountability Act) and/or ISO/IEC 27001 when working with healthcare-related data.
- **FERPA** (Family Educational Rights and Privacy Act) for working with student or educational information in the US
- **FCRA** (Fair Credit Reporting Act) for apps related to consumer reporting agencies such as credit companies, medical information companies or tenant screening
- **Section 508** compliance when working with US federal agencies, ensuring people with disabilities can access their electronic information technology (EIT.)
- **European Accessibility Act** guidelines for when developing for an EU country's government.

Individual country privacy laws may apply to your product, too.

Logging

Logging of data is an area which warrants careful thought:

- Logging PII data without end-to-end encryption can invite data breaches
- Aim to not log PII data. Anonymize this information in the logs, turning it into non-PII data
- Put guidance in place for what, when, and how to log, including a section on PII data
- Audit logs to ensure they comply with regulations
- User bug reports – including screenshots! – should not contain PII. You might need to take additional steps to ensure this is the case, so that information like credit card numbers does not circulate in ticketing systems, or be visible to customer support agents

As a helpful practice, regularly review what data is being logged and how, in order to ensure no PII is stored non-securely in any system.

Auditing

Your systems might need to be audited for regulatory compliance, such as GDPR or PII rules. Audits are done by vendors who specialize in this. Audit criteria tends to state what acceptable practices are. In reality, many of these requirements can be vague, without interpretation by a specialist.

When taking part or leading an audit, try to find folks who went through it before. If this isn't possible, consider making the case for hiring a consultant who can help prepare for the audit. Just as valid is the approach of preparing as best as you can for an audit and collaborating with auditors.

Preparing for an audit can be a significant undertaking, depending on the type of audit and how helpful auditors are expected to be. At Uber, we spent months mapping processes, making process and tool changes, and then auditing them ahead of the launch of GDPR. The amount of work and the scale of the changes made meant this project was one of the bigger undertakings by the company.

An audit tends to be most time-consuming and energy-draining the first time. Once you pass it and have the right processes in place, staying compliant is far easier.

6. Secure Development

Secure software development is a continuously evolving and vast topic, which this book doesn't cover in depth. As a staff+ engineer, you need to be intimately familiar with the secure development practices of your domain, and also with common threat vectors and how to mitigate them.

Secure coding practices can be language-agnostic, or language-specific. The most popular language-agnostic secure coding guideline is the OWASP secure coding practices reference guide[11].

On top of OWASP guidelines, you might be able to find secure coding practices for the language and framework of your choice. A few examples:

- Secure coding guidelines[12] for Java SE by Oracle
- Secure coding practices[13] for Go by OWASP
- Secure Rust guidelines[14], a community project

Dependencies as security vulnerabilities are an ever-present security threat. A library that one of your systems uses could one day be found to have a vulnerability. Until that library is patched, your systems could be insecure. One of the most impactful dependency vulnerabilities was discovered in 2021, which was the Log4j logging library's security vulnerability[15], which could be exploited to take backend systems offline with denial-of-service (DoS) attacks.

Penetration testing is the practice of testing a system by experts for vulnerabilities. If your team or company facilitates this, participating in it can be eye-opening in terms of learning how experts exercise your systems, and the unaddressed threats lurking within.

Security engineers are increasingly hired from medium-sized companies. Security is an over-arching focus that incorporates all parts of the software development life cycle. If you work at a medium-sized or large company, there's a fair chance a dedicated software security team is already in place.

Get to know them and aim to build a partnership. How do they improve secure engineering practices in your company, and how can you help? Identify situations when it would be helpful to involve the security team; for example, during project planning, or for certain key code changes.

---

[11] https://owasp.org/www-project-secure-coding-practices-quick-reference-guide
[12] https://www.oracle.com/java/technologies/javase/seccodeguide.html
[13] https://github.com/OWASP/Go-SCP
[14] https://anssi-fr.github.io/rust-guide
[15] https://builtin.com/cybersecurity/log4j-vulerability-explained

24

RELIABLE SOFTWARE SYSTEMS

There's a fair chance your organization implicitly or explicitly expects staff+ engineers to lead efforts to make systems more reliable.

In this chapter, we cover common approaches for building and maintaining reliable systems, including:

1. Owning reliability
2. Logging
3. Monitoring
4. Alerting
5. Oncall
6. Incident management
7. Building resilient systems

1. Owning Reliability

What role do you play in reliability as a staff+ engineer? In Big Tech, it's often an explicit expectation that you own reliability within your sphere of influence, be that on your own team or other teams. This means it's your responsibility to ensure reliability is measured, plans are put in place to improve it and to advocate for extra engineering bandwidth to improve reliability.

An OKR is often a helpful way to improve the reliability of systems. For example, you can capture objectives to make systems more reliable, performant, and efficient. Then you can define measurable key performance indicators (KPIs,) such as:

- Improve the p95 latency for System X by 10%
- Increase the throughput of the System Y by 30%, without changing the hardware resources
- Decrease the cold start time of System Z by 15%

You almost always need to partner with engineering managers to move the needle on reliability. At the end of the day, engineering managers are responsible and accountable for the performance of their teams and the reliability of their systems. However, as a staff+ engineer, you possess the skills to recognize when reliability is a problem and to employ various approaches to improve this. You can – and should! – bring data to engineering managers to highlight why it's important to invest in reliability, and what the return on this investment would be.

We covered more on OKRs and KPIs in Part V: "Understanding the Business."

2. Logging

Before we dive into logging approaches, let's put the record straight about why it matters. Logs are meant to help an engineering team debug production issues, by capturing missing but necessary information for future reference during troubleshooting.

Which logging strategy can help your team debug its production issues? Well, this depends on your application, platform, and business environment.

There's a logging toolset that can be helpful when deciding how and what to log:

- **Log levels**. Most logging tools provide ways to log various logging levels, such as "debug," "info," "warning," and "error." These are levels that can be used when filtering logs. How they're used depends on your environment and team practices.
- **Log structure**. Which details do logs capture, are local variables logged, do logs capture timestamps – down to milliseconds or nanoseconds – to make it easy to tell which one of two logging events happened first? Do these timestamps include timezones?
- **Automated logging**. Which parts of the system log automatically, so logging isn't dependent on an engineer remembering to do it?
- **Log retention**. How long are logs retained on client devices, and for how long are they on the backend? Retaining logs for longer can be useful, but takes up space and could end up costing more in data storage.
- **Toggling logging levels**. For applications, it's common practice to have "debug builds" where all log levels are outputted, but only warning or error log levels are logged on a production build. The details depend on platform-level implementation and team practices.

Make your logging practices explicit

Consider introducing logging practices if the teams you work with don't have any. Logging is an area which engineers often wish they'd pushed for agreement on what and how to log, when they're trying and failing to find information in the logs.

Putting a short logging guide together for the team is a matter of talking with a few engineers, and empowering a team member to make a proposal – or doing it yourself. For logging basics, agreeing on something is better than nothing, as long as the team knows it owns this guide and can change it.

A logging guide that's stood the test of time

The guide below is from 2008, by Anton Chuvakin[1], who was then chief logging evangelist at LogLogic. This logging guide remains relevant, and so with Anton's consent, here it is:

The best logs:

- Tell you exactly what happened: when, where, how
- Are suitable for manual, semi-automated, and automated analysis
- Can be analyzed without the application that produced them being to hand
- Don't slow the system down
- Can be proven as reliable if used as evidence

Events To Log

- Authentication/authorization decisions (including logoff)
- System access, data access
- System/application changes (especially privilege changes)
- Data changes: add/edit/delete
- Invalid input (possible badness/threats)
- Resources (RAM, Disk, CPU, Bandwidth, any other hard or soft limits)
- Health/availability: startups/shutdowns, faults/errors, delays, backups success/failure

What To Log – Every Event Should Have:

- Timestamp & timezone (when)
- System, application, or component (where); IP's and contemporaneous DNS lookups of involved parties; names/roles of systems involved (what servers are we talking to?), name/role of local application (what is this server?)
- User (who)
- Action (what)
- Status (result)
- Priority (severity, importance, rank, level, etc)
- Reason

---

[1]https://www.chuvakin.org

Have a framework that makes logging the "right" way easy

How does your team do logging, does everyone invoke logs however they see fit? This approach makes sense for very small teams with senior engineers, but on larger teams it tends to result in ad hoc logging approaches: devs log to the console, use a third-party logging vendor, or invoke an in-house logging solution.

A relatively straightforward way to improve consistency is to reach an agreement on the logging approach – for example, which strategies to use – and then make it really hard to log the "wrong" way by introducing a lightweight but opinionated logging framework.

But why put another framework in place, just for logging? Creating a simple interface helps abstract the underlying vendor in use, which could be especially relevant at larger companies where vendors change and it's helpful to make migrations far easier. It can also help analyze logging usage in future. Of course, don't build a new framework for its own sake; do it when it solves the problem of ad-hoc, inconsistent logging, and unclear guidelines for which frameworks to use.

3. Monitoring

How can you tell if a system is healthy or not? The most reliable way is to monitor key characteristics and trigger an alert when a metric seems unhealthy.

50th, 90th, 95th percentile

Percentiles are a key concept in monitoring and service level agreements (SLAs.) When monitoring things like load times or response times, it's not enough to look only at average numbers. Why not? They can mask worst-case scenarios that impact many customers. To avoid this, consider monitoring the following percentiles:

- p50: the 50th percentile or median value. 50% of data points are below this number, and 50% are above. This value represents the "average" use case pretty well.
- p95: the 95th percentile. This represents the worst-performing 5% of data points. This value is particularly important in performance-monitoring scenarios because the worst performing 5% of data points could refer to power users.
- p99: the 99th percentile. This number represents measurements which 1% of customers or requests see longer times for. It could be acceptable for this number to be an outlier in some use cases.

Things to monitor

So what should you monitor? There are plenty of obvious choices which provide health information about a system or app, including:

- **Uptime**. For what percentage of time is the system or app fully operational?
- **CPU, memory, disk space**. Monitoring resource usage can provide useful indicators for when a service or app risks becoming unhealthy.
- **Response times**. How long does it take a system or app to respond? What is the median, and what's the experience of the slowest 5% of requests or users (p95), and the slowest 1% (p99)?
- **Error rates**. How frequent are errors, such as exceptions thrown, 4XX responses on HTTP services, and other error states? What percentage of all requests are errors?

For backend services:

- **HTTP status code responses**. If there is a spike in error codes like 5XX or 4XX, it could indicate a problem
- **Latency metrics**. What are the p50, p95, and p99 latencies of server responses?

For web apps and mobile apps, additional metrics are worth monitoring:

- **Page load time**. How long does the webpage take to load? How does this compare across p50, p75 and p95?
- **Core Web Vitals metrics**. Google released "Web Vitals" in 2020, which are quality signals to deliver a great user experience. These metrics can capture a more detailed picture of web performance. The core signals are Largest Contentful Paint (LCP,) First Input Delay (FID,) and Cumulative Layout Shift (CLS.)

For a mobile app, additional metrics worth monitoring are:

- **Start-up time**. How long does it take for the app to start? The longer this takes, the more likely customer churn is.
- **Crash rate**. What percentage of sessions end with the app crashing?
- **App bundle size**. How does this change over time? This is important for apps because a larger size could mean fewer users install it.

Business metrics tell the "real" story of how healthy apps or services are. The metrics above are more generic and infrastructural; they indicate fundamental problems. However, the above metrics can look good, and a service or app can still be unhealthy.

Monitoring business metrics

To get a full picture of system health, you need to monitor business metrics that are highly specific to the product. For example, at Uber core business metrics for the Rides products were lifecycle events:

- How many people are requesting a ride?
- How long does a request stay in the "pending" state?
- How many of these requests are accepted or rejected?

Changes in metrics like a plummeting rate of rides being accepted could indicate an outage.

On my Payments team within the Rides product, the business metrics we monitored were:

- Number of successful additions of a new payment method (e.g., a credit card.)
- Number of errors during the add payment flow
- Time taken to complete the add payment flow – the p50 figure

We measured the business metrics for payment methods like credit card, PayPal, Apple Pay, and others. Business metrics are specific to your business unit, but some are widespread, such as:

- **Customer onboarding**. How many customers entered the sign up funnel, which ratio of exits are successful, how many people get "stuck" at certain steps, how long does a signup take?
- **Success and error rates for business-specific actions**. What is the ratio of successful and unsuccessful business-specific actions? For example, on Uber's Payments team the action is adding a payment method.
- **Daily/weekly/monthly active users (DAU, WAU, MAU.)** How many users are active per day/week/month?
- **Revenue**. What's the total revenue generated on a daily, weekly, and hourly basis? What about average revenue per user?
- **Usage numbers**. For how long does a user interact with the app or service, and how many actions do they make? Statistics like p50, p75, and p90 identify median users, frequent users, and power users.
- **Number of support tickets**. What is the number of total support tickets coming in, and how are they split by category? When splitting by category, it can be useful to track how this occurs, as spikes may indicate bugs or outages.
- **Retention and churn**. What percentage of users are retained on a weekly, monthly, and quarterly basis, i.e., what percentage return? What's the ratio of users who cancel, such as by deleting their accounts?

Monitoring alone isn't sufficient to ensure a system is reliable. Alerts need to be fired when the metrics look wrong, which an oncall engineer must receive, investigate, and mitigate.

4. Alerting

Decide which metrics need alerts assigned to them. There are many things to monitor, but which specific metrics should have alerting in place for when they trend in the wrong direction?

One way to answer this question is to start with the business and product. Ask questions like:

- **What does "healthy" look like?** Which metrics tell us things look good? Add alerts to metrics that indicate things are not good.
- **What outages happened previously?** Which metrics could indicate something is wrong, in the future? Add alerts to metrics which would alert for a previous outage.
- **What do customers notice when things are not working?** Add monitoring and alerting to catch them. You might need to look at percentiles like p95 to catch outlier use cases related to long latency.

Just by verbalizing what "healthy" and "unhealthy" states look like, you should be able to figure out which areas of a system to monitor and alert for.

Urgency of alerts

Not all alerts are equal. A system going down for all customers sounds like a very important alert, whereas a small functionality breaking for a fraction of users – for example, a ticketing system's 'import users' function – has a much smaller impact. For this reason, categorize the urgency of alerts. Here's a simple but efficient system:

- **Urgent alert**: fires alerts that need to be acknowledged and acted on, ASAP. This alert will send a push notification, attempt to call a phone number, and escalate along a chain of command if there's no response.
- **Non-urgent alerts**: this alert doesn't disrupt people outside of business hours. These alerts are important to check but can wait until office hours.

Alert noise

Track the "noisiness" of alerts and act on it. A noisy alert is one that's not actionable. It's stressful to be woken up in the middle of the night by an alert, and even worse when it's for no real reason. At the same time, missing an outage due to an alert not being sent is less than ideal. So what's the right balance to strike? Measuring precision and recall are two concepts that help.

Precision. This measures the percentage of alerts which indicate a real issue. A system with 30% precision means 3 in 10 alerts are outages, and the rest are noise. The higher the precision percentage, the less noisiness there is. A system with 100% precision fires only alerts which indicate outages.

Recall. This measures the percentage of outages for which alerts are fired. A system with 30% recall means alerts are fired for 3 in 10 outages. A system with 100% recall means alerts are sent for every outage.

The ideal oncall system has 100% precision with no noisy alerts, and detects 100% of outages. But in the real world there tends to be tradeoffs, such as:

- When you remove noisy alerts you boost precision, but risk missing outages due to alerts not firing. This reduces recall.
- To improve alerting of outages, it's common to add more alerts to boost recall. But this may reduce precision.

Measure both the precision and recall of alerts to see which area you need to focus more on. A common method:

- Have the oncall engineer record whether each alert is for an outage, or if it's noise. *Most oncall tooling helps track this. If not, build or buy this functionality.*
- In incident reviews, go through all recent outages and answer the question: "did an alert fire which indicated an outage was happening?" This will show the recall percentage.

Measuring precision and recall rates involves engineers following the two manual steps above. Engineers need to tag alerts to confirm if an alert was for an outage, and incident reviewers should tag whether an outage was preceded by an alert. Capturing this information might already be possible with your existing oncall system. If not, you might need to build this functionality or extend the oncall system.

Static thresholds vs anomaly detection

How do you decide when to fire an alert for a metric? There are two common approaches:

1. Static thresholds. Manually define a threshold for when to fire an alert. For example, put a rule in place stating, "if this metric drops to zero for more than 60 seconds: fire an alert," or "if this metric is above 500/minute where the usual number is 100, raise an alert."

The upside of static thresholds is that they are easy to define, and it's easy to understand exactly why an alert fired. They are also easy to tweak. The downside is that it's hard to predict in advance what static thresholds to set, and it's more common to put static thresholds in place after an outage which a static threshold alert could have caught.

2. Anomaly detection. Instead of manually defining thresholds, let a machine learning system detect anomalies in the traffic patterns related to a metric. The only configuration input is how sensitive these alerts should be.

The upside of anomaly detection is that it picks up on far more variance than static thresholds do. With a well-trained and well-configured anomaly detection system, alerts are fired in the case of unexpected traffic surges or traffic drops. Anomaly detection is also much less of an effort to deploy across a variety of metrics, assuming there's an anomaly detection framework to use.

The downside is that anomaly detection can be overly noisy when not trained or configured well, so that it fires too many alerts, even for normal traffic patterns. I remember when we first deployed anomaly detection for our payments system at Uber; during the first few weeks while the system was training and we were configuring it, we got so many alerts that it was necessary to turn off live alerts.

And anomaly detection can have the opposite problem of being too insensitive to detect real anomalies. Configuring anomaly detection is often more work than it seems, and you'll likely need to have this system take into account things like usual traffic patterns during different times of week. It could also fire alerts for predictably low or high traffic – such as a traffic surge or drop during Black Friday for an e-commerce business.

Use good judgment to decide which types of alerts to use, and when. It takes hands-on experience with both types of alerts to decide which one is more beneficial for a specific use case. Use both of these alerts on different projects if you've not done so already!

Often, the most practical approach is a mix of the two: anomaly detection for most metrics, combined with static thresholds for expected traffic increases/drops, and to capture key metrics dropping to zero.

5. Oncall

Until the 2000s, it was common for companies to operate an ops model, with "ops" meaning operations. Developers wrote and tested code, committed it to a "next release" branch in source control, and over weeks or months the Release Candidate would be finalized and tested. The ops team would then take over and ship the release by deploying the code across servers, and applying database schema updates. For downloadable applications, the ops team updated the binary, and the update scripts. Then ops monitored the application.

Today, with much shorter iteration cycles, engineering teams frequently deploy multiple times per day. It's no longer an ops team which monitors the code, but the engineering team that makes changes and defines oncall rotations.

Typical oncall rotations

At tech companies, a typical oncall setup looks like this:

- **Primary oncall**: the engineer who receives alerts for the team's systems in production.
- **Pager application**: the app that routes alerts to the primary oncall. The most popular pager application vendor is PagerDuty, and other solutions like ZenDuty, incident.io, Jeli, FireHydrant, and Spike, are also used. Some large tech companies build in-house pager applications.
- **Secondary and tertiary oncall**: when an alert comes in, the oncall engineer needs to acknowledge it within a given amount of time, say, 10 minutes. If there's no acknowledgment, the alert escalates and pages the next person in the oncall chain, who's the secondary oncall. If the secondary oncall doesn't acknowledge in time, then the propagation continues to the tertiary oncall, and so on.

Most tech companies define a primary and secondary oncall rotation comprising team members. The tertiary layer tends to be engineering managers, and then the engineering management chain – such as directors and VPs in the engineering organization.

Dedicated oncall team vs every team being oncall

At most of Big Tech, it's common for engineering teams to own their own oncall rotation and to both define and staff it. At smaller tech companies it's not uncommon to have a dedicated oncall team that handles all high-priority alerts. This is often a virtual oncall team, and engineers are usually compensated for their extra time and effort.

At more traditional companies, or those beginning a digital transformation, it's pretty common for a DevOps team to handle alerts, given runbooks are associated with alerts.

What's the ideal size of an oncall team? However an oncall team is staffed, it's typical for an engineer to be oncall for a week. This means a team size of at least 5, if no engineer is to be oncall more than once a month: given a month has 4.5 weeks, on average. A team size of 6 accounts for holidays and illness; a good rule of thumb is that there's at least 6 people in a healthy oncall rotation.

If engineers also serve as secondary oncalls on top of their primary oncall duty, then a healthy rotation has 10-12 people, so that members aren't oncall too often.

At companies with a single oncall team, it's usually easier to ensure it's of a healthy size. But at companies where every team is oncall, people will be oncall more than once a month if they're on a team of fewer than 6. In such cases, it's common for two smaller teams in related domains to merge their oncalls to create a healthier cadence.

Oncall runbooks

When an alert fires, it's typically the oncall engineer who gets the notification. They then take action to determine if the alert indicates an outage.

An alert runbook helps to debug alerts and take steps to mitigate an outage. "Oncall runbook" is the collective term for alert runbooks, or the "master" alert runbook. Oncall runbooks can also be called "incident response runbooks."

Having an alert runbook attached to each alert makes oncall much more efficient. A useful alert runbook contains the following information:

- **Diagnostic steps**. How can the oncall engineer determine if an alert indicates an outage? Which dashboards, metrics, or other resources should they access for this? Which steps should they take to definitively determine if there's an outage? Ideally, the runbook has direct links to resources for diagnosing the issue.
- **Pointers to mitigate an outage**. Assuming an alert indicates an outage, what are the steps to resolve it? Most alerts tend to indicate specific types of outages, and the runbook contains details about them.
- **Relevant previous incidents**. What outages did this alert indicate previously? A pointer to the outage document can help review diagnostic steps, as well as mitigation, and could be handy when an alert fires.

Alert runbooks need to be kept up to date. Unfortunately, it's not possible to write the "perfect" alert runbook which never needs updating! Alert runbooks need to be updated when new incidents occur, including details on how to diagnose outages, as well as when systems are changed.

A healthy incident review process includes updates of oncall runbooks as part of each and every oncall event, or at least a review of whether the runbooks should be updated.

There are similarities between documenting code and writing alert runbooks. Both are useful for future reference – like when an engineer wants to understand what's going on – but it's tempting to de-prioritize these documents in the present. This means it falls to engineers who've been burnt by a lack of oncall runbooks to lead by example and be proactive in writing them.

As a staff+ engineer, defining a "master" oncall runbook is an easy way to make oncall more efficient. Try and work with the engineering team to create runbooks for common alerts, and make reviewing and updating alert runbooks part of the incident response process.

Oncall compensation

Whether or not oncall is paid depends on a few things:

- **Regulation**. In countries like Spain and Brazil, oncall pay is clearly regulated and applies to software engineers.
- **Whether being oncall is the only job**. Some companies – mostly traditional ones – hire dedicated DevOps or oncall engineers whose sole job is oncall rotation. At these places, there is no additional compensation for oncall.
- **Is oncall voluntary**. At places where oncall is voluntary, it's common to incentivize people to volunteer by offering payment.

At Big Tech and other companies paying closer to the top of the market – Tier 3 or Tier 2 compensation packages, as per the categorization in the chapter, Part I: "Compensation" – being oncall tends to be a widespread practice with no extra compensation. The likes of Amazon, Meta, Apple, and Microsoft, all follow this model. The exception is countries where oncall compensation is mandated.

Google is the only Big Tech company that compensates oncall[2], and also limits the time spent oncall.

Companies with more "centralized" oncall rotations which engineers can volunteer to join, almost always compensate oncall. For a list of companies that pay, and how much, see my article, Oncall compensation for software engineers[3].

Companies that pay closer to the middle of the market or below it, tend to need to pay for oncall because it's an additional time commitment and a source of stress outside of normal work hours. At well-paying companies, engineers will often accept the additional responsibility as part of a decent compensation package. However, if engineers feel they are not compensated sufficiently for it, they may seek jobs which pay more, or that pay similarly but without oncall pressure.

Should engineers do "normal" work while oncall?

There are a few teams on which being oncall is like a fulltime job, with frequent outages taking up people's time on cleaning up and executing follow-up actions. But for most teams, the work is not so intense, and during "good" oncall weeks there's barely any additional work. So should an oncall engineer do "normal" work while oncall?

Ultimately, this is a decision for the team manager. Here are common approaches for defining the weekly work of the oncall engineer:

- **Combine oncall with support engineering**. If a team is customer-facing, there will be plenty of inbound support requests from customers. Many teams combine the

---

[2]https://blog.pragmaticengineer.com/oncall-compensation
[3]https://blog.pragmaticengineer.com/oncall-compensation

oncall role with support engineering, with the oncall engineer going through inbound requests which might be bug reports to investigate, data cleaning requests that involve writing and running scripts, and more. During oncall week, an engineer stops their "normal" work and oncall becomes their first priority. When not doing oncall work, they pick up support tasks.

- **Assume zero project work and only oncall work**. For teams where oncall is a major source of labor, the oncall engineer can work only on oncall-related tasks, and when not handling outages they work on improving the oncall system, for example, by reducing alerts' noisiness, improving system reliability, or writing and improving runbooks.
- **Assume an engineer has no capacity for project work while oncall**. A conservative approach is for a team to assume the oncall engineer is busy with oncall the whole week, and to plan accordingly. In reality, there will be additional time to contribute to project work, but strictly on a "best-effort" basis. This is a helpful approach, unless it's expected the engineer will spend most of their time working on a project, of course!
- **Assume the engineer will be at X% of capacity**. Some managers assume an engineer on call will have a certain amount of capacity for project work, which is fine when the oncall load is as expected. But the problem with oncall is that it's unpredictable!

As a staff+ engineer, you will likely be able to influence the decision of how to plan oncall. Take oncall load and team dynamics into account when deciding the best approach.

Oncall burnout

A common axiom states "people quit managers, not companies." Here's a related observation by me: People don't only quit managers, they also quit terrible oncall rotations.

"Oncall burnout" is very real and something I've seen several times. It tends to happen in a combination of two or more factors:

- Engineers go oncall more than once a week per month
- The oncall rotation is noisy, meaning most alerts are non-actionable
- Engineers are awoken at night more than once a week per rotation
- Many outages happen, with lots of fires to put out
- Engineers are expected to do "normal" work while oncall

People respond to oncall burnout in different ways. Some recognize it's happening and take steps to change their situation by moving teams or leaving the company. Others keep pushing on, but their performance is negatively impacted, which they may not even notice! The impact of a stressful oncall is familiar; it wears people down.

As a staff+ engineer, you're likely one of the few individual contributors whose voice is taken seriously by management. So if you observe a team or individual getting close to burnout, make a case to improve oncall dynamics. Managers are responsible for team health, but if a manager is hands-off it might be down to you to deliver a diagnosis on the state of oncall, and offer an improvement.

6. Incident Management

What happens when an alert is fired and the oncall engineer confirms it's an outage? This is when the incident management process begins. The goal of incident management is to restore the system to normal operation as fast as possible, and prevent it from happening again.

There are various frameworks related to incident management, and your workplace might already use one. Typical incident lifecycle steps are:

1. Detect an incident
2. Fix it
3. Follow-up after the incident

Detecting an incident

Monitoring and alerting are key ways to detect incidents quickly, ideally within minutes. Once an alert fires, the oncall engineer needs to assess whether an outage is happening.

Declaring an incident is the first step of the incident management process. This is done by creating a new incident with the company's preferred incident management tool.

Categorizing and prioritizing an incident often happens when it's declared. There's a big difference between an outage that impacts a small cohort of customers, and a system going down for all customers.

Incident levels and categorization is something most tech companies have in place from the early days. Some opt to define incidents by different levels. For example, Amazon defines levels by severity: SEV-0 is the highest impact and most widespread, with SEV-1, SEV-2, SEV-3 all increasingly lower priority. At Uber, level 5 (L5) was the most serious, and L4, L3, L2 were all lower by impact and percentage of users affected. Some companies define two parts of an incident: impact (High/Medium/Low,) and how widespread it is (High/Medium/Low)

There should be clear criteria for how to categorize an incident, which is based on easy-to-measure metrics like service level indicators (SLIs.) If you find your company is vague about how to categorize severity, it may be an opportunity to improve this area!

Fix it

Incident management roles should be clear from when an incident is defined. Who coordinates the incident response and who updates stakeholders? It's common enough for the "incident commander" role to be the response coordinator. This might not be the person who detected the incident. Most engineering teams quickly learn it's helpful to make this role explicit.

Most incident management tools require an assigned incident commander when declaring an incident. Like the severity of the incident, this role can be changed later. It's not uncommon for incident commanders to change, especially when an outage starts small, but develops into a more severe one.

Mitigation is the most pressing step after declaring an outage. Fixing an incident as quickly as possible is sometimes straightforward; for example, if it was caused by a recent code change, then rolling back that change may be a quick fix.

Mitigating efficiently tends to involve these steps:

- When mitigation steps are known, execute them. This is why runbooks are so valuable; they make mitigation much easier
- When mitigation steps are unknown, get people with relevant expertise involved and start mitigating. This could involve paging or calling them. Knowing who the right people are is easier with an oncall runbook.
- Communicate with stakeholders. Outage stakeholders are people in the management chain with an interest in what's happening with an outage, or business stakeholders, or customers
- Verify whether a mitigation step has worked. After attempting to mitigate, verify its effectiveness. Outages can be tricky beasts and may require multiple steps in order to be resolved. Occasionally, mitigation efforts can make an outage worse

Assessing the root cause of an outage isn't the biggest priority. A common mistake less experienced engineers make is trying to understand why an outage occurred, and to only start fixing it when they know. It is logical to not want to fix without first understanding the cause, but this approach can slow down efforts to mitigate an outage as quickly as possible.

If there are obvious mitigation steps that can be started, like rolling back a code change, or executing a rollback plan, **do these first**. Once the outage is mitigated, there will be plenty of time to understand its cause.

Follow-up after an incident

Once an incident is mitigated, it's time to take a breath. If mitigation took place outside of business hours, then take a well-earned rest and follow up the next workday.

Incident analysis/postmortem is typically the next step in the incident-handling lifecycle. Common questions include what caused the incident, what was the exact timeline of events, and how to avoid a repeat in future?

The incident review is a meeting in which a bigger group reviews the incident analysis documents of high-impact outages. Some companies have dedicated incident management teams for this, others hold weekly or bi-weekly meetings with some managers present, while others do it ad hoc.

Incident follow-up actions are those the team identifies as necessary to avoid similar incidents in future. But it's easy enough for these to be deprioritized after mitigation, especially if they require a lot of engineering work. Every team and company has a different way to track these items and ensure they are done. As a staff+ engineer, you can – and should! – help create time for the team to do this follow-up work, sometimes even at the expense of other tasks.

Blameless reviews are a common approach across the tech industry. When doing an incident analysis, avoid making it a witch hunt process of finding someone to blame.

Most outages are caused by configuration or code changes which someone made, and it's very easy to find out exactly who. But rather than directly or indirectly pinning blame on one person, go deeper and look into why systems allowed those changes to happen without feedback. If the conditions that allowed an incident to occur are unaddressed, they could easily trip up someone else in future.

Some people resist the idea of blameless postmortems. "Will this lead to a lack of accountability?", they ask. But accountability and a blameless culture are distinct things which go hand in hand, in my view. Accountability means people take responsibility for their work, and when things inevitably go wrong, they take ownership for fixing them. A blameless approach recognizes that it's counterproductive to blame someone for doing something which they were unaware would cause an outage, especially when they take accountability for addressing the causes.

Consider whether your incident review process prioritizes learning from incidents. In the article, Incident review and postmortem best practices[4], I talk with John Allspaw – former CTO of Etsy, and founder of Adaptive Capacity Labs. John helps companies improve their incident management processes, and shared an interesting observation:

> "Most incidents are written to be filed, not to be read or learned from. This is what we come across again and again. Teams go through incidents, they file a report, pat themselves on the back, and think they've learned from it. In reality,

---

[4]https://blog.pragmaticengineer.com/postmortem-best-practices

the learning has been a fraction of what it could have been.

> The current incident-handling approaches are only scratching the surface of what we could be doing. In some ways, tech is behind several other industries in how we architect reliable systems."

There are plenty of playbooks and tools for building an incident-management process that's in line with how most tech companies handle incidents. What there is a scarcity of, is companies that successfully use incident management as a learning tool to make teams and systems more resilient.

As a staff+ engineer, you're able to influence how the incident management processes in your workplace evolve. As you do, remember that learning from incidents and applying lessons across the organization should be the ultimate goals of any incident management system. It's the approach used by companies which are ahead of the pack.

7. Building Resilient Systems

How do you build a system that operates reliably? Design and code systems that are resilient, are a must-have. But resilience doesn't come from just thinking about future faults and use cases. Here are approaches for designing, building, testing, and operating resilient systems.

Planning phase

Resilient systems are designed to behave resiliently, obviously. During the planning phase, pay attention to these things:

- **SLIs**. Determine the system's uptime service level indicators (SLI). What will determine if a system is "healthy," what does "uptime" mean, and what is the uptime target? Define these as precisely as possible, as this definition will drive architecture decisions, as well as testing and operations choices.
- **Plan for failure**. What could go wrong and how will you respond?
- **Plan for load**. What load is the system expected to handle, what does peak load look like, what capacity does the system need to handle this initial load?
- **Plan for redundancy**. What are redundancy requirements, how will data be replicated and redundancy ensured?
- **Plan for what to monitor and alert for**. What are indicators of system health, and what anomalies do you want to alert oncall engineers to?

During the coding phase

As you build the system, a few areas are worth focusing on with resiliency in mind:

- **Code defensively**. Handle edge cases explicitly and not implicitly, where possible.
- **Pay attention to error states and error mapping**. What indicates errors in the system? These could be variables, API responses, or state. Record and log these errors, and – if it's sensible – alert on them. Pay attention to how systems map error states between one another.
- **Consider state management**. How is state handled within the application, and what parts of the application can modify state? The fewer places which can modify the state, the fewer things that can go wrong. This is a reason why frameworks offering immutable state – and declarative languages that don't support state handling via variables – tend to be easier to validate as working correctly.
- **Catch unknown states**. A state that's neither good nor bad, tends to be a hotbed for problems later. Be diligent in searching for unknown states and responses, log them, and consider alerting them.

Simulate failures and test the system's response

There are several ways to simulate a failure and confirm the system can handle it as expected. A few examples:

- **Graceful degradation**. Shut down a dependency of a system and validate that it responds by degrading some of its parts, as expected.
- **Retries**. When dependencies such as an external API go down, a resilient system retires requests and backs off, according to strategy.
- **Circuit breaker**. Simulate how a service handles getting into a degraded state. With a circuit breaker pattern, the system should switch to a "closed" state when it detects errors within one of its key dependencies. The system reopens itself when the degradation is resolved.
- **Data center failover**. Simulate a problem at a data center and the application failing over to operate from another location.
- **Disaster recovery**. Ensure secure data backups are in place, and that full service can be restored using them, in the event of a major outage or disaster.

Once the system is in production, keep checking how it performs, and alert when anomalies are detected. Have a clear incident management process that continuously tweaks and improves these systems because incidents inevitably occur.

25

SOFTWARE ARCHITECTURE

When thinking about what standout staff+ engineers do, always near the top of the list are software architecture and software design. Software architecture is the baseline for planning complex systems, while good software architecture is the foundation which reliable and maintainable systems are built upon.

Software architecture is so important at staff+ levels that traditional companies still refer to their most experienced software engineers as "software architects." Newer tech businesses have done away with this wording, favoring the staff/principal/distinguished engineer formulations, to emphasize the engineering part. However, while the word "architect" is out of fashion, there's still a clear expectation for staff+ engineers to be solid software architects.

The best software architects I've seen all became standout in this craft through a mix of experience in challenging projects, and ongoing learning. In this chapter, we don't cover how to become a standout software architect. I strongly believe this takes practice and the building of challenging real-world projects. What we do cover are areas to pay attention to when planning solutions for complex problems.

In this chapter, we cover:

- Keep it as simple as possible
- Architecture debt
- One-way door vs two-way door decisions
- The "blast radius" of decisions
- Know the jargon, but don't overuse it
- Scalable architecture
- Architecture vs business priorities
- Keep close enough to where work is done
- Software architect traits

1. Keep It as Simple as Possible

People are often surprised when I mention we didn't use "standard" software architecture planning tools for some of the largest projects I've worked on, like rebuilding Uber's payments system which processed $60B/year, or when building Skype for Xbox One, which had 1 million users at launch week. We could have used formal approaches and dedicated architecture frameworks for sketching out architecture like UML[1], the 4+1 model[2], architecture decision records[3] (ADR,) the C4 model[4], dependency diagrams[5], and more. But we didn't.

We used whiteboards, boxes, and arrows to draw out ideas, and documents to capture those ideas in simple language, which were then circulated for feedback. We also didn't make use of specialist language. This was despite the staff+ engineers having spent decades working at the likes of Google, VMWare, PayPal, and other large companies, and having architected large systems before.

When it comes to architecture, start simple and resist using complex jargon for its own sake. My point isn't that you should not use more formal approaches, but to do so only when you're *convinced* it adds value, and team members understand it.

The beauty of keeping architecture simple is that it keeps the discussions and ideas accessible to everyone, including entry-level software engineers. This is a great thing because the more people there are who understand the architecture, the more feedback and suggestions you can gather.

Coming up with complex architecture is often much easier than sketching something simple and efficient. I recall one of the best software architects I've met, who'd been a director of engineering and had built some of the largest payments systems on the planet, before we worked together. When we designed Uber's revamped payments system, he explained the proposed approach in simple terms, with a couple of diagrams that were easy to follow. I asked him how he could capture and express such complex systems so simply. And he told me that clarity comes from having built similar payments systems over and over again; starting with a complex version and distilling it into more efficient approaches.

2. Know The Jargon, But Don't Overuse It

Even though it can be helpful to not use jargon in cases when you can avoid it: as a staff+ engineer you still need to know the technical vocabulary relevant to your work: the "jargon!" This includes:

- **Software engineering-related jargon**. If you build distributed systems, you'll want to understand things like weak/strong consistency, idempotency, write-through-cache,

---

[1]https://en.wikipedia.org/wiki/Unified_Modeling_Language
[2]https://en.wikipedia.org/wiki/4%2B1_architectural_view_model
[3]https://github.com/joelparkerhenderson/architecture-decision-record
[4]https://c4model.com
[5]https://herbertograca.com/2019/08/12/documenting-software-architecture

reverse proxy, and many other terms.

- **Business jargon**. For example, if working in the payments domain you'll want to understand and be able to use terms like issuing bank, acquiring bank, payment gateway, PCI DSS, auth/hold, and much more.
- **Internal jargon**. Every company has its internal jargon. For example, at Uber we had Morpheus (experimentation system,) Bankemoji (payments system,) landing a diff (merging a pull request,) or commandeering an L5 outage (taking the lead in a high-impact outage.)

Find a way to organize and learn the jargon for your day-to-day work. When joining a new team or company, you'll hear new jargon. Find out what it means by doing research on industry or business language, and asking colleagues about internally-used terms.

There's some similarity between learning jargon and learning a new language, in that the more you practice it, the more natural it gets. An approach that has worked well for me is to keep a list of new terms, and figure out what it means later. I used terms in different settings to confirm the correct context.

Using too much jargon can exclude others who don't understand it. The single best way to make a less experienced software engineer feel inferior – and discourage them from participating in a conversation and sharing their ideas – is to use jargon they don't understand.

Don't be a "jargon architect." Yes, you should understand and be able to use the vocabulary of a domain, and yes, jargon does speed up communication when everyone understands it.

But in a group of varying experience, use simpler terms. Check that people are familiar with terms when using them for the first time.

Explaining jargon helps people to use it correctly, and you become better at switching between using it and simpler terms. Have you noticed how some of the best teachers can explain complex things in simple ways? Develop this skill by using basic terms instead of technical jargon. Next time you're about to use jargon, stop yourself and phrase it without using that term. Do this frequently enough and you will be an approachable engineer, not a slightly intimidating jargon architect.

3. Architecture Debt

Architecture debt is a form of tech debt, where old software architecture decisions slow down the extending of software or services, maintenance, and even operation.

No engineer or team sets out to create architecture debt, just as with tech debt. However, decisions that were once sensible can turn sub-optimal over time. Here are four examples of architecture debt:

Creating standalone services to move faster

A team needs to build a new functionality and the most obvious way to do this is to extend a backend service. However, the backend service in question is owned by another team, which pushes back on the proposed changes. To move quickly, a new service is built which enables the engineering team to launch its feature quickly.

This engineering team then does the same when launching other new services. In all cases, the decision enables faster shipping, and avoids negotiations with other engineering teams about how to extend or integrate with existing services.

As time passes, the downsides of a small, standalone service become apparent. Making a change to a feature means finding the right service, and figuring out which conventions it uses. Services might be written in different languages, which makes context-switching harder. Equally problematically, each service has its own dependencies, which use different versions of the same libraries.

In this case, the team inadvertently creates architecture debt by prioritizing pace above maintaining the system.

Not breaking up a monolith

The exact opposite approach can also create architecture debt. Take a team that has built a monolithic application to power all its products. At first, sticking with a monolith is sensible as it allows people to move faster, and only deploy a single codebase to their servers.

However, as the team grows, working on the same monolith becomes painful. If the monolith's structure is insufficiently granular, engineers might spend longer working on the same files while building very different features and need to resolve merge conflicts. If the monolith can only be deployed as one unit, the time to deploy can increase, with a higher likelihood of conflict between a team that doesn't want to deploy their changes yet, and another team that does want to push ahead.

Non-functional issues

Lots of architecture decisions work well when you build systems. However, as the load upon the system increases and more use cases are added, some non-functional characteristics of the system start to noticeably degrade, such as:

- Performance. System latency could become unacceptable, and resource optimization such as CPU or memory usage get out of hand, or the throughput of the system could struggle
- Scalability: as the load upon the system increases, its performance can significantly degrade, to the point where customers notice

- Reliability: outages or performance degradation which indicate the system has issues, become more common

Dated languages or frameworks

This is akin to tech debt, but the use of dated languages or frameworks that become unsupported can also be architecture debt. When using languages or frameworks which aren't actively supported or maintained, there can be security risks and problems with interoperability. In some cases, the performance of these languages or frameworks is significantly worse than modern alternatives.

Changing a language or framework is a significant undertaking, for which it's reasonable to consider whether some architecture decisions should be revisited as part of a rewrite. For example, when the online learning provider, Khan Academy, changed languages from Python 2 to Go, it also broke down its monolith into smaller services and moved from having REST API endpoints to GraphQL.

Note that using a dated language or framework does not automatically create debt. An underrated benefit of sticking with a stable if unfashionable language or framework, is that there are fewer surprises and blockers. When using frameworks and languages that are currently being developed, there's always the risk of uncovering problems few other teams encounter, or for which no fixes have been shipped at the language or framework level. This risk can be reduced by using stable versions of frameworks and languages and not development versions, or releases marked "alpha" or "beta."

4. One-Way Door vs Two-Way-Door Decisions

Software architecture involves lots of decisions, many of which are choices between tradeoffs. But not all decisions are equal, and one common way of thinking about them is as "one-way door" or "two-way door" decisions. This concept comes from online retail giant Amazon, as part of its "Day 1" culture.

Two-way door decisions

These are easily reversible decisions of limited impact. A few examples of two-way door decisions:

- **A/B testing of a feature**. Changes that are easily reversible by design, like conducting an A/B test, running an experiment, or using a feature flag.
- **Naming**. For example, the naming of classes and variables for internal use. Names are simple to change, thanks to most programming environments having powerful refactoring capabilities. As long as nothing external depends on a name, it's straight-

forward enough.

- **Whether to split one class into two classes**. Refactoring one class into two, or merging two classes into one, is another relatively easy task to reverse.
- **Choosing a CSS preprocessor**. When debating whether to use a cascading style sheets (CSS) preprocessor like SASS (syntactically awesome stylesheets,) or LESS (leaner CSS,) it's uncomplicated to reverse this decision thanks to similarities between the preprocessors. The decision is even easier when only a small part of the codebase was moved to a CSS preprocessor.
- **Choosing a testing framework**. When choosing a unit testing or other automated testing framework, you can walk back the decision later simply by introducing a new testing framework solely for new tests, without rewriting existing ones.
- **Choosing a new linter**. This change is a one-off. The work might be a little more complex, but it's just the tool that's changed and possibly some formatting of the code.

One-way-door decisions

In stark contrast to the above, these are decisions that are very hard to reverse, and should only be changed after serious consideration. It's wise to prototype such decisions when possible, or execute them in smaller parts of the codebase so that reversing them is easier.

In reality, there are very few true one-way-door decisions because software is reversible enough by nature. Exceptions to this include shipping software in a way that it cannot be modified later or is very challenging to do. Such software is almost always coupled with hardware, such as embedded software, or software embedded onto ROM (read-only memory) units. Most software decisions are perfectly reversible. For example, if choosing to consolidate 20 microservices into a monolith, this decision can be undone later, even if it would make little sense.

One-way-door decisions are those that are too expensive to reverse, and this is relative to your working environment. It usually means at least as much work is needed to reverse a decision as went into implementing it. Below are decisions which could be one-way doors due to the time and effort needed to reverse them:

- **Switching from a monolith to microservices, or vice versa**. Once the choice is made of a model for a monolith or microservice, migrating to the other approach becomes too expensive.
- **Choice of programming language**. Changing existing code can be very hard, as you'd have to rewrite all existing code. You might also have to train engineers and hire experts in the target language. There are languages which are easy enough to introduce another language to, like TypeScript into a Javascript web application.
- **Choice of framework**. Some application development frameworks are opinionated enough that choosing one is considered a one-way door. For example, in the frontend, choosing React, or Vue, or Svelte, locks you into these ecosystems. To move an

application off one of these frameworks could involve a full rewrite.

- **Cloud vs on-premises infrastructure**. Utilizing on-premises infrastructure or a cloud provider is a decision that's very expensive to change. You can make a change more easily by using abstractions such as containers. Still, switching infrastructure is an intense, often risky migration.

- **Relational vs NoSQL data storage**. Migrating between relational and NoSQL data models is much easier than migrating between NoSQL and SQL models. Choosing one is often considered a one-way door.

- **A force upgrade strategy of a native mobile/desktop app**. Native applications are interesting because they can run older versions of the client-side code. Deciding how to implement a "force upgrade" strategy to disallow running of certain, older versions is hard to reverse because business logic will run on the client.

- **Changes that lead to a full revert/rewrite**. If you'd need to undo all your work and do a full rewrite, it's usually a one-way door decision.

Two-way doors that become one-way doors

Some decisions that seem to be two-way doors actually become one-way doors over time, thanks to customer expectations. Here are a few:

- **Protocol choice**. Deciding which protocol a service exposes, is a decision that's very hard to reverse. For example, changing REST, GraphQL, Protobufs, Thrift, or similar protocols, is very expensive. All customers would have to migrate to the new protocol, or an adapter that keeps exposing the "old" protocol must be written for backwards compatibility.

- **Versioning strategy**. How will version numbers for an API or product be determined? Once this approach is decided and customers are used to one strategy, it can be very hard and often impossible to change without breaching customers' trust.

- **Exposing functionality as a public, stable API**. Customers will build on top of an API after they're exposed to it. Once the API is declared stable, customers will expect no breaking changes, and any change which is, must be launched as a new API endpoint, or as an endpoint with a new major version – assuming versioning accounted for this.

- **Launching a new, customer-facing service**. Similarly to APIs, services which customers use must be maintained, and often offer backward compatibility. For example, this is why Amazon Web Services (AWS) has a high bar for declaring a new service as "General Availability." Once AWS does this, it needs to maintain the service, even if it's loss-making. Services can be deprecated only on a very long timeframe of years, which makes launching a new AWS service a one-way door.

In-between decisions

Some decisions are reversible, but doing so can be somewhat expensive. Data migrations and introducing smaller frameworks are examples.

My advice is to decide whether a decision is a two-way door that's easy to reverse, or a one-way door which is expensive to reverse. For two-way doors, there's little point in debating the decision too much, or doing extensive prototyping. For one-way doors, do your homework: prototype or build a proof-of-concept to confirm the decision will work, and try to make the first phase of work easy enough to reverse.

Identifying what is a two-way door and a one-way door decision is a skill that takes time to learn. When in doubt, do your research, move forward with what looks sensible, and when it's complete, reflect on how the decision played out.

5. The Blast Radius of Decisions

How many teams and customers would be impacted by a decision you make? Some decisions have limited impact, like refactoring a system to clean up the code which only your team uses. The "blast radius" of this decision is small, which also applies to changes to systems that no other teams or customers depend on.

Other decisions have bigger blast radii. For example, retiring an API endpoint which 20 teams within the company use, will impact them and all customers who depend on those 20 teams. If it's a public endpoint that 100,000 customers use, then the blast radius is quite large.

A decision with a big blast radius is much harder to execute for a few reasons:

- Pushback from teams that would need to do work due to the change. For example, if all 20 teams have to change their code and test that things work as expected, expect several of them to push back on your team's proposed timeline.
- Impact on customers. If retiring an API means that functionality breaks for paying customers, then shipping this breaking change could create customer churn.

The blast radius of reversing a one-way-door architecture decision is often big.

Figure out ways to shrink the blast radius. There are almost certainly multiple ways to reduce any decision's blast radius. For example, by keeping an API endpoint externally alive while internally retiring an API endpoint, and putting an adapter in place that "translates" using the new API endpoint. Or motivating customers to move to a new endpoint with extra functionality so that the blast radius shrinks as a result.

It might not be the right choice to pick a decision with a smaller blast radius, given context and constraints. So list all options and consider their tradeoffs. Often, a decision that reduces a blast radius is the result of thinking "outside the box."

Good architecture decisions limit the blast radius of corrective future decisions. I wish there was a recipe for avoiding tricky situations where a large blast radius is unavoidable, which is unpopular with teams and customers dependent on your software. But there isn't one; you live and learn, and try to design more sustainable software next time!

6. Scalable Architecture

Staff+ engineers are often expected to produce scalable architecture. This expectation is commonly put in writing at Big Tech companies. But what does it mean? Scalability means building a system to handle growing amounts of work and accommodate further growth. Scalability is a potentially ambiguous term, but can be broken down to two main categories:

- Growth of new business use cases
- Growth in data, usage, traffic loads

Scalability of growth of new business use cases

Say you work on a ridesharing app, in the payments team. You're tasked with implementing a way for customers to pay by credit card. You build this payment option, and the business is happy with how it works. Over time, the app grows and the business asks for more new capabilities:

1. Paying using PayPal
2. Paying using cash
3. Paying using Apple Pay
4. Paying using PayTM (a digital wallet in India)

You could just implement support for each payment type from scratch, but this is not really a scalable approach. It's much more scalable to predict the types of request, and build an approach which makes it easier to add support for each one.

A scalable approach begins by recognizing the business will want to keep adding payment methods. You realize it takes around a month to create a new payment method by building code on the backend, web and mobile. So you design an opinionated framework, which might take a few months to build, but will cut the time it takes to add a new payment method down to a few days. Congratulations, you've put scalable architecture in place.

You cannot design for scalable business use cases without understanding two things:

1. How the business works. In the case of payment methods, you need to understand how payments work. For example, by studying the 20 most popular payment methods, globally, and going through their mechanics with a payments expert.

2. The company's roadmap. Is it worth investing to make it more scalable to add new payment methods? If the business only wants to add Apple Pay during the next two years, the answer is no. But if the plan is to add 10 payment methods within 12 months, then it's smart to get ahead of this. But you can't know whether to make systems more "business use case-scaleable," without first knowing the company's plans.

Scalability of growth in data, usage, traffic load

How will a video streaming system operate when it stores 100x more videos than it does today? How will the same system hold up with 100x more daily active users? These are typical scalability challenges. There is ample literature on how to build scalable systems, and somewhat different approaches are required for backend systems, web systems, and mobile or desktop applications. The bulk of scalability conversations tend to be about backend systems, including:

- Horizontal vs vertical scalability
- Sharding
- Caching
- Messaging strategies
- Database replication
- Content delivery networks

We don't go into depth on scalable architecture topics here, but there are books which do:

- Designing Data-Intensive Applications, by Martin Kleppmann
- Foundations of Scalable Systems, by Ian Gorton

7. Architecture Decisions vs Business Priorities

The more experienced software engineers get, the more they appreciate the importance of architecture decisions. It takes time for architecture decisions to play out, including your own. Many engineers build an appreciation of good architecture by making poor architecture decisions or being affected by them.

It's easy to fall into the trap of obsessing about "perfect" architecture which enables systems to scale for new business use cases and traffic patterns. However, there's a risk of over-engineering systems if account isn't taken of current business needs.

Align architecture decisions with the business's goals and growth

Architecture should not exist in a vacuum; in fact, good architecture is always coupled to the business. What are the goals of the business? The underlying architecture should enable these goals to be met, and if the current systems get in the way of these goals, then it's a worthwhile – and necessary! – task to change them.

How does the business plan to grow? Architecture decisions should help systems evolve and scale in line with the company's growth goals. However, spending time and effort building scalable systems for things the business has no need for, is a poor use of resources.

Let's take a specific example, re-architecting a payments system at an e-commerce company, to make it scale better. But what does "scale" mean here?

If the business has the pain point of not being able to add new payment methods quickly enough – for example, it takes 2 months but the business needs to add 20 new payment methods in the coming year to stay competitive – then investing in a re-architecture to add payment methods rapidly is a sensible approach.

If the business has the pain point of payment systems outages causing customer churn, then making changes so that systems operate more reliably, is the sensible approach. This could involve architecture changes, but will likely also include improvements to monitoring, alerting, and oncall.

But if the business has no payments-related pain points, then is there really a business case for making large architectural changes? Don't forget that changes involve effort and risk, so there should be an upside and a business reason for them.

And of course, improving engineering productivity and reducing engineering toil are valid business reasons. Just ensure they're high on the list!

Tie architecture changes to business initiatives

There will be many times when you notice that improving the architecture of systems could help reduce tech debt, and increase engineering productivity. However, this improvement is unlikely to be a good enough business reason to justify the work.

Consider coupling some improvements to business priorities, and projects that ship features and products which the business cares about. For example, when building a new feature, also improve the architecture related to the feature, which might make it more robust, or make similar additions easier and quicker in future.

Good enough may be better than perfect

Code and engineering processes can be modified or removed, and new code and processes introduced, when needed. Architecture can always be modified when needed, but architecture changes are more expensive, so it's helpful to be careful when making "one-way door" decisions.

Ultimately, it's sensible to balance building "perfect" architecture with the importance of having good enough structures in place. "Good enough" architecture allows the business to reach its goals and supports its growth. And architecture is rarely rigid; it can be tweaked and modified as the business changes.

The more you see business growth and change as being coupled with the evolution of architecture, the more you'll help software engineering to solve business problems, and use software and software architecture to do this.

8. Stay Close Enough to Where The Work is Done

The biggest challenge of becoming a staff-and-above engineer is that many things pull you away from where coding happens, like meetings, recruitment, and other priorities. You will feel the pull to spend much more time on "big picture" matters; understanding the business, talking with less technical stakeholders, and collaborating with a variety of teams.

Understanding the business and engaging in strategic discussions are much higher-leverage activities than writing code is. However, they're only high leverage if you are technical and hands-on enough to represent engineering effectively in such discussions.

Strike a balance in being close to where the work is done, and doing the work of engineers. Coding certainly won't be what you spend most of your time on, but aim to not become an archetypal theoretical software architect. Come up with ways to stay hands-on and close to the code, while also getting a deeper understanding of the business.

Keep being involved in architecture decisions, and support other engineers to become better architects. Good architecture continuously evolves, and it's software engineers who evolve it. As a staff+ engineer, even if you have many other priorities, take time to review and discuss architecture approaches and improvements that other engineers suggest.

As a strong architect, you shouldn't want to make architecture decisions because doing so makes you a bottleneck for the team. Instead, you should help other engineers make future-proof decisions by challenging and coaching them; asking questions and suggesting tradeoffs to consider.

9. Software Architect Traits

The terms "staff+ software engineer" and "software architect" are often interchangeable. Staff+ engineers may be the most senior engineers in a team, group, or organization. It's only natural they tend to be heavily involved in architecture and lead many efforts.

I've observed different types of architects or staff+ engineers. The traits of different types of architect can be aids for reflection about software engineering approaches, for an experienced engineer. Below is a roundup of architect archetypes.

Note these are descriptions of behaviors, and behaviors can change. For example, an architect might be more hands-on in one project, and less so in another. Also, individuals change over time, so an "ivory tower architect" can become an "approachable" one.

I do have a bias towards more practical traits because I've repeatedly observed that engineers who stay close to the code tend to consistently make better decisions than engineers who become detached from this core aspect of engineering. However, there's no single "good" or "bad" approach, and theoretical traits can be useful in many situations. More theoretical engineers often spend more time understanding the business and the industry, which can bring much-needed insights to decision-making.

More theoretical traits

1. Ivory Tower architect

A software engineer who's detached from day-to-day work, with few to no interactions with software engineers who implement their architecture ideas. This person is usually hard to reach and does not come across as approachable. Decisions by this person feel "top-down."

Being unapproachable means someone is often blissfully unaware when engineers don't understand their reasoning, or have valid objections.

2. Painfully precise

An engineer who pays excessive attention to the exact details of what people say and corrects them on that. This person tends to not take engineers seriously who fail to express themselves immaculately.

The issue many engineers face when dealing with a painfully precise colleague is that discussions often end up being about fine detail, and not the big picture. Less experienced engineers who are repeatedly corrected for improper usage of terms may avoid input from their painfully precise colleague.

3. Theory addict

This engineer is an avid reader of books, papers, and case studies, and suggests patterns or approaches they recently read about, and uses those resources as justification.

The issue with a theory addict is that they can lean too heavily on book learning, while lacking practical experience of the domain in which they work. In a setting where there's a more practical architect to challenge them, a theory addict can help a team by bringing alternative approaches. However, without pushback they might enforce impractical architecture approaches which cause pain points and engineering churn in future.

4. The philosopher

An engineer who seemingly brings a lot of value to every architecture debate by bringing up alternative approaches and counterpoints. The problem with this? Discussions involving this person seem to never end, nor reach agreement. This engineer often prefers an exhaustive debate, which can cause conflict with practically-minded engineers who seek a good enough decision, and want to start building.

5. The superior linguist

This engineer knows their technical jargon and never misses an opportunity to use perfect language in conversation. In a group setting with junior engineers present, a superior linguist may say something like:

> "Surely idempotency is not a strict requirement, given the system is likely not even weakly consistent. I would suggest we look at durability, but am unsure we have the right quorum for such discussion."

A superior linguist may assume an unbreakable link between engineering competency and the use of jargon. So they dismiss input from colleagues without the same command of technical jargon as they have.

The superior linguist and painfully precise archetypes share common traits, but the painfully precise engineer is usually less fixated on jargon than the superior linguist. The superior linguist is often also an ivory tower architect, as they disdain input from anyone they see as less fluent in technical vocabulary – which is usually almost everybody.

6. The walk-away advisor

An experienced engineer who provides advice during the early phases of a project, but then walks away from the implementation phase. The problem is that advice provided this way can cause more harm than good, as the assumptions on which this person's input is based, may turn out to be faulty when the work begins. Then a team is stuck; do they stick to the previous advice which looks less relevant, or do they ask the walk-away advisor for fresh input, or should they take things into their own hands because the walk-away advisor has chosen to have no skin in the game?

A walk-away advisor can say they're overstretched and lack time to get involved in the projects they'd like to, due to having too much on their plate. If you find yourself being a walk-away advisor, consider reducing the number of things you're working on, in order to see efforts through from start to finish.

More practical traits

7. The coding machine

An experienced software engineer who's heads-down with coding for much of the time. This person tends to get things done fast, and is naturally very approachable for software engineers because they work side by side with them.

Meta has a dedicated senior staff engineer archetype called the "coding machine," which was created for Michael Novati[6]. He shared with me how this archetype was created:

> "Facebook takes fairness as the #1 consideration. I was basically the "largest volume" committer at the company, but when they calibrated me against the E7 in other areas – which granted was a very small number of people, about 100 – they didn't feel like I was as impactful, or on par.
>
> I was pushing hard to have my contributions recognized more. I did also do 300+ interviews at that time, and worked on important things on the side. My understanding is that my director of engineering at the time wrote up the "coding machine" archetype and presented it to the calibration group that reviews all E7s. The committee accepted this, and added it to the list of archetypes."

Being a coding machine is not a trait most people easily associate with software architects, but I think it's important to bust the myth that architects can't be very hands-on with coding. Some of the largest tech companies like Meta recognize the existence and importance of such people.

8. The integrator

An experienced engineer who understands most of the company's systems, how they work, what they do, and how to easily extend and modify them. These engineers are hands-on and can quickly make modifications to most systems, and integrate new functionality, or one system with the other.

An integrator is an extremely useful person at places with many complex systems. Thanks to

---

[6]https://www.linkedin.com/in/michaelnovati

their hands-on knowledge, they can offer smart workarounds and elegant hacks that avoid large rewrite efforts.

There is a danger that integrators get too used to patching up systems as they go – after all, they are very good at this! Pairing an integrator with a more theoretical engineer could be a great way to go about large rewrites or re-architectures, as the integrator will push back on unnecessary rewrites. Both integrators and coding machines tend to be excellent at debugging and solving challenging bugs and outages, as both have deep understanding of the code and systems, and possess hands-on knowledge.

9. The approachable one

An experienced software engineer who's surprisingly approachable and available, often because they work on a team, participate in discussions with engineers, go oncall, and take part in chats where engineers hang out.

This engineer frequently mentors less experienced colleagues informally via code reviews and pairing, and sometimes more formally by meeting mentees regularly to discuss work and challenges.

10. The detailed documenter

An engineer who writes documents that help fellow engineers understand architecture, common concepts, and terms. This engineer is a proponent of RFCs, design docs, architecture decision records (ADRs,) runbooks, and other documents which capture and spread knowledge.

Note that depending on how practical the documentation is, this trait can be more practical or more theoretical. Many ivory tower architects are also detailed documenters.

11. The new, shiny chaser

An engineer who loves to jump to using the latest, greatest framework or approach which they just learned about. This approach tends to work well on less experienced teams, with members who are keen to be on the cutting edge.

Over time, the approach of – almost blindly – jumping on the latest technological bandwagon can cause issues because new and unexpected problems almost always arise with less battle-tested approaches.

12. The old schooler

The opposite of the new, shiny chaser, this is an experienced engineer who prefers the same toolset that's worked for decades, even though teammates see it as out of date.

Believe it or not, an old schooler may once have been a new, shiny chaser, who got burnt once too often and decided that jumping on bandwagons wasn't worth it.

The old schooler is not necessarily unpopular. They can advocate effectively for a helpful approach on a more experienced team which shares their understanding of battle-tested approaches that often lead to software development with few or no surprises. Their motto is "use boring tech."

However, The old schooler can create tension with team members who prefer modern approaches, and their presence could make it more challenging to hire engineers who like cutting-edge approaches.

Are architect traits useful?

You may recognize colleagues with the traits of one or more of the above archetypes. It can be useful to figure out which archetype your colleagues see you as, based on your current work.

And this is exactly the point of archetypes as tools for reflection. Would you be described as someone who's more theoretical, or more practical? Most importantly, are you perceived how you want to be?

Don't forget these traits describe behaviors, which can and do change. Most engineers can recognize themselves as a mix of the above archetypes, while the mix of traits changes by project and the dynamics of teams.

Pairing engineers with different traits can create great outcomes. For proof that there are no definitively good or bad traits, I recall the single best architect I've had the opportunity to work with. It was not one person, but a pair. One was a highly theoretical architect, and one was highly practical.

These two kept challenging one another. Their unique pairing led to practical architecture that was built with long-term maintainability and extensibility, all done elegantly. Along the way, each appeared to develop respect for the other's approach, so that the theoretical engineer grew more practical, while the practical engineer started to appreciate the value of research papers, books, and taking time to think, not just code.

Across a long enough career, you will likely find yourself operating as a few different archetypes. Recognizing the traits of each can help you reflect on whether people with certain traits are right for a current project and team.

Takeaways

The terms "staff engineer," "principal engineer," and other staff+ engineer titles can mean surprisingly different things at different companies. There will be places where a principal engineer title is what is considered a senior engineer role elsewhere, and also companies where a staff engineer role has a blast radius of around 50-100 engineers – which is well above normal. So instead of just focusing on the title, figure out what the expectations are at your current workplace, and at businesses you want to join.

Staff+ engineers are frequently partners with EMs and PMs, and tend to work across several teams. It's often an unspoken expectation that they uncover new problems worth solving, as well as fixing existing ones.

Balancing your time by dealing with context switches tends to become more of a challenge. Here's a visualization of how time spent changes for a software engineer, a senior engineer, and a staff engineer:

How do you typically spend your time in each role?

Software engineer

☑ Strategy & alignment

☐ Building software

☒ Other activities

Senior engineer

Staff engineer

How time spent changes, as engineers progress into more senior positions. Staff engineers tend to have less dedicated time for activities directly related to building software.

At this level, understanding the business is table-stakes, together with working well with a wide range of people, such as EMs, PMs, business folks, and other engineers.

At this level, you'll be expected to lead by example in building reliable and resilient software systems, utilizing industry practices, and putting ones in place that help your group execute better.

Even if you don't hold the title "software architect," you'll certainly play this role. Don't forget that doing so is not only an opportunity to make pragmatic long-term decisions, but also to get team members involved, and mentor and teach them to become better at long-term thinking.

The best thing about staff+ roles is how much of a positive impact you can have on the products you build, the group you are part of, and the engineers you work with. Keep learning, keep getting things done, and don't forget to meaningfully help other engineers by mentoring and sponsoring them, as well. And of course, enjoy the ride!

Writing is a skill that becomes increasingly important for staff+ engineers. This skill is especially in-demand when working within large organizations, when working remote, or working with distributed teams. While we did not go into detail on this topic in the book, you can read more in the online, bonus chapter for Part V:

Becoming a Better Writer as a Software Engineer

pragmaticurl.com/bonus-5

Part VI

Conclusion

26

LIFELONG LEARNING

What separates some of the best software engineers out there, from the rest? One thing is that the great ones never stop learning. As well as picking up new languages and technologies, they dive into new, interesting approaches.

Take Simon Willison, co-creator of the web Django framework, former director of architecture at Eventbrite, and an independent software engineer at the time of this book's publication. Simon has been coding for more than 20 years and is a very productive engineer, who's not stopped learning new approaches. A few months after the general release of ChatGPT, Simon documented his experiments[1] with the large language model, and what he'd learned about its applicability in helping him become a better developer. Not only this, he became an expert in exploring prompt injections into LLMs[2] in only months.

For me, Simon is a great example of a software engineer who never stops learning. He shows that there's always something new and interesting to understand and use.

Learning helps in any part of your career, whether you're just starting out, or are a veteran software engineer. There are approaches for this, and in this chapter, we cover:

1. Stay curious
2. Keep learning
3. Challenge yourself
4. Keep up with the industry
5. Give yourself a break

1. Stay Curious

No matter how much you know about tech and software engineering, there's always more to discover. One sure way to experience this is by asking questions.

---

[1]https://simonwillison.net/series/using-chatgpt
[2]https://simonwillison.net/series/prompt-injection

Ask questions

Always understand why you are working on something, and how things work. Ask "why?" and "how?" until you get answers, and don't be afraid to go down the rabbit hole to seek these out.

Here are some examples of questions you can - and should! - ask as part of your work.

"Why are we doing this project, who benefits?" As a software engineer, your job is not to complete tickets and write code, it's to create value for your team and the business. So start by understanding why your work matters, who benefits from it, and how.

For example, as you begin work on a ticket that says, "make the padding on the Submit 4 pixels wider," ask why this is being done. It could be that the app has accessibility issues and older users have issues navigating it. In that case, increasing padding might be one solution, but is it the most practical? Is it only the Submit button that has this issue, or all buttons? Could you solve a whole category of accessibility issues across the app with a smarter approach?

"Why does it work now: what changed?" Sometimes when trying to resolve a bug, an issue simply "fixes" itself. This is good news, right? You can get back to work and close the issue as "works for me," "cannot reproduce," or "probably already fixed."

Well, a questioning mentality doesn't leave it there. After all, you don't understand what really happened. Perhaps the issue is still present but only affects certain users, certain configurations, or certain regions. Perhaps another, unrelated code change fixed this issue? Perhaps it's an indeterministic issue?

Put your detective hat on and investigate what really happened. There is no such thing as a bug that fixes itself; there's always a reason why it happens. If you ask questions and investigate, you will find out what really happened, and become a better software engineer in the process. This is because you learn something valuable about tracking down these issues, how computer systems work, and edge cases you were unaware of.

"Which alternatives could we use?" Early in my career, working at a software consultancy, I was put on a project to build a simple enough CRUD (create/update/delete) business application to manage business records for a customer. A senior software engineer advising the project said I should use the in-house object-relational mapping tool (ORM) to store and retrieve data for this application.

I was unsure why I should do this, but didn't ask, and assumed the senior engineer knew best. I built the application using this wrapper. However, when it was time to hand over the project, I noticed something worrying; the application became very slow as soon as it had more than 50 records. Inserting or updating a record took 5 seconds, then 10, and then even longer. The issue was the custom ORM tool was terrible at dealing with even small data sets.

I asked the senior engineer which alternatives we could use, and what those alternatives would mean. As we discussed options, it became apparent that throwing away the ORM tool or using a mature ORM tool with no known performance issues would be more sensible. I ended up rewriting the application to use a popular, open source ORM tool at the data layer.

I would have saved so much time if I'd only questioned the initial approach and evaluated alternatives.

Other questions worth asking:

- **"How does this solution work, exactly?"** Dig deep and don't stop until you understand the exact details.
- **"What does this component do under the hood?"** In modern software engineering, it's very common for a library or framework to do the heavy lifting of building an application. However, if you don't understand how the tool, library, or framework works under the hood, then you're doing yourself a disservice and turning down a learning opportunity.
- **"What would it mean if we built our own solution from scratch?"** When building a project, you have the option to use existing components, vendors, or to build your own. I believe it's sensible to ask what it would mean to build your own solution, not because you necessarily want to, but because doing so might reveal what the components or vendors need to do.

Stay curious and be humble

People I observed to be lifelong learners share the traits of being humble and approachable, even when they're senior. They have an appetite for learning, and are flexible in changing their opinions when they discover new facts and information.

An example of this is Kent Beck, creator of "Extreme Programming," and a major advocate of Test Driven Development (TDD.) He joined Facebook in 2011, aged 50, and thought he'd seen it all in tech. Here's his impression of the company after he finished Bootcamp, from an interview[3] with Software Engineering Daily:

> "I see this place, it's crazy. It looks like a clown show, and yet things are working really well. They weren't doing the things in my books. (...)

---

[3] https://softwareengineeringdaily.com/2019/08/28/facebook-engineering-process-with-kent-beck

> In the back of my mind there is the mystery of this bumblebee. In theory, this process should be a disaster. In practice, it's working extremely well at doing two things at the same time: scaling and exploration."

After he joined, Kent hosted a class on Test Driven Development as part of a Hackathon. Colleagues were not using TDD, so he expected they'd show up to learn about it. Nobody came to Kent's class on TDD. Meanwhile, the Argentinian tango dance class was oversubscribed, with a waitlist.

Kent was accomplished and respected across the industry, and TDD was a widely-accepted best practice for software, but Facebook didn't use it. A different kind of software engineer could have tried to force TDD on the company, or have left for another place. Kent Beck did neither: he took the humble, curious approach and set about understanding how Facebook operated one of the world's largest sites without TDD.

This approach led him to appreciate how Facebook prioritized moving fast, while relying on advanced experimentation and rollback systems, and how, in the case of Facebook, moving fast without tests was possible. Kent Beck went on to have a fulfilling career at Facebook; being respected in the workplace and mentoring hundreds of engineers. None of this would have happened if he was not humble and curious.

2. Keep Learning

Pairing and shadowing

Working together with another engineer to solve a problem by pair programming, or pairing to sketch out a solution, is a superior way to solve a problem and learn from a colleague.

Pair programming is a practice that a minority of experienced software engineers swear by because they see how much more efficient it is. However, most engineers don't do it, while many have never tried it.

When you are stuck on a problem, consider asking a teammate to pair with you to solve it together. That's all there is to pairing!

Once you're experienced in pairing sessions, you can proactively offer to pair with engineers whom you notice are stuck.

Shadowing involves experiencing an activity, meeting, or event, which you otherwise would not. For example, there are plenty of meetings at work to which you don't get invited, but if you're curious you may think you could learn something from attending one. So, ask a person who is invited if you can shadow them by going along. Just remember, shadowing means observing and not having input.

Situations that lend themselves to shadowing:

- A job interview, if you're inexperienced at interviewing. Ask to shadow an interview to observe how it's conducted.
- A meeting in which software engineers don't have direct input, like a strategy meeting for product managers, or an incident review for directors at which a teammate is attending.
- Another team's regular event. For example, joining another team's weekly update meeting as a tech lead, to observe how it's run and what the dynamics are.

When you hear of an interesting meeting or event you're not invited to, but which you think is a learning opportunity, ask the organizer if you can shadow it. The worst they can say is no!

Mentorship

Having a mentor to learn from and mentoring others are great ways to keep learning and growing. Mentorship is a two-way relationship, wherein mentors learn from mentees while they give them the benefits of their experience.

We go into detail on mentoring in Part III: "Collaboration and Teamwork."

Self-guided learning

Learning by yourself is an essential skill in tech, which empowers you to be more autonomous, and to unblock yourself when you don't know something, by just learning it!

Within software engineering, there's no shortage of resources online for learning languages, frameworks, and approaches, including:

- Reference documentation for languages, frameworks, and libraries. These resources are usually pretty "dry," but are typically the most up-to-date.
- Educational resources like articles, books, videos, and courses. There's an ever-growing quantity of these, both as free and paid-for. The more niche the field, the more likely it is that paid resources are most helpful. These resources tend to pay for themselves in their educational value. Also, your employer might have a learning and development budget, meaning you don't need to spend your own money.
- Forums and Q&A sites where you can ask for support and help, like StackOverflow, Reddit, Discord servers, and other programming communities.
- Artificial Intelligence tools. Large language models (LLM) like ChatGPT and Bard are surprisingly helpful tools that can help understand and explain programming context. But don't forget, these tools sometimes make things up, so blindly don't trust them!
- Learning by doing. I've left the most efficient approach until last: build something using the technology or approach you want to learn! For example, if you want to learn

a new language like Go, build a service or rewrite an existing one in this language. Nothing beats first-hand experience of typing code and debugging issues. The other resources in this list can help with this.

As you become more experienced in a field, your learning process changes:

- As a beginner in a field such as the programming language TypeScript, guidance is very helpful. This may come from opinionated resources, or from an experienced engineer who acts as a guide.
- At the intermediate level, it's more useful to explore an area yourself and seek out expert resources. For example, if you have experience with TypeScript, you could try out its more advanced features like union types, the keyof keyword, and Required and Partial utility types. It's useful to consult advanced resources that go into detail on how advanced language features work, and are implemented under the hood.
- When you are an expert in a field, teaching others and pushing boundaries are ways to grow. Taking TypeScript as an example, teaching engineers how the language works, and creating for them written or recorded resources are good ways to deepen your own understanding of it. Taking on advanced projects like writing an compiler for Type-Script is a challenge that would push both your understanding of the language and the understanding of how compilers work. Getting involved in widely-used projects written in the language is another way of doing so.

Share what you learn

A great way to learn something in-depth is to teach it because this requires you to:

- Understand how it works
- Break it down into simple enough terms
- Answer questions, including ones that didn't occur to you

Speaking personally, my own understanding of concepts, frameworks, or systems, deepens when I explain them, and I've frequently discovered gaps in my own knowledge from doing so, meaning I needed to understand them better. Of course, upleveling other people is the main benefit of teaching. It's a bonus that doing this also makes you more of an expert in the subject.

Here's a useful life hack; If you really want to force yourself to learn something well, give a presentation, or hold a session about it. I did this at Uber when I wanted to understand how its dozens of systems worked together, which about 10 teams owned. So, I volunteered to put together an onboarding presentation for new joiners about what each system did, and how they worked together. For this, I needed to piece together the parts and get a deep understanding of each part of the system.

Hoard knowledge

Simon Willison has an interesting observation about the value of hoarding knowledge. He told me:

> "I think a big part of succeeding in tech is just constantly hoarding new things that you know how to do, then looking out for opportunities to combine and apply them."

This is why it's useful to dip your toes into areas which aren't closely related to your "main" expertise. For example, if you're a frontend engineer, dig into a different platform like backend, or embedded. Play around with new technologies like large language models or machine learning. Learn about a different area and "hoard" this knowledge. It might not be useful right now, but could come in handy later!

How you learn changes over time

Approaches to learning are more effective or less effective, depending on whether you're a newcomer to the industry, or are an an expert in areas. No single approach is right for everyone, but here are a few things I've observed:

- Guided learning, where someone pairs with you, or you follow tutorials, is often more efficient when starting out in a new area,
- When you have a deep interest in an area, self-guided learning often works well.
- Needing to solve a problem can be a very strong motivation, which pushes you to use the most efficient ways to figure out how a given technology works (or doesn't work!)

I've had times when I preferred different mediums for learning new things. I've gone from using books to learn a new language/technology, to video tutorials, to using reference documentation, to going back to books, and now using AI tools. I suspect my preferences will continue to change over time.

And it's not just your own preferences that change. Team dynamics can have a large influence on learning from colleagues' knowledge. If they are open to helping you and have relevant experience in areas you need to make progress in, you can often learn faster this way.

Embrace the fact that your preferences and approaches to learning change over time, and don't shy away from trying out new approaches!

3. Keep Challenging Yourself

There is a learning curve when discovering and understanding how something new works, like a technology or system, or how to navigate a new team or workplace. At first, the curve is steep as you take on and organize a lot of new information. Over time, this curve flattens as you become an expert. Drawing this progression out:

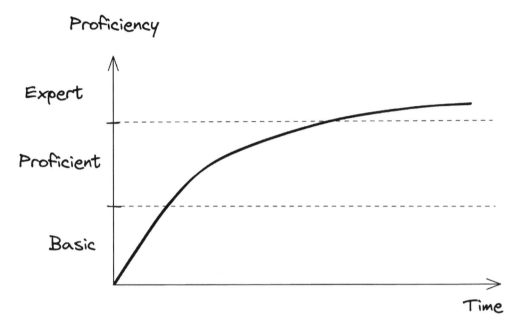

A typical learning curve

There are three distinct learning phases. To illustrate them, let's take the case of learning to use a new framework:

1. Onboarding/beginner. You're just getting started with the framework, and reading the code or making simple changes using it. Initially, you have trouble with the basics, but you quickly cross this hurdle; quickly compared to phases 2 and 3, at least.
2. Proficient. You know the basics, and as you use and learn about the framework, start to discover and use more advanced features. At first, your progress is equally rapid as before, but this slows over time. You look under the hood of the framework, debug challenging bugs, and over time reach a point where few things surprise you.
3. Expert. After working with the framework for a long time, you become an expert. There's not much left to learn. Well, this would be true if the framework never changed, but it does! When a new version of the framework comes out, your level drops back to "proficient."

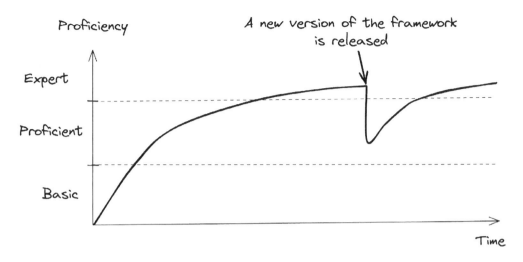

The typical learning curve for a framework, library, or even a language. When new versions are released, there's more learning to do!

Once you reach "expert" level, the learning curve tapers off. Sooner or later, you get to this stage with any technology, or team you work on, or company you work at. The only places where you can never really feel like an expert are fast-changing environments, like the forefront of a rapidly changing industry, or at a startup experiencing hypergrowth.

Still, most engineers do reach the "expert" phase, and when you do, you feel it. So, what next? There are options:

- Do nothing. Stay the expert you are and enjoy being a go-to person for the technology. Keep up with the occasional change like new versions, and gain an expert understanding of these.
- Teach more. Remain the expert you are, and help others to level up. By teaching, you continue your own learning.
- Engage with the industry. If you're a renowned expert in an area within your company, you could probably learn more outside the company. Engaging with industry-leading figures and events and publishing your learnings, are ways to do this. Of course, you might need some support from your manager and employer to pursue these. However, doing so could establish both yourself and your company, as industry-wide known figures in a given technology.
- Challenge yourself with new technology. For example, if you're an expert in building backend services in Go, consider onboarding to new languages or using new frameworks.
- Challenge yourself in a new area or platform. A bolder move is to change not just the technology, but your area or platform. For example, if you feel you are an expert backend engineer, you could explore working on the frontend, get deeper into

machine learning and AI, or another area you're a beginner in.

There is no right or wrong approach to what to do next when you're an expert. I suggest that if you are an expert, it's beneficial to decide what you want to do, instead of just going with the flow. Are you content with staying as the expert, do you want to teach more, or is it time for a new challenge and to feel the thrill of learning something new?

4. Keep up with the industry

The one constant in technology is change. Technologies change, new languages and frameworks come out, and existing ones are improved; likewise for approaches and platforms. Sometimes change happens over years, other times in a matter of months.

An example of a change that took months to spread is large language models. ChatGPT launched publicly in November 2022, and only 3 months later had 100 million monthly active users, including many software engineers using it to write code more efficiently.

There are ways to keep pace with change:

- **Through work**. One reason to work at "modern" companies that use cutting-edge technology, is that you keep up-to-date just by showing up at work! If your team uses the latest version of a modern language and the latest stable versions of popular frameworks, then you keep yourself up to date via your job. This is one reason that companies with modern tech stacks are attractive to developers.
- **Keep up with tech news**. Read newsletters and websites, listen to podcasts, and watch videos that summarize the latest news in tech and your segment. For example, if you're a backend engineer using Go and Rust at work, find resources on these niches. There's no shortage of publications for keeping engineers up-to-date. You can also use aggregators like Feedly to subscribe to several websites that cover interesting topics and read relevant articles every now and then.
- **Build side projects**. Side projects done in your personal time and prototyping at work, are two of the surest ways to avoid being left behind. If you don't have the opportunity to do these at work, consider spending time outside of work on building proof-of-concept projects. Try out new frameworks, languages, platforms, and approaches.
- **Tinker with tech, even at work!** Find excuses to try out a new technology or interesting approach, even if it's not strictly related to your day-to-day work. You could prototype a simple tool for your own use or your team's, with a framework you've always wanted to try. Or you could play around with a piece of technology and then do a lunch and learn session with your team, sharing what you've learned.

5. Give yourself a break

The advice contained in this chapter may give the impression that it's necessary to be learning for every waking minute of your life. This could not be further from the truth!

It's great to learn something new regularly, but there will naturally be times when this doesn't happen in the course of your work, or you lack the willpower or opportunity.

You need to give yourself a break, just like athletes don't train every day, or train at full intensity each time. Obviously, the tech industry moves fast, so it's understandable to feel FOMO (fear of missing out) if you don't keep up with things. However, my view is that to always keep learning in order to not fall behind, risks burnout.

Sometimes you just need to give yourself a break from it all. Don't feel guilty about doing so!

27

FURTHER READING

You've reached the end of the book: congratulations! Here are recommendations on what to read next.

Bonus chapters

There is still more to the book in the form of online, bonus chapters. There are 10 bonus chapters totaling 100 more pages. Access these here:

Online, Bonus Chapters

pragmaticurl.com/bonus

Keeping up-to-date with the industry

All books, by nature, will get somewhat outdated, over time the years. To keep up-to-date with how the industry is changing, look to more realtime resources:

The Pragmatic Engineer Newsletter is where I cover how the software engineering industry is changing: with industry trends, deepdives, and insights from software engineers and engineering leaders at some of the most exciting companies. If you enjoyed this book, you'll probably like the newsletter as well: as it's also written by me! The topics are more "realtime," and the examples are very specific to what is happening, right now. It's a weekly newsletter, free to subscribe – you can always upgrade for a paid plan for more content – and you can subscribe here:

The Pragmatic Engineer Newsletter

pragmaticurl.com/newsletter

Software engineering-related newsletters are a solid way to stay up-to-date with what is new and worth paying attention to as a software engineer. Here are the ones I personally read and recommend:

pragmaticurl.com/newsletters

Books

While frameworks change quickly and languages evolve relatively speedily in software engineering, there are plenty of things that change much slower. The fundamentals of how software systems work, and the nature of how people work together (or have problems working together) are examples of such areas. Below are books that helped me grow into a better software engineer – and engineering lead – and I recommend them. Browse all of them here:

pragmaticurl.com/recommended-books

ACKNOWLEDGMENTS

So many people have helped directly or indirectly with this book:

I owe a great deal of thanks to my former developer peers, managers, and mentors I've been lucky enough to work with throughout my career. While software engineering can be done alone: I've always found that it's both more interesting, and more exciting to do it with a team. I've learned the most while working shoulder-to-shoulder with other people, solving challenging projects. If I've worked with you in the past: thank you. One or more of our interactions directly or indirectly might have just made its way into this book!

A shoutout to people I spent extended time with at Sense/Net, Scott Logic, the TEXAS team at JP Morgan, Skype London (Durango / Xbox One, Outlook.com and Skype for Web), Skyscanner (TripGun and TravelPro), and at Uber (PPP, Helix, RP, Payments and Money).

Thank you to the early reviewers of the book: Anton Zaides, Basit Parkar, Bruno Oliveira, Cecilia Szenes, Chris Seaton, Giovanni Zotta, Harsha Vardhan, Jasmine Teh, John Gallagher, Katja Lotz, Luca Canducci, Ludovic Galibert, Martijn van der Veen, Michael Bailey, Modestas Šaulys, Nielet Dmello, Oussama Hafferssas, Radhika Morabia, Rodrigo Pimentel, Simon Topchyan, Stan Amsellem and Yujie Li.

A special thanks to my editor Dominic Grover and his tireless work to get this book even more enjoyable to read.

Finally, thank you to my family for supporting the writing of this book and the long hours and weekends that came with it. And to my parents for their ongoing support and advice, and their cautioning on spending too much time writing this book – which I did in the end, anyway.

INDEX

A

B

C

Made in the USA
Las Vegas, NV
01 December 2023

81923284R00227